St. Louis Community College

Forest Park
Florissant Valley
Meramec

Instructional Resources
St. Louis, Missouri

School of American Research
Advanced Seminar Series

JONATHAN HAAS, GENERAL EDITOR

SCHOOL OF AMERICAN RESEARCH
ADVANCED SEMINAR SERIES

Available from Cambridge University Press

Dreaming: Anthropological and
Psychological Interpretations
BARBARA TEDLOCK

Available from the University of New Mexico Press

**Reconstructing Prehistoric Pueblo
Societies
WILLIAM A. LONGACRE

New Perspectives on the Pueblos
ALFONSO ORTIZ

Structure and Process in Latin America
ARNOLD STRICKON and SIDNEY M.
GREENFIELD

The Classic Maya Collapse
T. PATRICK CULBERT

**Methods and Theories of
Anthropological Genetics
M. H. CRAWFORD and P. L. WORKMAN

**Sixteenth-Century Mexico: The
Work of Sahagun
MUNRO S. EDMONSON

**Ancient Civilization and Trade
JEREMY A. SABLOFF and
C. C. LAMBERG-KARLOVSKY

**Photography in Archaeological
Research
ELMER HARP, JR

**Meaning in Anthropology
KEITH H. BASSO and HENRY A.
SELBY

**The Valley of Mexico: Studies in
Pre-Hispanic Ecology and Society
ERIC R. WOLF

Demographic Anthropology:
Quantitative Approaches
EZRA B. W. ZUBROW

**The Origins of Maya Civilization
RICHARD E. W. ADAMS

**Explanation of Prehistoric Change
JAMES N. HILL

**Explorations in Ethnoarchaeology
RICHARD A. GOULD

**Entrepreneurs in Cultural Context
SIDNEY M. GREENFIELD, ARNOLD
STRICKON, and ROBERT T. AUBEY

The Dying Community
ART GALLAHER, JR and HARLAND
PADFIELD

**Southwestern Indian Ritual Drama
CHARLOTTE J. FRISBIE

**Lowland Maya Settlement Patterns
WENDY ASHMORE

**Simulations in Archaeology
JEREMY A. SABLOFF

Chan Chan: Andean Desert City
MICHAEL E. MOSELEY and KENT C.
DAY

Shipwreck Anthropology
RICHARD A. GOULD

Elites: Ethnographic Issues
GEORGE E. MARCUS

The Archaeology of Lower Central
America
FREDERICK W. LANGE and DORIS Z.
STONE

Late Lowland Maya Civilization:
Classic to Postclassic
JEREMY A. SABLOFF and E. WYLLYS
ANDREWS V

**out of print

The Anasazi in a changing environment

THE ANASAZI IN A
CHANGING
ENVIRONMENT

EDITED BY
GEORGE J. GUMERMAN

A SCHOOL OF AMERICAN RESEARCH BOOK

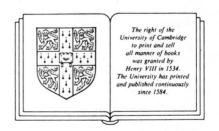

The right of the
University of Cambridge
to print and sell
all manner of books
was granted by
Henry VIII in 1534.
The University has printed
and published continuously
since 1584.

CAMBRIDGE UNIVERSITY PRESS
Cambridge
New York · New Rochelle · Melbourne · Sydney

Published by the Press Syndicate of the University of Cambridge
The Pitt Building, Trumpington Street, Cambridge CB2 1RP
32 East 57th Street, New York, NY 10022, USA
10 Stamford Road, Oakleigh, Melbourne 3166, Australia

© Cambridge University Press 1988

First published 1988

Printed in Great Britain at the University Press, Cambridge

British Library cataloguing in publication data
The Anasazi in a changing environment.
(School of American Research advanced seminar series).
1. Pueblo Indians
I. Gumerman, George J.   II. Series
979'.00497   E99.P9

Library of Congress cataloguing in publication data
The Anasazi in a changing environment.
(School of American Research advanced seminar series)
"A School of American Research book."
Bibliography.
Includes index.
1. Pueblo Indians – Antiquities – Congresses.
2. Indians of North America – Southwest, New – Antiquities – Congresses.
3. Paleoecology – Colorado – Southwest, New – Congresses.
4. Southwest, New – Antiquities – Congresses.
I. Gumerman, George J.   II. Series.
E99.P9A52 1988   97'.01 87–25692

ISBN 0 521 34631 2

wv

Contents

vii

Contents

Illustrations

Illustrations

Tables

Foreword

The Advanced Seminar program at the School of American Research is set up to allow scholars to come together for a week of intense interaction and discussion of a specific topic. Sometimes the topics are very general, as in "Trade and Civilization" (see Sabloff and Lamberg-Karlovsky 1975), for example, and sometimes they are specific, as in "Southwestern Indian Ritual Drama" (see Frisbie 1980). Both types of seminar have proven to be successful in the past, and both have produced results that have contributed to a greater understanding of the human condition.

When the seminar on "Anasazi Cultural Developments and Paleoenvironmental Correlates" was held in 1981, it was intended as a "specific-type" seminar that would lead to new insight into prehistoric cultural developments in the northern Southwest. The seminar certainly accomplished its immediate ends. For the first time in the Southwest, the paleoenvironmental data were brought together in a comprehensive way with the archaeological data.

Both of these data sets are in many ways unparalleled anywhere in the world. The kinds and quality of information extracted from tree rings, pollen, and hydrology by Dean, Hevly, and Karlstrom, respectively, are rarely available elsewhere, and nowhere do they provide such an accurate reconstruction of past environment as in the Southwest. The archaeological data base utilized by Euler, Powell, Plog, and the others, in turn, is almost unequaled. The Southwest has been an archaeological training ground and laboratory for much of American archaeology for a full century, and the excellent data reflect the breadth and intensity of research in this area. Bringing these two kinds of data together in a lucid and provocative model of prehistoric cultural development across the Colorado Plateaus represents, by itself, a significant achievement in the archaeology of the Southwest. I expect it to stimulate both active discussion and future directed research across the region.

On a parallel track with the specific accomplishments of the volume run the broader implications of the research presented by Gumerman and his colleagues. The ramifications of this volume extend far beyond the borders of the southwestern United States, and spread from the archaeological past into the anthropological present. The authors truly provide an outstanding study of the relationship between human beings and their environment. To what extent is human behavior determined by environment, demography, and the technological foundations of culture? How do humans respond to both short- and long-term changes in their environment, and what is the impact of the environment on the long-term evolution of cultural systems? These are questions that have assumed critical importance in the field of anthropology in the past forty years as we seek to understand the ultimate causes underlying patterns of human thought and action.

Gumerman and his colleagues have provided a new and extra-ordinarily valuable data base for addressing these questions empirically. They demonstrate, for example, that human social systems adjust to short-term fluctuations in the environment without undergoing major changes, and that the real evolutionary transformations occur in the face of the long-term trends in rainfall, erosion, temperature, and demography.

Such information offers a new dimension of insights into the modern world, as we are attempting to assess such things as the impact of cyclical droughts in Africa or the effect of a long-term warming trend resulting from increased carbon dioxide in the atmosphere. Droughts and broad climatic changes (although today perhaps stimulated by human actions) are not unique phenomena, and we need not turn to conjecture or crystal balls to estimate how humans are likely to respond in general ways to such phenomena. The authors in this volume have outlined a thousand-year chronicle of environment, demography, and culture history which stands out as an experimental baseline for explaining broad patterns of interaction between humans and their environment in the past and for predicting similar patterns in the future. *The Anasazi in a Changing Environment* sets a new standard in archaeological research, and at the same time it serves to link the ancient past with the modern world. This is anthropology at its best.

JONATHAN HAAS
School of American Research

Preface

The genesis of this volume occurred in 1966 when Thor Karlstrom, who was with the U.S. Geological Survey in Flagstaff, asked archaeologists at the Museum of Northern Arizona to look at some sites south of the Hopi villages. The study area was the Hopi Buttes where the U.S. Geological Survey was training astronauts and testing equipment for the proposed lunar landing. Karlstrom was interested in dating surficial deposits and caliche formations, and he believed some of the buried sites in the area had the potential for providing ceramic-derived dates. The USGS therefore found itself funding an archaeological study.

This initial cooperative venture provided a model for the many years of interaction by the authors of this volume. Karlstrom could have gotten the information he needed by having archaeologists put in a few test trenches. However, he realized that better cooperation would result from allowing the archaeologists great latitude to explore not only those areas of interest to the USGS, but those of the archaeologists as well.

Over the years all of us have pursued our own research directions but have recognized the common need for an area of overlap where all our interests coincided. When funds were available we would help one another – not viewing other disciplines as ancillary and demanding strict adherence to narrowly focused paleoenvironmental research. Rather, individual researchers were given free rein, in the expectation that some of our efforts would contribute to the common cause. It was only in this fashion that it was possible to sustain an informal research effort over so many years with scholars from different disciplines in widely scattered places.

Throughout the 1970s and early 1980s we worked on developing a detailed cultural and environmental sequence for the Christian era for the Black Mesa region of northeastern Arizona. Karlstrom developed the hydrostratigraphic curve, Hevly the pollen record, Dean the dendroclimatic curve, and Euler and Gumerman the archaeological sequence. The pan-Colorado Plateaus implications of our work became obvious because it was apparent that it was necessary to use published data from throughout Anasazi country in order to interpret our more localized data. It seemed clear to us that there were regular, predictable patterns between the reconstructed environmental conditions, demography and culture change throughout the Colorado Plateaus.

The Anasazi-wide implications of our work were not immediately apparent nor did we have in mind a well-articulated goal for our collective research. Rather, the need for a volume of this type grew as our general patterns became more apparent, and it was obviously necessary to support our conclusions about human and environmental linkages with our data.

The large number of researchers involved in our informal group made it difficult for all of us to meet for more than a day or two to discuss the ramifications of the independently derived but highly interrelated aspects of our work. The need became obvious for a week-long meeting to contemplate the articulation of the alluvial, plant, and tree-ring records with human demography and behavior in an atmosphere such as provided by the School of American Research's Seminar House.

In addition, we felt it was necessary to have discussants for each of our disciplines who held opposing view to ours or at least were somewhat skeptical about our approach or results. This was a necessity also because over the years we have not only generated some skepticism among our colleagues, but some of us also felt inadequate to evaluate competently all the details of disciplines other than our own. The result was an Advanced Seminar entitled "Anasazi Cultural Developments and Paleoenvironmental Correlates" held in October 1981.

The composition of the seminar participants was not the same as represented by the authorship of this volume, and some of the roles of the participants have changed. Fred Plog was invited as a discussant because he was somewhat skeptical of our earlier efforts. His contributions at the seminar and the subsequent meetings to draft the final synthesizing chapter of this volume, as well as his "conversion," prompted us to recognize him as more than a discussant to our papers; therefore he is the senior author on the summary chapter. Because of the change in Plog's role, after the seminar we requested Jim Judge to evaluate our efforts in relationship to Southwestern archaeology. Shirley Powell's contribution was solicited after the seminar because of our realization that the volume would be improved with a more thorough discussion of the role of demography in culture change. Pat Kirch, who has published widely on cultural evolution and adaptation, was asked to participate in the seminar as someone who could provide a non-Southwestern perspective to our research.

A summation of some of the results of the Advanced Seminar has been published (Dean, J. S., R. C. Euler, G. J. Gumerman, F. Plog, R. H. Hevly, and T. N. V. Karlstrom, "Human Behavior, Demography, and Paleoenvironment on the Colorado Plateaus," *American Antiquity* 1985). This article is also known more widely but more informally as "The Gang of Five, Plus One, Minus Two, Meet Bombay Gin Martinis at Sweeny's," the result of a Dean, Euler, Gumerman, Plog (the latter is "the plus one") meeting (minus Hevly and Karlstrom) at a bar/restaurant (Sweeny's) in Durango that provided inspirational martinis.

The organization of this volume reflects the cooperative venture. Unlike most edited volumes, this monograph is not a compilation of articles about a single topic. While each paper can stand alone, the value of the studies is that they are essential segments of a whole. Each article is a building block for understanding the total edifice of the Anasazi in relation to their changing environment. After the first chapter, a historical perspective on culture and its relationship to environment, a model is presented for understanding the relationships between environment, demography, and behavior. Data from the fields of hydrogeology, pollen, tree rings, population, and archaeology are then presented. Finally, there is a chapter in which the natural and cultural data presented in earlier chapters are analyzed and attempts are made to explain how the Anasazi reacted to their changing environment. This is accomplished by describing different environmental and demographic situations and then predicting appropriate behavioral responses. The fit of the predicted response to the real situation is then examined.

As in all our earlier published work, we do not view this as the final word on the relationship between the Anasazi and their environment. Archaeologists' early views on Southwestern culture and environment were hampered by a paucity of hard data. In many instances, the implications of our work became obscured by the diversity and immense quantity of data and it was necessary for us to adopt a synthesizing view. It is our hope that Anasazi scholars can use this method, data, and the theory represented by this volume to refine further our understanding of past peoples and environments on the Colorado Plateaus.

All the seminar participants are greatly indebted to Douglas W. Schwartz and the personnel of the School of American Research for their encouragement and hospitality. Special thanks go to Jane Barbarousse, whose warmth and congeniality made the Seminar House a homey refuge that encouraged stimulating thought and conversation. O. J. Sarah and the kitchen crew at the Seminar House can be blamed for our more spherical shapes at the end of the week. Jane Kepp, Director of Publications for the School of American Research, helped shepherd the manuscript through the publication process.

The final preparation of this manuscript was aided at Southern Illinois University by Barbara Cohen, Lee Hill, and Susan Wilson who did the technical editing, by Kathy Zeh, who directed the manuscript typing and assembly, and by Terri Mathews who did most of the typing. The drawings were rendered by Carole Prowse and Karen Schmitt. Special thanks for financial support go to Peabody Coal Company of St. Louis, Missouri, and to the Office of Research, Development, and Administration at Southern Illinois University at Carbondale.

GEORGE J. GUMERMAN

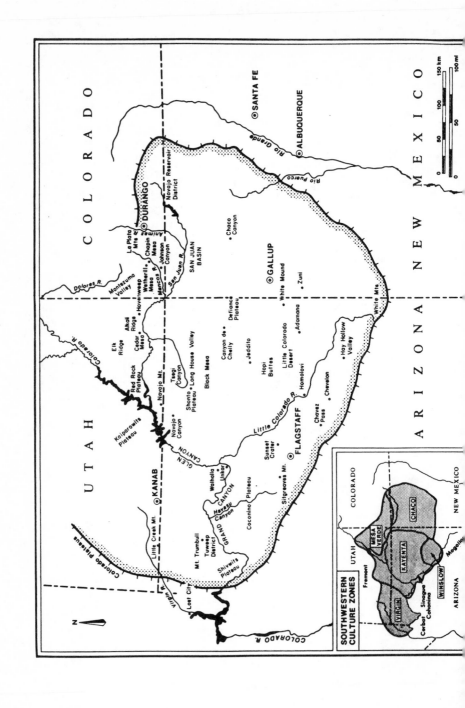

1
A historical perspective on environment and culture in Anasazi country

GEORGE J. GUMERMAN

Department of Anthropology
Center for Archaeological Investigations
Southern Illinois University at Carbondale

Observations concerning the relationships between environment and human behavior are hardly a new arena of inquiry for archaeologists – or anyone else, for that matter. This volume, however, represents the culmination of an ambitious long-range attempt on the part of the contributors to bring to bear a tremendous amount of natural and cultural data on explanations for the development of Anasazi culture and perhaps the evolution of complex societies in general. It is an effort, called informally by us the Paleoenvironment Project, to come to grips in a realistic fashion with the universal problem of large-scale ecological studies – the testing of the fit between diverse voluminous data and cultural–ecological models. It is not the purpose of this volume to develop a universal model for the testing of all ecological–cultural linkages. Nor shall we detail the historical foundations of an ecological anthropology. Numerous summaries have documented the evolution of method and theory in ecological anthropology (i.e., Anderson 1973; Harris 1968; Jochim 1979; Vayda and McCay 1975). In order, however, to understand and evaluate the methods and the models that are developed for our purposes, it is necessary to set our study in an evolutionary perspective.

In many ways, the evolution of anthropologists' conceptual under-

1

standing of the coupling of environment and culture is an outstanding example of the general development of the entire discipline. Whether environment is ignored or given deterministic qualities, whether it is viewed in its grossest global terms or in single organismatic caloric units, the view anthropologists have of the culture–nature link is a fairly accurate reflection of both the sophistication of our general anthropological models and the precision of our methods. The American Southwest with its semiarid environment, generations of intensive field exploration, and prehistoric continuity provides an ideal subset of the ecological–anthropological sample, reflective of the evolution of anthropological method and theory.

In order to comprehend more clearly the development of understanding about climate and population in the prehistoric Southwest, it is profitable to examine how refinement in (1) techniques and methods, (2) conceptual frameworks, and (3) changes in the scale of observation and analysis have influenced our present perception of the problem.

Methods and techniques of course are the tools we use for describing and measuring the environment and human behavior. These involve not only anthropology but numerous other disciplines. The details of the strengths and weaknesses of the methods and techniques of those other disciplines as well as their underlying assumptions, which form the basis of the conceptual frameworks of these disciplines, are discussed in following chapters.

The conceptual models which ecological anthropologists employ determine, in large part, the interpretation of the data which have been accumulated by various techniques and methods. The conceptual model by which we are constrained or liberated structures our perception of the relationship between human beings and the environment. It is the construct which not only allows us to interpret the data, but determines how the data are interpreted.

The scale of observation and analysis is the breadth or focus of a specific unit of study. Scale here is used in the mundane sense referring to the relative size of something or the scope of activity. It is the narrowness or broadness of a scope of inquiry on any level of investigation. The scale of observation (whether determined by the limitations of methods and techniques or conscious selection, collection, and analysis strategies) often profoundly affects the interpretation of the data. Change or continuity may be masked or enhanced by the division of archaeological phases; the collection units or sampling intervals for

2

pollen, soil samples, and artifacts; averaging of tree-ring width indices on a five-year, decadal, or century basis. Scale of observation and analysis is pertinent to and cross-cuts both techniques and conceptual models and affects the collection of data and their interpretation.

The very triteness of the observation that variation in the scale of observation and analysis affects our perception of what we are investigating has perhaps dulled our conscious sensitivities of its importance. In any case, scale is a convenient gauge with which to judge the effectiveness of cultural–ecological studies because it is a yardstick that can be applied to methods and techniques as well as conceptual models.

A BRIEF HISTORY OF ECOLOGICAL ANTHROPOLOGY IN THE SOUTHWEST

In the Southwest, one of the earlier calls for understanding the people in the context of their environment came from Lyndon Lane Hargrave, who, in a report on the Rainbow Bridge–Monument Valley Expedition (1935:24), declared archaeology inseparable from human ecology. It took no brilliant insight, of course, to establish that this semiarid, nearly barren land, raked as it is by incredible variations in precipitation and temperature, profoundly affected the behavior of its past and present human inhabitants. The Rainbow Bridge–Monument Valley Expedition exemplifies for the Southwest the difficulty of reconciling method with theory in ecological anthropology. Notwithstanding its lofty goals for studying past human ecology, the published reports on the project provided little analysis of human and natural environment (Beals, Brainerd, and Smith 1945).

Most early archaeological and anthropological studies used a broad scale of both observation and analysis in terms of the interpretation of the relationships between the natural environment and culture. Beyond general musings about population variabilities in the Southwest, most early efforts to explain demographic shifts were quite specific as to the locality of population movements and the possible causes of the movements. This early period of scientific exploration in Southwestern cultural ecology was characterized by *particularistic explanations*.

Beginning in the 1950s, improved methods and new techniques were developed for estimating populations and determining past environments. Conceptual models were devised that treated culture and environment as a holistic entity. Nevertheless, these schemes were

3

usually static, with both the natural environment and culture viewed as relatively homogeneous entities in homeostasis. This period may be called one of *mechanistic cultural–ecological explanations*. Although culture and the natural environment were viewed in a quasi-systems sense, the variability between culture and environment as well as the number of variables impinging on the relationship was minimized. Furthermore, there was little in the way of testing conceptual models against the data during the period. What data existed tended to be interpreted in terms of gross scales of analysis.

By the late 1960s, anthropologists were using much finer scales of observation and analysis and viewing culture and environment as much more heterogeneous, often in a state of systemic disequilibrium. It was understood that in many habitats continual cultural adjustments had to be made to accommodate a perpetually fluctuating natural environment. The nuances of cultural buffering of environmental perturbations began to be more widely appreciated. In addition, concerns about the appropriate scale of observation and analysis began to take on added importance. This stage is characterized by much more *dynamic cultural–ecological explanations*.

While these three types of explanations tend to follow one another in historical progression, this is not always the case simply because in some instances investigators see "causes" for cultural change in a restricted area or are constrained by inadequate data. Most southwestern scholars, regardless of the type of explanation they employ, are at least peripherally interested in the kinds of population adjustments in space and time which characterized much of the Anasazi occupation of the Colorado Plateaus. As a result, changing views of population movement and abandonment provide an effective yardstick by which to measure the scale and sophistication of different explanations.

PARTICULARISTIC EXPLANATIONS

Conceptual models

Many of the earliest explanations for variations in population size or population movement were attempts to link specific populations to unique, usually catastrophic events, such as Frank Hamilton Cushing's heartfelt assertion in 1890 that earthquakes caused the abandonment of many of the large prehistoric towns in southern Arizona (Haury 1945).

4

Less fanciful was Harold S. Colton's (1932) hypothesis that the eruption of Sunset Crater in the mid-eleventh century was a major factor in population movements around the San Francisco volcanic field near Flagstaff, Arizona. Colton hypothesized that people were initially driven from the area of the erupting volcano, but later were attracted to the region because the cinders provided a suitable mulch for the agricultural fields. While Colton's hypothesis has recently been criticized (Pilles 1979), his formulation is remarkable for tying the abandonment of a restricted geographic area to a specific environmental event, and for linking the repopulation with environmental changes caused by the volcanic eruption and with the prehistoric farming technology. Furthermore, he was able to date the volcanic eruption by the newly discovered technique of dendrochronology because volcanic ash covered structures containing datable beams. Colton's scale of analysis was quite detailed over a limited region and for a narrow span of time.

This early era of particularistic environmental explanations for population movement and demographic change was not necessarily limited to climatic fluctuations, as the earthquake and volcanic theories demonstrate. Colton (1936: 337–43) felt that some apparent population declines resulted from the spread of epidemic diseases caused by crowded pueblos and unsanitary conditions. However, few, if any, archaeologists and epidemiologists now view disease as the sole cause of site abandonment on the Colorado Plateaus at any particular time, although they do agree that it may have been a contributing factor in some instances (Kunitz and Euler 1972).

More pervasive in the literature than disease as a reason for population decimation and movement is the spectre of "enemy peoples" arriving in the northern Southwest (Jett 1964, 1965). Population movements are viewed, not as the result of natural environmental factors, but as the consequence of cultures impinging on one another through increased competition for scarce resources. Warfare and feuding undoubtedly caused some displacement of populations in the Southwest, yet few archaeologists accept the view that large-scale population movements evidenced in the archaeological record are due to the incursion of enemy peoples or internecine warfare (Davis 1965). It makes more sense, as in the case of disease, to posit warfare as one of the results of a disequilibrium between population and resources than to see it as a cause for the disequilibrium.

Methods and techniques

The development of dendrochronologial and dendroclimatological techniques in the late 1920s and early 1930s by A. E. Douglass and archaeological colleagues eventually led to the development of more geographically widespread and more dynamic models of culture change linked to environmental events. The retrodiction of past climate, especially precipitation, as the result of dendro studies not only permitted an evaluation of each year's climate, but, because of the chronological aspect of the method, it permitted archaeologists to relate population movements over large areas to one another and to specific climatic trends. These first efforts in the 1930s, as might be expected, were searches for dramatic climatic shifts which were echoed in major population shifts with a very direct cause-and-effect linkage between environment and population movement. This culminated in delineating events such as the "Great Drought" between A.D. 1276 and 1299, which was supposed to account for a great deal of population movement.

In order to link population movements with environmental factors, there had to be some quantification of population size at specific times, but methods for determining prehistoric populations were in their formative stages. Since sites could be relatively dated by means of their ceramic assemblages and, later, by dendrochronology, early scholars were able to discern that sites of certain periods were much more numerous than sites of other periods. In addition, it was obvious that many localities with evidence of past human occupation were not presently occupied nor did they seem to have been during the Spanish *entradas*. But these observations were vague and imprecise.

Colton (1936) made the first efforts at quantifying population estimates. He estimated the number of sites for an area, the number of rooms for an average site, the number of families per room, and the number of individuals in a family. While he realized the inaccuracy of his figures, he felt that his method could at least demonstrate demographic trends. Colton's method, while crude, is still the basis for most demographic studies in the Southwest.

Although these first attempts to correlate environment with population shifts and site abandonment were characterized by simple particularistic models of the relationships between the two variables, the technique that was used remains unchanged. This method involves

6

developing a population curve and a climate or precipitation curve, by whatever methods; dating the events; and noting correspondences, for example, between increasing population and wetter climatic regimes or between decreasing population and dryer climatic regimes.

MECHANISTIC CULTURAL–ECOLOGICAL EXPLANATIONS

Conceptual models

The term *mechanistic*, as applied to this type of model, is not meant to carry a pejorative connotation. The researchers who used these models saw culture and environment in a holistic, integrated manner, but were often constrained by methods which did not allow them to use very fine-grained scales of observation and analysis, by the use of general ecological principles which were not sufficiently developed for a sophisticated understanding of the natural environment, and by inadequate data. Furthermore, they perceived both culture and the environment as relatively homeostatic with only major change in one or the other causing disequilibrium.

It was Julian Steward who devised a conceptual model of cultural ecology by means of which it became possible to conduct a detailed study of the interplay between culture and environment. Steward was the first modern scholar to apply concrete examples in landmark early studies (1936, 1937) of cultural phenomena to the broader conceptual models of what he called "cultural ecology" (1955). Steward was one of those individuals who was capable of testing large-scale cultural ecological theory through a fine-scale analysis of data, a rare accomplishment even today. Steward's concept of the relationship between environment and culture, especially technology, was important because it assumed the systemic relationship between various aspects of culture. Among his contemporaries, only Leslie White had the same vision. Technology was conditioned by the natural environment, as were sociopolitical institutions and ideology. It was Steward's explorations of the relationship between environment and culture which introduced a new era into archaeological interpretation and has subsequently exerted a profound influence upon the modern generation of archaeologists.

The lure of Steward's, and to a lesser extent White's, concept for the archaeologist springs from several points. In the first place, the very idea

7

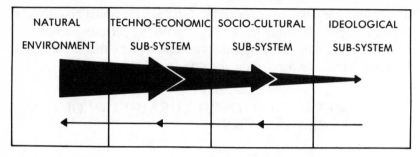

Figure 1.1 Mechanistic model of cultural–environmental relationships. While the subsystems of culture were seen as articulating with one another and with the natural environment, the strengths of the relationships were seen to vary, with the strongest relationships (wide arrows) being the environment and techno-economic subsystem and the weakest (narrow arrows) the natural environment and ideological subsystems. The cultural subsystems were generally seen to have no major influence on one another and on the natural environment (left-pointing arrows), especially the ideological subsystem.

of the interrelatedness of the various aspects of culture rekindled hope among archaeologists that the reconstruction of the nonmaterial aspects of culture could be accomplished. Following the reconstruction of the techno-economic system, according to this view, it should be possible to infer related aspects of a sociological and ideological nature. Secondly, archaeologists tended to feel that the material culture related to subsistence, which Steward stressed, was most plentiful in the archaeological record and also the easiest to interpret. Thirdly, both White and Steward's conceptual models are inextricably linked with cultural evolution. As many scholars have noted since then, evolution provides the theoretical basis for ecological studies (Jochim 1979:78; Kirch 1980). Hence, contemplating White's and Steward's ideas about the primacy of technology and environment, the presumed relative ease of extracting environmental and technological data from the ground, and the coupling of cultural ecology and evolution, archaeologists were having visions of whole extinct cultural systems dance in their heads (Binford 1965; Kushner 1970; Fritz 1972) (Figure 1.1).

Steward was followed by other ethnographers and theoreticians, such as Titiev (1944), Eggan (1950, 1966), Dozier (1970), and Ford (1972), who provided detailed descriptions of the interaction between Puebloan peoples and their environment, as well as models for archaeologists to test.

Demographic conceptual models during this period were usually based on relatively simple schemes, mostly Malthusian in nature, or more recently, based on the schemes promulgated by Boserup (1965; see Zubrow 1975, for a review of anthropological, demographic, and economic models). The number of conflicting hypotheses concerning demographic processes, as well as misinterpretations of these hypotheses, have resulted in confusion rather than clarity. Suffice it to say that the view has prevailed since the 1950s and 1960s that increases in population are a source of culture change and only a small number of archaeologists continue to see culture change as a cause of demographic change.

The single overriding commonality among demographic studies of the mechanistic cultural–ecological model is that they view population and resources as normally being in a state of static equilibrium with only occasional states of disequilibrium. Dean (Chapter 2 below) provides a fuller statement on the role of demography in culture change.

Methods and techniques

Concomitant with the development of conceptual models for formulating an ecological anthropology in the Southwest was the refinement and discovery of techniques for reconstructing paleoclimate, estimating extinct populations, and dating both. Techniques such as radiocarbon dating, palynology, and surficial geology were initially largely divorced from the development of conceptual models. Instead they were most often used to develop local sequences and to sketch in general ways local climate variations. Established variations in climate were used as explanations for culture change when both cultural and climatic changes appeared to be coincident.

Tree-ring studies over the years continued to refine the relationship between ring growth and climate (Fritts 1976), so that many local dating and climate sequences were constructed. Radiocarbon dating complemented dendrochronology, especially for early sites and depositional units which contained no datable artifacts or beams. Palynology became a very important technique for paleoclimate reconstruction, especially when studies were done on a regional basis (Hevly 1964a; Martin 1963;

9

Schoenwetter and Dittert 1968). Schoenwetter and Dittert's landmark study was a vital step in understanding the linkages between climate and culture, because they made interpretations about culture change not only on the basis of climate and more specifically rainfall, but on the seasonability of the precipitation.

Hack's (1942) study of the surficial geology and hydrology of the Hopi country built on the early pioneering work of Bryan (1925; 1928; 1954) and contemporary work of Bryan (1954) and Antevs (1952; 1955) provided the baseline study in the northern Southwest for using the very recent geology for reconstructing climate. Hack's work also permitted the relative dating of sites found in similar depositional units. In addition, Hack, a geologist, produced in the same volume an excellent exposition of the relationship between environment, technology, and social organization. The Hopi, Hack showed, were able to adapt to a high-risk environment by planting in a great diversity of environmental niches, usually ensuring the successful maturation of crops in at least several of the niches. The strength of Hack's study lies in its use of a relatively fine scale of observation and analysis to address larger questions of adaptation, combined with the use of precise analytical techniques, in this case surficial geology, to test concepts of cultural adaptation.

Each of these techniques, as with dendro studies, was first applied to gross problems, with little knowledge of limitations in methodological applications and interpretations. Later, increasing refinement of the various techniques, coupled with better understanding of their strengths and weaknesses, permitted a more realistic appraisal of the relative value in reconstructing paleoenvironments.

Parallel to the development of these various techniques was the evolution of increasingly refined archaeological techniques, such as finer provenience control, and improved screening and flotation in order to recover proxy data for paleoclimate and demographic trends.

Until the mid-1970s archaeological methods for estimating population were mechanistic and, as I said earlier, assumed that static equilibrium was the normal condition. Estimations of population size from this period were based on cemetery body counts, room and site counts, room size, size of cooking vessels, and amounts of food refuse, among other things. But few archaeologists gave actual population figures for an area; instead, relative figures for different periods were the rule, and for most purposes that sufficed. But mechanistic models also

10

usually showed smooth curves with few perturbations because of the assumed population-to-resource balance, the use of a relatively large temporal scope of observation and analysis, and imprecision in determining population figures.

Increasing refinement of techniques in the natural sciences and in archaeology itself led scholars to the ironic situation of having more data than they could handle, often of a conflicting nature, and which had been collected and analyzed at different scales. This situation made the testing of general cultural–ecological models extraordinarily difficult. No individual or even single large field research project could control enough environmental and cultural data or standardize it enough to test broad hypotheses about human–environmental relationships on a pan-Colorado Plateaus level.

Two different and continuing attempts have been made to grapple with the problem of voluminous, nonstandardized data to explain Anasazi behavioral patterns.

The Southwestern Anthropological Research Group (SARG) is a consortium of scholars who, while conducting individual research projects, gather data in a comparable manner in order to address questions of common concern and to attain common goals (Gumerman 1971; Euler and Gumerman 1978). The researchers have attempted to understand regional settlement systems throughout much of the Anasazi country and ultimately to derive universally applicable laws for understanding settlement location. Much of the data collected in SARG's standard format and placed in SARG data banks is therefore concerned with the natural environment. The difficulty of working with very fine-scale units of analysis to test hypotheses on a large regional basis was overcome by holding individual members of SARG responsible for data collection at a local level. The problems of implementing the initial SARG research design were primarily ones of operationalization, standardization of data and sample size, and difficulties in hypothesis testing.

The second major effort at using a very fine scale of analysis to understand regional cultural–environmental correlations is the informally structured Paleoenvironmental Project (Euler *et al.* 1979) which forms the foundation for this volume. Its primary goal is to identify these relationships empirically. Geological, palynological, and dendroclimatological data have been collected specifically for the project or obtained from other earlier and ongoing studies conducted by other

11

scholars. These data have been buttressed by scores of tree-ring and radiocarbon dates and measured against prehistoric population fluctuations in eleven different localities on the Colorado Plateaus. There appears to be a strong positive correlation between mesic periods and population increase and xeric episodes and population movement and abandonment. As has been stated by many individuals, however, demonstrating correlations among the variables of climate and population change may be suggestive but does not constitute proof of underlying relationships nor explain those relationships.

The strength of the Paleoenvironmental Project study is that each line of evidence – archaeology, geohydrology, dendroclimatology, and palynology as well as the dating methods – is independently derived. The data for each technique are evaluated independently and the concordance builds confirming evidence, one source against all the others. While this method does not constitute absolute proof, it does establish the existence of potentially significant relationships.

While the method stands the test of scrutiny, there have been some problems with the data, especially regarding variations in scales of observation and analysis used by different investigators; not all the local archaeological sequences used in the study are securely dated; archaeological phase boundaries previously used by us to indicate behavioral change were often determined by stylistic breaks rather than by period of rapid culture or population change; population figures in different locales were often derived by different methods; dating of natural and cultural events varies in accuracy from a single year to a century or more; and finally, every method used for reconstructing climate and prehistoric populations in the study needs an assessment of the adequacy and the quality of the samples used (Dean, Chapter 2 below). Most importantly, it is apparent that the study must take the next logical step and *explain* the relation between the observed population and environmental change.

Both of these large-scale research projects have attempted to come to grips with fine-scale data of incredible magnitude in different ways. Interestingly, both projects have had the charge of environmental determinism leveled against them. While both have noted in their early stages that the relationship between environmental change and cultural change is very complex, the juxtaposition of demographic or population spatial distribution with climatic trends or environmental variables implies a causal relationship. In a sense such criticism, while perhaps valid at the time, is premature since both projects are very long-term endeavors at publishing, with the intention of disseminating results to obtain reaction in order to modify and refine the research schemes. The early SARG meetings stressed the need for the endeavor to be a long-term effort – at least a decade. The individuals involved in the Paleoenvironment Project, begun informally in 1966, only gradually realized the scale of the efforts and the amount of time necessary to accomplish the objectives of understanding Anasazi culture change and its relationship to environment. Both projects recognize without question the need to provide more dynamic cultural–ecological explanations and both are endeavoring to do so.

DYNAMIC CULTURAL–ECOLOGICAL EXPLANATIONS

By the early 1970s it became apparent that static conceptual models for explaining the interrelation between culture and environment were inadequate. As late as 1968 Vayda and Rappaport (1968:492) advanced the idea of a single science of ecology with laws and principles that applied to all organisms, including humans. In short, they advanced the concept of true systems ecology.

More recently dynamic ecological models are characterized by (1) a realization of the importance of *all* subsystems in the cultural and natural system, (2) an understanding that disequilibrium between population and resources is the normal state, rather than a delicately balanced equilibrium, (3) an appreciation of the role of cultural and environmental variability in both spatial and temporal vectors when considering cultural adaptation, (4) a greater understanding of cultural buffering mechanisms, (5) the knowledge that humans do not always act to optimize their energy return from the environment nor do they always have the necessary knowledge about their environment to make optimizing decisions.

Conceptual models

Truly *systemic models* have been developed for understanding the relationship between cultural and natural subsystems without resorting to the primacy of one subsystem over another (Figure 1.2). Most mechanistic explanations for culture change focus on the techno-

13

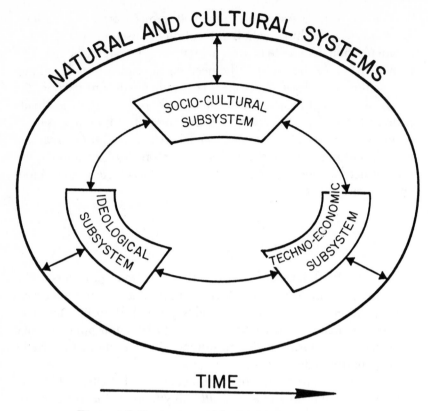

Figure 1.2 Dynamic model of cultural–environmental
relationships. The cultural subsystems are viewed as having
more equal interaction with one another, with the natural
environment and with other cultures. Furthermore, the systems
are not viewed as inherently stable homogeneous units.

economic aspect of culture and on the competition for the production of
energy. Vayda and Rappaport (1968), Kent Flannery (1972), James
Anderson (1973), and Roy Rappaport (1979) have been especially
persuasive in their arguments that ecological systems studies have to
include aspects of culture, such as humanistic variables, previously
considered outside the sphere of ecological studies. Flannery (1972:424)
even goes so far as to say that, in the study of the evolution of
civilizations, humanistic and ideological concerns may be more
important than the manner in which these complex societies produced
their food. This view has been challenged by others (Sanders and

14

Webster 1978) who continue to view the techno-economic subsystem as having primacy. Nevertheless, the point is clear; noneconomic, nontechnological phenomena are critically important for an understanding of the dynamic relationships of the various subsystems of culture and environment. Kinship systems, values, and beliefs, as well as exchange networks, all have important roles in a systems ecology.

Related to the concept of a total systems ecology has been the realization of the impact of culture on the environment and the sure knowledge that some environmental change detected in the archaeological record was culturally induced. Correspondences between culture change and environmental change in prehistoric situations therefore do *not* indicate whether culture or environment was the causative agent – or indeed if either of them was (Euler *et al.* 1979:1089).

Flannery (1968) was also instrumental in forcing archaeologists to look at the role of *dynamic disequilibrium* in cultural systems. More and more scholars have begun to recognize that the normal state for many cultural systems is dynamic disequilibrium, that there is seldom a delicately balanced relationship between resources and people, and that population–resource imbalance is a fact of life (Dean, Chapter 2 below; Vayda and McCay 1975; Winterhalder 1980). Accompanying this understanding has been the current realization that there is never an absolute population capacity at an exact point in time for a given technology (Kirch 1980:144). In short, as equilibrium-centered views in ecology have come to be viewed as essentially static and lacking in insight for transient systems (Holling 1973), some anthropologists have come to accept this dynamic view for cultural systems (Vayda and McCay 1975).

While archaeologists have recognized the need to go beyond normative theory to more realistic models of past patterned human behavior, they and other anthropologists, with few exceptions, have tended to conceptualize the natural environment in a normative and nondynamic fashion (Winterhalder 1980). Dynamic explanations have demonstrated that the concept of average for most environmental variables has little meaning for effective human adaptation. More important than concepts centering on average or normal conditions are those which focus on the degrees or range of the many environmental properties of temporal variability and spatial heterogeneity. The ability of a cultural system to respond to the range in spatial and temporal variation in the natural environment is one index of cultural adaptation (Slobodkin and Rappaport 1974; Vayda and McCay 1975). This does not imply that environmental change is an adequate explanation for culture change only if the environmental deviation from the norm is exceptional as Slobodkin (1972) has indicated, or that "hazards" research (Vayda and McCay 1975) should focus on catastrophic events rather than chronic hazards. Instead this view emphasizes that environmental properties deviate from a norm in spatial and temporal frameworks, and a culture has to cope and make evolutionary adjustments in response to these deviations.

Dynamic equilibrium models have focused on three broad categories of environmental and cultural variables with reference to past human behavior: (1) relative spatial heterogeneity; (2) temporal variability; and (3) coping strategies. A number of ways have been suggested in which spatial and temporal variability can be categorized and evaluated in relation to past human behavior, based on concepts generated in biology and the systematic ecology (Winterhalder 1980). Plog et al. (Chapter 8 below) provide examples of the anthropological use of spatial hetero-geneity and temporal variability. These ecological concepts permit an increasingly fine scale of observation and analysis and encourage the viewing of an ecosystem as dynamic, taking historical processes into account. The implication for archaeologists is that finer analysis of spatial and temporal variability of the natural environment is necessary if we are going to understand the persistent human coping behavior that is necessary in an environment in dynamic disequilibrium.

While it is necessary in many cases to rely on the talents of ecologists to evaluate the environment adequately, coping strategies can best be addressed by archaeologists. Adjustment to an existing dynamic environment is of immediate advantage to a human population. However, whether or not this short-term adaptation is advantageous in the long run is purely a matter of chance. "Preadaptation" within an existing environment is defined as the ability of a population to respond or fail to respond to future conditions (Kirch 1980:123).

Because short-term responses to daily, seasonal, or annual change seem to have produced the vast majority of the archaeological record (Cordell and Plog 1979:409), archaeologists have to be attuned to detecting subtle shifts in almost any aspect of the archaeological record. Unfortunately slight modifications or shifts in emphasis in lifeways are more difficult to detect archaeologically than is innovation. A minor increase in collected wild plant foods because of decreasing crop yields may go undetected by the archaeologist because of sampling error, differential preservation, the fact that different segments of a society may stress different strategies, or the fact that the perceived environment may be different from this actual environment (Anderson 1973: 211; Rappaport 1979). The introduction of a new cultigen or replacement of the atlatl by the bow and arrow is more obvious.

Any attempt to explain regional relationships between the cultural and natural environments requires a much finer scale of observation and analysis than archaeologists are used to or maybe even capable at this time of dealing with. The issue becomes even more complicated if we recognize the variety of ways any society can attempt to accommodate environmental change.

Societies reduce the stress caused by environmental perturbations by cultural buffering mechanisms, which compensate for the effects of environmental change. Many examples of cultural buffering have been cited, but it is only relatively recently that the extent and degree of this dampening of the effects of environmental fluctuations have been recognized (Braun and Plog 1982; Jorde 1977; Judge *et al.* 1981). Cordell and Plog have categorized three broad adaptational strategies and their buffering characteristics: demographic, productive, and organizational.

Demographic strategies include population limiting strategies, such as infanticide and postpartum taboos, population movement, and the manipulation of the distribution of population over the landscape. Similarly, productive strategies include decisions concerning the use of particular resources, specialization in production and subsequent exchange, storage, and the intensification of production. Finally, organizational strategies include variations of social roles, social institutions, social decision making, social contact, and social stratification. (1979:409)

For any given cultural system, a large number of behavioral variables must be considered in order to understand how that system mitigates environmental changes. The following consideration of these buffering, or adaptational, strategies within the context of the Anasazi Southwest provides an opportunity to examine these processes.

Demographic buffers relate to the relationship between human population, cultural behavior, and resources. Recent anthropological literature dealing with demographic buffers has been fraught with determinism, conflicting and opposing views, and with glib generalizations (Powell, Chapter 6 below). The cause-and-effect nature of most of the models dealing with the relationship between population and resources (Boserup 1965; Cohen 1977) seems to be an attractive aspect to archaeologists, individual scholars picking models which best suit their needs at the time. Dean (Chapter 2 below) and Powell (Chapter 6 below) have most adequately addressed the demographic situation for the Anasazi.

The important point here is that most recent evidence suggests that the Anasazi populations were constantly undergoing subsistence stress (El-Najjar et al. 1976; Martin et al. 1982), except perhaps for the earliest periods when population density was low. The implication is that there were constant resource–population imbalances and that this situation required constant fine-tuning of coping techniques in order to dampen the subsistence stress.

Cordell and Plog (1979:411) have suggested that conscious population-limiting behavior, "voluntary" in Dean's terms (Chapter 2 below), such as postpartum taboos and infanticide, had little effect on population size. At present, however, there is no evidence either to support or refute this hypothesis.

A major premise of many Southwest studies has been that people tend to move in order to take advantage of ameliorating climatic conditions or to lessen the effects of deteriorating ones (Euler, Chapter 7 below; Powell, Chapter 6 below). But, like many human demographic situations, the movement of populations is not simply a resources–population equation, but is profoundly affected by social factors. Even when decisions to move have to be made, the "abandonment" process is buffered by organizational factors. As has been noted before (Gumerman and Euler 1976), in some instances the last period of occupation of an area is characterized by the virtual absence of whole artifacts, including even metates which are so prominent otherwise, suggesting a nearby move to a known location. In other cases whole pueblos are left with all the appurtenances of daily life remaining, and in still other instances, much of the household inventory was destroyed before moving, suggesting different kinds of "abandonment" processes were operating.

The contemporaneous occupations of Betatakin and Kiet Siel are one example of different occupational histories only a few kilometers apart (Dean 1970). Betatakin was probably settled in a preplanned move by a group of people who already constituted a community. Thereafter

18

Betatakin grew largely by internal population growth rather than by immigration. Kiet Siel, on the other hand, was settled as a result of various immigrations into the cliff shelter with the probability that people arrived from different places. Dean infers this from the great variety of architectural styles, the large number and style of kivas and the fact that there seems to be no overall village planning, but a gradual accretion of individual households (1970:161).

These types of "abandonment" suggest that the term masks a great variety of behavior, which is probably internally related to productive and organizational buffering systems. Decisions to move, where and when to move, and the manner in which the abandonment of an area is undertaken are probably closely related to organizational systems.

Productive buffers to moderate population–resource imbalances have always been a staple of archaeological inquiry. A whole recent literature has developed that stresses Anasazi productive behavior as (1) much more diverse than previously thought (Judge *et al.* 1981; Nelson 1980; Powell 1983), and (2) that Anasazi villages were not autonomous, but were involved in a complex network of trade and other forms of interaction (Braun and Plog 1982; Deutchman 1980; Judge *et al.* 1981; Plog and Powell 1981; S. Plog 1980b).

The realization of these two important facts has great implications for our understanding of Anasazi adaptability. Early archaeologists first used a broad scale of observation and analysis, discussing adaptational transformations such as the origins of agriculture and increasingly settled life. Later the scale was narrowed to include such buffers as water and soil control systems. Finally archaeologists recognized the great adaptability afforded by the mixed economy which varies annually or seasonally and which has been demonstrated archaeologically. For example, conceptual models about adaptation have been profoundly affected by both the ability to detect seasonal occupation in the archaeological record and the recognition of the social and economic effects of seasonally occupying different environments (Powell 1983). This narrowing of the scale of observation and analysis does not mean that the investigation of productive strategies, such as adoption of agriculture or agricultural intensification, are no longer of interest in understanding productive buffers. They have simply been absorbed into a larger repertoire of productive buffers archaeologists can investigate.

The ability to detect intercommunity social and economic ties made it possible to postulate the existence of highly developed networks of alliances. The proposal of a nonautonomous economic status for thousands of Anasazi habitation sites suggests that individual small communities shared in an increased, broader resource base. By forging social and economic links with a number of communities in the highly heterogeneous environment of the Colorado Plateaus, the Anasazi were able to spread the economic risks and benefits of production in a constricted geographical range.

This kind of adaptation in a spatial framework is especially important in a patchy environment such as the Southwest. As Kirch (1980:135) has noted, human behavior assumes the structure of a nested spatial hierarchy. On the most spatially constricted level is the site and site catchment. Second in size is the larger sustaining unit of the group, and finally the broader regions which contain several societies. Mobility on a daily and seasonal basis, structures of exchange networks, kinship-system population size, as well as traits of the environment all affect the physical size of the nested hierarchy and adaptational characteristics. A network of social and economic alliances has the effect of increasing the site catchment for individual sites, as well as the larger sustaining area of the community. Different productive strategies for varied environments and demographic situations require different adjustments in the size and intensity of social and economic networks.

For years the Western Pueblo and more specifically the Hopi have provided an example of how organizational structure has been a buffering mechanism from the vagaries of climatic fluctuation (Bradfield 1971; Hack 1942; F. Plog 1978). Only recently archaeologists have recognized the true importance of the social organizational aspects in the process of adaptation (Cordell and Plog 1979; Low 1981; Powell 1983).

The two most salient features of the Hopi organizational system are the interrelatedness of the parts and the ability of the system to adapt to changing environments and demographic variables. The Hopi cultural system, often characterized as structurally very rigid, is a highly flexible organization functionally, which allows effective coping behavior in an extremely patchy environment. The effects of drought, torrential summer rains, short growing season, violent sandstorms, and highly localized showers can be minimized by a social and religious organization which stresses community welfare, sharing, and cooperation. For example, since clans own the productive agricultural land and since that land is divided among many different environmental zones, such as

20

irrigated plots, sand dunes, and arroyo bottoms of various sizes, some crops in some environments are bound to reach maturity. The individual household does not have to assume the entire risk of crop failure by maintaining a single large plot in one environment. Instead, the clan acts as an insurance system, spreading the risks and stabilizing through diversification.

There is a great deal of archaeological evidence to suggest Anasazi organizational systems were even more diverse and flexible than they were historically. The contrasting environments of the Hopi Buttes and northern Black Mesa suggest different ways of intervillage integration (Gumerman 1975). Neither area could support large communities, but in an era of expanding population the Black Mesa environment could support "mother" villages with the expanding populations forming "daughter" populations, which maintained religious, social, and probably economic ties to the "mother" village. In the Hopi Buttes area, an even more xeric environment, villages were smaller and more scattered, necessitating a single large ceremonial and storage center. Both systems permitted social cohesion and encouraged economic interdependence by taking advantage of the diversity of environmental situations which required small and scattered communities. Each area, however, adapted to its particular environmental situation differently.

Another example of differential adaptation is suggested by the form and number of what the archaeologist calls kivas. Many sites which could support no more than twenty individuals have kivas, some of equal size have none, and in some instances sites of no more than ten habitation rooms have three kivas. These reflect local social and religious differences. In addition, some regions have many great kivas which have been hypothesized to integrate localities not only religiously but also economically and socially. Other very large areas are without a single great kiva. These examples of variations in the number and size of kivas suggest that the kiva associations described by ethnographers for the Western Pueblo did not pertain to most, if any, of the Anasazi.

In sum, the variations in the archaeological record usually thought to be the result of differential contacts with other groups, historical accident, or stylistic differences are often in all probability local organizational adaptations to a heterogeneous environment. Nevertheless, it must be kept in mind that humans do not necessarily perceive and respond to environmental change instantaneously. Furthermore,

21

social groups may not always desire to maximize their exploitation of the environment and, even if they did, their knowledge of the environment may be imperfect or incorrect.

Cultural buffers to environmental fluctuations are so great in number and often so subtle, sometimes involving nothing more than a slight but strategic shift in emphasis along any demographic, productive, or organizational line, that the variety of coping devices is almost infinite. Our current awareness of the importance of cultural buffers is so pervasive that one scholar suggests climatic factors are only an indirect influence on population movement (Low 1981). He sees climate as an external influence that creates a disequilibrium allowing the system to "work out an evolution dependent more on internal structure than on characteristics of climatological input" (1981: 281). While it is true that the relationship between population movement and environment is buffered by a large number of productive and organizational strategies, which determine the form that the adaptive behavior takes, the fact of environmental change and its influence on people cannot be denied.

Methods and techniques

The era of dynamic cultural–ecological explanations has been characterized by a refinement of techniques rather than the development of new ones. Infinitely more data are available which help stress the great variety of adaptations in the Colorado Plateaus area. Local variations are highlighted as well as regional commonalities.

Perhaps the greatest amount of new data relevant to human adaptation in the present era comes from the refinement of archaeological techniques for the recovering of floral and faunal material for reconstruction of past climates and subsistence behavior. Not only have flotation and screening with fine mesh screens become the required techniques, but so has the collection of samples in a standardized fashion. By systematically collecting and analyzing a specific sample size from each feature it is possible to make observations about the contents of different sites in a quantifiable way. The scale of observation and analysis can be the same for sites in different areas, and consequently conclusions become more demonstrable and verifiable.

Trace element studies for lithic and ceramic materials began to be used with greater frequency and precision. These techniques helped to establish the social and economic alliances that developed between

22

communities (Deutchman 1980; Green 1982; S. Plog 1980b). They enable the archaeologist to determine the nested spatial hierarchy, the site catchments and the larger sustaining units, and to distinguish networks of social and economic alliances.

Techniques were developed for more accurately estimating populations (Layhe 1981; F. Plog 1975), although, as Powell (Chapter 6 below) demonstrates, there are still many conceptual and methodological problems in understanding the demographic situation. Recent studies showed the existence, not of smooth curves of population increases and decreases, but of more logically defensible trends with deviations from the general trend. The realization of short-term deviations from population trends helped establish the population–resource disequilibrium as a fact of life.

By and large, methods and techniques helped to establish the great variability in adaptive techniques throughout the Colorado Plateaus and the fact of a cultural and natural disequilibrium.

PROSPECT

The increased sophistication of models and the large increase in the data base bode well for retrodiction of the relationship between environment and culture change. Cordell and Plog (1979) are correct in their assessment that the great cultural and natural diversity of the Colorado Plateaus dictates studies of adaptation at a local level, while broader cultural patterns necessitate the study of regional alliance systems and organizational forms. They are perhaps too pessimistic about our ability to recover the data necessary to perceive slight shifts in adaptation. They are not as pessimistic, however, as Walter Taylor who, in a study entitled *The Pueblo Ecology Study: Hail and Farewell* (1958), came to the conclusion that no site with enough perishable material was left intact to test the "Great drought hypothesis." I do not, however, underestimate the difficulty of our task.

With the realization that an almost infinite number of cultural and natural variables can and apparently do effect cultural and demographic change, it may appear that the task is hopelessly difficult. The models discussed have all been deterministic, i.e., they all seek underlying cause for cultural and demographic events, even the system models such as that promulgated by Low (1981). Few scholars, however, continue to see human adaptational behavior as a simple cause-and-effect relationship. The Anasazi did not respond in a mechanical way, as a barometer changes in ambient pressure. "Causation" is probably best viewed as the result of a multitude of interrelated processes, none of them having dominance over the others and therefore making prediction difficult.

This does not mean that the study of patterns is futile. Through an awareness of the variables and with cautious effort to work from local situations to regional generalizations, it should be possible, in an attempt such as this volume, to be able to test the data against the conceptual models of the systemic relationships between culture change and environment. We should not allow the complexity of the task to deter us. Ecologists themselves bemoan the fact that the studies of entire ecosystems are still in their formative stages, with investigators unable to come to an agreed-upon approach (Pomeroy 1981:1368). The intrusion of the cultural elements makes our task the more difficult.

Breakthroughs will occur when the conceptual models no longer outstrip our ability to test those models and when there is a reconciliation of method and theory. Clearly, the study of the complex relationships between environment and human behavior on a regional rather than a local level requires a long-term commitment by a number of individuals using fine-scale data, as the SARG and this volume attempt. Sometimes the results can seem like "archaeology by committee," but, if archaeologists and others concerned with past environment–human behavior relationships are to answer the questions they say are their concern, the attempt has to be made.

2
A model of Anasazi behavioral adaptation

JEFFREY S. DEAN

Laboratory of Tree-Ring Research
The University of Arizona
Tucson, Arizona

INTRODUCTION

A fortunate combination of circumstances provides archaeologists working in the Colorado Plateaus region of the American Southwest with greater control over the physical variables that affected prehistoric human populations than is available nearly anywhere else in the world. Intensive geomorphological, palynological, and dendroclimatic research in the region has produced a broad range of accurate, well integrated paleoenvironmental reconstructions that are related to one another by independent, high-resolution temporal controls provided by dendrochronology, ceramic placement, and radiocarbon dating. Even so, relating this paleoenvironmental knowledge to past human behavior remains a formidable problem. Any such exercise requires a theoretical orientation based on general conceptions ("models") of "universal" relationships between human behavior and the physical environment. Many such models are possible (Gumerman, Chapter 1 above); however, the most useful for our purposes are those that are focused on long-term behavioral (cultural) change.

Conceptual models of general processes of culture change enjoy wide application in contemporary archaeology (Gumerman, Chapter 1 above). This emphasis on culture process derives in part from the conviction that archaeology is unique among the behavioral sciences in controlling time spans of sufficient duration to permit long-term "systemic" culture change to be differentiated from impermanent, short-range variations in human behavior. Models of culture process that have been employed to explain Anasazi culture change differ from one another mainly in the independent variables advocated as causes of change in the dependent variable – patterned human behavior. Commonly, these constructs emphasize the role of one or another of three kinds of independent variable: environmental, demographic, and sociocultural.

While these formulations stress the causal primacy of one kind of variable over the others, interactive models that incorporate the dynamic interrelationships among several kinds of variable more accurately reflect the nature of human adaptive systems. Presented here is a provisional integrative formulation that applies relevant aspects of universal culture process models to the specific problem of Anasazi culture change in the environmental setting of the Colorado Plateaus. This is accomplished by delineating possible interrelationships among environmental, demographic, and behavioral variables that prevailed on the Plateaus during the last two millennia.

Two caveats are in order before elaborating this model of Anasazi adaptive processes. First, given the purpose of this volume, it is not my intention to create yet another universally applicable model of culture process. Rather, I propose only to develop a framework for examining the relationships, specifically, between Anasazi culture change and the documented paleoenvironmental variations on the Colorado Plateaus. Secondly, the model is a conceptual construct designed to direct attention to points of articulation between the environmental, demographic, and behavioral components of Anasazi adaptive systems. By specifying such critical points, the model provides a basis for qualitatively evaluating the effects of changes in one component on the others. The existence of a specific, integrative model of this type also underscores some of the problems that arise in relating Anasazi prehistory to the high-quality paleoenvironmental data available for the Colorado Plateaus.

THE MODEL

The Anasazi adaptation model is derived in part from broader anthropological and archaeological formulations concerning culture process in general. Three aspects of recent developments in human ecology are especially important in this regard. First, the modeling of human subsistence in terms of interactions among technology, behavior, and organization (Earle and Christenson 1980; Jochim 1976, 1981; Netting 1965, 1974, 1977) has established the explanatory power of a perspective that treats human subsistence within the larger context of whole adaptive systems. Secondly, investigation of the cultural contexts of general demographic processes (Boserup 1965; Hassan 1978, 1981; Spooner 1972) has integrated population dynamics into the study of culture stability and change. Finally, attempts to specify the inter-relationships among population, subsistence, social organization, and other aspects of culture (Adams 1981; Jochim 1981; Netting 1974, 1977) provide a foundation for systemic models of processes of cultural maintenance, adaptation, and change. Among these formulations, the Anasazi model is unique only in its exclusive concern with environmental, demographic, and behavioral variables known to have operated on the Colorado Plateaus during the last two millennia.

The Anasazi adaptation model is based on the postulate that prevailing environmental conditions limit the number of individuals that can be supported by a particular subsistence technology. Thus, three general classes of variable are important in this formulation: environmental, demographic, and behavioral. Variables of these classes (plus others not considered here) interact to form a set of relationships that define the adaptive system at any point in time. While it may be theoretically useful to conceptualize such a system as tending toward "equilibrium," the degree of equilibrium attained varies in time and space and must be assessed situationally. It seems entirely plausible to suppose that long-term equilibrium was never achieved by the Anasazi populations of the Colorado Plateaus (Cordell and Plog 1979). Fluctuating relationships among environmental, demographic, and behavioral variables characterize and account for many of the observed changes in Anasazi culture.

The three variable classes are related to one another by a modified concept of carrying capacity: the maximum human population that can be permanently supported by a given economic system under particular environmental conditions (Hassan 1978:73). Although easily conceptualized, carrying capacity has proved virtually impossible to quantify in any specific archaeological situation, because many of the relevant variables cannot be accurately measured. Because this definition entails dynamic interrelationships among several classes of variables, carrying capacity is not viewed as a static, measurable attribute of a particular environment. Rather it is considered to be an integrative variable that, because it is directly affected by changes in one or more of the components of the adaptive system, can increase or decrease rapidly and substantially. As a consequence of these considerations, carrying capacity is used in this paper as an expression of the interrelationships among the variable classes rather than as a quantifiable analytical tool.

Boundary conditions that regulate human adaptive systems such as those that prevailed on the Colorado Plateaus during the last 2000 years are established by interactions among the variables that determine carrying capacity. Limits on such adaptive systems vary as changing circumstances alter the relationships among the variables. Liebig's "law of the minimum" is applicable to the consideration of limits on human adaptive systems. Paraphrased for greater relevance to this investigation, the "law" states that the least abundant element necessary to the functioning of a system establishes the boundary conditions that regulate the system. Thus, in certain situations a variable (or variables) from any one of the three variable classes can establish the thresholds that bound the system. Parenthetically, other kinds of variable can also limit human behavioral systems; I emphasize these three because they seem to be the most pertinent to relating Anasazi prehistory to environmental stability and change. Change from one limiting variable to another, and even from one variable class to another, can be rapid and sometimes ephemeral. Thus, the regulatory career of a particular variable can be brief, perhaps too brief to be detected archaeologically, a circumstance that may account for much of the "unexplained" variability in the archaeological record.

Change in behavioral adaptive systems often occurs in response to the violation of the boundary conditions that regulate the system. When systemic limits are exceeded, population–resource imbalances (Cordell and Plog 1979) are created that strain the adaptive system. If severe enough, these imbalances and stresses require behavioral responses on the part of the affected society. Those responses that help alleviate the stress become institutionalized and contribute to the development of a new adaptive system defined by new carrying-capacity thresholds. The new system persists with only minor, adjustive modifications until the boundary conditions that regulate it are surpassed to create a new stress situation (Dean 1978b:108).

Because the boundary conditions that regulate an adaptive system are determined by interactions among the three variable classes, change in any one of the components of the adaptive system – environmental, demographic, or behavioral – can breach thresholds and trigger systemic culture change. Although culture change can result from variability in any of the three variable classes, environmental and demographic variables are usually viewed as being independent, while behavioral variables are considered to be dependent. That is, changes in the physical environment and in population that surpass systemic thresholds are seen as creating situations that require adaptive behavioral responses on the part of human societies. While this is probably true in most cases, it need not always be thus; because behavioral variability imposes constraints on the system, it can also trigger true systemic culture change.

The conception of culture change embodied in the provisional model has three attributes that facilitate the task of relating Anasazi culture changes to reconstructions of paleoenvironmental variability on the Colorado Plateaus. First, permanent systemic culture change occurs when thresholds defined by the limiting conditions are exceeded, which creates a qualitatively new situation to which the existing system is not adapted. Secondly, as long as the boundary conditions are not exceeded, nonadaptive behavioral fluctuations, mostly of a "stylistic" nature, characterize the system. Such fluctuations can be cumulative and lead to systemic culture change through their effects on the boundary conditions. Thirdly, change in any one of the components of the adaptive system can breach thresholds and trigger culture change. Thus, changes within each class of variable can be causes or results of adaptive transformations in the system as a whole.

The following examination of the three variable classes as they relate to human adaptation on the Colorado Plateaus establishes the range of variability encompassed by the provisional Anasazi adaptation model and exemplifies the model's potential for elucidating the relationships between Anasazi prehistory and changing environmental conditions.

Environmental variability

Environmental factors fall primarily into the category of independent variables, if only because people at the technological level of the Anasazi have little overt control over the natural processes that produce, maintain, and alter the physical environment. Natural processes of two basic kinds are recognized as causing environmental change on the Colorado Plateaus. Low-frequency processes (LFP) are characterized by periodicities longer than one human generation (ca. 25 years). Low-frequency processes are responsible for phenomena such as alternating episodes of erosion and deposition along streamcourses and major fluctuations in alluvial water-table levels. LFP environmental variability on the Colorado Plateaus is comprehended through alluvial chronostratigraphic and some palynological investigations. High-frequency processes (HFP) are characterized by shorter periodicities and are responsible for phenomena such as the cycle of the seasons, year-to-year climatic variability, and fluctuations in wild food resources. HFP environmental fluctuations on the Plateaus are specified by dendroclimatic analysis and by some high-resolution palynological, macrobotanical, and faunal studies. Extremely rare events, such as the destruction of crops by insects or hail, while sometimes catastrophic, are momentary phenomena of little long-range adaptive significance.

Human behavioral adaptation to LFP environmental variability is different from adaptation to HFP fluctuations. Most LFP variability is unlikely to be apparent to humans and probably is comprehended as stability. Basic economic and social adaptations are made to the environmental conditions established by low-frequency processes. HFP environmental variability on the other hand is much more likely to be explicitly recognized by human groups. If people are to persist in an area, the basic adaptation to LFP environmental conditions (perceived as "stability") must be flexible enough to handle expectable HFP variations. Most behavioral "buffering mechanisms," discussed below, are adaptations to "predictable" HFP environmental fluctuations.

The importance of LFP and HFP environmental variability to a particular adaptive system varies in response to a number of factors. One of the most important of these is how close the system is to carrying capacity. When the population is well below the local carrying capacity, HFP fluctuations probably are of little consequence and can be readily coped with through short-term adjustments such as the temporary expansion of farming areas or the increased exploitation of wild plant and animal resources. Exceptionally severe or prolonged adverse conditions may have more serious effects, but in the long run HFP variability should have relatively minor adaptive significance. As population levels

30

approach the long-term carrying capacity of the local habitat, HFP environmental fluctuations become more critical to survival. HFP variations that could have been easily accommodated by a small population can have much more serious consequences for a larger population that is already straining the supportive capacity of the local habitat. Similarly, when LFP environmental processes (whose *effects* can be sudden even though the process is a gradual one) lower the carrying capacity by reducing the limits on the number of people that can be supported in an area, HFP environmental variability becomes more limiting to the adaptive system as a whole. Such changes in systemic "equilibrium" produce stresses that may require adjustive or, in extreme cases, major adaptive responses. Local disequilibria of this sort may be responsible for many of the behavioral and demographic changes evident in the prehistory of the Colorado Plateaus (Cordell and Plog 1979).

Adaptive consequences are much more severe when LFP environmental change lowers the boundary conditions *below* levels required for the maintenance of the existing population. Under such circumstances, the carrying capacity is reduced to such an extent that the population can no longer be sustained by the extant subsistence system. As noted above, such transformations can be fairly abrupt, even though the natural processes that control them are of a low-frequency, gradual nature. Changes such as these demand rapid and often drastic responses on the part of the affected populations to stave off what sometimes can be major disasters. Some of the widespread demographic and cultural changes during the last 2000 years on the Colorado Plateaus may have been caused by LFP environmental transformations that upset carrying-capacity relationships throughout the region. Major cultural and demographic changes of the late twelfth century may represent adaptations to relatively abrupt LFP environmental changes that began around A.D. 1150.

Demographic variability

As with environmental processes, low- and high-frequency aspects of demographic variability can be recognized. There are, however, two important differences between the frequency attributes of the demographic and environmental components of a human adaptive system. First, the distinction between high- and low-frequency phenomena is more clear-cut in reference to environmental processes, primarily because of the magnitude of low-frequency environmental periodicities. Secondly, and more fundamentally important, the frequency characteristics of demographic variability are attributes more of effect than of process. That is, the same basic processes are responsible for both low- and high-frequency demographic variability. Thus, for heuristic purposes, low-frequency demographic variability can be defined as the trend in population size over two or more human generations. The relative population curves presented by Euler (Chapter 7 below) reflect low-frequency demographic variability. High-frequency variability involves short-term fluctuations around the general population trend. Changes in the high-frequency component of demographic variations can affect the low-frequency component enough to alter the general trend.

Demographic variability has long been viewed as an important cause of culture change. Most frequently, population growth is seen to trigger more productive exploitation of local habitats so that larger populations can be supported. Thus, population growth is viewed as a stimulus to behavioral practices that, in effect, raise the carrying capacity of an area (Boserup 1965). In the Anasazi adaptation model, gradual population growth is a low-frequency process that has the same eventual effect as LFP environmental fluctuations that lower the carrying capacity of an area. As population approaches a "stable" LFP environmental threshold, HFP environmental fluctuations become more limiting to the functioning of the adaptive system. A crucial difference between population growth and changes caused by low-frequency environmental processes is that the former tends to be more gradual than the latter. Therefore, the adaptive consequences of population increases that strain the boundaries of an adaptive system are more likely to be anticipated by the affected human groups than are the possible effects of LFP environmental transformations. Because of this, behavioral responses to population growth are likely to be more gradual, and possibly more effective, than responses to abrupt LFP environmental changes.

Population size is also a dependent variable in that it can be adjusted downward to alleviate stress created when a carrying-capacity threshold is approached or surpassed. Such demographic adaptations generally involve modifications of high-frequency fluctuations that have the effect of stabilizing or reducing the total population. Voluntary population adjustments involve practices such as increased birth spacing, infanticide, abortion, emigration, and warfare. Such adjustments are commonly viewed as the results of self-regulating processes inherent in cultural systems. This type of self-regulation seems most likely to occur when gradual population growth toward a carrying-capacity threshold allows sufficient time for appreciation of the problem and the development of population regulatory responses. Gradual environmental deterioration could produce similar responses. The increasing constraints exerted by HFP environmental variability as systemic limits are approached could stimulate population adjustments of the type described above.

If "voluntary" population adjustments fail, either through lack of sufficient time for implementation or as a result of the severity of the reduction of carrying capacity, "involuntary" population adaptations may be imposed on the affected groups. Such involuntary responses involve birth-rate reduction and increased mortality as results of malnutrition or, in more dire circumstances, of starvation. In the most extreme case, "adaptations" of this sort can result in the extinction of the population. In most instances, however, behavioral adaptations or emigration occur before physical extinction takes place.

Behavioral variability

For certain purposes, it is convenient to recognize that the cultural component of an adaptive system is also characterized by low- and high-frequency variability. This distinction acknowledges the fact that, under all but the direst of circumstances, certain aspects of culture tend to change more slowly than others.

The low-frequency component of behavioral variability results from the tremendous inertia of tradition, or the tendency toward intergenerational continuity in human societies. The importance of low-frequency behavioral variability is exemplified by the persistence for at least a thousand years of the Pueblo cultural tradition, which has survived in recognizable form the vicissitudes of environmental change and degradation, spatial dislocation, predation, conflict, epidemic disease, catastrophic depopulation, religious persecution, and political subjugation. Low-frequency behavioral variability embodies the basic adaptation to LFP ("stable") environmental conditions. Thus, the basic Pueblo adaptation to the habitats of the Colorado Plateaus has served for

33

at least a thousand years and remains distinct from other identifiable traditional adaptations – such as that of the Navajos – to the same environments.

High-frequency cultural variability includes the numerous behavioral options that are available to any society for solving situational problems. In the context of adaptation, such options allow people to cope with spatial variability and short-term temporal fluctuations in resource availability. Thus, high-frequency cultural variation provides the adaptive system with enough flexibility to maintain the low-frequency aspects of the total sociocultural system. The high-frequency component also serves as a source of traditionally acceptable alternative behaviors that can be employed to modify the low-frequency component with the least possible disruptive effect when adaptive stress requires such modifications.

Behavioral (or cultural) variables are commonly viewed as mechanisms of adapting human populations to their physical and social environments; therefore, they are usually seen as being results, rather than causes, of systemic culture change. However, under certain circumstances, purely cultural factors can transform the adaptive situation sufficiently to cause systemic culture change. Behavioral or technological innovations that increase the efficiency or productivity of the subsistence system can raise the carrying capacity and thereby trigger permanent change in the adaptive system. Momentous culture changes on the Colorado Plateaus at the beginning of Basketmaker II times are often attributed to the introduction of new, more productive races of maize. Contacts – either direct or indirect, coercive or noncoercive – with other populations can alter the adaptive situation enough to cause systemic culture change. The incorporation of the Pueblos into the Spanish empire had enormous adaptive consequences (Wilcox 1976, 1981), as did the expansion of Athabaskan groups into environmental niches formerly exploited by the Pueblos (Wilcox 1981). It is well known that human activity – such as agriculture, stock grazing, or air pollution – can change the environment sufficiently to trigger behavioral adaptations. More relevant to our purposes here, "normal" (high-frequency) behavioral variability within the bounds of a "stable" LFP-controlled adaptive situation can be cumulative (sometimes perhaps due to chance alone) and cause configurational changes in the cultural component of the adaptive system. Changes made possible by the

34

increasing mechanical efficiency of seed-grinding technology (Plog 1974:139–41) may fall into this category.

Despite the fact that behavioral variability can cause systemic culture change, patterned behavior is primarily a response mechanism that endows human groups with the flexibility to exploit and survive in a wide variety of habitats and to adapt to environmental and demographic changes. High-frequency human behavioral and technological variability acts as a "buffer" against expectable (usually HFP) environmental fluctuations (Jorde 1977). It also acts as a reservoir of potential responses to LFP environmental or demographic changes significant enough to alter the boundaries of the adaptive system. Initial responses to such changes often involve the subsistence system, which, if possible, is modified to increase carrying capacity sufficiently to sustain the population. Changing from a primary reliance on hunting and gathering to an emphasis on food production is one such response. Agricultural intensification to increase the productivity (yield/acre) of the subsistence system is another (Boserup 1965). Other subsistence mechanisms for accomplishing the same objective are the use of higher-yield varieties of food plants, monocropping, expansion of the area under cultivation, water and soil control, the use of fertilizer, and mechanization. "Spread the risk" farming strategies, such as locating fields in a wide variety of habitats so that even in bad years some crops are produced, offset unpredictable HFP spatial variation in crop production. Varying the degree of reliance on wild food resources helps compensate for unpredicted temporal variability in crop production.

Behavioral practices not directly associated with food procurement can serve to adapt human groups to stresses caused by systemic disequilibrium. Many such responses function to offset HFP environmental variability, which becomes more limiting as systemic boundaries are approached. Improved storage practices, or merely an increase in the amount of food produced and stored annually, buffer increased year-to-year variability in crop yields. Centralized storage and redistribution of surpluses is another means of compensating for unpredictable variability in food production. "Banking," or the accumulation in times of excess food production of "luxury items" to be exchanged for food in leaner times (Bronitsky 1977), is another possible response. Trade among widely dispersed communities also offsets spatial and temporal variability in food production. Predation on other groups also

35

may result from stress on an adaptive system (Griffin 1969). Responses such as these should increase as systemic thresholds are approached and HFP environmental fluctuations become more limiting to the adaptive system.

Any or all of these behavioral responses to stress have organizational consequences that may themselves trigger further systemic culture change. Agricultural intensification, increased storage, the redistribution of food among the members of a community, trade, banking, and warfare all require the integration of people into larger cooperating social units than would have been necessary before such adaptive responses were employed. The organization of people into larger groups requires mechanisms of conflict resolution, task apportionment, and resource allocation that can lead to the development of part- or full-time task and craft specialists and administrative personnel. The increasing differentiation of society that results from these processes can create further systemic stresses that must be coped with if the society is to survive. Depending on a number of factors, these processes of societal intensification can lead to higher levels of organization, to the dissolution of the society into smaller units capable of sustaining themselves in the area, or to the absorption of the local group into larger, more highly organized societies.

IMPLICATIONS OF THE MODEL

Five major aspects of attempts to relate Anasazi prehistory to reconstructions of paleoenvironmental conditions on the Colorado Plateaus are elucidated by the Anasazi adaptation model. These considerations lead to a critical evaluation of the ways in which the events of Anasazi prehistory have been related to environmental variability.

First, the model clearly specifies the degree of difference between environmental transformations caused by low-frequency natural processes and those caused by high-frequency natural processes. Changes due to the former are generally more severe and less predictable than are those due to the latter. As a result, LFP transformations are likely to require major adaptive change on the part of societies whose livelihood depends on conditions established and maintained by low-frequency processes. It should, therefore, be fairly easy archaeologically to recognize culture changes caused by LFP environmental transformations.

HFP environmental fluctuations often constitute the "normal" variability within a "stable phase" of the LFP cycle. Thus, it should be more difficult archaeologically to perceive behavioral responses to HFP environmental variability. The chief exception to this expectation occurs during intervals of adaptive stress caused by LFP environmental change or by population exceeding systemic limits. At such times HFP environmental variability becomes much more important to survival and may even become the primary limiting factor to the functioning of the adaptive system. Recognition of the vastly different effects of LFP and HFP environmental variability on human adaptive behavior is crucial to adequate evaluation of the impact of environmental stability and change on Anasazi prehistory.

Secondly, because patterned human behavior acts as a buffering mechanism to mitigate the direct impact of (primarily HFP) environmental variability, we should not expect exact correspondences between observed environmental variability and prehistoric human behavior. Storage simulations undertaken by Burns (1983) graphically illustrate this point. Burns calibrated tree growth and crop production in southwestern Colorado and used the calibration to retrodict annual corn and bean production per acre for the area back to A.D. 652. Using these crop-yield retrodictions as input, Burns simulated potential annual storage amounts for each year from A.D. 652 to 1968 for a set of "ideal" storage capacities ranging in half-year increments from 1.5 to 5 years. This simulation reveals periods of storage surpluses and deficits; that is, intervals in which there would have been a surplus of food above what could have been accommodated in the granaries and periods in which food production would have been so low that withdrawal from the storage system would have far exceeded input. Periods of major storage deficits do not correspond exactly to intervals of decreased tree growth in the area. Put another way, dendrochronological "droughts" (some of them quite severe) do not always equate with storage deficits. This is so because the *timing* of "bad" years is often more important in producing storage deficits than is the severity of the average decade departure value. One good year can offset two or three moderately bad years. Conversely, a few moderately bad years (which do not produce a significant tree growth departure), unrelieved by a peak year, can devastate a storage system. In the southwestern Colorado case, and undoubtedly in others for which we have no data, storage behavior moderates or temporally

37

displaces the effects of high-frequency variability in crop production to such an extent that no one-to-one relationship exists between climatic variability, as measured by tree growth, and human behavior.

Thirdly, attempts to use archaeological estimates of population growth and decline to measure response to environmental variability (Euler *et al.* 1979) are probably doomed to failure for several reasons. Not the least of these is the questionable nature of such estimates, which are usually based on dubious assumptions and inadequate data. Furthermore, it is doubtful that such estimates would measure relevant variability even if they were accurate. Except in the most extreme cases, population change is probably not closely related to environmental variability. Thus, attempts to relate human behavior to environmental variability should focus on behavioral variables that can be better perceived archaeologically and that have the potential of being more closely related to the environment. Things such as population movements, changes in subsistence behavior, organizational transformations, changes in the scale of social integration, trade relationships, and others seem more promising in this case than do inferred population curves.

Fourthly, attempts to relate phase boundaries to environmental variability (Euler *et al.* 1979) likewise seem questionable. Behavioral responses to environmental transformations generally involve substantial adaptive changes. Phase boundaries, on the other hand, reflect all sorts of changes in the archaeological record, most of which are *not* major adaptational changes. Most phase boundaries are defined on the basis of stylistic criteria that are useful for dating but do not reflect important cultural changes. Figure 2.1 illustrates several possible archaeological criteria for defining phase boundaries. Only one of the transitions shown represents the kind of transformation that is likely to have resulted from a major adaptational shift. It should come as no surprise therefore that most observers perceive little correlation between the environmental fluctuations and the phase boundaries depicted by Euler *et al.* (1979, Fig. 5).

Fifthly, in light of the truly formidable array of sources of systemic change in human adaptive systems, it seems to me that the problem of human behavioral response to environmental change must be treated situationally, especially in regard to HFP environmental variability. Environmental, demographic, behavioral, and other variables must be considered as potential sources of stimuli for systemic culture change,

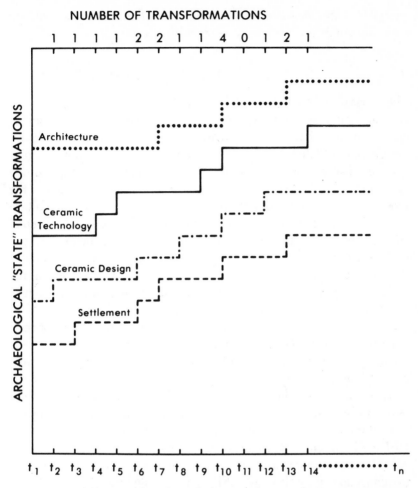

Figure 2.1 Phase boundaries vs. adaptive transformations. Most of the transitions from one state to another in any one of the represented archaeological data categories would be sufficient to define a phase boundary. Only the point at which all four categories change together (t_{10}) is of a magnitude likely to represent the kind of adaptive transformation specified by the Anasazi adaptational process model.

and each variable category must be carefully evaluated in each case to see which provided the trigger for an observed instance of culture change. Only in this way can environmentally induced culture changes be differentiated from those due to other causes. Such differentiation is

39

crucial to an adequate understanding of the processual role of environmental variability in Anasazi culture history.

EVALUATION OF THE MODEL

The Anasazi adaptation model and its implications provide a conceptual foundation for the consideration of Anasazi responses to environmental changes revealed by paleoenvironmental research on the Colorado Plateaus. Circumstances under which adaptive culture change is likely to occur are identified by the interrelationships among environmental, demographic, and behavioral variables specified by the model. Once the attributes of situations conducive to systemic culture change are identified, the archaeological and paleoenvironmental records can be searched for congruences that indicate the existence of such situations. Thus specified, likely situations can be examined in depth to evaluate the model's performance as a predictor of the occurrence of systemic culture change and of the nature of the new adaptive systems created by the adaptive process.

The model allows adaptive situations to be ranked in terms of their potential for stimulating systemic culture change. Obviously, the highest potential for change exists when an abrupt LFP environmental degradation coincides with a population level that approaches the carrying capacity of the adaptive system. Second in severity are situations in which the population grows beyond the limit established by the environmental and behavioral components of the system. Third are HFP environmental fluctuations and high-frequency demographic and behavioral variations that occur when an adaptive system is near carrying capacity. Fourth are LFP environmental transformations that affect a system that is well below carrying-capacity thresholds. Fifth are HFP environmental fluctuations that occur when the adaptive system is well within its boundary limits. Sixth, a host of high-frequency demographic and behavioral variations should have little effect on a system that is not crowding its limits. In addition, historical events can trigger major adaptive change independently of the causal factors specified by the model. The ravages of epidemic disease, the conquest and exploitation of the population by an outside group, and other such circumstances can destroy existing systemic interrelationships and require the development of new adaptive arrangements.

Karlstrom's (Figure 3.2; Euler *et al.* 1979, Figure 5) hydrologic curve

40

is the best synthesis of LFP environmental variability during the last 2000 years on the Colorado Plateaus. This record reveals four major episodes of depressed alluvial water tables and stream entrenchment that could have been detrimental to carrying-capacity interrelationships for adaptive systems dependent on the farming of alluvial floodplains. The adaptive impact of these episodes began respectively at approximately A.D. 200, 750, 1250, and 1850. Secondary hydrologic minima – characterized by depositional hiatuses, minor surface erosion, and lesser groundwater fluctuations – occurred between the major episodes at about A.D. 550, 1150, and 1700. Relative demographic curves for several areas on the Plateaus (Euler, Chapter 7 below) disclose fairly low population levels throughout the region before ca. A.D. 900. After A.D. 900, regional population grew steadily, and in some places rapidly, to reach a peak in the middle twelfth century. Although quantification is impossible, the demographic trends indicate that for the first time population was potentially large enough to approach or breach carrying-capacity thresholds in many localities. Many local populations declined rapidly after A.D. 1150, and some areas were totally depopulated at this time. In other areas, population continued to grow until around A.D. 1300 when the entire San Juan drainage was virtually abandoned. After A.D. 1300, extremely large population concentrations developed along the Little Colorado River, in the vicinity of the Hopi Mesas, in the Zuni area, and in localities in New Mexico presently occupied by Pueblo groups.

Given the demographic and LFP environmental trends outlined above, the interval beginning at about A.D. 1250 is easily identified as the most likely period to have been characterized by substantial adaptive changes. At this time a major LFP environmental disruption of carrying-capacity thresholds, caused by depressed alluvial groundwater and widespread stream entrenchment, coincided not only with a peak in general population magnitude but also with extremely high local population densities caused by settlement agglomerations that followed A.D. 1150. In addition, this interval was characterized by the Great Drought, an HFP environmental phenomenon that could only have aggravated the adaptive problems of the time. As predicted by the model, major transformations in Anasazi culture occurred between A.D. 1250 and 1350. As mentioned above, the entire San Juan drainage basin was vacated as Anasazi populations concentrated in areas that, for various environmental reasons, were able to support large agricultural

41

communities under a hydrologic regime characterized by arroyo cutting and depressed alluvial water tables. Major sociocultural changes underlay the development of large villages through the amalgamation of smaller communities and fragments of communities (Eggan 1950). Thus, the Anasazi adaptation model correctly predicts a major adaptive transformation in the prehistory of the Colorado Plateaus.

In light of the preceding, it is interesting to note that many of the demographic and behavioral transformations of the early fourteenth century are recognizable outcomes of processes set in motion 150 years earlier in the middle twelfth century. It has long been recognized that major demographic and behavioral changes took place on the Colorado Plateaus (and elsewhere in the Southwest) shortly after A.D. 1150. Many areas were abandoned, and large settlements and high population densities developed in the localities that remained inhabited (Euler, Chapter 7 below). These twelfth-century changes coincide with a regional population maximum (Euler, Chapter 7 below), one of the secondary LFP depositional hiatuses identified by Karlstrom (Chapter 3 below), and a severe and protracted HFP dendroclimatic drought (Dean, Chapter 5 below). These correspondences suggest that by A.D. 1150 population was sufficiently close to systemic limits that a secondary LFP hydrologic perturbation, coupled with an HFP drought, reduced the carrying capacity enough to create systemic stresses that triggered major adaptive responses. Subsequent LFP hydrologic transformations at the end of the thirteenth century reduced the carrying capacity even further and triggered even more drastic behavioral accommodations. Problem-oriented investigations will reveal whether these explanations derived from the model are correct. What is important is that the model of Anasazi adaptive processes is capable of yielding testable hypotheses about human adaptive behavior on the Colorado Plateaus.

Not all major LFP environmental transformations produce systemic culture changes. In fact, only one of the four major hydrologic minima is accompanied by widespread population dislocations and behavioral transformations. The impact on native American populations of the latest such minimum, which began late in the nineteenth century and which continues into the present, was mitigated by the participation of these groups in the American economy. Nevertheless, the economic impact of the recent epicycle of erosion was not inconsiderable, and permanent adaptive responses were required of Navajo farmers

42

(Gregory 1917:130), Hopi agriculturalists (Bradfield 1971), Anglo– and Mexican–American stock raisers, the citizens of Tucson (Cooke and Reeves 1976), and most other segments of the Southwestern population. Fewer adaptive changes are evident in the archaeological record pertinent to the hydrologic minimum that began around A.D. 750. Undoubtedly, this is a consequence of nonstressful population levels ensuring the adequacy of high-frequency behavioral adjustments in lieu of major low-frequency cultural adaptations. The lack of obvious adaptive responses to the hydrologic minimum of the third to fifth centuries is probably due to the small populations of the time coupled with a lesser dependence on the farming of alluvial floodplains. The Anasazi adaptation model, with its integration of different kinds of variables, is capable of explaining apparently anomalous situations in which LFP environmental transformations are not accompanied by systemic culture changes. Because of the effects of the demographic and behavioral components of the adaptive system, the environmental changes do not stress the system sufficiently to require permanent response.

In the absence of other sources of systemic stress, HFP environmental variability is unlikely to cause major adaptive change. It is no accident that the Great Drought appears to have had a greater impact on human behavior than earlier and later droughts that were more severe. The Great Drought came at a time when Colorado Plateaus adaptive systems were under the twin stresses of high population levels and major LFP environmental degradation. The substantial and widespread drought of the late twelfth century undoubtedly exacerbated systemic stresses caused by high population and a secondary LFP hydrologic minimum. That other HFP dendroclimatic droughts apparently caused no major systemic disruptions should come as no surprise if they did not coincide with other more severe sources of systemic stress. One of the common arguments against the so-called drought theory of culture change on the Colorado Plateaus is that not every known drought is accompanied by site abandonments or population movements (Jett 1964). The Anasazi adaptation model clearly indicates why each and every drought should not be expected to cause such behavioral changes. Whether or not a particular drought (or any other HFP environmental event) helps trigger systemic culture change is due largely to situational factors and to the existing interrelationships among the environmental, demographic, and behavioral variables that determine an adaptive system.

The foregoing brief evaluation of the Anasazi adaptation model establishes that the construct has considerable heuristic value. The model specifies criteria for identifying situations in which adaptive behavioral change is likely to occur, identifies pertinent variables that can be recognized by archaeological and paleoenvironmental data, indicates the potential impact of these variables in particular circumstances, specifies possible behavioral responses that can alleviate systemic stresses caused by the independent variables, and isolates many of the pitfalls involved in an effort to understand human adaptation to environmental change on the Colorado Plateaus. Furthermore, the model has demonstrated considerable explanatory power. It successfully predicted periods of high systemic stress with great potential for adaptive demographic and culture change. Testable hypotheses regarding human behavioral responses to adaptive stresses created by environmental and demographic variability on the Colorado Plateaus can be derived from the model and evaluated against pertinent archaeological data. In addition, the model provides logical and testable explanations for the failure of certain primary and secondary LFP environmental changes and HFP environmental fluctuations to trigger significant changes in the behavior of the inhabitants of the region. Further evaluation of the model, through specifically focused regional-scale and locality-level tests of propositions derived from it, will permit the reformulation and refinement of the construct. In this way, the model can be transformed into a powerful analytical tool for the study of Anasazi behavioral adaptation to environmental variability on the Colorado Plateaus.

Alluvial chronology and hydrologic change of Black Mesa and nearby regions

THOR N. V. KARLSTROM

Department of Geology
Northern Arizona University
Flagstaff, Arizona

The main objectives of this paper are (1) to derive an empirical model of the environmental relationships that control the deposition and erosion of floodplain sediments, (2) to describe the chronostratigraphic method that underlies my use of the model to reconstruct past hydroclimatic variability on the southern Colorado Plateaus, (3) to illustrate the application of the method in four drainages in the Black Mesa area of northeastern Arizona, (4) to characterize the hydrologic and aggradational changes reconstructed for the last two millennia, and (5) to establish the regional relevance of the Black Mesa-area hydroclimatic reconstruction.

Mapping of alluvium on Black Mesa by the author and by Cooley *et al.* (1969) indicates a high degree of geomorphic variability. Both undissected and dissected valley floors in various parts of the same and different drainage basins have different numbers and heights of terraces. Comparable variability in terraced and unterraced valley floors occurs throughout the Southwest (Kottlowski *et al.* 1965). By assuming that this geomorphic variability reflects corresponding variability in depositional history, Kottlowski *et al.* (1965) conclude that the number, magnitude and duration of the represented episodes of erosion and deposition differ from basin to basin and along reaches of the same

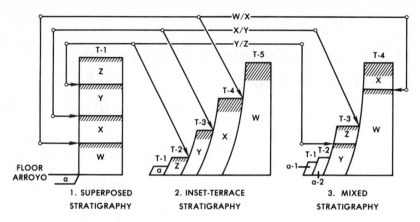

Figure 3.1 Possible geomorphic–stratigraphic relationships.

stream, an interpretation repeated by Cooley *et al.* (1969) for Black Mesa. These authors, however, do not exclude the alluvial–erosional sequences considered by Bryan (1940) and Hack (1942) to reflect climatic change. Instead, they propose (1) that these sequences only occur along certain types of Southwest streams, and (2) that the associated geomorphic variability may be indicative "of controls of the type and amount of erosion and alluviation by such physiographic characteristics as gradient, size, shape of watershed, and other factors" (Kottlowski *et al.* 1965: 289).

My chronostratigraphic research on Black Mesa was designed specifically to determine whether geomorphic variability necessarily corresponds one-to-one with depositional history. The data indicate that, because of local physiographic factors, geomorphic variability does *not* correspond one-to-one with depositional history (Figure 3.1; Karlstrom 1978). Others, however (Schumm 1977; Womack and Schumm 1977; Patton and Schumm 1981; Boison and Patton 1983), believe that it does; therefore, they use geomorphic variability to support a nonclimatic, "episodic erosion," model of floodplain variability. A contrasting, "periodic erosion," model of fluvial processes is presented here.

STREAM FLOW, GROUNDWATER HYDROLOGY, DEPOSITION, AND EROSION

Many researchers have interpreted the Southwest meteorological and hydrologic records as primarily reflecting random spatial and temporal

46

distributions of precipitation. Most conclude that the cycles revealed by various levels of smoothing also reflect this random, nonsecular distribution (Cooke and Reeves 1976). Gatewood *et al.*'s (1963) study of a large number of regional precipitation, hydrologic, and dendroclimatic records demonstrates too many internal parallels to be dismissed as representing random events. Only two per cent of 99 correlation coefficients among 24 gage records from the Great Basin–Colorado Plateaus meteorological zone were below the adopted lower limit of 0.72 (Gatewood *et al.* 1963:B27). The number of year-to-year agreements in common trends, shown in Figure 3.2 by shaded bands and summed as percentages in row 12A, is much greater than would be expected from a corresponding number of random-number series (Row 12B). The data assembled in Figure 3.2 graphically illustrate the high degree of concordance between the hydrologic and dendroclimatic records of the southern part of the Colorado Plateaus.

The regional historical and dendroclimatic data (Stockton 1975) establish the relationship between recorded climatic and hydrologic changes as possible analogs for the longer-term hydrologic trends defined in the regional alluvial record. From these data, I conclude that the flow regimes of regional streams respond primarily to broadly parallel, regional changes in year-to-year and longer trends in annual (particularly winter) precipitation. I further conclude that these hydroclimatic relations provide the most reasonable analog for interpreting the earlier, longer-term hydrologic trends geologically defined in the region.

Because of the equilibrium between water-table levels in valley fills and surface flow in the region, any increase in precipitation and recharge rates causes alluvial ground water to rise and intersect increasingly longer segments of the generally low-gradient channel floors. The result is appreciably lengthened reaches of permanent flow, such as those observed by Gregory (1916) during the wetter, early decades of this century.

Hydrologic thresholds (Schumm 1977) are involved as well; any increase in precipitation above threshold values (recharge = discharge) supplies increasing amounts of water to the valley bottom (Figure 3.3). Once the amount of water supplied by precipitation, and indirectly through seeps and springs, exceeds even slightly the amount that can be stored, transmitted or evaporated away, water-table levels rise and permanent-flow reaches lengthen. Conversely, when discharge from

47

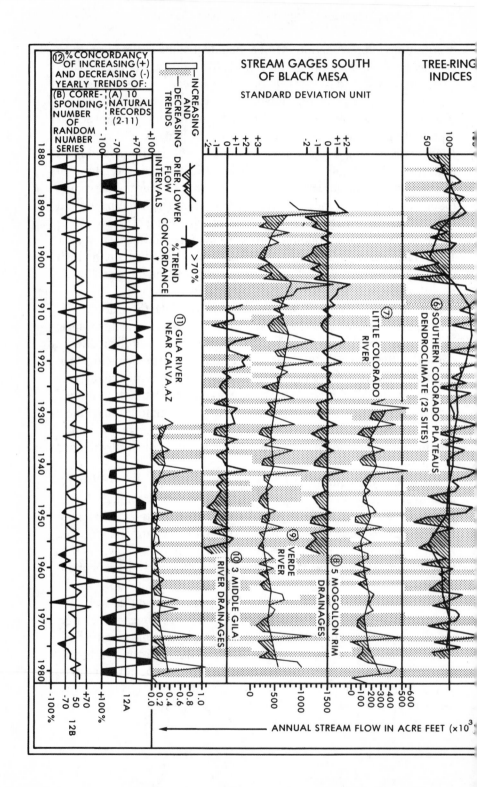

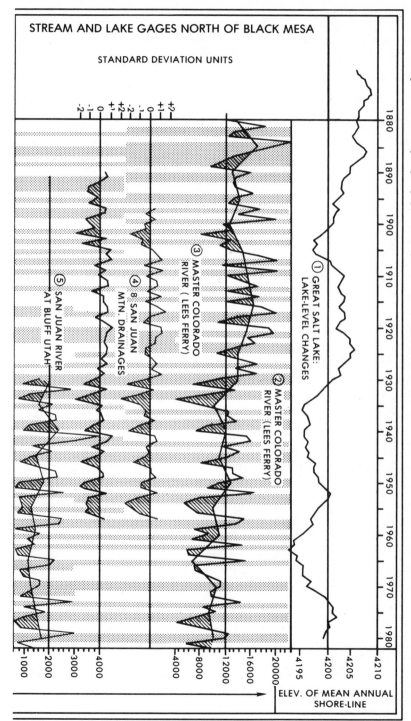

STREAM AND LAKE GAGES NORTH OF BLACK MESA

STANDARD DEVIATION UNITS

① GREAT SALT LAKE: LAKE-LEVEL CHANGES

② MASTER COLORADO RIVER (LEES FERRY)

③ MASTER COLORADO RIVER (LEES FERRY)

④ 8 SAN JUAN MTN. DRAINAGES

⑤ SAN JUAN RIVER AT BLUFF UTAH

ELEV. OF MEAN ANNUAL SHORE-LINE

Figure 3.2 Comparison of historical hydrographs north and south of Black Mesa with regional dendroclimatic record.

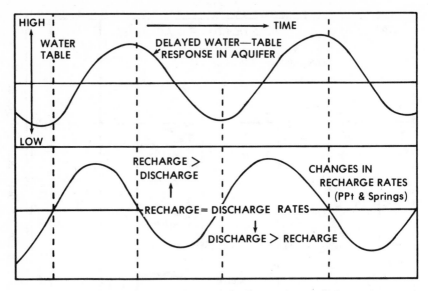

Figure 3.3 Groundwater (hydrologic) climatic relationships.

the fills exceeds recharge, water-table levels begin to drop and permanent-flow reaches shrink until the critical threshold values are again exceeded. Time-lags between precipitation input and hydrologic responses are thus an inherent part of the system, and can be expected to vary in duration (weeks to decades) from place to place, depending on such factors as variable discharge rates from aquifers of different storage capacity and permeability.

Based on the information presented above, I assume that shifts from general ephemeral-flow to permanent-flow conditions in the streams of the region resulted in changes from largely channel-confined flooding and erosion (the present condition) to channel filling and general valley-bottom aggradation accompanying a progressive rise in water-table and base-flow levels during wetter periods of the past. As discussed below, such base-level changes are recorded by the heights, stratigraphy, bedding structures, finer textures, and intercalated soils of the older fill deposits in the region.

INTERPRETIVE MODEL OF
HYDROCLIMATIC PROCESSES

The Holocene alluvial record on Black Mesa is characterized by a series of contemporaneous depositional events on valley-floor and alluvial

Table 3.1. *Processes governing alluvial disposition and erosion*

Past climate	Hydrologic response	Hydrogeologic work		Vegetation	Eolian activity
		Slope	Valley floor	Regional	
(1) $P_p t^-$ (Drier climate)	$\hookrightarrow Qr^-$, EF^-, WT^-, SF^-, PFS^-	$\rightarrow C^-$, SW^-, $G^- \rightarrow Qs$	$\rightarrow DS \rightarrow Vf$	$\rightarrow Vr^-$	E^+ $\rightarrow E^-$
(2) $P_p t^+$ (Wetter climate)	$\hookrightarrow Qr^+$, EF^+, WT^+, SF^+, PFS^+	$\rightarrow C^+$, SW^+, $G^+ \rightarrow Qs$	$\rightarrow A \rightarrow Vf$	$\rightarrow Vr^+$	E^- $\rightarrow E^+$

fans that were interrupted by intervals in which previously aggrading surfaces were dissected and soils formed on resulting stabilized terrace surfaces. The hydroclimatic implications of these buried soils and overlying vertical accretion deposits seem clear. Flood levels during the period of dissection and soil formation must have been generally low and channel-confined to permit subaerial weathering of bordering lowlying surfaces. The progressive burial of these soil horizons by vertical accretion deposits of well-stratified, well-graded clay, silt, and sand must in turn record intervals of progressively higher effective flooding and episodic overbank deposition that were preceded and accompanied by filling of preexisting, deep erosional channels.

From these and other pedologic and stratigraphic relations, and from the historical evidence of generally positive correlations between regional precipitation, natural runoff, and groundwater levels, I derive the climatic, hydrologic, geologic, and biologic linkages for deposits in the ephemeral drainage basins of the region shown in Table 3.1. Past periods of valley-floor dissection and soil formation (DS) are correlated with intervals of decreased precipitation (Ppt⁻) and runoff (Qr⁻), lower effective-flood (EF⁻) and water-table (WT⁻) levels, diminished spring flow (SF⁻), and shortened permanent-flow segments (PFS⁻) (Equation 1). Conversely, the succeeding periods of valley-floor aggradation (A) correlate with intervals of increased precipitation (Ppt⁺), and runoff (Qr⁺), high effective flood (EF⁺) and water-table (WT⁺) levels, augmented spring flow (SF⁺), and lengthened permanent-flow segments (PFS⁺) (Equation 2).

Accordingly, valley-floor aggradation during past wetter periods must reflect, despite tendencies toward denser regional vegetation-cover (Vr⁺), increased sediment yield (Qs⁺) from valley slopes and upland mantles by accelerated colluvial (C^+), slope-wash (SW^+), and gully (G^+) processes. Conversely, sparser regional vegetation (Vr^-), decreased rates of colluvial (C^-), slope-wash (SW^-), and gully (G^-) activity, and lessened sediment yield (Qs^-) should have occurred during drier periods.

Little agreement exists on the mechanisms governing alluvial deposition and erosion (Cooke and Reeves 1976; Graf 1983). Most Southwest researchers have based their divergent anthropogenic, hydrologic, and climatic interpretations on historical climatic and hydrologic records and on scattered observations of recent arroyo cutting; few have considered the depositional and erosional evidence of the associated alluvium. Using such evidence, however, both Hack (1942) and Haynes (1968) suggest that changing water-table levels governed alluvial processes by establishing alluvial base levels.

Lake level changes are generally recognized as base-level controls on alluvial processes in the lower reaches of tributary valleys. Considering the relationship between lake and water-table levels, on the one hand, and between water-table levels and surface-water hydrology throughout a drainage net, on the other, I assume that changing water levels in near-surface groundwater reservoirs function much like lake-level changes in imposing similar-sign base-level constraints on alluviation throughout a drainage basin. Base-level controls, viewed as a function of regional water-table changes, provide an explanation for the near-synchrony of depositional events in upper- to lower-reach sites, as well as for the uniform concave-upward terrace profiles of some Southwest streams. During wetter periods of basin-wide aggradation and of partial to complete damming of main-stem drainage segments by tributary fans, stream gradients would tend toward smoother, more uniform curvilinear profiles. During drier periods, when bedrock exposures rather than groundwater levels limited downcutting, as of today, stream gradients would have been more irregular, with step-like profiles produced by locally exposed bedrock floors.

In terms of process, the most critical hydrogeologic relationship is that between increasing precipitation and runoff and increasing sediment yield. This correlation is consistent with Schumm's (1977) suggestion that in past shifts from arid (15° C, 250 mm) to subhumid (10° C, 500 mm) climates, protection of sediment sources by expanding vegetation may not have kept pace with accelerated erosion. In the Black Mesa region, abundant moderate to steep slopes underlain by thick

52

interbeds of erosion-prone, fine-grained bedrock established the marginal slopes as principal sediment sources during the wetter periods of valley-floor aggradation. During these periods, preexisting valley-floor vegetation would have been largely destroyed by episodic burial (V_f^-) in sediments derived from the unstable slopes. During drier periods, greater slope stability would have diminished the supply of slope sediments to bordering streams, thus facilitating stream dissection and the resulting soil development on vegetation-stabilized valley floors (V_f^+). The relations expressed in Equations 1 and 2 indicate that regional vegetation controls (Vr) were subordinate to those of the geologic slope- and valley-floor processes directly affecting *local* vegetation cover, sediment yield, and eolian activity.

Given that both deposition and erosion represent geologic work by running water, the critical question becomes, what were the main hydrologic factors that facilitated deposition during wetter periods and dissection during drier periods? One such factor is channel morphology, which appears to be dominated by varying discharge/sediment load ratios (Leopold, Wolman, and Miller 1964; Schumm 1977). Other factors being equal, relatively decreasing discharge ($Qr<Qs$) leads to stream overloading and deposition; relatively increasing discharge ($Qr>Qs$) to stream underloading and dissection. The valley fills of Black Mesa record wider channel or depositional cross sections and higher effective-flood levels during periods of aggradation. This in turn required both greater volumes of water and greater sediment supplies ($Qr^+ Qs^+$ but with $Qr<Qs$). Conversely, the narrower cross sections of buried channels and the pedologic evidence for lower floods during the drier periods of dissection required both lesser volumes of water and diminished sediment supplies ($Qr^- Qs^-$ but with $Qr>Qs$).

Although less water was available during drier periods, its progressive confinement to narrower cross sections and diminished sediment load would have increased its effective velocity and erosive capability for channel deepening and widening. During periods of dominant down-cutting, channel-confined higher floods would erode more than lower floods unless the hydrogeologic threshold ($Qr=Qs$) was more closely approached or exceeded by increased sediment supply. Local physiographic factors differentially affecting sediment supply and discharge would result in varying hydrogeologic thresholds in different parts of a drainage net. Varying thresholds could explain entrenchment in some but not all parts of a drainage net during an exceptionally high flood

(Swift 1926). In the model, predominant eolian activity is equated with generally wetter intervals of valley-floor aggradation rather than, as is usually the case, with the generally drier periods of erosion. The extensive longitudinal dune-sand mantle of Black Mesa records effective wind transportation from the southwest (Hack 1941; Cooley *et al.* 1969) and can be traced to primary sources in the broad floodplain of the Little Colorado River. Cliff-head, or ridge, dunes on the margins of tributary canyon rims point to primary source materials in nearby canyon floors. Thus, deposition of eolian silt and sand should have been accelerated during periods of valley-floor aggradation and diminished during periods of valley-floor dissection and vegetation encroachment on previously aggrading valley-floor surfaces.

Equation 2 indicates the importance of largely vegetation-free aggrading valley floors (Vf^-) as primary sediment sources for enhanced eolian activity (E^+). During the drier intervals (Equation 1), dissection and resulting soil formation on vegetation-stabilized floodplain surfaces (Vf^+) diminish the role of these bottomland environments as sediment sources for wind activity (E^-). Other areas, such as vegetation-free slope, upland, and friable, silty, sand bedrock outcrops then become potentially more important sediment sources for continuing wind transportation and deposition.

Water-table (base-level) control of near-surface aquifers combined with the hydrogeologic discharge/sediment-yield threshold mechanism appears adequate to explain the recorded systematic shifts from aggradation to degradation. During periods of falling water-table, shrinking water supplies, and diminishing slope erosion and sediment yield, surface water would have been increasingly concentrated into channels inherited from the previous period of aggradation. Continuing channelization of diminishing volumes of underloaded water ($Qr>Qs$) would lead to progressive channel deepening, headcut erosion, and side-wall erosion. Side-wall erosion would be concentrated around outside bends of migrating meander loops and in areas of shallow bedrock that inhibited downcutting. This dominant erosive mode would continue until hydroclimatic conditions shifted across the hydrogeologic threshold ($Qr=Qs$) to a dominant aggradational mode characterized by rising water-table levels, increasingly groundwater-augmented surface-water supplies, and accelerating slope erosion and sediment yield.

The proposed model, as expressed symbolically in Equations 1 and 2 above, is reconstructed primarily from empirical data and historic

54

analog. The model defines (1) geomorphic–stratigraphic variability as a primary function of local physiographic factors; (2) positive correlation between precipitation and sediment yield as the result of erosional slope processes dominating opposing trends in regional vegetation cover; and (3) parallel depositional histories in upper- to lower-reach sites as a product of hydroclimatic mechanisms, including regional water-table (base-level) changes and varying discharge/sediment-load threshold conditions. The model is directly testable (1) against the results of comparably detailed chronostratigraphic (Point Boundary) analyses of alluvium in other regions; (2) through comparison with other types of paleoclimatic records of comparable resolution; and (3) by extended research on hydrologic process and base-level mechanisms. The composite alluvial–colluvial–eolian model represents an extension of the alluvial–colluvial model communicated to E. Karlstrom (1983) and forms the basis for the reconstruction of the low-frequency process environmental changes related to prehistoric human behavior in Chapter 8 below (Figure 8.1).

CHRONOSTRATIGRAPHIC RESEARCH IN THE BLACK MESA REGION

Geologic observations on Black Mesa were begun in 1970 to define the physical nature of an area affected by surface coal mining and to develop a better understanding of the geomorphic history of the southwestern United States. Chronostratigraphic research was primarily designed to (1) provide a detailed alluvial chronology of the Holocene and (2) assess whether this record is climatic or nonclimatic in origin by considering its internal characteristics and by comparing it with historical and other paleoclimatic evidence; and (3) assess possible interaction between environmental change and cultural dynamics, through comparison with archaeological chronologies (Chapter 8 below). Dating and correlation of the alluvial deposits exposed in the walls of the existing arroyos throughout Black Mesa and the surrounding region provides a chronology for the Holocene events that have affected the land surface.

The study region

Black Mesa is a high, moderately dissected plateau of about 7800 km^2 that occupies the approximate center of the Black Mesa structural basin

55

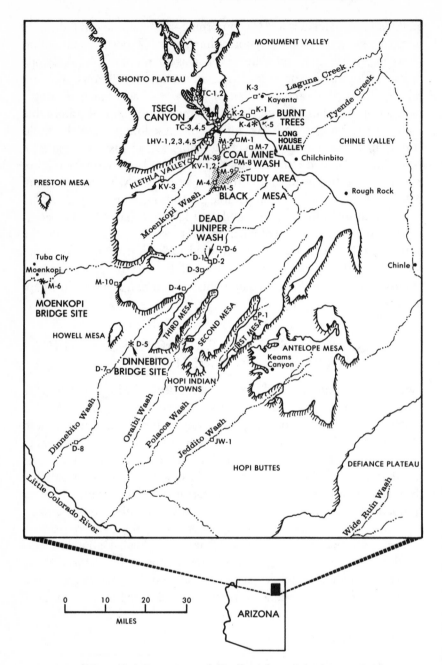

Figure 3.4 Locations of 40 alluvial stratigraphic sections.

in the southern Colorado Plateaus Province (Figure 3.4). Black Mesa owes its topographic prominence to resistant sandstone strata within the Upper Cretaceous Mesa Verde Group. Surficial deposits laid down by stream, wind, and slope processes mantle extensive areas of the Black Mesa region. Alluvial deposits that range from Pleistocene to Holocene age fill valleys in the area. Older Pleistocene and Tertiary sediments are locally preserved as stratified terrace deposits 50 to 100 m above present valley floors and as gravel caps and channel fills on interfluves.

Black Mesa is drained by several southwesterly flowing ephemeral streams known as the Tusayan Washes (Gregory 1916) and by the upper reaches of Moenkopi Wash and its tributaries, including Coal Mine Wash and Yellow Water Canyon Wash. All flow to the Little Colorado River and may be relicts of a more ancient drainage system that came from now disjunct highlands to the northeast.

These intermittent streams are fed by runoff from winter snow, winter frontal precipitation, and sporadic and scattered thunder storms in summer and early fall. Most of the runoff is ephemeral, responding directly to the irregular precipitation. My own observations on Black Mesa suggest that the flows of longest duration occur mainly during and following winter and spring snowmelt and precipitation. These more sustained flows (weeks to months) are generally of clear water, suggesting primary sources from winter-replenished and filtered ground-water supplies. The shorter-term and more localized summer floods generally carry higher sediment load, suggesting increased contributions from surface runoff and slope wash. Cooley *et al.* (1969:A37) estimate that about 50 per cent of the runoff in the southern Colorado Plateaus is lost to the surface by infiltration into underlying materials and by evaporation and transpiration.

Ground-water aquifers include alluvium beneath valley floors and several bedrock formations. Water levels (the potentiometric surfaces) in the bedrock aquifers slope generally south and southwest, and springs are most abundant toward the south and west parts of Black Mesa (McGavok and Levings 1974). The presence of permanent-flow stream segments where channels intersect the bedrock aquifers (Cooley *et al.* 1969) indicates the important contribution of stored ground-water to surface hydrology in the region. Permanent alluvial aquifers in the area are supplied in large part by discharge from underlying bedrock aquifers. Recent studies by Peabody Coal Company's Environmental Quality Division (Steve Hamilton, personal communication, 1981) indicate that the alluvial aquifers on Black Mesa average about 3 m below valley floors but intersect the surface in some washes. Water-table levels in these shallow aquifers respond quickly to precipitation and snowmelt and are generally higher in late spring than in late summer.

The Holocene alluvium in the region occurs in two main depositional environments: (1) Valley-bottom fills that may be either dissected or undissected; and (2) alluvial fans that form at abrupt changes in slope, such as near the base of the Black Mesa scarp, and on canyon floors near the mouths of some tributary streams.

The valley-bottom fills on Black Mesa generally occupy bedrock canyons and range up to 30 m thick, as exposed locally in deep arroyos cut entirely in alluvium. They range in texture from coarse bouldery gravel near bedrock outcrops to varve-like silty clay in valley-floor depressions. Most, however, are alluvial deposits of graded sand, silt, and clay that were laid down in horizontal and lenticular beds that commonly become finer upward. The bedding and the fine textures show that the valley fills were formed primarily by vertical accretion during successive overbank floods. Most arroyo-wall exposures include a series of these vertical accretion units separated by channels, diastems, incipient to moderately developed soils, forest litter zones, and fine-grained organic layers. These nondepositional features indicate interruptions in alluvial deposition contemporaneous with arroyo-cutting and organic accumulation and subaerial weathering on bordering valley-bottom surfaces. At the times represented by these nondepositional features, the streams were generally confined to their channels and rarely overtopped their banks.

Hack (1942) divides the Black Mesa alluvial record into three formations, Jeddito, Tsegi, and Naha. The Jeddito is considered late Pleistocene on the basis of enclosed elephant fossils. Using a paleoclimatic model of postglacial time, Hack dated the Jeddito/Tsegi interval of erosion and soil formation between 5000 and 2000 B.C. and equated it with the period of maximum postglacial warmth (the European "climatic optimum" or the "Altithermal" of the western United States [Antevs 1948]). The Naha was considered to be younger than the abandonment of the San Juan drainage by the Anasazi around A.D. 1300. The end of Naha deposition was placed at the beginning of the modern arroyo-cutting episode historically dated between the late 1880s and early 1900s. Hack's observations, time-stratigraphic subdivisions, and correlations have been broadly confirmed by subsequent investigations (Cooley 1962; Malde 1964; Baumhoff and Heizer 1965; Haynes 1968; Hevly and Karlstrom 1974; and Karlstrom 1982), although his units have been further subdivided.

Soils of differing maturity are distinguished by thickness of oxidized zones (B-horizons) and degree of calcium carbonate enrichment. Pedologic analyses indicate the thick (1–2 m) soil on the Jeddito formation to be a polygenetic mature Haplargid soil, whereas the much weaker and thinner soils (generally less than 30 cm thick), intercalated in the overlying Holocene deposits, are immature Fluventic Camborthid, Ustollic Camborthid, Typic Haplargid or Cumulic Haplaquoll Soils (E. Karlstrom, personal communication 1977, 1981; E. Karlstrom 1983).

Chronostratigraphic method

The geomorphic variability characteristic of Black Mesa, the numerous discontinuities and rapid facies changes typical of alluvial deposits, and the discontinuous exposure and preservation of alluvium and associated terraces make it impossible to trace equivalent beds or terraces over long distances within one drainage basin or across drainage divides. In the general absence of geomorphic and lithologic criteria for intersite correlation, only the geologic criterion of parallel stratigraphic sequence remains. Application of this geologic criterion, however, assumes that parallel stratigraphic sequence reflects parallel depositional history. This assumption must be independently tested to determine whether horizons matched on the basis of stratigraphic sequence in fact represent contemporaneous events. In the Black Mesa research, independent chronometric dating of numerous sections in different drainages was used to resolve the geomorphic–stratigraphic variability, and to confirm time correlations suggested by parallel stratigraphic sequence. Direct dating of numerous stratigraphic sections in various parts of studied drainage basins circumvents the circular reasoning implicit in parallel-sequence correlations and curve fitting (Karlstrom 1961:333). This procedure also resolves the problem of homotaxis (NASC 1983), the possibility of intrabasin variability, and thus distinguishes between depositional histories characterized by either synchronous, diachronous, or systematic upvalley- or downvalley-lagging events.

Simple parallel-sequence correlation also assumes complete strati-

59

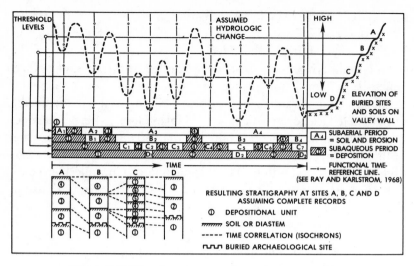

Figure 3.5 Site elevation as a factor in geomorphic–stratigraphic relationships.

graphic records, which is difficult to demonstrate in cut-and-fill–alluvial situations without physical tracing or independent temporal criteria. Depositional sequences with varying numbers and durations of events can be produced within a single valley system under the same hydrologic regime (Figure 3.5). This effect can result from elevation alone because sites lower in the valley are buried earlier than and exposed later than upper valley sites during any succession of aggradational and degradational epicycles (Figure 3.6). Depending on epicycle amplitude, sites at upper and lower elevations in a valley may fall beyond the range of changes recorded in the more sensitive intermediate elevation sites. Most of the dated Holocene sections on Black Mesa appear to occur in the most sensitive depositional environment represented by Site C (Figure 3.5).

Although correlative soil horizons can vary in duration, the contemporaneity of their midages is generally retained. These geometric relations justify the use of time-frequency analysis of dates from horizons of corresponding hydrologic sign to assess the timing of regional events. The placement of reference time lines at basal contacts, if consistently applied, permits more precise chronocorrelations among all types of oscillatory time-transgressive paleoclimatic sequences (Ray

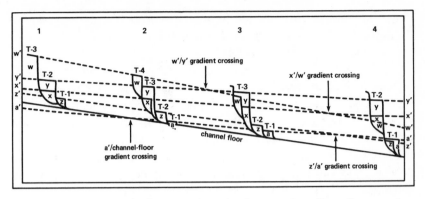

Figure 3.6 Schematic diagram showing the effect of converging and diverging terrace gradients on geomorphic–stratigraphic geometry.

and Karlstrom 1968). The recent North American Stratigraphic Code (NASC 1983) emphasizes the importance of basal contacts in chronostratigraphic analysis and refers to them as *Point Boundaries*.

Fortunately, many of the alluvial sections on Black Mesa contain materials datable by archaeological, C-14, and tree-ring methods. Ceramic dating was done mainly by archaeologists who in most cases independently collected or recorded buried sites or artifacts and reviewed the stratigraphic relations with me. Most of the radiocarbon samples were analyzed by the Isotopes Laboratory of New Jersey. Tree-ring dating (Dean, Chapter 5 below) was done by the Laboratory of Tree-Ring Research at The University of Arizona.

The resolution of dating depends on sample quality and dating method and generally ranges from less than 25 years for tree rings to less than 200 years for radiocarbon and archaeological samples. Although it is technically possible to date dendrochronologically the germination and death of a buried tree to the year, practical problems (principally center rot and missing outer rings) reduce the attainable resolution. Extrapolations based on ring curvature and distance of samples above roots and on the number of sapwood rings present on fragmentary samples provide estimated germination and death dates considered accurate to within 25 years (Euler *et al.* 1979:1099). The error in ages based on tree-ring calibrated ceramic dates is estimated to be not less than about 25 years for the most sensitive pottery associations and not

61

larger than about 200 years for the least diagnostic sherd assemblages. All dates associated with alluvial stratigraphic sections in the study area are presented in Karlstrom (in press).

Most of the datable material is associated with unconformities and nondepositional horizons marked by soils that vary in degree of development. The stratigraphic interpretation of the chronometric samples depends on sample type, stratigraphic position, and on whether they represent *in situ* (autochthonous) or transported (allochthonous) materials. The *in situ* soil dates provide maximum ages for overlying deposits and minimum ages for underlying deposits. The range of germination ages of trees rooted in the soils along with length of habitation of buried structures provide minimum durations for subaerial conditions between depositional events. Dating of the outermost ring of a standing buried tree provides a maximum age for when the tree died. Wide variation in tree death dates suggests that trees differ in their tolerance to burial. Judging from partly buried living trees, some are able to survive long intervals (100–700 years) of burial to depths of more than three meters. Thus, median tree ages derived from bulk C-14 samples cannot be directly related to either minor nondepositional or depositional intervals. Dated detrital wood and sherds from overlying and underlying alluvium provide contemporaneous to broad maximum ages for the enclosing sediments as a check on the intervening soil dates. Dated surface structures, trees rooted in the tops of sections, and historical accounts provide close minimum ages for the topmost deposits and help date the beginning of modern arroyo-cutting at different localities.

Geologic observation and independent dating were concentrated in several drainage basins on and around Black Mesa (Jeddito Wash, Dinnebito Wash, Moenkopi Wash, Klethla Valley, Long House Valley, Tsegi Canyon) and in tributaries of Laguna Creek near Kayenta. Independent dating by C-14, archaeology and tree rings greatly extended the number of Point Boundaries that could be dated, but many observed Point Boundary horizons remain undated in the absence of appropriate chronometric samples. These undated horizons are temporally positioned by the conventional geologic procedures of *interpolation* between overlying and underlying dated horizons and of *sequential correlation* to corresponding horizons directly dated in other sections. Although work was concentrated on dating valley-floor alluvium and alluvial fans, local exposures permitted direct dating of associated colluvial and eolian deposits.

Space limitations preclude detailed presentation of the chronostratigraphic data and analyses that are the basis for the reconstruction of past hydrologic variability in the study region. Because these data are not available elsewhere and because the reconstruction can be understood only through comprehension of the data and analyses that underlie it, examples of the application of the chronostratigraphic method to the alluvial sediments of four drainages in the Black Mesa area are presented in the Appendix, pp. 70–91 below.

Analytical results

Application of the chronostratigraphic (time-frequency) method outlined above and illustrated in the Appendix to the analysis of more than 40 stratigraphic sections produced a detailed chronology of synchronous alluvial events for the Black Mesa area. The chronostratigraphic data confirm Hack's (1942) subdivision and dating of the Black Mesa alluvial record into three main depositional units or formations: the Jeddito (late Pleistocene), Tsegi (early and middle Holocene), and Naha (latest Holocene). The major break in the alluvial sequence is represented by the Jeddito/Tsegi boundary, which is marked by an unconformity associated with a mature Haplargid soil with pronounced argilic B and calcic horizons (calcium carbonate Stage II-III:E. Karlstrom 1983). In middle Tsegi Canyon a detrital log from near the base of Tsegi deposits radiocabon dates ca. 3330 B.C. (Figure 3.12), slightly older than two buried forest layers in early Tsegi deposits in upper Tsegi Canyon (Figure 3.12) and along Laguna Creek near Kayenta (2780 and 2930 B.C., respectively) (Karlstrom in press). These results are consistent with the provisional radiocarbon age of about 4600 B.C. from calcium carbonate root casts in a truncated mature soil beneath early Holocene sediments in Dead Juniper Wash (Figure 3.10). This dating is congruent with Hack's placement of the Jeddito/Tsegi interval between 5000 and 2000 B.C. but suggests that Tsegi deposition in the lowest parts of canyon floors may have commenced around 3000 B.C.

Hack's archaeological dating of the termination of Tsegi deposition around A.D. 1300 or earlier is confirmed by tree-ring and radiocarbon

63

dates of A.D. 1390 to 1475 for buried trees rooted on the Tsegi/Naha unconformity in lower Tsegi Canyon (Figure 3.12). Thus, Tsegi deposits can be closely positioned by Point Boundary dates between greater than or equal to 3000 B.C. and about A.D. 1450. The dated Tsegi/Naha Point Boundary and the historical evidence that post-Naha arroyo cutting began in the late 1880s to early 1900s place Naha deposition between about A.D. 1450 and 1900. The tree-ring dating of the Z/a boundary at ca. A.D. 1900 in Klethla Valley (Figure 3.11) is consistent with the historical dating of modern arroyo cutting in the region.

The clustering of 119 dated Point Boundaries in restricted time intervals (Figure 3.7) strongly suggests essentially synchronous shifts from nondepositional to depositional conditions in different parts of the same and different drainage basins. Since the temporal spacing of the regional cluster pattern is replicated in many upstream-to-downstream sections with two or more Point Boundary dates consistent with sequential position, I interpret the evidence as recording essentially parallel depositional histories throughout the Black Mesa region. If systematic upstream or downstream lags in deposition are involved, these appear to be too short to be discriminated by present dating resolution.

The chronostratigraphic data strongly suggest primary and secondary depositional cycles of about 550 and 275 years. The ranges of independent dates associated with the generally weak X/Y and Y/Z soil horizons suggest intervals of nondeposition and subaerial weathering as much as 200 years in duration. The range of dates associated with the even weaker soil horizons of Y-$\frac{1}{2}$ and Z-$\frac{1}{2}$ age suggest soil formation during shorter intervals of around 100 years. Presumably, older primary and secondary soil horizons positioned on the bases of fewer dates or of sequential correlation record nondepositional intervals of roughly comparable durations.

Shorter subaerial intervals that interrupted the course of Z deposition are locally dated by germination and termination ages of buried trees at about A.D. 1525, 1600, and 1800 (Figures 3.10, 3.11, and 3.12). A subordinate nondepositional interval during Y-1 time is dated about A.D. 1000 by buried archaeological structures in four sections in Dinnebito Wash (Figure 3.10), Tsegi Canyon (Figure 3.12), Long House Valley, and the Kayenta area (Karlstrom in press).

REGIONAL REPRESENTATIVENESS
OF THE BLACK MESA
CHRONOSTRATIGRAPHIC RECORD

The hypothesis that the Black Mesa record is generally representative of conditions throughout the southern Colorado Plateaus (Euler *et al.* 1979) is supported by parallelisms in three main types of published information: (1) historical climatic and hydrologic records and dendroclimatic sequences relating to higher-frequency components of regional change (Gatewood *et al.* 1963; Stockton 1975); (2) moderate- to high-resolution pollen and bog sequences that reflect lower-frequency components of the hydroclimatic record; and (3) time-frequency analysis of dates from Point Boundary samples recording essentially contemporaneous regional and extraregional shifts from nondepositional to depositional conditions. The extraregional data replicate (1) the broader postglacial hydrologic trends; (2) elements of the intermediate frequency 550–275 year cyclical pattern; and (3) some of the higher-frequency components of the Black Mesa chronostratigraphic record.

Because of the general discontinuity and partial exposure characteristic of the alluvial record and the scattered occurrence of datable material, it is unlikely that all the main Holocene events have been, or can be, identified or dated in restricted areas. However, taken together, the partly dated Holocene sequences from Black Mesa (n=119, Figure 3.7, Column 2), from Chaco Canyon in New Mexico (n=17; Hall 1977, Figure 3.7, Column 3), and from the Pecos River Valley in Texas (n = 27; Kochel and Baker 1982, Figure 3.7, Column 4) provide a complete post-"Altithermal" sequence of directly dated, stratigraphically separated nondepositional horizons that are contemporaneous with the regional clustering of dates. These correlative nondepositional horizons are currently best dated statistically by the modal peaks in the time-frequency diagram combining the mutually exclusive Black Mesa and Southwest data sets (n = 384; Figure 3.7, Column 5).

Analysis of alluvial Point Boundary dates from the Southwest suggested strong, in-phase recurrences at 550-year intervals and a few at intermediate 275-year intervals (Karlstrom, Gumerman, and Euler 1974). Inclusion of dated depositional events recording burial of basal vegetation by glacial, alluvial, lacustrine, eolian, and colluvial (GALEC) processes provides larger and more regionally representative

65

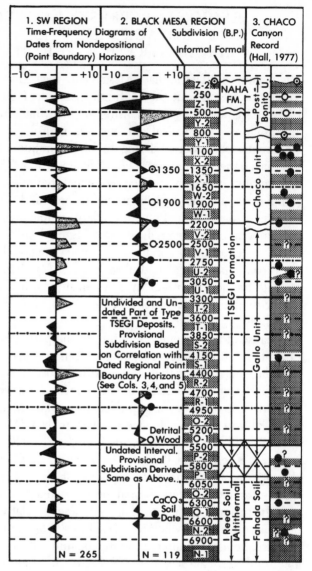

Figure 3.7 Regional comparisons.

samples. Analyses of these samples indicated generally similar cluster patterns (Hevly and Karlstrom 1974). Spectral analysis (Hereford, written communication, 1976) of GALEC Point Boundary dates from the southwestern, northwestern, and midwestern sectors of North

66

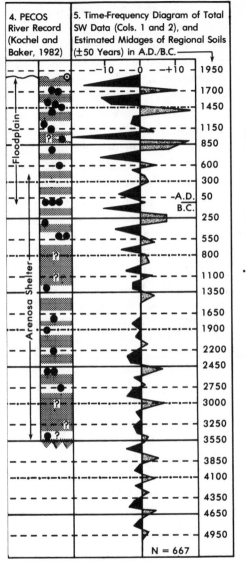

4. PECOS River Record (Kochel and Baker, 1982)	5. Time-Frequency Diagram of Total SW Data (Cols. 1 and 2), and Estimated Midages of Regional Soils (±50 Years) in A.D./B.C.

EXPLANATION

Dating Control

● Radiocarbon

⊙ Archaeology and History

○ Interpolated Age

▨ Buried Nondepositional Horizon (Soil, Culture or Organic Layer; or Unconformity); and 100yr. Class Interval with Excess Number of Regional Dates.

▧ Alluvial Unit; and 100yr. Class Interval with Deficient Number of Regional Dates.

•— — Reference Time-Line (See Fig. 6)

? Absent, Undetected or Undated Horizon; or Apparent Anomalous Mean Age, or Out-of-Phase Local Event.

America described in the radiocarbon literature through 1973 defines, at the 95 per cent confidence level, cycles of the harmonically related 1100–550–275-year cyclic series (Karlstrom 1980). Apparently, the larger samples are more representative of short-rank events and compen-

67

sate better for undetected anomalous dates, thereby tending to cluster-define the shorter cycles with greater precision.

Similar recurrence patterns are indicated by the clustering of 265 Holocene Point Boundary dates from the western United States published in the *Radiocarbon* volumes through 1983. By description, these dates are associated with buried soils, archaeological features and structures, organic-rich layers, and erosional contacts and appear to date local hydrologic shifts from nondepositional to aggradational conditions. Their analysis, therefore, permits the distinction of comparable-sign contemporaneous events of widespread regional occurrence from those that may represent either local facies changes or dating inaccuracies. To compensate for the greater number of samples in the late Holocene and to emphasize relative density differences between 100-year class intervals, the time-frequency data are differenced according to the formula $(\mathcal{E}X - \mathcal{E}X^{-1})$. The mutually exclusive data sets (Figure 3.7, Columns 1 and 2) produce comparable cluster patterns, and the larger regional sample suggests extension of the 550–275-year cyclic series throughout the post-"Altithermal" Holocene. The strong clustering of the independent Black Mesa and regional data sets indicates that the Holocene depositional history of Black Mesa is essentially representative of changing hydroclimate conditions throughout the larger region.

That these results are not the product of selection bias is indicated by similar cluster patterns that result from analysis at comparable 100- and 200-year class intervals of Point Boundary dates tabulated by other researchers (Karlstrom 1980, from data in Porter and Denton 1967; Denton and Karlen 1973, 1977; Pirazzoli 1982). Denton and Karlen (1973) propose a broadly defined 2500-year Holocene cycle. Time-frequency analysis of their Point Boundary data strongly suggests shorter cycles of 1100, 550, and 275 years in phase with the Black Mesa evidence.

Summary and conclusions

High-resolution dating (tree-ring, archaeology, and radiocarbon) of more than 40 Holocene alluvial sections throughout the Black Mesa Region reveals parallel depositional histories (chronotaxis) despite different locations in several drainage basins, and association with differing numbers and heights of terraces. Typical geomorphic/stratigraphic variability results from varying combinations of superposed- and inset-

68

terrace-stratigraphy. This variability evidently results primarily from varying physiographic (cross-sectional) controls on local depositional–erosional processes and includes elevation thresholds and crossing longitudinal terrace gradients.

The Black Mesa chronostratigraphic data support the classic interpretations of a major postglacial drought (the "Altithermal" of Antevs [1948]) culminating 6000–5000 years B.P., and followed by wetter and cooler climate (the "Little Ice Age") punctuated by secondary droughts. The Holocene droughts are marked by incipient- to moderately developed-geosols (buried soils) and diastems that are intercalated in alluvium of Tsegi and Naha age overlying a mature carbonate-rich (State II–III) geosol capping Jeddito sediments of late Pleistocene age.

Geologic relations in the valley fills indicate that the intercalated valley-bottom geosols must have developed during *drier* climatic periods with lower groundwater levels, headward and laterally widening arroyos, lower generally channel-confined floods, relatively stable valley-margin slopes, and decreased sediment yield (Qs^-). Thus, arroyo cutting evidently results from the combination of lowering groundwater levels, and progressive confinement of resulting lower floods (with lower sediment loads [$Qs<Qr$]) to narrow and deep channels. The overlying well-bedded and stratified vertical accretion (overbank) deposits represent progressively higher and wider valley-floor aggradation during *wetter* climatic periods with rising groundwater- and flood-levels and relatively unstable valley-margin slopes (Qs^+:colluviation$^+$ opposing trends towards denser vegetation cover$^+$). In the Black Mesa region, and in many other regions of the Plateaus, the dominance of colluvial process over that of expanding vegetation during wetter periods is facilitated by abundant moderate-to-steep valley slopes and outcrops of easily eroded and landslide-prone finer-grained clayey formations.

Time-frequency analyses of geosol (Point Boundary) dates from Black Mesa ($n = 119$) and from surrounding Southwest areas ($n = 265$) reveal parallel cluster patterns that imply synchronous timing of regional droughts of differing rank with average recurrence intervals of ca. 550 and 275 years. Comparisons with extraregional records of comparable resolution indicate that this Southwest hydroclimatic cyclicity may reflect wider hemispheric or global climatic trends.

Coincidences between the dated drought intervals and cultural changes, translocations, and abandonments suggest that the expanding Anasazi culture of the Southwest was responding differentially to lower-

69

and higher-frequency recurrences of environmental stress (Euler *et al.* 1979). This hypothesis and alternate socioeconomic and organizational hypotheses are explored in depth in Chapter 8 below.

APPENDIX: DATED SECTIONS AND CHRONOSTRATIGRAPHIC CORRELATIONS

More than 40 dated sections are available from Black Mesa and immediately surrounding areas (Figure 3.4; Karlstrom in press). The stratigraphy of sections in four representative drainages in northeastern Arizona exemplify data and procedures used in the chronostratigraphic analyses. A series of correlation diagrams (Figures 3.9–3.12) shows dated and undated soils and unconformities relative to thickness of intervening deposits, to height of associated terraces and geomorphic surfaces, and to level of arroyo floors. Synchronous depositional histories defined by dated sections in three other drainage basins (Moenkopi Wash, Long House Valley, and Kayenta area) are described and correlated in Karlstrom (in press). The symbols used to distinguish between different types of deposits, soils, erosional surfaces, chronometric samples and dating results are defined in Figure 3.8.

The stratigraphic subdivisions are those of the informal classification introduced by Karlstrom, Gumerman, and Euler (1974) in which the capital letters U (oldest), V, W, X, Y, and Z (youngest) designate the primary depositional units, and terms such as Z-1 and Z-2 designate main subdivisions of a primary unit. The intervening nondepositional intervals (depositional contacts or Point Boundaries) are designated by symbols combining the letters and numbers of the underlying and overlying deposits such as Y/Z and Z-1/2. The symbol *a* designates the contemporary sediments of the modern arroyo floors as well as modern (post-A.D. 1900) deposits laid down on adjoining uplands and low terraces by sheetwash and overbank floods. The associated terrace levels are numbered from lowest (T-1) to highest.

The lines in the correlation diagrams that represent the modal ages of nondepositional intervals (Point Boundary horizons) show my correlation of the stratigraphic sections. Solid arrows connect dated horizons of equivalent age. Dashed arrows connect undated horizons whose age or stratigraphic position is inferred from closely contiguous dates or from stratigraphic sequence. Dashed lines without arrows indicate the absence of a stratigraphic horizon (or the failure to find or identify a particular horizon) that is present in other sections. The absence of an equivalent horizon may indicate important differences in local depositional history or may simply reflect too casual field examination, undetected gaps, mantling of critical parts of a section, or absence of an event due to local threshold conditions (Figure 3.5).

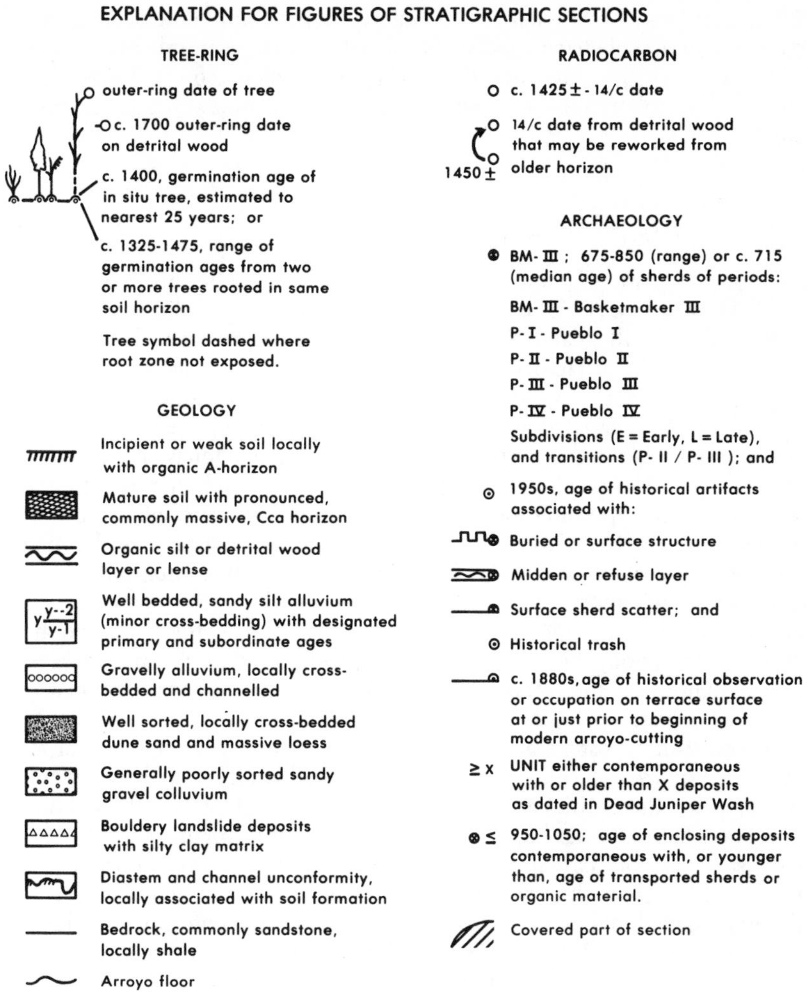

EXPLANATION FOR FIGURES OF STRATIGRAPHIC SECTIONS

TREE-RING

O outer-ring date of tree

-O c. 1700 outer-ring date on detrital wood

c. 1400, germination age of in situ tree, estimated to nearest 25 years; or

c. 1325-1475, range of germination ages from two or more trees rooted in same soil horizon

Tree symbol dashed where root zone not exposed.

GEOLOGY

Incipient or weak soil locally with organic A-horizon

Mature soil with pronounced, commonly massive, Cca horizon

Organic silt or detrital wood layer or lense

Well bedded, sandy silt alluvium (minor cross-bedding) with designated primary and subordinate ages

Gravelly alluvium, locally cross-bedded and channelled

Well sorted, locally cross-bedded dune sand and massive loess

Generally poorly sorted sandy gravel colluvium

Bouldery landslide deposits with silty clay matrix

Diastem and channel unconformity, locally associated with soil formation

Bedrock, commonly sandstone, locally shale

Arroyo floor

RADIOCARBON

O c. 1425 ± - 14/c date

O 14/c date from detrital wood that may be reworked from
1450 ± older horizon

ARCHAEOLOGY

BM- III ; 675-850 (range) or c. 715 (median age) of sherds of periods:

BM- III - Basketmaker III

P- I - Pueblo I

P- II - Pueblo II

P- III - Pueblo III

P- IV - Pueblo IV

Subdivisions (E = Early, L = Late), and transitions (P- II / P- III); and

1950s, age of historical artifacts associated with:

Buried or surface structure

Midden or refuse layer

Surface sherd scatter; and

Historical trash

c. 1880s, age of historical observation or occupation on terrace surface at or just prior to beginning of modern arroyo-cutting

≥ x UNIT either contemporaneous with or older than X deposits as dated in Dead Juniper Wash

⊗ ≤ 950-1050; age of enclosing deposits contemporaneous with, or younger than, age of transported sherds or organic material.

Covered part of section

Figure 3.8 Key for figures of stratigraphic sections.

The estimated midpoint ages of the nondepositional intervals are derived from time-frequency analysis (100-year class-intervals) of the dated Holocene soils on Black Mesa and elsewhere in the region (Euler *et al.* 1979; Hevly and Karlstrom 1974; Karlstrom, Gumerman, and Euler 1974, 1976). The Black Mesa soil dates (n = 119) cluster in restricted time intervals and suggest average recurrence intervals of about 550 and 275 years (Figure 3.7, Column 2). The accuracy of the estimated temporal midpoints (± 50 years) of the buried nondepositional horizons shown in the correlation diagrams is directly related to the number of dates and the

71

dating methods. The modal ages therefore are generally more accurate for the younger alphabetized subdivisions dated by a larger number of samples and by combined archaeological, tree-ring and radiocarbon methods than for the older subdivisions defined by less accurate and fewer radiocarbon samples.

JEDDITO WASH

Jeddito Wash, one of Tusayan Washes, drains the southernmost part of Black Mesa. Hack (1942) designated the Jeddito Valley as the type locality of the Jeddito (Fill-1) and Naha (Fill-3) Formations, respectively of late Pleistocene and late Holocene age. A deposit of intervening Holocene age (Fill-2) was named Tsegi by correlations with a corresponding deposit in Tsegi Canyon designated as its type locality. Hack interpreted the depositional sequence as recording three main aggradational periods separated by region-wide drier climatic intervals in which arroyo cutting and sand-dune deposition took place. The formations were subdivided primarily on the basis of color and weathering characteristics, fossil content (mammal bones and artifacts), and conformable and unconformable stratigraphic relations. Because of local physiographic factors affecting gradient and axial positions of streams, and resulting depths of erosion and ensuing deposition, the valley fills as mapped and interpreted by Hack (1942, Figures 29 and 30) occur in various combinations of superposed and inset terrace relations.

Arroyo-wall exposures between Hack's Jeddito Valley Stations L and K examined in 1976–8 (Figure 3.9) clearly showed his three-fold sequence and revealed that a thick mature calcareous soil developed on the Jeddito formation before burial beneath the Tsegi formation (Figure 3.9). As reconstructed from partial exposures, the Jeddito formation is a bedded russet red to yellowish-gray sandy gravel in its lowest part, grading up through bedded and lenticular gravelly sand to an unconformity overlain by a variably thick (3–6 m) unit of well sorted, locally cross-bedded eolian sand. Overlying this eolian sand unit is a variable thickness (1–3 m) of horizontally bedded sandy silt alluvium in which the capping mature soil is largely developed. At least three deep channel fills associated with soils on buried interchannel divides occur in the lower to middle part of the formation, and record significant periods of erosion and weathering that interrupted Jeddito aggradation. The eolian sand unit and underlying unconformity near the top represent another interruption in alluvial deposition, which in turn was followed by further alluviation and, finally, by deep soil formation during the major Jeddito/Tsegi erosional epicycle. Pedologic analysis of the Jeddito/Tsegi ("Altithermal") soil indicates that it is a polygenetic mature typic Haplargid soil (E. Karlstrom 1983). The degree of calcium carbonate accumulation suggests that the soil is

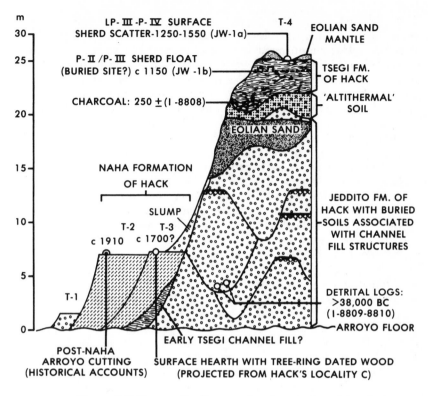

Figure 3.9 Composite diagram showing stratigraphic relations in Jeddito Wash.

somewhat less well developed than stage II carbonate soils in New Mexico considered to be pre-4000–5000 B.C. in age (Schultz 1983; Wells, Bullard, and Smith 1983).

About 3–6 m of uniformly bedded, brownish-gray silty sand alluvium mapped as Tsegi in age by Hack overlies the mature soil capping the Jeddito. The deposit underlies Terrace-4 and includes many thin beds and lenses of organic-rich silt, some diastems, and, locally near the base, several channel-fill structures. These features collectively record episodic interruptions in progressively higher overbank deposition of the detrital alluvium.

Three inset terraces are locally preserved in the bottom of the arroyo. The lowermost terrace (T-1) is underlain by about 1.5 m of coarse-grained, unweathered gray sand and gravelly sand of modern (a) age. The uppermost terraces (T-2 and T-3), which are of nearly equal height, are underlain by more than 7 m of stratified gray to brownish-gray silty sand alluvium mapped by Hack as the Naha Formation. Deposits of Terrace-2,

73

Terrace-3, and Terrace-4 are separated by steep erosional unconformities recording intervening epicycles of erosion down to or below present arroyo-floor levels. Unconformably underlying deposits of T-3 is a basal remnant of a well-bedded silty sand and gravel unit that I provisionally interpret as representing basal channel-fill deposits of early Tsegi age. However, in the absence of more critical information, it is not possible to exclude rigorously the alternate possibility that this oldest inset deposit is of early Naha age, deposited following the Tsegi/Naha rather than the Jeddito/Tsegi epicycle of erosion.

A few of the many nondepositional horizons exposed in Section JW-1 were associated with datable materials. Wood from two large detrital logs collected from a channel fill near the middle of the Jeddito radiocarbon date older than 38,000 years B.C. (I-8809 and I-8810). These results are consistent with Hack's fossil (*Elephus*) assignment of the Jeddito to the late Pleistocene. Charcoal collected from one of the channel-fill deposits near the base of the overbank deposits of Tsegi age dates A.D. 250 ± 100 years (I-8808), or relatively late within Hack's assigned interval of the Tsegi (2000 B.C.–A.D. 1300). Only sherds of late P-III and P-IV age (JW-1d) were found on the partly dune-mantled surface of the Tsegi deposits, but a local float concentration of transition P-II/P-III sherds (JW/1b) was found on partly mantled slopes within 1.5 m of the top of the arroyo wall. Although no buried structures were found in place, the position and age of this sherd concentration strongly suggest that a P-II/P-III site was buried in the upper Tsegi deposits, and in a stratigraphic position comparable to that of the buried P-II/P-III site 16 km upvalley at Hack's R location (Hack 1942:Figure 34). If so, the last Tsegi depositional event recorded at two places within Jeddito Valley can be dated between about A.D. 1150 and A.D. 1300, or equivalent in age to the uppermost part of the Tsegi Formation as dated at its type locality in Tsegi Canyon. Hack dates the Naha in Jeddito Valley as younger than about A.D. 1100–1300 on the basis of sherds associated with uppermost Tsegi deposits, and older than A.D. 1700 on the basis of tree-ring dates of charcoal collected from a surface hearth on the Naha terrace near his locality C. I have not found the hearth described by Hack. Dates for alluvium correlated with the Naha suggest that the hearth was probably on a surface equivalent to the T-3 terrace of Section JW-1. Based on historical accounts, Hack dates the beginning of the modern, post-Naha arroyo-cutting episode in Jeddito Valley between 1908 and 1918, or about two decades later than arroyo initiation in the northern part of the Black Mesa region (Gregory 1916).

Two of the earliest radiocarbon samples from the Southwest were collected in Jeddito Valley and attributed to the Naha and Tsegi Formations. These dates have been repeatedly used in correlation of the Southwest alluvial sequence with the postglacial record of the Rocky Mountains (Haynes 1968; Kottlowski et al. 1965; Richmond et al. 1965). Sample W-622 (A.D. 910 ± 250 years) is from charcoal associated with a white-ware sherd in a buried hearth. This hearth was exposed in an axial gully cutting a side-tributary alluvial fan of presumed Naha age. However, the date is significantly older than the terminal age of the Tsegi deposits exposed along Jeddito Wash. If the charcoal is of contemporaneous wood and validly dates the nondepositional interval represented by the buried hearth, the underlying as well as the overlying deposits should be of Tsegi age. This assignment is supported by the associated white ware sherd in the hearth, and by the description of inset Naha terrace deposits locally preserved in the same axial gully upstream from the sampled site. Sample W-621 (1150 B.C. ± 250 years) is charcoal from a nonceramic hearth buried in deposits attributed to the Tsegi. The results are compatible with Hack's dating and interregional correlation of the Tsegi formation and with the present chronometric dating of the type Tsegi deposits in Tsegi Canyon between about 3000 B.C. and A.D. 1450 (Karlstrom 1982; above, pp. 58–9).

DINNEBITO WASH

Dinnebito Wash drains the central part of Black Mesa and is separated from Jeddito Wash by Polacca and Oraibi Washes. Beyond reconnaissance observations, I have not dated sections in these intervening drainage basins. Descriptions of alluvial sections are provided by Hack (1942) and Thornthwaite, Sharp, and Dosch (1942). Whereas Hack views the alluvial sequences in these basins as supporting his regional climatic model, Thornthwaite, Sharp, and Dosch interpret the geomorphic–stratigraphic variability in Polacca Wash as a product of erratic nonclimatic processes.

Eight stratigraphic sections associated with varying numbers and heights of terraces have been dated in different parts of the Dinnebito drainage basin (Figures 3.4, 3.10). The Dead Juniper Wash section (D-1) is the most closely dated of these. Here the first buried forest in the region was discovered and later carefully sampled by personnel of the Black Mesa Archaeological Project (BMAP), the U.S. Geological Survey and The University of Arizona Tree-Ring Laboratory. Sampling was done to determine whether the buried juniper trees were datable against the regional dendrochronological record. Many of the trees proved datable, and this dating technique was subsequently applied with varying degrees of success at numerous other buried forest localities in the region. The resulting increase in dating precision enabled more detailed chronostratigraphic subdivision of the alluvial record and contributed to the development in Dead Juniper Wash of the informal alphabetic subdivision of the record into primary W, X, Y, and Z depositional units as an initial standard for comparison with other dated sequences in the region.

The Dead Juniper Wash stratigraphic record is exposed beneath two main terrace levels (Figure 3.10). Deposits beneath the upper terrace include a gravelly limonitic mottled basal unit capped by a truncated

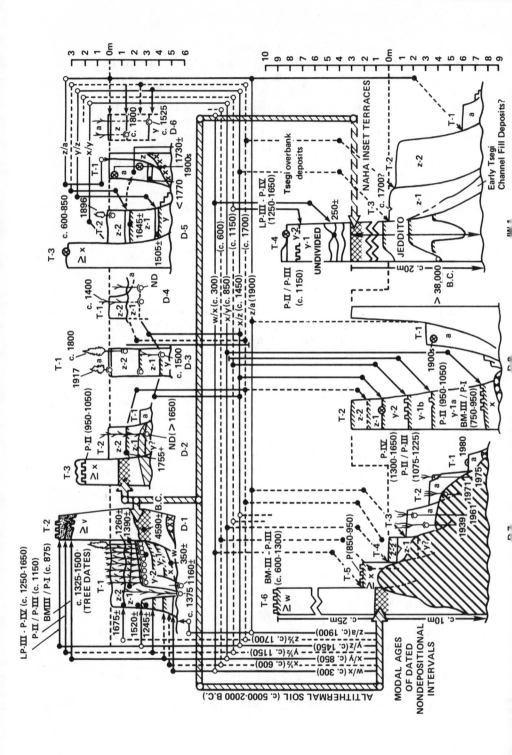

mature Cca soil. This soil is in turn overlain by a ca. 5 m thick section of bedded reddish to gray gravelly to sandy silt alluvium mantled by eolian sand. Archaeological refuse and structures buried near the base, middle and top of the mantling eolian sand deposit date by associated sherds respectively BM-III/P-I (A.D. 750–950), Late P-II (A.D. 1100–1200) and Late P-III and P-IV (A.D. 1250–1650). Calcium carbonate root-casts from the buried mature soil date 4590 B.C. ± 115 years (I-6918). Comparable degree of soil development and stratigraphic position support correlation of this Dead Juniper Wash soil with the late Pleistocene/Tsegi soil in Jeddito Wash; the radiocarbon age of ca. 4600 B.C. is consistent with Hack's estimated placement of this boundary between ca. 5000 and 2000 B.C. By this correlation the deposits underlying the mature soil in Dead Juniper Wash are Jeddito in age, and the overlying Holocene alluvium, dated sometime prior to A.D. 750 (buried BM-III/P-I horizon), correlates with the lower part of the Tsegi Formation as this is dated at Jeddito Wash between A.D. 1250 and older than A.D. 250 ± 80 years (I-8808).

The alluvium exposed below the lower terrace in Dead Juniper Wash is subdivided into four main depositional units (W, X, Y, and Z) separated by unconformities and weak soils. The W/X boundary is dated ca. A.D. 350 ± 85 years (I-7298) and a channel fill associated with a minor soil horizon in the Y deposits is dated ca. A.D. 1160 ± 80 years (I-6950). Germination ages of eleven buried trees rooted in the overlying and better-developed Y/Z soil horizon range from ca. A.D. 1325 to 1500 (DJW-1, 3–9, 12–13, 15) and provide a minimum duration of about 175 years for development of this soil prior to burial by the overlying Z sediments. An internally consistent radiocarbon age of A.D. 1390 ± 80 years (I-7535) was obtained from a root collected below the Y/Z horizon. That the duration of this soil-forming interval in Dead Juniper Wash may have been appreciably shorter than 300 years is indicated by radiocarbon ages of ca. A.D. 1250 (I-6951 and I-8522) and ca. A.D. 1520 ± 80 years (I-7521) on wood or forest litter collected respectively from within uppermost reddish Y deposits and lowermost yellowish-gray Z deposits. These dated nondepositional horizons define minor depositional events that immediately preceded and followed the Y/Z soil-forming interval.

The Z deposits record at least four main depositional units grading upward from bedded silty clayey sand to clayey sandy silt sediments. These subunits are separated by discontinuous diastems, forest litter layers or incipient soil profiles with minor $CaCo_3$-enrichment. Wood associated with the middle nondepositional horizon dates A.D. 1675 ± 85 years (I-6949) and along with equivalent dates from corresponding horizons in other sections was accepted as dating the defined Z-1/2 boundary at about A.D. 1700 (Karlstrom, Gumerman, and Euler 1974).

The detailed dating of Dead Juniper Wash stratigraphy clarifies the utility of germination and terminal ages of buried trees in alluvial dating. The unexpected finding that many of the trees survived long intervals of incremental burial required confirmation by independent dating of overlying deposits. Placed within the resulting chronostratigraphic framework (Figure 3.10), the wide range of terminal ages of those trees that germinated in the Y/Z erosion and soil-forming interval indicates that eight (DJW-5, 7–9, 12–13, 15, 21) died at various times during Z-*1* deposition between A.D. 1500 and 1700; three (DJW-2–4) survived Z-1 deposition and Z-1/2 erosion and then expired sometime during Z-2 deposition between A.D. 1700 and the beginning of the modern arroyo-cutting episode; and one (DJW-1) with an unexposed root system survived either one or both Z-*1* and Z-2 deposition and is still living (1983). Similar variable age relations of buried trees to dated overlying sediments are recorded in other sections. Thus it is evident that only germination ages could be used to date associated buried soil horizons, and that the divergent terminal ages must reflect different survival capabilities of individual trees to local burial history.

To survive burial, tree height must exceed that of depositional levels. This is best documented by the deeply buried tree DJW-21 rooted in the floor of a deep channel cut below the Y/Z terrace surface. Pith ages of the basal stem and the top branch 20 ft (6 m) above excavated root level are respectively A.D. 1396 ± and 1456 ± indicating that the tree had attained a height of more than 6 m prior to the beginning of Z-*1* deposition around A.D. 1500. Thus the tree crown was still more than 2.5 m above rising depositional levels when it died in the mid-1600s, following burial by more than 3 m of sediment. In contrast, tree DJW-13, since it occurs as a stump dated between A.D. 1350 and 1520, evidently was broken off near its base during early phases of Z-*1* flooding and deposition.

At section D-2 a stratigraphic sequence similar to D-1 is exposed 0.5 mi (2.4 km) downstream; here, however, the arroyo-floor deposits include a small terrace (T-1) (Figure 3.10). One of several dead juniper trees buried in the Z deposits beneath T-2 was sampled for dating. The sample (CPG-35) did not cross-date because of erratic ring patterns. Simple ring counts indicate a lifespan of significantly more than 300 years, and it is probable that the buried trees here are rooted in a buried horizon equivalent to the Y/Z soil exposed upstream. Large charcoal fragments from a discontinuous charcoal layer exposed in the upper part of the Z deposits dated A.D. 1755 ± 80 years (I-7534) or, within limits of dating error, contemporaneous with the dated Z$-\frac{1}{2}$ horizon in D-1. A surface structure covered by eolian sand mantling Terrace-3 dates by associated P-II sherds ca. A.D. 950–1050.

Three buried tree horizons are exposed in and beneath Z deposits in Section D-3 located in a side canyon 1½ mi (2.4 km) southwest of D-1. Trees in the lowermost zone are rooted in a weak soil comparable in development and in stratigraphic position to the Y/Z soil exposed in D-1. One of three trees sampled (CPG-32) proved cross-datable and provides a germination age of ca. A.D. 1500. An immature tree from the middle horizon marked by a discontinuous thin oxidized zone was too disintegrated to sample; whereas three living trees with buried roots nearer

78

Alluvial chronology and hydrologic change

the top but 5 ft (1.5 m) down in the section provide germination ages of around A.D. 1800 (CPG-25, 26, and 27). An immature tree growing in the top of the alluvial section and buried by a thin layer of slope-wash deposits germinated in A.D. 1917 (CPG-31). These results are therefore consistent with the correlation of the lowermost tree zone with the Y/Z horizon, the intermediate zone with the Z-$\frac{1}{2}$ horizon and the uppermost zone with a previously undated interruption in deposition during late Z time that may be represented by the upper diastem in Section D-1. The tree rooted in the top of the section indicates that Z deposition following ca. A.D. 1800 ceased prior to 1917.

Numerous other buried forests are represented in the area by wind-scoured tree trunks projecting above undissected to little dissected surfaces underlain by the grayish valley-floor deposits of Z age. To determine whether these trees were rooted within or below the Z deposits, tree sections were obtained from two localities (D-4 and D-6). A sample (CPG-36) from the projecting trunk of a deeply wind-scoured dead juniper at D-6 provides a germination age of ca. A.D. 1525, suggesting that an essentially complete section of Z deposits is present at depth in the area. A sample from a partly buried pinyon (CPG-38) provides a germination age of ca. A.D. 1800, suggesting shallower burial in the Z deposits and germination during the same nondepositional interval recorded in the upper Z deposits of Section D-3. A buried juniper tree sampled at Section D-4 provides a germination date of ca. A.D. 1400 (CPG-32), and therefore represents a pre-burial period of nondeposition and tree germination that was contemporaneous at least in part with that associated with the Y/Z soil-forming interval at Dead Juniper Wash (D-1).

Section D-5 is located along the main stem of Dinnebito Wash where the wash is crossed by a bridge on State Highway 264. The record is of three terraces. The higher terrace (T-3) forms the main floor of Dinnebito Valley and predates A.D. 600–950 (BM-III and P-I surface sherds; Robinson in Schafer *et al.* 1974). The intermediate terrace (T-2) is underlain by Z-type deposits overlying basal deposits capped by a weak oxidation profile. A detrital wood layer deposited on this soil is dated A.D. 1505 ± 80 years (I-7522) and represents the beginning of Z deposition at this locality. Two closely spaced buried tree (Cottonwood) horizons occur in the upper part of the section, the lower one of which is dated A.D. 1645 ± 80 years (I-69196). A few mature cottonwood trees are rooted in the top of the section. The oldest tree cored has a germination age of A.D. 1896 and records cessation of Z deposition prior to that time. In 1970 an unusually high flood overtopped the terrace (Schafer *et al.* 1974) and deposited a discontinuous veneer of gray sand on the vegetated terrace surface.

A remnant of a coarser-grained terrace deposit (T-1) is preserved on the west side of the arroyo and is about the same height as the Z terrace on the east side. Based on equivalent height, it was originally assumed that these terrace deposits were also of Z age (Karlstrom, Gumerman, and

79

Euler 1974). Subsequent observations and sampling of new exposures indicate inset relations to the Z deposits, diagnostically coarser-grained lithologies and presence of tin cans, plastic, and fragments of road macadam recording deposition in the last century. Sample I-6915 (A.D. <1770), originally thought to date a Z event, instead relates to post-1900 *a* deposition. Insofar as the Z deposits at the site are dated between A.D. 1896 and A.D. 1505, the detrital wood in *a* deposits, finitely dated A.D. 1730 ± 68 (I-7523), is either dated too old or, most probably, represents wood reworked from the older Z deposits. The latter possibility is suggested by the dashed source arrow in Figure 3.10.

The internally consistent chronostratigraphy of D-5 indicates that Y, Z, and *a* deposition in the main stem drainage were essentially contemporaneous with aggradational events defined in the side-tributary drainages upstream at D-1, D-2, D-3, D-4, and D-6.

Section D-7, located 10 mi (30 km) downstream from D-5 and near Dinnebito Springs, occupies a canyon cut into and below the Jurassic Navajo sandstone aquifer. The deeply dissected, uncommonly thick alluvial record is associated with at least six terraces, the lowest three of which were unweathered, bedded, light grayish sand and gravel incorporating partly buried living saltcedars. Since saltcedar is an exotic plant introduced in the area at the turn of the century (Hereford 1983) these deposits must postdate 1900.

The dune-sand mantled upper Terrace-6 is underlain by more than 100 ft (31 m) of reddish- to brownish-gray alluvium with a more deeply weathered and gravelly lower part separated by a polygenetic mature soil from the upper part. Pedologic analysis of this soil indicates it is a mature Haplargid soil (E. Karlstrom 1977, Appendix 1) or comparable to the buried late Pleistocene/Holocene soil in Jeddito Wash. Numerous archaeological structures and sherds of BM-III to P-III age on Terrace-6 indicate that alluvian deposition ceased sometime before A.D. 600. Inset Terrace-5 is capped by a weak soil with a conspicuous calcium-carbonate cemented horizon. A rock-lined cist and associated sherds of P-I age at the surface indicate that deposition of Terrace-5 ceased sometime before A.D. 850–950. Inset Terrace-4 is capped by a less well developed soil with inconspicuous $CaCO_3$ concentration, and is underlain by less oxidized, more friable brownish-gray sediment than that underlying Terrace-5. A buried hearth, 1½ ft (45 cm) below the T-4 surface included a small obsidian projectile point of uncertain age. Germination ages of partly buried saltcedars in the three recent terrace deposits indicate that T-1/T-2 dissection took place sometime between 1975 and 1980, T-2/T-3 dissection between 1961 and 1975, and T-3/T-4 dissection prior to 1940.

Although additional exposure and dating is required for more definitive subdivision and correlation to this section, the available minimum ages, stratigraphic sequence and differences in weathering favor correlation of the upper sediments of T-4 with the Z-1 and Z-2 deposits, and those of T-5 with X or older deposits as these are dated upvalley at Section D-5.

According to Hack's classic subdivision, the deposits below the mature CCa soil are of Jeddito age, those above and including the T-5 terrace deposits are of Tsegi age, and at least the uppermost exposed parts of Terrace-4 deposits are of Naha age. Sequential correlation with Section D-5 also suggests, as shown in Fugure 3.10, that these Z or Naha age deposits of T-4 probably overlie Y deposits (A.D. 850–1450) of late Tsegi age.

Section D-8 is located 18 mi (29 km) downstream from Section D-7. The section is exposed in the axial channel of a large alluvial fan-shaped deposit that apexes in a reentrant of the low Wingate Sandstone scarp where crossed by Dinnebito Wash above its confluence with the Little Colorado River. The stratigraphic record is of at least five main aggradational units separated by diastems and weak soils locally associated with buried archaeological structures and sherds. The alluvial context of these buried sites was observed jointly in the field with Mike Berry, Mike Windham, and Dave Deschambre, former BIA archaeologists who first located them. Dating of the buried sites is by Mike Windham: the lowermost site is dated to the BM-III/P-1 transition (A.D. 750–950), the intermediate site broadly to P-II time (ca. A.D. 950–1100) and the highest to the P-II/P-III transition (ca. A.D. 1100–1200). A few Jeddito yellow sherds (P-IV ca. A.D. 1300–1650) were subsequently found by the author associated with the uppermost weak soil in the section. These ages are therefore consistent with direct correlation to the X/Y, Y-$\frac{1}{2}$ and Y/Z horizons as dated upstream. In addition, the site stratigraphy provides evidence of a previously undated nondepositional interval ca. A.D. 1000 in mid Y-1 time, a subordinate event also recorded in drainage basins to the north (see Sections TC-2 and K-3 below).

KLETHLA VALLEY

Klethla Valley lies between the Black Mesa scarp to the south and the largely eolian-sand-mantled Navajo Sandstone uplands of the Shonto Plateau to the north (Figure 3.4). Drainage is from headwaters feeding off the largely landslide- and alluvial-fan-mantled Black Mesa scarp and from deep canyons cut into the Navajo Sandstone. The mainstem drainage is underfit and locally dammed by dune and alluvial sand. Much of the seasonal runoff is interior and trapped in the ephemeral Red Lake, although major floods overtop the shallow lake basin and flow into the Moenkopi drainage via Begashibito Creek. Alluvium along the north side of the valley is primarily of pinkish-brown well-sorted sand derived from the Navajo Sandstone; whereas that along the southern side is primarily finer-grained, more poorly sorted yellowish- to bluish-gray sediment derived largely from the unstable clayey Mancos Shale that outcrops in the middle to upper part of Black Mesa scarp.

Buried forests and archaeological sites occur locally within the dissected

81

alluvial fans and channel-fills of Holocene age at the base of Black Mesa. These deposits cover or are inset within more weathered alluvium and landslide deposits of Pleistocene age or rest directly on bedrock. Sampling of three buried-tree sites provides the bases for reconstructing the late Holocene chronology of alluvial fan development and dissection (Figure 3.11).

The exposed stratigraphy is comparable to that from the interior of Black Mesa in that it reveals a multiple sequence of more weathered (reddish) depositional units that flank and underlie a thick, essentially unweathered bluish gray, bedded deposit (Z) that was laid down just prior to the beginning of the modern arroyo-cutting episode in the region.

Section KV-1 (Figure 3.4) is of an alluvial fan that apexes above a drainage reentrant cut into the Dakota sandstone that forms a discontinuous structural bench at the base of the Black Mesa scarp in this area (Figure 3.11). The record is of axial dissection and tree germination on the newly exposed arroyo floor prior to channel filling and burial by as much as 4.6 m of bedded Z deposits. Buried trees exposed in the shallow arroyo cut in alluvium on the Dakota sandstone bench are rooted at a depth of 0.6–1.5 m in a Fluventic Camborthid soil beneath Z deposits, whereas those exposed in the deeper arroyo cut downvalley from the Dakota Sandstone scarp are buried by more than 15 ft (4.6 m) of Z deposits exposed below the same terrace level. Of sixteen standing buried trees sampled, nine proved datable and provide germination ages ranging from ca. A.D. 1300 (CPG-10 and CPG-13) to ca. A.D. 1475 (CPG-1 and CPG-3) and including intermediate germination ages of ca. A.D. 1425 (CPG-2), ca. A.D. 1375 (CPG-5, CPG-12; and CPG-14), and ca. A.D. 1325 (CPG-6). Thus it is evident that the nondepositional interval preceding Z deposition here was broadly equivalent in minimum duration (175 years) and contemporaneous with all or most of the Y/Z interval as defined in the Dead Juniper Wash section (Figure 3.10).

A transported branch associated with a diastem near the middle of the Z deposits is dated by outer rings A.D. 1675–1700 (CPG-9) or contemporaneous with the Z-1/2 horizon as dated between A.D. 1657 ± 80 and A.D. 1755 ± 80 at D-1 and D-2, ca. A.D. 1645 ± 80 at D-5 within the Dinnebito drainage area; and ca. A.D. 1700 at M-2 and ca. A.D. 1740 ± 80 and A.D. 1715 ± 80, at M-5 within the Moenkopi drainage area. Development of the associated incipient to weak Z-1/2 soil required surface stability (neither net erosion nor net aggradation) over a relatively short but significant time interval. The regional tree-ring and C-14 dating of this horizon is internally consistent in suggesting that the Z-1/2 nondepositional interval averaged roughly 100 years in duration, or about half the duration of the preceding Y/Z soil interval.

As in Dead Juniper Wash (D-1), the trees of KV-1 rooted in the Y/Z soil horizon show a wide range of terminal ages. Trees CPG-5, 10, 12, 13, and 14 evidently died between ca. A.D. 1615 and 1625. Tree CPG-6 died ca. 1675 and tree CPG-3 ca. 1880. Buried trees CPG-1 and CPG-2 were

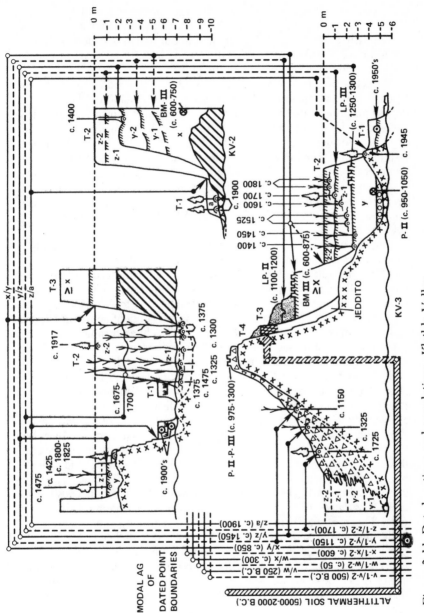

Figure 3.11 Dated sections and correlations, Klethla Valley.

still living when last observed in 1982. Thus, placed within the chronostratigraphic context of overlying sediments, five of these trees died during early to middle Z-1 deposition; one during late Z-1 deposition or in the following Z-1/2 nondepositional interval; one during or following late Z-2 deposition; and two survive to the present.

At Section KV-1, a germination age of A.D. 1917 (CPG-15) for a juniper rooted at the top of the Z terrace records cessation of latest Z deposition prior to that time. Another living juniper rooted on a rock ledge exposed in the modern arroyo wall and ca. 1.5 m below the top of the Z deposits, provides a germination age of A.D. 1800–1825 (CPG-8). The position of this dated tree indicates that local channel dissection to a depth of at least 1.5 m below the terrace top took place near the beginning of the nineteenth century, or contemporaneous with tree germination, incipient soil and diastem intervals dated in the Dinnebito drainage basin and at another site in the Klethla valley (KV-3) and in Tsegi Canyon (TC-5).

The a deposits at the KV-1 site are represented by arroyo-floor sandy gravel sediments containing tin cans, plastic, and other junk items recording deposition in this century. A recent wave of headward arroyo-cutting of these floor deposits commenced in the early 1970s, exposing the underlying stratigraphy of well-bedded gravelly sand to silty sand layers. The exposed section is of more than 1.5 m of sediment above an irregular bedrock surface. At ca. 55 cm depth is a well-defined organic layer containing immature sagebrush in growth position recording a brief interruption in deposition during a mid-a time interval.

Section KV-2 is located along a tributary drainage 0.3 km east of KV-1 (Figure 3.4), and represents a superposed alluvial sequence laid down near the apex of a large alluvial fan just prior to dissection by the modern arroyo-cutting episode (Figure 3.11). Nine to eleven m of regularly bedded Z deposits fill a channel and overlap the bordering fan surface. Away from the buried axial channel, 1.5–4.5 m of Z deposits disconformably overlie three depositional units separated by weak Fluventic Camborthid soils. A burned stump rooted in the upper soil and buried by the Z deposits germinated ca. A.D. 1400 (CPG-21), or within the Y/Z nondepositional interval as dated at D-1, KV-1, and elsewhere. The outermost ring is dated ca. A.D. 1775 (CPG-21) marking the tree's demise by a forest fire.

By stratigraphic sequence, the underlying soils correlate to the Y-1/2 and X/Y nondepositional intervals. Transported Lino Gray (BM-III) sherds collected from the middle of the lowermost unit (X) provide a maximum age of A.D. 500–700 and, consistent with sequential correlation, indicate that the enclosing sediments cannot be older than X (A.D. 300–850) in age.

Arroyo-floor alluvium includes one meter-high terrace and floor deposits of unweathered sandy gravel and sand. Two partly buried trees rooted near bedrock beneath the terrace deposits provide germination ages of ca. A.D. 1900 (CPG-16, and CPG–17). Two other living and partly buried trees in the arroyo bottom could not be dated because of erratic and false rings, but provide crude estimates of about 80 rings (CPG-20), and 53 rings (CPG-19). The date of ca. A.D. 1900 defines a minimum age for post-Z arroyo-dissection and a maximum age for commencement of arroyo-floor aggradation in the area. If, as historically recorded in nearby Tsegi Canyon, post-Z erosion was initiated here in the late 1880s, more than 10 m of rapid dissection down to bedrock took place prior to A.D. 1900, or within a brief period of a decade. As dated, the trees germinated near the culmination of the major drought interval recorded near the beginning of the century by the regional hydrologic and dendroclimatic indices (Figure 3.2). Thus the preceding period of rapid dissection evidently took place during the late 1800s interval of rapidly falling precipitation and hydrologic levels, and the subsequent burial by *a* deposits during one or more of the ensuing intervals of wetter climate and rising hydrologic levels.

At section KV-3 (Figure 3.4) the Z deposits occur as an irregularly shaped fan inset below at least three older terrace levels situated in turn below partly debris-mantled bedrock ridges (Figure 3.11). T-3 predates A.D. 600–875 on the basis of BM-III surface sherds and structures. Archaeological structures on a higher ridge of Dakota sandstone are dated between P-II and P-III (A.D. 975–1300) and record repeated, if not continuous, occupation of the area during this period (Euler, Chapter 7 below). A buried late P-II site (A.D. 1100–1200) occurs at a depth of 1 m in dune sand that locally mantles the T-3 surface.

The alluvial sequence exposed below Terrace-2 is of 1.6–2.4 m of uniformly bedded Z deposits overlying as much as 3.6 m of bedded reddish-brown to gray Y deposits enclosing near the base a few P-II (A.D. 975–1075) sherds. The weak Y/Z soil horizon is discontinuously exposed in the arroyo walls and is locally associated with check dams and sherds of late P-III (A.D. 1250–1300) age, and with rooted buried trees. Of six trees sampled from this horizon two proved datable and provide germination ages of ca. A.D. 1450 (CPG-78) and ca. A.D. 1400 (CPG-66) or within the Y/Z interval as dated at D-1 and KV-1. The record is therefore of late P-III farming on the Y fan surface prior to dissection, tree germination, and soil development in turn before final burial by Z deposition.

Tops of numerous buried trees project above the undissected surface of the Z fan near its head. Ten of these trees were sampled by excavation down to root crowns, and associated incipient soil horizons are, respectively, ca. A.D. 1525 (CPG-71, CPG-79), ca. A.D. 1600 (CPG-70), ca. A.D. 1700 (CPG-77); and ca. A. D. 1800 (CPG-76, CPG-80). Since trees cannot germinate on surfaces undergoing either active erosion or aggradation, these tree-dated horizons should represent brief but distinct intervals of nondeposition and surface stability that episodically interrupted the course of progressively higher Z deposition at the site. As dated, these subordinate nondepositional intervals occurred during pronounced decadal droughts recorded by the regional dendroclimatic indices and suggesting sensitive hydrologic responses to secondary climatic trends during "Z"-time

(Euler *et al.* 1979). That these subordinate "Z" events represent regional rather than random local responses is suggested by essentially contemporaneous nondepositional events, as these are directly dated in other sections of the region. The ca. A. D. 1800 nondepositional event is evidently represented by dated buried trees in the Dinnebito drainage, and in section TC-5 of Tsegi Canyon. The ca. A.D. 1525 event is represented in the Dinnebito and Moenkopi drainages. The ca. A.D. 1600 event dated in KV-3, however, has no directly dated counterpart in the other sections of the region.

Trees partly buried by slope deposits above the margins of the KV-3 fan were also sampled. A dead tree partly buried in landslide debris germinated ca. A.D. 1150 (CPG-73). A living tree partly buried by sandy slope-debris germinated ca. A.D. 1725 (CPG-60). A more deeply buried dead tree germinated ca. A.D. 1325 (CPG-59). Since these trees must have germinated during intervals of slope stability prior to burial, it is considered significant that all germinated during the nondepositional intervals recorded in the alluvial record, or contemporaneous with the Y-1/2 and Y/Z and the Z-1/2 Point Boundary horizons. Thus conditions of increased slope instability and debris movement evidently occurred during the intervening intervals of active Y-2, Z-1, and Z-2 aggradation on adjacent valley-bottom floors.

The *a* deposits of section KV-3 occur as terrace- and floor-deposits inset below the Z surface. The *a* terrace (T-1) ranges in height above the arroyo floor from 1.6 m to 3.2 m and is traceable as a geomorphic feature up to the headcuts of the present arroyo system. Above these headcuts, the drainage lines on the undissected parts of the fan are marked by shallow narrow trenches that feed into the arroyo heads. The *a* deposits here, as elsewhere in the region, are generally uniformly bedded and locally contain tin cans, plastic, and other historical artifacts indicating deposition during the present century. A buried trash accumulation at 0.6 m depth in the terrace deposits contains pop bottles, plastic, tin cans, and car parts of mid-century vintage (Alexander Lindsay, personal communication, 1972), suggesting a nondepositional interval centered in the 1950s that stratigraphically corresponds with the buried sagebrush horizon in Section KV-1.

As dated, this nondepositional interval in *a*-time occurred during the pronounced 1950s drought interval defined in the regional dendroclimatic and hydrologic records (Figure 3.2). Three living junipers rooted on a bedrock ledge exposed in the modern arroyo walls ca. 3.1 m below the top of the Z deposits germinated around A.D. 1940 (CPG-82–84), and provide a broad minimum age for the beginning of the recent arroyo dissection in the area.

TSEGI CANYON

Tsegi Canyon is the type locality of the Tsegi formation which, as defined by Hack (1942), underlies the higher of two terraces that characterize the deep alluvial fill of the canyon and its numerous tributary canyons. The canyon is drained by the spring-fed, permanent Laguna Creek, which flows on or close to bedrock in a deep arroyo cut through alluvium of predominantly horizontally bedded, grayish to reddish, gravelly to clayey sediment. The twofold terrace sequence records two main intervals of active canyon-floor aggradation following periods of deep dissection down to present bedrock-floor levels. The higher Tsegi terrace lies 12–30 m above present grade. Following post-Tsegi dissection, the development of the lower terrace (Naha) represents an interval of renewed aggradation to within 3–6 m of the Tsegi terrace level. Terrace gradients are less than the stepped, bedrock-controlled longitudinal profile of Laguna Creek, and deposits exposed below both terraces generally increase in thickness downcanyon.

Based on geologic correlations and associated archaeological materials, Hack (1942) broadly dates the commencement of Tsegi deposition around 2000 B.C., and its cessation sometime prior to the construction of surface structures of P-II age broadly placed by sherd types between A.D. 900 and 1200. The Tsegi/Naha interval of arroyo-cutting is dated as concurrent with and/or following the abandonment of the region by Pueblo peoples around A.D. 1300. Historical observation in the canyon indicates that Naha aggradation had ceased by the mid-A.D. 1800s, and that the modern arroyo-cutting episode abruptly commenced in the late 1880s (Gregory 1916). These historical observations thus suggest an interval of several decades of relatively stable floodplain conditions between cessation of Naha aggradation and the commencement of the recent arroyo-cutting episode in the area.

Tsegi Canyon section TC-1 (Figures 3.4 and 3.12) is reconstructed from observations near the mouth of Kiet Siel Canyon. Here the record is of four terrace deposits, the lower two of which are of unweathered grayish-sandy gravel of post-A.D. 1900 (*a*) age. Inset T-3 (Naha) occurs as discontinuous remnants 8–9 m above present grade along the right bank of the trunk canyon. These deposits have been largely removed by post-Naha dissection in the lower reaches of Kiet Siel Canyon. The 12–15 m high Tsegi Terrace is better preserved and is nearly continuously traceable along trunk canyon margins and up Kiet Siel Canyon. Whereas Naha Terrace surfaces are generally undissected and unmantled by wind deposits, the older Tsegi Terrace surfaces are in part covered by thick reddish dune deposits, and where unmantled are generally gullied and surficially stripped by slope wash and by piping processes concentrated in $CaCO_3$-cemented upper horizons.

Where best exposed by recent slumping of arroyo walls, both the Tsegi and Naha formations are primarily characterized by horizontally bedded

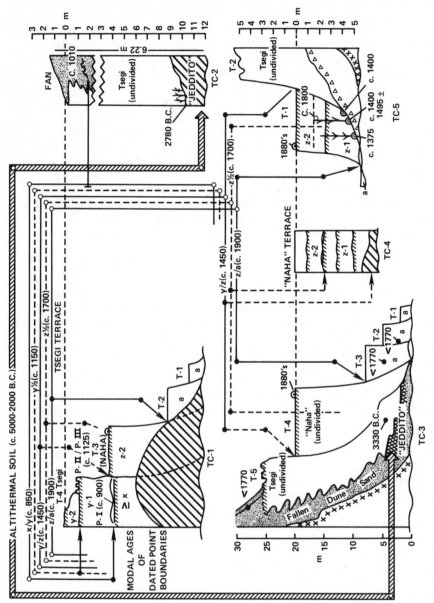

Figure 3.12 Dated sections and correlations, Tsegi Canyon.

sandy alluvium intercalated with several soil horizons and numerous thin beds and lenses of organic silt and peat (cienega or marsh-type deposits). Both the soils and the horizontally extensive cienega deposits record repeated interruptions in general histories of progressively higher overbank deposition. The soils mark intervals when base-flow levels and associated water-table levels fell sufficiently below stabilized floodplain surfaces to permit subaerial weathering of surface material lying generally above the water-saturated zone. The cienega horizons, in contrast, mark those interruptions in alluvial sedimentation when lowered flood- and water-table levels remained sufficiently high for accumulation of organic material and vegetation in floodplain depressions that intersected a shallower water-saturated zone.

The intercalation of cienega beds and soils from base to top of the formations thus clearly requires a general pulsatory rise in base-flow and water-table levels from present grade to positions 12–15 m higher during Tsegi time; a fall in such water levels to present grade during the Tsegi/Naha arroyo-cutting interval; a progressive hydrologic rise to levels 8–9 m higher during Naha time; and a final fall in base-flow and water-table levels to present grade during the current post-Naha arroyo-cutting interval. In the absence of local or regional geologic evidence suggesting other possible types of base-level controls such as regional tilting or volcanic damming (Gregory 1917), the recorded pronounced changes in volume of the spring-supported ground-water reservoirs in the canyon may be most directly related to aquifer recharge rates, and thus to past changes in climatic conditions.

Tsegi deposits (T-4) exposed immediately north of the trail in the mouth of Kiet Siel Canyon locally enclose buried pueblo structures and trash horizons. These occupation horizons occur near the top of the section on a stripped $CaCO_3$-enriched soil horizon, and at a depth of about 4.6 m. Preserved remnants of bedded alluvium on the upper stripped soil horizon indicate post-habitation burial by at least 1.6 m of alluvium prior to stripping. This exhumed habitation horizon is dated by ceramics between A.D. 1075–1200, or ca. A.D. 1125 (J. S. Dean, site AKa 8lb, unpublished survey notes, 1981) or contemporaneous with comparably dated buried structures in Long House Valley and Dinnebito Wash (Figure 3.10, D-8) and in the Kayenta area (Karlstrom in press). The lower trash horizon dates to P-I or ca. A.D. 900 (J. S. Dean, site AKa 8lb, unpublished survey notes, 1981), or contemporaneous with a buried hearth in Long House Valley, buried pit houses near Kayenta, and buried structures in the Moenkopi drainage (Karlstrom, Gumerman, and Euler 1976), and in Dinnebito Wash (Figure 3.10, D-8).

These results differ but slightly from Hack's interpretation of Tsegi deposition as predating A.D. 900–1200, in that the presented evidence indicates a later Tsegi depositional event (Y-2) that can now be more precisely bracketed between the P-II/P-III transition (ca. A.D. 1150) and late P-III (A.D. 1250–1300) periods. Unfortunately, the P-II structures described as constructed on the Tsegi Terrace were not recovered in the field, and confirmation of ceramic age and stratigraphic position was not possible.

A buried pueblo structure (NA7521) is exposed 3.0–3.5 m below the surface of a marginal alluvial fan that is graded to the Tsegi Terrace level about 4 km upcanyon from TC-1, along the left bank of Kiet Siel Creek (Figures 3.4, 3.12, TC-2). The ceramic age of P-II is directly supported by tree-ring dates between A.D. 1000–1020 derived from associated charcoal (Bannister, Dean, and Robinson 1968). The mid-Y-1 (ca. A.D. 1000) nondepositional interval stratigraphically defined by dated buried structures in Dinnebito Wash, Long House Valley, and near Kayenta evidently has a counterpart in the Tsegi Canyon alluvial record. Downstream from site TC-2, a recent slump exposed 21–24 m of stratified Tsegi deposits overlying a basal forest horizon. Mature ponderosa pine, Douglas fir, and softwood trees were identified (Dean). A sample from the forest horizon dates 2780 B.C. ± 100 (W-10725), and provides an age at or near the beginning of Tsegi deposition in the canyon.

Reconnaissance in the lower part of Tsegi Canyon recovered the main stratigraphic units described by Hack. These features (Figures 3.4, 3.12, TC-3) include: (1) the deeply oxidized fallen dune deposits underlying Tsegi alluvium interpreted as marking the Jeddito/Tsegi ("Altithermal") dry interval; and (2) the inset relations recording dissection to bedrock-floor levels during the Tsegi/Naha interval.

As in the upper part of the Canyon, the Tsegi deposits, here underlying the 24–28 m high T-5, are more dissected and more oxidized than the younger Naha deposits, here underlying the 18–22 m high T-4. Wood from a detrital log was collected from the base of a partly exposed section near the mouth of Dowozhiebito Canyon. Stratigraphic relations indicate that the log may have been enclosed in a remnant of basal Tsegi alluvium overlying weathered red dune sand, and unconformably separated from the overlying more grayish, less weathered deposits exposed beneath the Naha Terrace. The radiocarbon age of 3380 B.C. ± 115 years (I-7540) is consistent with this stratigraphic interpretation and is accepted as providing a closer maximum age for commencement of early Tsegi deposition than that obtained near Section TC-2. Stratigraphic position and age of these samples support correlations of the Jeddito/Tsegi soil boundary in Tsegi Canyon with that in Jeddito Wash and with the comparably buried mature soil dated at about 4600 B.C. in Dead Juniper Wash.

The fine-grain lithologies and bedding structures of the Tsegi and Naha deposits in the lower part of the canyon are generally similar to those exposed in upper canyon reaches, and record the same pulsatory rise and fall in hydrologic levels. Traced into side gullies cut below the Tsegi Terraces, the inset Naha deposits, however, rapidly coarsen toward gully heads and bedrock sources. A section measured in a side gully near the confluence of Long House Valley outlet drainage with Laguna Creek (Figure 3.12, TC-4) is of five main depositional units predominantly of bedded silty sand and gravel separated by diastems and incipient to weak Camborthid soils. Based on parallel sequence, provisional correlation may be made with the comparable number of tree-ring-dated nondepositional intervals in the Z deposits of Section KV-3 in Klethla Valley (Figure 3.11).

Some changes have evidently taken place in the lower part of the canyon since Hack's observations in 1938. The fallen-dune sand deposits described as stabilized with vegetated surfaces above the Tsegi Terrace level are now covered by 60–90 cm of bare reddish dune or colluvial sand resting on an iron-stained horizon associated with plant remains and scattered angular fragments of reddish sandstone derived from nearby bedrock (Wingate) cliffs. A radiocarbon result of < 180 years B.P. (I-8757) from wood from this soil horizon is compatible with the interpretation that this horizon may represent the vegetation-stabilized dune surface observed in 1938.

Section TC-5 is located at the mouth of Tsegi Canyon in a short tributary arroyo draining the Black Mesa scarp (Figures 3.4, 3.12). The arroyo exposes the basal unconformity separating the inset Naha deposits from the higher, more eroded Tsegi Terrace deposits. Tree-ring dating of buried dead juniper and pinyon trees rooted below the weakly weathered Tsegi/Naha unconformity provide germination ages of ca. A.D. 1375, ca. A.D. 1400 and ca. A.D. 1400 (CPG-22, CPG-23, and CPG-24). A radiocarbon age of A.D. 1495 ± 80 (I-8528) was obtained from the inner to middle part of the CPG-22 tree. This tree evidently survived about 1.8 m of Naha deposition prior to a nondeposition interval in which it was burned off to ground level. One and a half meters of late Naha deposition followed this interval of subaerial burning that is dated by outermost rings to about A.D. 1800.

These results confirm Hack's broader dating of the Tsegi/Naha interval of dissection as occurring around or following A.D. 1300, and his correlation of this Tsegi Canyon boundary with his similarly designated boundary dated between A.D. 1300 and A.D. 1700 in Jeddito Wash. The data further demonstrate the temporal equivalence of this classic Tsegi/Naha boundary with the Y/Z nondepositional horizon as this is correspondingly and most precisely positioned between A.D. 1325 and 1500 in the Dead Juniper Wash Section and between A.D. 1300 and 1475 in Section KV-1. The late Naha nondepositional horizon dated ca. A.D. 1800 in Section TC-5 was evidently contemporaneous with the subordinate late Z-2 nondepositional intervals defined by germination ages of buried trees in the Dinnebito and Klethla Valleys (Figures 3.10 and 3.11).

4
Prehistoric vegetation and paleoclimates on the Colorado Plateaus

RICHARD H. HEVLY

Department of Biological Sciences
Northern Arizona University

This study will attempt reconstruction of the paleoenvironment of the prehistoric inhabitants of the Colorado Plateaus, utilizing biotic remains, especially pollen, recovered from a variety of depositional environments and will distinguish, when possible, some of the interacting factors that contributed to this record.

While the collective sites of the Colorado Plateaus provide data spanning the period between 10,000 B.C. to A.D. 1900, emphasis will be placed on the millennium with the greatest number of sites yielding pertinent data: A.D. 350 to 1350. This millennium is also the one within which Pueblo culture flourished and changed dramatically. Within this period, data exist from hundreds of sites on the southern Colorado Plateaus, but only a few localities provide adequate temporal control, similar time depth, and a variety of comparable paleontological data. For this study, data will therefore be primarily derived from only a few localities (Figure 4.1).

MODERN CLIMATES, BIOGEOGRAPHY, AND CARRYING CAPACITY

In regions of great relief, such as the Colorado Plateaus, a striking zonation of biotic communities occurs in response to temperature and

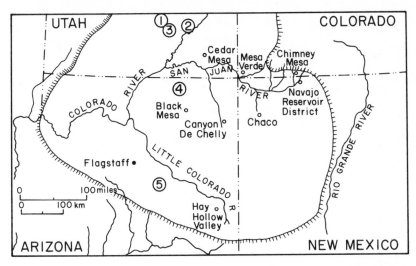

Figure 4.1 The Colorado Plateaus of the American Southwest, showing the locations of the major study sites utilized in the recovery of paleontological data employed in the evaluation of environmental change and the response of prehistoric human populations to such change. The locations of pithouse and pueblo sites are named while the locations of Archaic sites are indicated by number: 1 = Sudden Shelter; 2 = Cowboy Cave; 3 = Joe's Alcove; 4 = Dust Devil Cave; 5 = O'Haco Shelter.

precipitation gradients (Figure 4.2). Within the Little Colorado River Basin, with increasing elevation, six principal vegetation types are recognized: Sage Desert (Northern Desert Scrub), Short Grass (Plains Grasslands), Pinyon–Juniper Woodland, Pine Parkland, Mixed Coniferous, and Spruce–Fir Forests (Lowe and Brown 1977; Nichol 1952).

Comparison of vegetation and long-term, local meteorological records from the same area suggests that the principal vegetation types may be associated with arid, semi-arid, mesothermal, and microthermal climates as described by Trewartha (1954). This vertical zonation of climates is controlled by altitude, slope, and exposure (Figure 4.2). For each 333 m (1000 ft) increase in elevation, there is a corresponding decrease in temperature of approximately 2.5°C (3.5°F). Accompanying this decrease in temperature is a pattern of increasing precipitation, the distribution of which depends on exposure, prevailing winds, and distance from mountains (Smith 1956). Wind velocities, March through June, are usually the highest for the year and average

93

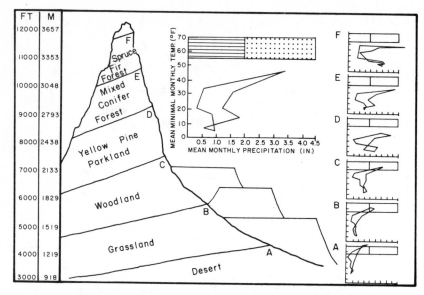

Figure 4.2 The major plant communities of the Colorado Plateaus, illustrating their vertical zonation. (Climatic data are from Sellers and Hill 1974 and Smith 1956.) Representative climographs of each of the major plant communities (A–F) relative to the climatic requirements for corn agriculture (horizontal box associated with each climograph) are also shown. Each of the twelve points of a climograph documents the mean monthly precipitation and temperature found at a weather station in the indicated plant community (climatic zone) (Dansereau 1957). If the summer climate (right hand points of a climograph) does not extend into the box, corn cannot be grown at that locality. If the summer climate extends into the left hand side of the box, irrigation will be required to grow corn. Climates for crops such as corn are marginal or inadequate in most areas of the Colorado Plateaus above 7000 feet today but may have differed in the past as sites of prehistoric agriculturalists occur above 7000 feet.

about eleven miles per hour (Smith 1956). Prevailing wind direction at present is principally from the southwest, particularly during the spring and summer flowering seasons. Alignment of both stable and moving sand dunes would suggest that it has been so for many thousands of years (Hack 1942).

On the Colorado Plateaus, rainfall occurs during two principal seasons, July–September and December–March, which are separated by a pronounced dry season, April through June, and a less pronounced dry season in October and November (Sellers and Hill 1974; Smith 1956). Winter precipitation arises from Pacific Polar Maritime sources and is typically widespread, persistent, and gentle, while summer rains arise from Tropical Maritime sources in the Gulf of Mexico and are usually local, of short duration, and torrential (Trewartha 1954).

The interaction of precipitation and temperature produces a vertical zonation of vegetation in which the upper altitudinal limit of a species is usually determined by its ability to function in low temperatures and its lower range is controlled by its resistance to drought (Daubenmire 1954; LaMarche 1973; Pearson 1931). The forest and parkland vegetation types, in addition to having lower temperatures and greater precipitation, seem to have the precipitation distributed in a slightly different manner from that of the lower steppe and desert communities (Figure 4.2). Thus, stations below 6500 feet on the west and northwest sides (or 7000 feet in the rain shadow on the east and northeast sides) of mountains, receive eight to eighteen inches of precipitation, and 50 per cent of this is delivered in the form of torrential thunderstorms during the three-month summer rainy season, with 13 per cent to 18 per cent delivered in each of the remaining three seasons. Stations above these elevations receive 20 to 30 inches of precipitation, of which 50 per cent or more is delivered during the fall and winter months, with only about 40 per cent during the summer rainy season.

The significance of such seasonal differences in the distribution of precipitation in determining lower altitudinal limits is more apparent when the phenological record of the major arboreal species is examined. Root and stem elongation, flowering, and to a certain extent radial growth occur during spring, the driest season of the year, and are apparently dependent largely on residual soil moisture from winter precipitation and stored food from the previous growing season (Fritts 1976; Johnsen 1962; Pearson 1950). The drought tolerance of juniper and pinyon pine, being greater than that of yellow pine, fir, or spruce, permits their survival and perpetuation at lower elevations in areas of less effective moisture than at higher elevations (above 6500 feet) where low temperature coupled with greater winter precipitation (including fall rains) permit the survival of yellow pine and other conifers.

While the distribution of major vegetation types is largely controlled by the elevational distribution of temperature and precipitation, local edaphic factors also exert a profound influence, and it is possible for more than one vegetation type to develop under a single climate (Nichol 1952; Pearson 1931). For example, both Juniper–Pinyon Woodland and Grassland may occur under a steppe climate (Hevly 1968). The Woodland is better developed in shallow, coarse-textured, well-aerated soils or on rock outcrops, while Grassland thrives on deeper, finer-textured, more poorly aerated soils (Johnsen 1962). Seasonal character-istics of climate are also of significance, particularly in regard to the germination of the seeds of annual plants and the development of seedlings into mature plants (MacDougal 1967). For example, corn, beans, and squash are dependent on residual winter moisture for germination, combined with warm temperature and summer moisture for maturation.

The prehistoric distribution of humans was likewise limited to those environments in which food could be acquired by gathering and/or by cultivation. The greatest diversity of native plant and animal resources that were commonly consumed as food items occurs between 4500 and 6500 feet elevation on the Colorado Plateaus. Corn, beans and squash, the principal cultigens grown by the prehistoric inhabitants of the Colorado Plateaus, can be grown at any elevation below 7000 feet, but currently require irrigation below 5500 feet. Corn, beans, and squash provide a nutritionally balanced diet, but the development of strains of these cultivars adapted to the environments of the Colorado Plateaus did not occur simultaneously nor was cultivation of these plants always successful. Therefore it is not surprising to note in archaeological sites the persistent occurrence of the remains of both native and cultivated biotic resources, the proportions of which depended no doubt on their availability and the individual preferences of the humans exploiting such resources. Aside from the creation of very local microhabitats resulting from prehistoric human disturbance, the availability of such resources was probably largely controlled by natural factors such as climate and alluvial history (Euler et al. 1979; Young 1980).

LOCALITIES AND SAMPLING PROCEDURES

Nature of sites chosen for study

Paleontological data can be recovered from a variety of depositional environments, each of which affords the investigator particular advantages as well as disadvantages. Archaeological sites were chosen for this study because they afford better dating control than other depositional environments. Their paleontological records may be biased, however, by various cultural activities (e.g., disturbance of biotic community in the vicinity of the site or selective gathering of biotic materials). The nature and magnitude of such biasing can often be predicted and obviated or even utilized to answer specific questions (Hevly 1981).

The sites chosen for this study are situated within Pinyon–Juniper Woodland or its ecotones with grassland or pine forest. Ecotone communities were probably exploited by prehistoric peoples because of the sympatric occurrence of the biotic resources of two communities. Such communities can also be sensitive areas for paleoecological studies, since environmental shifts, even of a relatively minor magnitude, are likely to have been reflected by proportional changes of biotic composition or productivity (Adam and Mehringer 1975; Hevly 1964a). Fossil assemblages recovered from sites in such communities can be used to reveal such proportional changes in biotic composition or productivity and to reconstruct past environments, providing the materials are chronologically assignable to a relatively brief period of time (e.g., one to two human generations) and relatively unbiased by cultural activities. Small, briefly occupied sites provide chronologically suitable materials that, while understandably biased by direct and indirect cultural activity, appear less biased than records from large or long occupation sites (Hevly 1981). The availability of numerous sites within a small area with nearly uniform environment permits replicate sampling of comparable ages and simplifies comparison of fossil and modern data.

Recovery and analysis of data

On the Colorado Plateaus, archaeological sites have been selected that will provide floor samples, the fossil records of which could be chronologically assigned to periods whose duration did not generally exceed one-half century. Floor samples and samples recovered in association with artifacts resting on the floor have been employed to reconstruct the paleoenvironment of occupation, since they could be more precisely dated than samples obtained from archaeologically sterile fill. Furthermore, the pollen records obtained from such fill seem to record only the events of very local secondary succession (Hevly

1964a; Martin and Byers 1965; Schoenwetter 1962). Additional sources of paleontological data did, however, include trash or midden deposits, groundstone surfaces, and coprolites, particularly for the recovery of dietary information.

Utilization of pollen from archaeological sites to reconstruct past environments and human behavior has been a procedure developed, to a large extent, in the American Southwest. Pollen is easily recovered from sediments, groundstone implements, and coprolites, and because of its microscopic size, appears less subject than macroscopic materials to direct bias by cultural activities (Bohrer 1981). Pollen grains are also very resistant to decomposition and therefore provide a record of plant materials not so subject to the variables of preservation as the macroscopic record (Gasser and Adams 1981; Halbirt 1985; Hevly 1981; Struvier 1977). However, the pollen record was undoubtedly modified by plant manipulation and local alterations of the plant community resulting from edaphic disturbance (Adam, Ferguson and LaMarche 1967; Berlin *et al.* 1977; Bohrer 1972, 1982; Ford 1981; Hevly 1981; Jelinek 1966; Kelso 1976; Leopold, Leopold, and Wendorf 1963; Lytle-Webb 1978; Schoenwetter 1962).

Analysis and interpretation of fossil pollen data present a number of problems related to pollen production, transport, and preservation relative to prehistoric as well as modern samples, when used for comparative purposes. Ideally, the pollen records from archaeological sites should be compared with pollen records from comparable modern Indian villages, but unfortunately this has not been possible. Pithouse villages no longer exist, cultural adjustments to environment are no longer the same, and the extant pueblos do not occur in a suitably wide spectrum of habitat types. Therefore, modern soil-surface sampling techniques, which have provided useful data elsewhere in the Southwest, were utilized as the principal source of modern pollen records, particularly below the forest boundary.

In each archaeological area and at all other stations where modern soil samples were obtained, a mixture of fifteen to twenty subsamples (each about 2 g in weight) were combined from an area about 20 to 30 m in radius, avoiding wherever possible the canopy of major pollen producers. This collection technique was followed to reduce the problem of local overrepresentation, which can be pronounced in soil-surface samples collected from a small area or under plants producing abundant pollen (Adam and Mehringer 1975). At the time of collection

98

of most of the modern pollen samples (June), *Juniperus* had released pollen several months earlier, and other major pollen producers, such as "Cheno–Ams" (Chenopodiaceae and *Amaranthus*), Asteraceae, and many of the Poaceae, were not expected to flower until later in the summer. It is thus felt that variation in the modern pollen rain caused by different flowering periods of major pollen producers should have been minimized.

Fortunately, the major pollen types that characterize the major plant communities on the Colorado Plateaus are wind transported and hence are well represented in both modern soils and archaeological sediments. However, pollen transport into prehistoric rooms is not totally similar to transport onto soils nor are conditions of preservation necessarily the same. Archaeological samples therefore often exhibit characteristic differences from modern soils. Generally, archaeological samples contained less pollen per aliquot of extracted sediment and more non-arboreal pollen than did modern or prehistoric soils obtained outside structures. Preservation of pine, which was equivalent to that of many modern samples, combined with the generally low concentration of pollen, suggests that the pollen was rapidly buried (and therefore less subject to oxidative corrosion) and reflects some degree of attenuation (and therefore reduced probability of stratigraphic leakage and mixing from more recent horizons [Hevly 1981]).

The nonarboreal pollen of archaeological sites, which often appears to be overrepresented, is primarily composed of taxa typically associated with disturbed ground and/or known human utilization: Cheno–Ams, Asteraceae, and Poaceae (Lambrechtse 1982; Stiger 1977). Therefore ratios of arboreal pollen to nonarboreal pollen, which prove valuable in characterizing modern plant communities, could be potentially invalidated by prehistoric disturbance of the surrounding plant community and/or biased by plant manipulation and/or storage within rooms. While providing useful information on prehistoric cultural activities, the paleoecological information contained in such pollen records can be extracted only by obviating the apparent overrepresentation of nonarboreal pollen. Several methods have been developed to accomplish this: adjusted pollen sums, ratios of selected indicator taxa, and more sophisticated computer statistical analysis (Fall, Kelso, and Markgraf 1981; Hevly 1981; Schoenwetter 1970, 1980).

MODERN COMPARATIVE DATA

Analysis of many modern sediment samples from the Colorado Plateaus has yielded about 60 pollen types. Twelve of these pollen types account for more than 2 per cent of the pollen in any single 200-grain count, and six of these types, *Pinus, Juniperus, Quercus,* Poaceae, Cheno–Ams, and Asteraceae, were noted in all samples and accounted for 70 per cent or more of each count. A selection of the pollen spectra from a few of the numerous samples is shown in Figure 4.3 and, as noted in other studies, each environment yields a characteristic pollen assemblage that permits recognition and comparison with fossil data (Bohrer 1972; Diggs 1982; Dixon 1962; Hevly 1968; Maher 1963; Potter and Rowley 1960; Schoenwetter 1962; West 1978).

The meso- and micro-thermal coniferous forests and the semiarid Pinyon–Juniper Woodland are characterized by relative abundances of arboreal pollen (AP) exceeding 50 per cent. In the coniferous communities, pine pollen is the dominant arboreal type; spruce, fir, and oak pollen constitute more than a few per cent only when they grow in the immediate vicinity (Potter and Rowley 1960). With the possible exception of grass, nonarboreal pollen is an unimportant element of the pollen rain. The Pinyon–Juniper Woodland can be distinguished palynologically from the coniferous forest communities by the abundance of juniper pollen and by small-size pine pollen mostly referable to pinyon pine (Figure 4.3). The desert, grassland, and the ecotone between them as well as the ecotone between grassland and woodland (Juniper Savanna) are characterized by nonarboreal (NAP) pollen proportions exceeding 50 per cent. Arboreal pollen is often of limited utility in the separation of these communities, necessitating reliance on additional pollen proportions (Hevly 1968).

Within the woodland and its ecotones with grassland and pine

Figure 4.3 Comparison of selected modern pollen spectra →
from canopy and meadow areas within Yellow Pine Parkland, Woodland, Juniper Savanna, Grassland, and Desert vegetation. PAP denotes the conifer genera *Picea, Abies,* and *Pseudotsuga.* The Asteraceae (=Compositae) or Sunflower family includes the following pollen types from left to right: *Artemisia* or sagebrush (solid); Low-Spine (*Ambrosia* or ragweed type) and High-Spine (Aster type) (open) and Liguliflorae (*Taraxacum* or dandelion type) (solid).

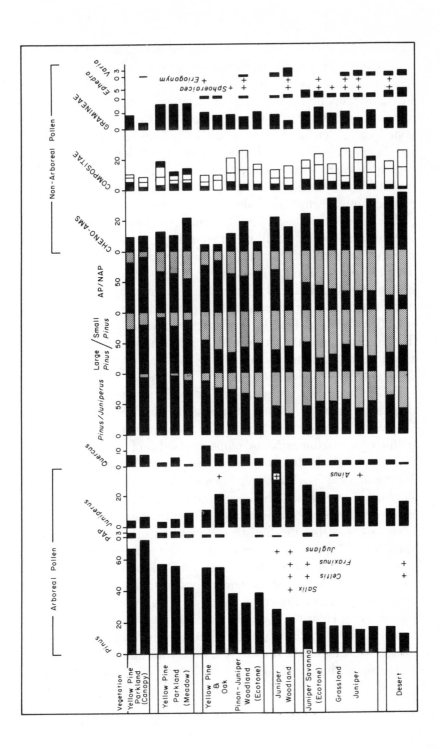

parkland, considerable variation exists in the proportions of pollen types from sample to sample. However, as density and cover of arboreal species increase, pollen proportions of arboreal taxa also increase. Increased proportions of arboreal pollen may also occur in situations of sampling beneath or in too-close proximity to trees and in situations of poor local pollen production where long-distance transport becomes significant (Diggs 1982; Fall 1981; Scott 1979; Solomon, Blasing, and Solomon 1982). Poor local pollen production can be the result of unsuitable substrate (rock or hard-pan soils) or disturbance of the local plant community by fire, chaining, or grazing (Figure 4.4).

The pollen assemblages described above that characterize each major environment are the result of differential production, transport, and preservation of pollen from the respective plants growing in a given area. Tremendous variation exists between species as to the amount and quality of pollen produced. Those species that rely on wind for dispersal and transport of their pollen generally produce large amounts of small, smooth pollen that tend to be overrepresented in sediment samples. Those species relying on animals for the transport of their pollen produce small amounts of large, rough pollen that tends to be under-represented in sediment samples.

Pollen production is also influenced by those climatic factors which condition growth, namely temperature and effective moisture. Unfavorable moisture and temperature have been observed to delay pollination, to reduce size and probably viability of pollen grains, and to result in total abortion of pollen (Hevly and Renner 1984; Kurtz, Liverman, and Tucker 1960; Leiberg, Rixon, and Dodwell 1904). Production of pollen by shallow rooted annual weeds is probably most strongly influenced by conditions of the current growing season; it has been observed that the floristic composition of weed populations is variable and apparently dependent on the seasonal distribution of moisture (Bohrer 1975; MacDougal 1967). Production of pollen by more deeply rooted woody perennials has been shown to correlate with climatic trends as reflected by tree rings (Daubenmire 1960; Hill and Hevly 1968). However, radial growth (and presumably pollen production) is highly correlated with the climate both during and prior to the current growing season (Fritts 1965; Fritts, Smith, and Stokes 1965).

The zonal climatic conditions in a mountainous region are reflected, not only by the zonal distribution of plants, but also in proportions of

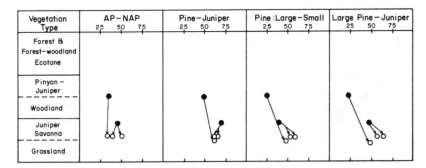

Figure 4.4 Effects of human disturbance on plant communities and the pollen composition of their soils. In each ratio the proportion of the first-named item is plotted. Solid circles are data recovered from relatively undisturbed habitats, while open circles are data recovered from more severely disturbed habitats of the same type shown by solid circles immediately above. Fig. 4.4a (upper figure) illustrates the effects of chaining (which occurred more than 20 years ago) and subsequent grazing (data from Dickey 1971; Hevly 1964a, and previously unpublished sources; Rosenberg and Gish 1975). Figure 4.4b (lower figure) illustrates the effects of burning the local plant community. The fires occurred ten or more years ago and the burned habitats have no pine trees. Juniper saplings are present but appear to produce no pollen as yet. The data points connected by arrows were collected within a few hundred yards of one another and reflect both the change in floristic composition and proportions of selected pollen types obtained from soil samples within adjoining burned and unburned habitats of the same plant community.

103

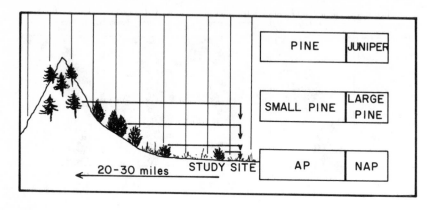

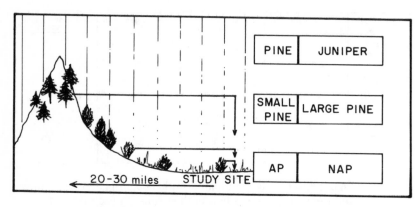

Figure 4.5 The effects of environmental factors on the proportions of pollen types selected. In the upper figure a broad slope is illustrated with Yellow Pine Forest at higher elevations, Pinyon–Juniper Woodland at middle elevations, and a Juniper Savanna at the base. With favorable environmental conditions pollen production is high in all communities. In ratios of selected pollen types, arboreal pollen (AP) is more abundant than non-arboreal pollen (NAP), pine more abundant than juniper, and small pine (mostly pinyon) more abundant than large pine (mostly yellow pine). Local pollen production is more significant than long-distance transport; hence juniper and pine are well represented, since they produce more abundant and more transportable pollen than grasses and forbs. With unfavorable environmental conditions (lower figure) pollen production is diminished in lower- and middle-elevation communities. The more drought-tolerant and earlier-pollinating junipers produce more pollen than pine. Long-distance transport of large pine is more significant than the

104

pollen (Figure 4. 5). For example, relative effective soil moisture may be adequate in the early spring for juniper pollen production but be so reduced by late spring that pine pollen production is essentially nil due to abortion. Under such conditions in a pine : juniper ratio, juniper pollen would predominate. In ratios of conifer pollen types, such relative pollen production would be reflected in fossil data by high-frequency oscillations whose duration or wave length is less than that necessary for growth of trees to sufficient maturity for pollen production. Low-frequency oscillations whose period is greater than necessary for growth of trees to pollen-producing maturity may then reflect changes of floristic composition in the local community, owing to either climatic or cultural factors (Hevly 1981). To be biologically significant, the amplitude of such low- and high-frequency oscillation should exceed the mean of the particular pollen statistic by at least one standard deviation.

Not only does the amount of pollen produced vary, but so does the capability of pollen to be transported long distances. The plant species that normally rely on pollen transport by animals produce it not only in smaller quantities, but it also travels less far than the pollen of species transported by wind. In the present study of modern pollen, it was noted that the wind-transported pollen of Cheno–Ams (including *Sarcobatus*), *Juglans*, and *Ephedra* occurred sporadically in Parkland and Forest soils where the species do not occur (Hevly 1964a, 1968). Recovery of these pollen types in modern conifer-dominated communities indicate that there is pollen transport from lower to higher elevation, but that in the present study area its effect is negligible, since the types are rare items at stations above which they grow (Hevly and Renner 1984; Maher 1963).

Caption to Figure 4. 5 – *cont.*

diminished production of small pine pollen. Nonarboreal pollen proportions are usually high.

Comparison of *prehistoric* changing arboreal pollen composition and growth trends reflected by tree-ring data suggest the relationship of pollen production and climatic perturbations shown in this diagram (Fall 1981; Hill and Hevly 1968). Comparison of *historic* climatic and/or hydrologic data with changing arboreal pollen composition supports this suggested relationship, utilizing data from Davis, Hevly, and Foust (1985); and Smith and Stockton (1981).

Long-distance transport of pollen from high elevations to low elevations is a more important phenomenon, as reflected by the occurrence of as much as 10 per cent conifer pollen in desert samples where only riparian, nonconiferous species occur (Hevly 1964a, 1968). Although *Juniperus* occurs sporadically in the adjoining grassland, the majority of pine pollen probably originates from the downwind conifer-clad ridges and mountains forming the southern escarpment of the Colorado Plateaus. Other anemophilous pollen types encountered occasionally in the modern records from stations at or below the woodland boundary, such as *Picea, Abies, Pseudotsuga, Ulmus*, and *Carya*, were probably transported from nearby areas of cultivation.

Long-distance transport could also be reflected in ratios of fossil pollen types. For example if local pollen production was diminished, it would be anticipated that in a ratio of pine pollen types the proportions of long-distance transported, non-pinyon types would increase, reflecting in all probability poor rather than favorable growing conditions (Figure 4.5).

Because of differential transport, various pollen types are deposited in different concentrations within and around various pollen traps, such as cattle tanks, rock shelters or fissures, and even archaeological sites (Hevly 1981). The proportions of such transported types may differ within and around pollen traps because of the natural mode of pollen transport or because of secondary transport by water and animals, including humans (Hevly 1981; Tauber 1967).

In addition to differential pollen production and transport, pollen is also differentially preserved (Hall 1981; Havinga 1971; Lindsay 1980 a,b). The pollen of *Populus*, for example, is extremely rare in pollen samples obtained from soil samples even when it was abundant in air samples only months before (Hevly and Renner 1984). Both Potter (1967) and Bradfield (1973) have suggested that the failure to find juniper pollen in the same proportions inside and outside such traps as cisterns and cattle tanks is related to differential preservation of juniper pollen within the different depositional environments. However, other studies (Hevly 1968; Hevly and Renner 1984) have been unable to demonstrate such differences, and Havinga (1971) has furthermore demonstrated that many of the pollen types found in the present study, including juniper and pine pollen, are about equally preserved in soils. Hence, while differential pollen preservation is a real phenomenon, it has been assumed for this study that it has no effect on the use of conifer pollen ratios from soils.

PREHISTORIC DATA

Paleoecology

Paleontological data, including pollen and the macroscopic remains of both plants and animals, have been recovered from a variety of depositional environments on the Colorado Plateaus, including lakes, caves, valley fills, and archaeological sites. Pollen records collectively spanning the past 50,000 years have been obtained from several lakes and have been interpreted as indicative of major, multiple century- to millennia-long environmental changes similar in magnitude and duration to those observed elsewhere in North America during the same period of time (Hall 1985; Hevly 1985; Hevly and Karlstrom 1974; Jacobs 1985).

With the waning of continental and alpine glaciers approximately 10–12,000 years ago (depending on elevation), the modern biotic communities assumed their present composition and geographic distribution as indicated by both macro and microscopic remains recovered from numerous sites. However, these biotic communities have undergone several major, centuries-long departures in floristic composition from modern toward either more xeric or more mesic conditions. While the data are often historically discontinuous, the major events, where dating is adequate, appear to be synchronous, parallel in trend and often of similar magnitude over a considerable range of geographic area and elevation on the Colorado Plateaus.

Superimposed on these major trends of Holocene climate are more minor oscillations whose durations are measurable in decades. The nature, magnitude, synchroneity, and biotic significance have remained uncertain and are the focus of this paper. For this analysis, emphasis will be placed on pollen derived from alluvial and archaeological contexts of the last two millennia, particularly aboreal pollen since these wind-transported types are derived from plant communities whose geographic area exceeded the most significant local impact of prehistoric human populations.

107

Pollen has been obtained from numerous lacustrine environments on the Colorado Plateaus, but only a few have yielded data which are radiometrically or archaeologically dated to within the past 2000 years and which can be shown thereby to be temporally correlative with the major episode of Basketmaker and Pueblo occupation. The most continuous of these (Beef Pasture, La Plata Mts., Colorado, Peterson 1985) is diagrammed below by assumption of uniform sedimentation between dated horizons (Figure 4.6). It may be seen that the proportion of spruce in a sum of spruce and pine fluctuates both above and below modern values (shown by the dotted line) for periods of time whose duration appears to be on the order of one or two centuries. Similar trends of arboreal pollen which may be temporally correlative may be observed in the data from Walker Lake and Red Rock Lake (Hevly 1985; Maher 1963).

Alluvial pollen deposited during the past 2000 years has also been studied at several localities including Black Mesa, Canyon DeChelly, Chaco Canyon, and Navajo Reservoir (Fall 1981; Hall 1977; Hevly this paper; Schoenwetter and Eddy 1964; Schoenwetter 1966). The AP proportions in alluvial records (e.g. Navajo Reservoir, Figure 4.6) fluctuate both above and below modern levels and generally periods of alluviation are characterized by increased proportions of AP while periods of diminished deposition (including nondeposition and erosion) are characterized by decreased proportions of AP. The alluvial pollen records are more complex than the lacustrine pollen records, being interrupted by episodes of erosion, and also the entire record reveals still more minor oscillations of AP pollen proportions than observed in the lacustrine data, owing perhaps to turbation-mixing of lacustrine sediments (Solomon, Blasing, and Solomon 1982). The more minor oscillations of AP pollen proportions in alluvial sediments might reflect differential sorting or redeposition of pollen (Fall 1981). Nevertheless, the major, century-long trends observed in the lacustrine data appear to be reflected also in the alluvial data and in some instances have been more accurately and precisely dated in the latter.

Century-long trends of selected AP proportions may also be observed in archaeological pollen records from Hay Hollow Valley, Black Mesa, Chuska Valley and Flagstaff (Figure 4.6). In addition, the archaeological pollen records also exhibit short-term (several decades) oscillations of AP proportions similar to those observed in the alluvial pollen records, particularly when the proportion of pine in a sum of pine and juniper is

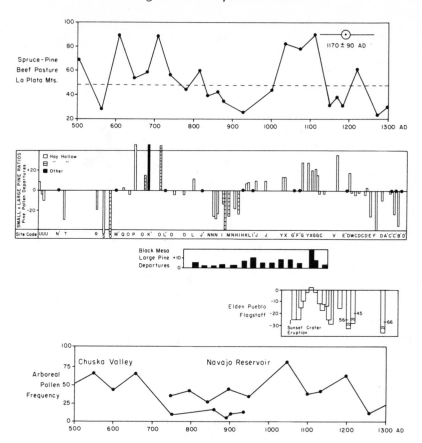

Figure 4.6 Long-term oscillations exhibited by arboreal pollen in a lacustrine pollen record from Beef Pasture (La Plata Mountains, Colorado), and archaeological and alluvial pollen data from Arizona (Flagstaff–Elden Pueblo, Black Mesa and Hay Hollow Valley) and New Mexico (Chuska Valley and Navajo Reservoir). Data from Hevly 1981; Hevly *et al.* 1979; Peterson 1985; Schoenwetter 1966, 1967; Schoenwetter and Eddy 1964. Please note that different pollen types have been used at different localities to illustrate these long-term trends which appear to be generally parallel over a wide geographic area.

plotted (Figure 4.7). It is interesting to note that at least at Black Mesa a general pattern of parallelism is manifest in both the archaeological and alluvial records of pine in a sum of pine and juniper. However, the unadjusted AP proportions from archaeological sites often appear to be

109

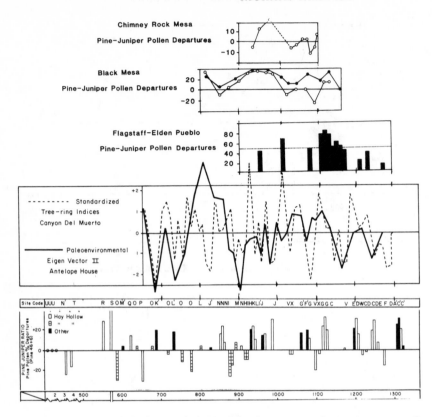

Figure 4.7 A comparison of the proportion of pine in a sum of pine and juniper from Chimney Rock Mesa (Buge and Schoenwetter 1977), Black Mesa (Hevly this paper), Elden Pueblo at Flagstaff (Hevly *et al.* 1979), and Hay Hollow Valley (Hevly 1964a; Dickey 1971) with tree-ring and pollen data from Canyon de Chelly (Canyon Del Muerto and Antelope House, Fall, Kelso and Markgraf 1981). Data are plotted as departures of the mean pollen or tree-ring values for the particular study area (horizontal line at 50 per cent in Elden Pueblo data is the average value of pine in a sum of pine and juniper).
Departures of pine proportions from the modern mean by more than 15 per cent, like departures of more than one standard deviation in the Canyon de Chelly data, are significant.

at or below modern values and even below the AP proportions in contemporaneous alluvial sediments.

These fluctuations of pine in pine:juniper ratios occur within relatively short periods of time (probably a few decades at most) and,

110

while difficult to date with great accuracy and precision, appear to be generally contemporaneous at least at five localities where this type of study has been done: Hay Hollow Valley, Black Mesa, Flagstaff–Elden Pueblo, Chimney Rock Mesa, and Antelope House.

Generally, this kind of data has been pieced together from a number of sites within a single locality. However, at Antelope House and Elden Pueblo, the samples come from stratigraphic series within a single room. Such situations provide good temporal sequences for comparative studies without the uncertainties attached to sequences constructed from many sites. Occasionally it has been possible to obtain exceptionally well dated series of samples from profiles within middens (Picuris Pueblo and Antelope House). In these later situations accurate and much more precise dating permits very detailed comparisons with other pollen records and tree-ring sequences.

While the above changes appear to be generally synchronous and parallel over broad regions of the plateaus, a final pattern of change in the AP is shown by a comparison of juniper pollen relative to large-size pine pollen. In Hay Hollow Valley, the proportion of juniper pollen diminishes below modern levels particularly during the final three centuries of prehistoric occupation (Figure 4.8). This change has not yet been demonstrated at other localities. It is conceivable that this change reflects human impact on the local juniper population, whose wood was used for construction and firewood and whose berry-like cones and seed were used for food and jewelry.

PALEOENVIRONMENTAL RECONSTRUCTION

The prehistoric environments of the Colorado Plateaus were influenced by a variety of factors that affected the biotic communities. Such factors included fire, climatic change, disease, and the cultural impact of humans. It is not easy to distinguish these factors, as more than one factor or combination of factors may result in similar disruption of the biotic communities. However, the nature, magnitude, duration, and regional extent of environmental change may often indicate probable involvement of particular factors such as humans or climate. Comparison of different paleoenvironmental indicators with each other and with records of human demography may still further elucidate the

111

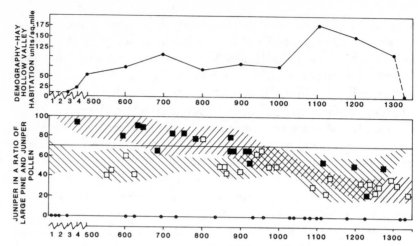

Figure 4.8 The proportion of juniper (most common fuel and construction wood) pollen in a sum of juniper and large pine pollen (mostly referable to ponderosa pine, a species whose nearest populations occur about 25 miles away). Horizontal line indicates the modern proportion of juniper in this sum. Black squares and white squares indicate analysis by different investigators (data from Hay Hollow Valley by Hevly 1964a; Dickey 1971). Note the general decline of juniper pollen in post-A.D. 1000 samples, generally mirroring the trend of increasing human population and construction activity (population data from Zubrow 1971).

relationships between climatic change, subsistence, and human demography.

The fossil pollen record of most archaeological sites was found to be characterized by more NAP than in modern samples from the respective study areas, suggesting an environmental degradation. Several factors may have contributed to such apparent degradation and will be examined below: (1) harvest of trees, (2) enhanced growth of pioneer species caused by disturbance; and (3) climatic changes modifying the composition of the local plant community or at least of pollen production (Hevly 1981; Peterson 1985; West 1978).

Both modern observations and ethnographic data indicate that human populations on the Colorado Plateaus can drastically alter the density of trees in the local plant community as the result of harvesting trees for construction timbers and firewood (Hack 1942; Samuels and Betancourt 1982). Such changes can be observed in modern pollen

112

records (Figure 4.4) and would be anticipated in prehistoric records if the modification of the local plant community was of sufficient magnitude. Periods of human population growth could result in harvest of trees in excess of their capacity for regeneration to pollen-producing maturity. Such human impact might then be reflected in fossil pollen records by diminishing AP proportions relative to NAP. Resurgence of AP in subsequent periods could reflect diminished harvest during episodes of stable or declining human population (Martin and Byers 1965). To assess further the apparent impact of human populations on the local pine and juniper populations (pine and juniper are principal charcoal types recovered from sites), comparisons were made of the ratios of selected indicator types and trends of human population in Hay Hollow Valley and Black Mesa. The proportions of pine in pine: juniper ratios fluctuate rapidly through time and do not exhibit any relationship to human demography. However, the proportion of juniper relative to large pine, while fluctuating, does diminish during the occupation history of Hay Hollow Valley, particularly coincident with a major population increase in the 12th and 13th centuries (Figure 4.8). This trend for juniper, the principal charcoal type, is not parallel to the AP proportions in AP/NAP ratios (Hevly 1964a; Dickey 1971) or to pine proportions in pine:juniper ratios (Figure 4.7) and is opposite in the 12th and 13th centuries to the proportional trends of pinyon pine pollen relative to large pine (Figure 4.6). This trend for juniper probably reflects human impact on the local plant community by harvest of juniper trees. Depression of AP in AP/NAP ratios and of pine in pine: juniper ratios in archaeological sites from Black Mesa coincident with increasing human population suggests that such effects may have been very local when compared to adjoining alluvial pollen data (Figure 4.9).

Rather than reflecting actual change in the density of local woodland, it is conceivable that overrepresentation of local, abundant, nonarboreal pollen-producers could swamp the normal arboreal pollen rain, resulting in an apparent decline of these pollen types (Leopold, Leopold, and Wendorf 1963). Weedy Cheno–Ams and Asteraceae species undoubtedly invaded the cornfields and other disturbed habitats about occupation centers and may even have been tolerated or encouraged for utilitarian purposes (Dobyns 1979; Ford 1984; Minnis 1978). Fossil pollen rain resulting from such situations would appear to reflect (due to local overrepresentation of herbaceous pioneer taxa) the usual proportion of pollen types recovered from grasslands or even deserts,

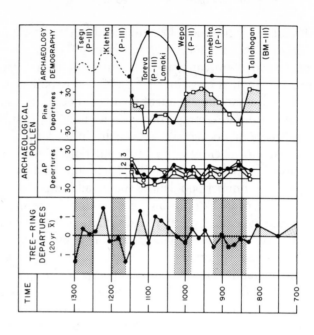

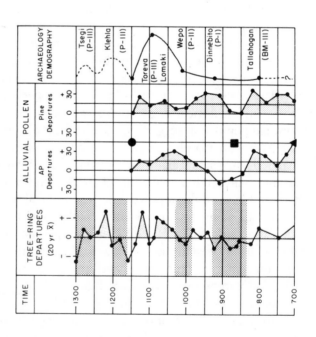

← Figure 4.9 A comparison of tree-ring growth trends, arboreal pollen proportions and prehistoric demography on Black Mesa in Northern Arizona for the time period A.D. 700–1300. Superimposed on the diagram of tree-ring growth is a screen pattern indicative of the general alluvial history, the shaded portions representing episodes of non-deposition, the clear portions representing episodes of deposition. All episodes of deposition correspond with periods characterized by above average growth of trees indicative of increased effective moisture. Likewise all episodes of increased effective moisture are also reflected in the pollen data by increased proportions of AP and of pine proportions in a sum of pine and juniper in alluvial pollen data.

Archaeological pollen data manifest similar trends of pollen data so far as pine proportions in a sum of pine and juniper but not so far as the proportions of AP in a sum of all pollen, perhaps reflecting the effect of prehistoric cultural activities enhancing the production of NAP. Significant suppression of all AP (even pine in a sum of pine and juniper) occurs coincident with the period of greatest numbers of prehistoric peoples in the area as indicated by recorded number of sites and rooms per site, the building of which resulted in the prehistoric exploitation of many trees. The effect appears to have been local as it is not manifested in the alluvial pollen data.

The elevation of the study site is 6500 feet. The modern vegetation is pinyon pine and juniper with flat openings of sagebrush (*Artemisia*), rabbit brush (*Chrysothamnus*) and saltbush (*Atriplex*). Mean average modern AP proportion 45 per cent, mean average proportion of pine in a sum of pine and juniper 50 per cent. The alluvial pollen data were recovered from a stratigraphic sequence in which buried trees and a buried archaeological site have yielded tree-ring dates (circles), radiocarbon dates (triangles) and archaeological dates (squares) based on ceramic typology. The archaeological pollen data were recovered from the floors of a number of nearby sites where similar dating techniques were employed. Archaeological and alluvial pollen data (Coal Mine Wash) are from Hevly 1983. Tree-ring data are from Navajo National Monument (Fritts 1965). Alluvial data are from Karlstrom, Chapter 3, above. Demographic trends are from Sessions (1978). The multiple curves of AP departures in the archaeological pollen data reflect alternative methods of calculating this pollen proportion.

115

when actually there would have been no decrease in the density of trees in the vicinity of what may have been a Juniper–Savanna or Woodland (Figure 4.9). Periods of increased relative abundance of arboreal pollen would then coincide with periods of less extensive development of the weed patches. Such an explanation necessitates a broad regional development of Cheno–Ams and/or Asteraceae to explain the widespread simultaneous occurrence of changes in the relative abundance of nonarboreal pollen. It does not seem likely that different populations would independently and simultaneously decide that utilization and encouragement of weeds is desirable for many decades and then abandon the idea, only to return to it a few decades later, unless forced to by some common environmental control such as climate.

The occurrence of climatic change, including nature, duration, and magnitude, can be evaluated by examination and comparison of tree-ring, geological, and pollen data. The geological data reflect long-term (more than one century) hydrological trends (Chapter 3 above). The tree-ring data reflect short-term (annual to several decade) trends of relative moisture or temperature, utilizing lower elevation versus upper elevation records (Chapter 5 below). Pollen data from the Colorado Plateaus appear to contain records reflecting both long- and short-term trends.

The changing proportion of pine in the pine:juniper ratio is a short-term phenomenon, the duration of which apparently does not exceed a half century and might be considerably less. The duration of each oscillation of pine proportion is probably less than that necessary for maturation of trees to significant pollen production size (Figure 4.7). Each oscillation in pine production is therefore most likely to reflect relative pollen production rather than altered floristic composition. A comparison of the changing proportions of pine pollen in a pine:juniper ratio with the lower elevation tree-ring record from the Colorado Plateaus suggests probable temporal parallelism, provided adequate precision exists in the temporal placement of the archaeological pollen data.

In contrast to the above trends, the proportions of other AP pollen types manifest long-term trends exceeding a century or more (Figure 4.6). The proportions of pollen of tree taxa which are scarce or absent at the sites of fossil pollen collection are above modern proportions A.D. 600–700 and 1000–1100. The proportions of these taxa are below modern levels A.D. 500–600, 800–900, and 1200–1300.

116

The decreased pollen proportions of such AP taxa could be attributed to any one of several factors, including periodic massive destruction of the forest by fire, harvest, disease or long-term change of relative effective moisture, affecting the composition of the local flora. It is unlikely that massive synchronous destruction of the forests occurred over such a large geographic area. A comparison of the changing proportions of AP pollen types with the hydrologic trends inferred from geological data suggests probable parallelism (Figure 8.1 below) and therefore probable climatic control.

Increased proportions of such AP pollen types are temporally correlated with periods of inferred high water tables. Elevated water tables could buffer climatic extremes so far as tree-growth is concerned and be reflected in the tree-ring record by low-amplitude variation. Depressed water tables could offer only limited, if any, buffering effect so far as tree growth is concerned and would therefore be reflected by high-amplitude variation in the tree-ring record. Such periods are likely to be edaphically more unstable than those characterized by elevated water tables and low-amplitude variation of tree-rings.

SUMMARY AND CONCLUSIONS

The pollen remains from a variety of depositional environments on the Colorado Plateaus permit recognition of biotic response to changing environments. These responses were of different orders of magnitudes, duration, and genesis. The microbiotic remains reveal the existence of long- and short-term variation in composition and proportion of types. These variations appear to be synchronous and of wide geographic occurrence. They therefore appear not to reflect local catastrophic events such as disease, fire, or volcanism, but instead appear to be closely related to climatic change and human activity (West 1978).

The long-term variations (usually many decades in duration) either parallel or mirror major demographic and hydrologic trends (Figure 8.1 below). Changes in population size or in location of population concentrations are closely tied to the local carrying capacity of an area (if not due to simple aggregation or dispersal), particularly for humans in the marginal environments of the Colorado Plateaus. Episodes of increased population size in most instances indicate increased carrying capacity resulting from technological adaptations, new or improved food resources, climatic change, or some combination of these.

117

The short-term variations (only a few decades long at most) do not parallel or mirror the long-term demographic or hydrologic trends. The short-term trends were of sufficient magnitude to elicit behavioral responses in humans, such as shifts in dietary emphasis probably related to the effects of minor climatic perturbations on production and carrying capacity of local biotic communities (Pulliman 1981; Ward 1975; Young 1980). These short-term trends were not of adequate duration or magnitude for compositional or proportional changes of taxa within biotic communities, unlike the long-term trends that were of greater significance and resulted in biotic (including human) relocation and significant changes in population density on the Colorado Plateau and adjoining areas (Berry 1982; MacKey and Holbrook 1978; Minnis 1985; Peterson 1985; West 1978; Metterstrom 1987).

5
Dendrochronology and paleoenvironmental reconstruction on the Colorado Plateaus

JEFFREY S. DEAN

INTRODUCTION

Each of the paleoenvironmental reconstruction techniques considered in this volume has its own body of theory, methods, and data. As a result, each discipline makes a unique contribution to our knowledge of paleoenvironmental conditions and changes. Synthesizing the disparate reconstructions provided by these techniques into an integrated picture of past environmental variability is a task of formidable complexity. Crucial to any such integration are the relationships among the various disciplines involved and the results of their research. Similarly, an understanding of the relevance of paleoenvironmental reconstructions to past human behavior depends on conceptions of the relationships between human behavior in general and those aspects of the environment that are revealed by each of the paleoenvironmental disciplines (Dean, Chapter 2 above). Heretofore, too little attention has been paid to these complex interrelationships, and attempts to relate Southwestern prehistory to Southwestern paleoenvironment have suffered as a result.

Three general issues, each composed of several subsidiary considerations, are critical to any attempt to specify the relationships among the various paleoenvironmental techniques and the relevance of their reconstructions to the study of human behavior. The first concerns the capabilities and limitations of the techniques involved. Each technique can be conceptualized as comprising three hierarchical components, each based on and encompassing the level(s) "below" it. The fundamental level or component consists of the actual observations and measurements made on the phenomena of interest to the discipline; that is, the raw data. The second level includes the reconstructions of paleoenvironmental conditions that are derived from the raw data. The third component is a model (or models) that conceptualizes the natural processes that explain the occurrence and nature of the observed, real-world phenomena. Thus, the model specifies interrelationships among variables that provide the basis for the inferences that convert the raw data of the first level into the paleoenvironmental reconstructions of the second.

Given this view of paleoenvironmental research, the most critical conceptual issue is the relationship between the hierarchical components of a particular discipline and paleoenvironmental "reality". Clarification of this issue is especially crucial for understanding the effects of environmental stability and change on human behavior, because human groups adapt to actual conditions, not to reconstructed conditions or to the models that explain the reconstructions. Thus, it is important to determine which of the hierarchical components of a paleoenvironmental discipline – the data, the reconstructions, or the model – most closely reflects conditions to which human beings had to adapt their behavior in order to survive. To use an example from paleohydrology, which most accurately indicates environmental conditions that would have impinged on human behavior: the stratigraphic and temporal relationships of the deposits, soils, and disconformities (the data); the inferred alternating episodes of aggradation and degradation (the reconstruction); or the hydrologic curve (the model)? Selection of the proper component is important because each generates a unique set of hypotheses regarding human behavioral response to hydrologic and depositional change.

Other considerations are pertinent to specifying the nature of the various paleoenvironmental disciplines. To what aspects of the total range of environmental variability is a particular technique sensitive? To what aspects of the environment is the technique insensitive? In what units (qualitative or quantitative) are the technique's reconstructions expressed? What is the temporal resolution of the technique, and

120

how precisely and by what methods are its reconstructions dated? The second general issue important in the study of the impact of environmental variability on past human behavior is the interrelationships among the various paleoenvironmental disciplines. Conceptual and methodological differences and similarities among the disciplines require that the degree of equivalence among these techniques be carefully assessed to obviate inappropriate comparisons of analytical results. Similarly, the less-than-total overlap in the ranges of environmental variability to which the techniques are sensitive dictates the precise delineation of how the reconstructions produced by each technique differ from or resemble those of the other techniques. Rigorous attention to the interrelationships among the paleoenvironmental disciplines clarifies the nature of the paleoenvironmental information extracted by each technique individually and maximizes the total amount of information that the methods produce in conjunction with one another.

Thirdly, resolution of the many problems of relating various paleoenvironmental reconstructions to human behavior is critical to the understanding of human cultural adaptation to environmental variability. Important in this regard is the specification of the ways in which human behavior relates to the environmental phenomena subsumed by each paleoenvironmental discipline. Also crucial is determining which of the hierarchical components of each paleoenvironmental technique – data, reconstructions, and models – is most relevant to the study of human behavior. A provisional model of Anasazi adaptive processes (Dean, Chapter 2 above) is a preliminary attempt to specify possible systemic relationships among the kinds of environmental variability revealed by the various paleoenvironmental techniques and prehistoric human behavioral and demographic variability on the Colorado Plateaus.

Obviously, a host of additional issues could be raised in this context, but the foregoing should provide some intimation of the magnitude of the task of relating human behavior to environmental conditions and changes. In this chapter I examine some of those issues as they apply to dendrochronology in the Southwest. The nature, capabilities, and limitations of dendrochronology provide a basis for discussing the contributions of this discipline to paleoenvironmental studies on the Colorado Plateaus. The relationships of dendrochronology to other paleoenvironmental disciplines provide a conceptual basis for evaluat-

121

ing the reconstructions produced by one technique against the results of the others. These considerations provide a dendrochronological foundation for tests of postulated relationships between prehistoric human behavior and environmental stability and change on the Colorado Plateaus (Dean *et al.* 1985; Plog *et al.*, Chapter 8 below).

MODERN SOUTHWESTERN CLIMATE

Because most of the environmental information preserved in tree-ring series is climatic in nature, relationships between dendroclimatology and any other measures of paleoenvironmental variability must rest primarily on the climatic element common to both. Similarly, dendroclimatic reconstructions are most relevant to specifying relationships between past *climatic* variability and human behavior. Before discussing possible relationships of these kinds, a brief examination of those attributes of modern Southwestern climate pertinent to such comparisons is appropriate. This examination is limited to precipitation and temperature, the two climatic variables most closely related to the various techniques of paleoenvironmental reconstruction.

Lying in the rain shadow of the Coast Ranges and the Sierra Nevada, the Southwest is characterized by general aridity. Nevertheless, considerable spatial, annual, and seasonal diversity in rainfall exists within the limits of the regional pattern. In general, annual precipitation varies directly with elevation. Driest are the low deserts of southwestern Arizona and the plateau country of northeastern Arizona and northwestern New Mexico, where average annual precipitation commonly is less than 180 mm. Wettest is the broad mountainous region of central Arizona and west-central New Mexico, where annual precipitation exceeds 500 mm. Other, less massive mountain ranges, such as the San Francisco Peaks and the Sangre de Cristos, have orographic effects that create more localized areas of high precipitation, ranging from 300 mm to more than 500 mm a year.

The seasonal distribution of Southwestern precipitation is determined primarily by the region's location between two major sources of atmospheric moisture, the Pacific Ocean and the Gulf of Mexico. Rain that falls during the sometimes violent convectional thundershowers of the summer months comes into the region from the Gulf of Mexico and the Pacific Ocean. Winter precipitation results mainly from large-scale frontal storms that originate over the northern

122

Pacific Ocean and sweep eastward across the region. About once every four or five years, hurricanes centered off the west coast of Mexico impel large quantities of moist tropical air into the region during the late summer and early fall. Storms resulting from relatively stationary pockets of low atmospheric pressure separated from the main hurricanes produce some of the heaviest rainfalls recorded in the Southwest. The general Southwestern climatic regime creates a bimodal precipitation pattern that is unique in western North America. Precipitation maxima in the summer and winter are separated by intervals of reduced rainfall in the fall and spring. The latter constitutes the Southwestern "spring drought," a three-month period (April through June) that commonly sees no rain whatsoever.

Because air masses of different origin account for summer and winter precipitation, there is little correlation, positive or negative, between the seasonal components of the annual total (McDonald 1956; Rose, in preparation). Winter precipitation at any locus is more variable from year to year than is summer rainfall, which, despite its apparent spatial variability, is more stable from one year to the next (Sellers and Hill 1974:16). As a result of these circumstances, abnormally wet years tend to occur when the winter precipitation component is greater than average. In short, the winter component accounts for much of the variability in annual precipitation in most areas of the Southwest.

The relative strength of the summer and winter precipitation components varies spatially as well as temporally (Figure 5.1). The summer component is strongest in the southeastern part of the region, and the winter component is strongest in the western area (Horn *et al.* 1957). Thus, the southeastern area tends to exhibit a unimodal pattern with a strong summer peak and a fairly attenuated winter component. To the west and north, a more truly bimodal distribution prevails, with the winter component predominant in the extreme northwest and southwest. The demarcation between these two patterns (Figure 5.1) is best represented as a sinuous transitional zone that trends eastward from Yuma, Arizona, to the New Mexico border, loops back to the westward along the Little Colorado valley, swings northeastward to the Four Corners, turns eastward along the San Juan River, then runs southeastward to an anchor point at the southern end of the Rocky Mountains. The boundary between these two patterns is depicted as a broad zone because the actual boundary swings back and forth from year to year in response to the relative strengths of the air masses that bring moisture

123

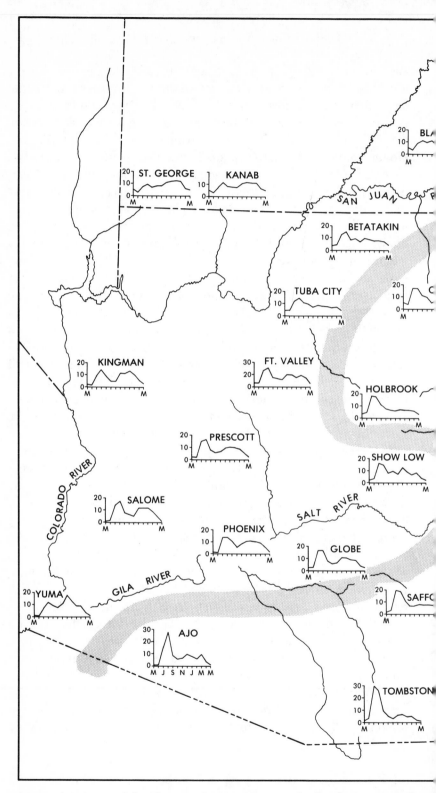

Figure 5.1 Seasonal distribution of precipitation in the Southwest; vertical sca

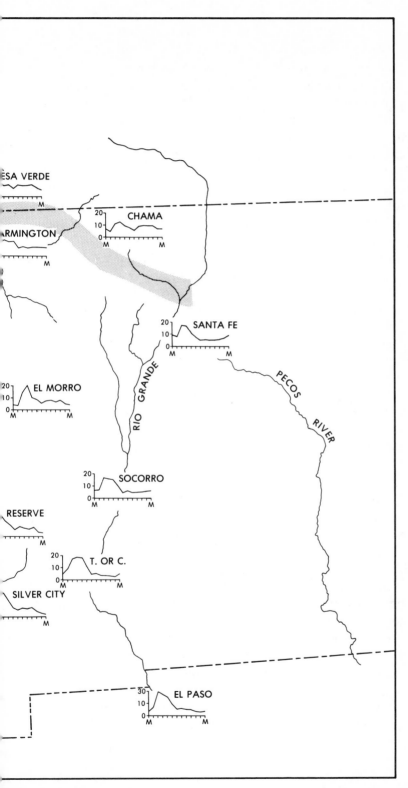

ESA VERDE

RMINGTON

M

M

20
10
0
M   M
CHAMA

20
10
0
M   M
SANTA FE

20
10
0
M   M
EL MORRO

RIO GRANDE

PECOS

RIVER

20
10
0
M   M
SOCORRO

RESERVE

M

20
10
0
M   M
T. OR C.

SILVER CITY

M

30
10
0
M   M
EL PASO

t of annual precipitation, horizontal scale = months from May through May.

into the region from the northwest or the south and east. This fluctuation is especially strong along the San Juan River extension of the zone (Mitchell 1976), perhaps because of the absence in this area of a strong topographic control on the movements of the masses of moisture-laden air.

Temporal and spatial variability in temperature tends to parallel that of precipitation, although the relationship between these two phenomena generally is inverse rather than direct. Thus, mean temperatures tend to decrease with increasing latitude and elevation as precipitation increases. Generally, this relationship means that cloudy, wet weather is accompanied by cool temperatures and clear, dry weather by warm temperatures. The major exception to this relationship occurs in the winter when the cloud cover associated with wet intervals decreases heat radiation from the earth's surface and thereby maintains higher-than-average temperatures. Thus, winter weather may be characterized by a direct relationship between precipitation and temperature, with wet periods characterized by relative warmth and dry intervals by colder temperatures.

DENDROCHRONOLOGY

Bannister (1969:191) defines dendrochronology as "the method of employing tree-rings as a measurement of time . . . and . . . of inferring past climatic conditions that existed when the rings were formed." Dendrochronology is an absolute chronometric technique (Smiley 1955) because it produces dates that are expressed in standard units of time mensuration, calendar years, and that have no associated statistical error. Because dendrochronology is capable of discriminating events only one year apart, it is a high-resolution chronometric technique (Ahlstrom 1980) that specifies high-frequency variability in phenomena to which tree-ring dates can be related.

The subdiscipline of dendrochronology that is concerned with the relationships between tree growth and the environment and with the reconstruction of past environmental conditions from tree-ring data is called dendroclimatology, even though nonclimatic environmental variables (such as run-off) can be retrodicted from tree-growth data. Although dendroclimatic reconstructions of past environmental variability have a resolution of one year, such reconstructions usually are collapsed into fewer intervals of longer duration. Longer periods (10,

20, 25 years) are used for two reasons. First, general patterns are difficult to distinguish in the welter of high-frequency (annual) values. Longer time intervals reveal such patterning. Secondly, longer periods are used to bring the dendroclimatic retrodictions into conformity with the resolution levels of reconstructions based on less temporally sensitive paleoenvironmental indicators (Euler *et al.* 1979:1095). This procedure facilitates comparison.

Chronological control

Dendrochronology provides the basic temporal control for most studies of paleoenvironmental variability during the last 1500 years in the northern Southwest, primarily as a by-product of the dating of archaeological sites. A substantial body of literature thoroughly covers the principles and techniques of archaeological tree-ring dating (Bannister 1962, 1969; Dean 1969, 1978a, 1978b), and there is no need to belabor the topic here. Suffice it to say that tens of thousands of tree-ring dates from nearly 5000 Southwestern archaeological sites provide a solid foundation for the temporal placement of many sites and of the materials associated with them. Thus dated, time-sensitive attributes of associated materials – primarily ceramics (Breternitz 1966) – are used for the chronological placement of additional thousands of sites that lack datable wood or charcoal. The principles and techniques of archaeological dating, which are based largely on tree-ring dates, can be extended to nonarchaeological contexts with which time-sensitive archaeological materials are associated. For example, in some cases tree-ring dates from archaeological features buried in alluvium are applied directly to the enclosing sediments. More commonly, the temporal placement of buried archaeological features and of the enclosing alluvial deposits is based on associated tree-ring dated ceramic types. Thus, archaeological dendrochronology contributes both directly and indirectly to the dating of the stratified alluvial deposits that provide the data for chronostratigraphic reconstructions of past sedimentary and hydrologic events on the Colorado Plateaus (Cooley 1962; Euler *et al.* 1979; Hack 1942, 1945; Hevly and Karlstrom 1974; Karlstrom, Chapter 3 above; Karlstrom, Gumerman, and Euler 1976). Many Southwestern pollen curves are based on samples from archaeological contexts dated by associated tree-ring dates or by tree-ring dated ceramics. Similarly, sedimentary deposits dated by tree-ring samples or ceramics associated with buried archaeological features have produced pollen samples used to reconstruct vegetational changes.

Perhaps the most significant recent chronometric contribution of dendrochronology to Southwestern paleoenvironmental research is the direct temporal placement of sedimentary events through the dating of living and dead trees partially buried in alluvial deposits (Euler *et al.* 1979; Karlstrom, Gumerman, and Euler 1976). Early attempts at the dendrochronological dating of alluvial deposits, such as that of Brady (1936) on the Rio de Flag and that of Antevs in Tsegi Canyon (Sears 1937, 1961), failed because the buried wood was not suitable for tree-ring analysis. These failures led subsequent workers to assume that all alluvial wood was undatable. Consequently, no further studies of this nature were undertaken until the early 1970s, when a veritable forest of dead juniper trees buried in the alluvium of Dead Juniper Wash, a tributary of Dinnebito Wash on Black Mesa in northeastern Arizona, was discovered. Many of the buried trees proved to be datable using standard dendrochronological techniques. The dates provide a detailed chronology of aggradation and erosion during the last 600 years along this drainage (T. Karlstrom 1983, Chapter 3 above).

The success of the Dead Juniper Wash research raised the possibility of like results from other drainages, and subsequent searches discovered buried tree localities throughout the Black Mesa region. To date, 280 tree-ring samples have been collected from 28 of these "buried forests", and 152 samples representing seventeen buried forests have been dated (T. Karlstrom 1983, Chapter 3 above). The dated buried forests represent several washes in five major drainage systems – Moenkopi, Dinnebito, Polacca, Jeddito, and Laguna. The remarkably consistent dates from these diverse drainage systems provide a high-resolution chronology of synchronous alluvial events over a large area of the Colorado Plateaus.

The congruences among stratigraphic sections dated by buried archaeological remains or by buried trees permit the construction of a composite stratigraphic diagram (Figure 5.2) that depicts the relationships common to all these localities. In Figure 5.2, the depositional formations are labeled according to the letter-number system developed by Karlstrom for the preliminary description of these units (Euler *et al.* 1979; Hevly and Karlstrom 1974; T. Karlstrom 1983, Chapter 3 above; Karlstrom, Gumerman, and Euler 1976). Breaks in the depositional sequence are designated by combinations of the letters and numbers, as

128

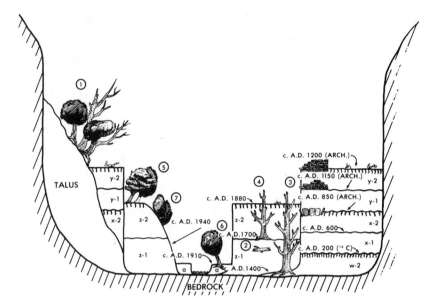

Figure 5.2 Schematic representation of the archaeological and dendrochronological dating of alluvial units in the Black Mesa region.

X-1/X-2, Y/Z, and so forth. In terms of the established nomenclature of named units, Karlstrom's X and Y units correspond to the upper part of Hack's (1942, 1945) and Cooley's (1962) Tsegi formation, and the Z unit is equivalent to their Naha formation.

Alluvial units older than ca. A.D. 1300 are dated primarily on the basis of buried archaeological features (Figure 5.2) and on radiocarbon dates derived from associated organic materials (Euler *et al.* 1979:Figure 4). Archaeologically dated depositional breaks occur around A.D. 850 (X/Y), 1000 (mid Y-1), and 1150 (Y-1/Y-2). Seven situations in which dendrochronology contributes directly to the dating of post-1150 alluvial events are illustrated in Figure 5.2. The oldest trees on the talus slopes above and adjacent to the drainages (Situation 1) germinated between 1150 and 1300, a period of extensive erosion. Detrital wood fragments (Situation 2) usually date earlier than trees rooted at lower levels, a circumstance that emphasizes the irrelevance of most detrital wood for refined alluvial dating. Trees rooted in soils formed during the Y/Z depositional hiatus (Situation 3) generally germinated between 1350 and 1450, indicating that the land surface had stabilized by 1350

129

and that the deposition of the Z unit did not begin before 1450. Synchronous tree-death events at Dead Juniper Wash and changes in wood morphology in buried living trees on Jeddito Wash suggest that in these two widely separated localities a major Z-1 depositional impulse occurred in the middle of the seventeenth century. Germination dates of trees rooted on the Z-1/Z-2 contact (Situation 4) indicate a pause in deposition around 1700. Historical records and the germination dates of trees rooted on the currently exposed surface of the Z-2 unit (Situation 5) specify cessation of deposition and achievement of surface stability by 1880. This brief interlude of stable conditions was soon followed by the present episode of channel incision. In some areas, historical records and photographs precisely document the headward erosion of the arroyos. Germination dates in the early 1900s for trees buried in a low terrace (the a unit) in the present arroyo channels (Situation 6) indicate the rapidity of the most recent arroyo cutting. The present arroyos were cut between 1880 and 1910. Since 1910, downcutting has virtually ceased, and the alluvial system has been fairly stable with only minor episodes of erosion and aggradation in the channels. In some localities, lateral erosion also has diminished, and arroyo bank slumping has begun to soften the sharp profiles of the channel sides. Trees growing on these healed arroyo banks (Situation 7) germinated in the 1940s. The current presence of juniper trees and seedlings on the terraces testifies to the continuing stability of the alluvial system during this interval of maximal arroyo cutting.

The existence of scores of buried forests consisting of juniper and pinyon trees rooted at three levels (Y/Z, Z-1/Z-2, and the present ground surface) in the stratigraphic columns of several major drainages on the Colorado Plateaus has environmental as well as chronological implications. Obviously, each of these levels represents conditions conducive to the growth of juniper trees on the floodplains. The processes of juniper reproduction provide some clues as to the nature of these conditions. Once juniper seeds have fallen from the trees, they lie dormant for a year or more until a winter freeze cracks open their tough outer shells, at which point they germinate and take root. Disturbance of the floodplain surfaces would preclude the establishment and survival of these trees. Erosion would wash away the seeds before they could germinate, while aggradation would bury them too deeply for germination. Furthermore, seedlings could not resist erosion, burial, or the saturation of the soil by ground water. Thus, due to adverse environmental conditions – excessive heat or cold, too much or too little water, predation, competition, erosion, or burial – most of the seeds fail to develop into trees robust enough to withstand the geological processes that affect floodplain surfaces. However, the few mature trees that survived these attritional processes could withstand a considerable amount of environmental abuse (moderate lower-stem burial, periodic saturation, drought, and erosion) before succumbing. Thus, minimal conditions for juniper establishment and survival on floodplains include a stable, well-drained ground surface coupled with a depressed water table.

Given these conditions for the establishment of juniper trees on floodplains, the widespread occurrence of buried forests indicates the equally general distribution of stable alluvial conditions during the three intervals represented by the stratigraphic positions of the forests. Stratigraphic studies establish that these forests germinated during breaks in the depositional sequence. Two of these breaks, the Y/Z hiatus and the current one, were characterized by extensive arroyo cutting and soil development. The third, the Z-1/Z-2 hiatus, is marked by an unconformity and, locally, by incipient soils. Geologically, each of the intervals during which floodplain forests developed was characterized by erosion followed by surficial stability and depressed water tables (T. Karlstrom 1983, Chapter 3 above). The erosional intervals are separated by periods, represented by the Z-1 and Z-2 deposits, in which aggradation and high groundwater precluded the survival of juniper trees on the floodplain. During these intervals, some floodplain junipers, as at Dead Juniper Wash and Marsh Pass, withstood considerable burial before dying, probably as a result of saturation of the roots by the rising groundwater.

Recent research (Hereford 1984) reveals that the pattern of tamarisk (salt cedar) establishment and survival on the confined floodplain of the Little Colorado River since 1900 is virtually identical to that inferred for the junipers. Tamarisks colonize the floodplain during brief periods of low precipitation and low runoff when the surface of the floodplain is undisturbed by erosion and deposition. These intervals are separated by equally brief episodes of higher precipitation, greater runoff, and aggradation during which no new trees are established on the flood-plain. Most of the older trees that germinated during the nonaggrada-tional periods survive their burial in the accumulated sediments. During succeeding low-water intervals, additional tamarisks germinate on the surface of the higher terrace. This process, which produces

131

several layers of tamarisks rooted at different stratigraphic levels, reproduces on a short time scale the buried juniper situation in which trees are rooted on stable surfaces separated by depositional units. Thus, buried forest data that represent two different environments and two different temporal ranges confirm and elaborate environmental inferences drawn from geological assessments of stratigraphic sequences on the Colorado Plateaus.

Environmental reconstruction

In addition to dating, dendrochronology provides direct estimates of past environmental (mainly climatic) conditions. This is possible because those aspects of the external environment that limit the physiological processes of tree maintenance and growth leave a permanent record of their effects on growth in the annual rings of the trees. Variability in radial growth, as measured by the widths of the annual rings, can be used as an estimator of variability in the limiting environmental factors. Chronological control is provided by the annual nature of the rings and by the circumstance that crossdating permits each annual increment in a ring series to be assigned to the calendar year in which it was produced. Dendroclimatic reconstructions, therefore, have a resolution of one year with climatic retrodictions for each year represented by a ring in the tree-ring sequence. Crossdating also allows ring series from many different trees to be averaged into composite sequences that are longer than any of their individual sample components. Averaging suppresses individual variability and maximizes the variation common to all the trees. The common variability is caused by factors external to the trees and is referred to as the climatic signal. Composite chronologies, consisting of sequent, absolutely dated annual ring-width values, provide the basis for the dendroclimatic analyses discussed here.

The basic principles and techniques of dendroclimatic analysis are discussed in detail elsewhere (Fritts 1976; Rose, Dean, and Robinson 1981) and need be only briefly summarized here. Eighty years of research into the relationships between climate and the radial growth of lower-forest-border trees in the American Southwest (Douglass 1914; Fritts 1976; Schulman 1956) establish that these trees respond to the climate of the year prior to the current growing season and of the current growing season itself. Secondary responses differ from species to species and provide one basis for the dendroclimatic reconstruction of seasonal

132

variations in climate. This research has produced a model of the complex interactions between arid-site tree growth and a host of environmental variables, the most important of which are precipitation and temperature (Fritts 1976:231-8). In general, Southwestern tree growth varies directly with precipitation and inversely with temperature. This model underlies all dendroclimatic retrodictions of past environmental variability in the Southwest.

Dendroclimatology provides the most direct and highest-resolution reconstructions of past environmental conditions now available. A wide variety of reconstructions is possible within the conceptual and analytical limits of the method. The simplest of these involves the use of tree-growth variability as a direct measure of relative fluctuations in past environmental conditions during the period of dendrochronological record. Qualitative reconstructions such as these have been produced for western North America from 1500 to 1940 by Fritts (1965) and for the Southwest from 680 to 1970 by Dean and Robinson (1977). Quantitative retrodictions of various environmental parameters involve calculating a mathematical relationship between synchronous time series – the relevant environmental variables and the tree-ring chronologies – for the period in which they overlap. The relationship is then used to estimate incremental values of the shorter (environmental) time series from the known values of the longer (tree-ring) series for the period in which only the latter is available. Considerable success has been achieved in retrodicting annual and seasonal variability in precipitation and temperature (Fritts 1981; Rose, in preparation; Rose, Dean, and Robinson 1981; Rose, Robinson, and Dean 1982), atmospheric pressure pattern anomalies (Blasing 1975; Blasing and Fritts 1976; Fritts 1971; Fritts *et al.* 1971), Palmer Drought Severity Indices (Meko, Stockton, and Boggess 1980; Mitchell, Stockton, and Meko 1979), surface runoff (Smith and Stockton 1981; Stockton 1975) and crop yields (Burns 1983; Garza 1978).

Despite these accomplishments, dendroclimatology has limitations as a technique for reconstructing past environmental conditions (Rose, Dean, and Robinson 1981:92-4). These limitations must be taken into account when dendroclimatic retrodictions are compared to paleo-environmental reconstructions produced by other techniques. Some constraints are created by the process of constructing tree-ring chronologies. Most of the Southwestern chronologies are composed of samples from living trees and from archaeological sites. Before the archaeological and living tree-ring series can be combined into a single chronology, it must be shown that both represent the same statistical population. Otherwise, relationships between the living tree segment and various environmental variables cannot legitimately be transferred to the segment made up of archaeological samples. Specimen depth – the number of samples per year – is a major limiting factor in that the accuracy of dendroclimatic retrodictions increases with the number of samples in the chronology. Problems arising from statistical inequivalence and insufficient specimen depth are minimized in the chronology-building process (Dean and Robinson 1977:3–6; Rose, Dean, and Robinson 1981:7).

Even when the tree-ring chronologies are suitable for analysis, dendroclimatic retrodictions have certain limitations. The amount of retrodicted climatic variance is less than 100 per cent of the variance in the actual climatic series (Rose, Dean, and Robinson 1981:87–8, Figures 30, 31) because there is not a perfect correlation between tree growth and climate. Tree-ring records are better predictors of low precipitation values than of high ones because low effective moisture inhibits growth directly by constraining the physiological processes of trees. High effective moisture frees the trees from external climatic control and allows them to respond to other, less universal factors such as competition and individual physiological capacity. Although tree-ring chronologies are excellent predictors of low moisture levels, the degree of water stress may at times be underestimated. Because a ring cannot be smaller than zero (absent), it is impossible in the case of missing rings to estimate how far effective moisture levels fell below a zero-growth threshold. These problems are minimized by maintaining maximum possible specimen depth throughout the tree-ring sequence.

Tree-ring chronologies are poor estimators of low-frequency (long-term) climatic variability. The standardizing procedures used to make individual tree-ring records comparable to one another tend to remove low-frequency variability from the composite growth index chronologies used for dendroclimatic reconstruction (Fritts 1976:267–8). Combining samples of different lengths into longer, composite chronologies eliminates trends longer than the average length, in years, of the component samples. These problems are reduced by incorporating the longest individual ring series available. In the Southwest, we usually cannot resolve trends of greater than 200 years because of the minimum ages of samples incorporated into the composite chronologies.

Finally, problems arise in comparing dendroclimatic retrodictions with reconstructions based on other techniques. Many of these problems derive from the higher-frequency (annual) temporal scale of dendroclimatology, a degree of resolution unmatched by any other technique. To achieve rough comparability in resolution, seasonal and annual dendroclimatic retrodictions are averaged into longer periods. The properties of dendroclimatic reconstructions constrain the usable length of such averaged periods, and intervals of 10 or 20 years are usually used. Dendroclimatology's relative insensitivity to low-frequency climatic variation also reduces comparability with the results of other paleoenvironmental techniques, which generally reveal low- rather than high-frequency environmental trends. These differences in resolution can produce systematic differences between dendroclimatic and other paleoenvironmental reconstructions. For example, the insensitivity of most nondendroclimatic paleoenvironmental measures to high-frequency natural processes can obscure lags in response to environmental change. Another comparability problem originates in the relatively short geologic time span encompassed by dendroclimatic reconstructions. The longest Southwest tree-ring sequence is just over 2300 years; however, the maximum range of accurate reconstructions for most of the Plateaus is more like 1500 years. Thus, the temporal and paleoenvironmental relevance of dendrochronology is limited to the most recent fraction of the time range covered by techniques, such as alluvial chronostratigraphy, that deal in millennia. As a result, the relationships between dendroclimatic reconstructions and those based on other techniques must be carefully weighed before one set of reconstructions is used to evaluate another.

Dendroclimatic variability on the Colorado Plateaus

Lacking quantitative dendroclimatic retrodictions for all areas of the southern Colorado Plateaus, high-frequency environmental (climatic) variability in the region is characterized through the use of qualitative reconstructions that encompass the northern Southwest (Dean and Robinson 1977). In such reconstructions, tree-growth variability is employed as a direct measure of relative fluctuations in climate, particularly total "annual" precipitation and average "annual" temperatures for the 14-month "tree year", previous June through current July. The reconstruction used for characterizing temporal variability in Colorado Plateaus dendroclimate is based on a regional tree-ring chronology produced especially for this volume. This chronology of annual tree-growth indices, which extends from A.D. 1 to 1976, is composed of 21 of the 25 archaeological–climatic tree-ring chronologies constructed for the Laboratory of Tree-Ring Research's Southwest Paleoclimate Project (Dean and Robinson 1977, 1978, 1979). Four of the 25 chronologies (Central Mountains South, Reserve, Rio Grande North, and Chupadero Mesa) are omitted from the regional composite sequence because they are not located on the Colorado Plateaus. Thus, the area covered by the regional composite ring series extends from Santa Fe, New Mexico, on the east to the Grand Canyon on the west, and from the Mogollon Rim on the south to north of the San Juan River (Figure 5.3). Merging the 21 chronologies suppresses the considerable intraregional dendrochronological variability that characterizes the Colorado Plateaus and enhances the variability common to the entire region.

Using standard dendrochronological analytical techniques (Dean and Robinson 1977:7; 1979:81–2; 1982:52–3; Rose, Dean, and Robinson 1981:92), the annual indices of the 21-station composite chronology were converted into 10- and 20-year departure values, which are expressed in standard deviation units. The resultant sequences (Figure 5.7A, B) represent departures of tree growth from the mean of the regional chronology. The high correlation between Southwestern tree growth and precipitation establishes the departure sequences as accurate records of relative variation in precipitation and temperature across the Colorado Plateaus from A.D. 1 to the present. Positive departures indicate greater-than-average rainfall and lower-than-average temperatures; negative departures reflect lower-than-average precipitation and above-average temperatures.

Two kinds of HFP paleoclimatic information are contained in the Colorado Plateaus regional tree-growth departure sequences. First, the amplitudes of the departures specify the relative magnitude – high, average, or low – of total precipitation and average temperatures that characterized the individual decades or 20-year intervals. Expressing the departures in standard deviation units permits an objective assessment of the statistical significance of a particular value. For example, a

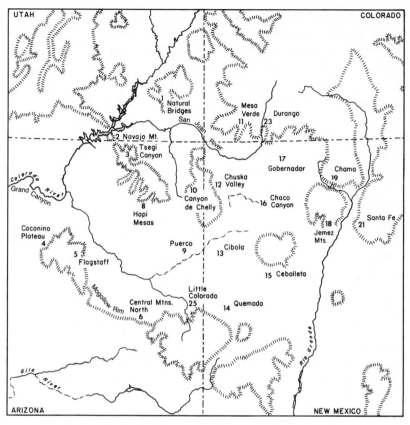

Figure 5.3 Local climatic tree-ring chronologies included in
the Colorado Plateaus regional composite chronology.

value greater than 2.0 in either direction indicates that the departure lies
outside the range of 95 per cent of the total variability around the
chronology mean. What such a value signifies in terms of other natural
systems or of human behavior is less objectively assessed and, indeed,
probably varies in response to different circumstances.

A reference of two standard deviation units has previously been
employed to denote potential significance for biological and cultural
adaptive systems (Dean and Robinson 1977:7; 1982:53). However, this
limit, which defines as potentially important only 2.5 per cent of the
variability above and 2.5 per cent of the variability below the mean,
seems excessively restrictive. Because variation in tree growth under-
estimates the full range of climatic variability (see above), a particular

tree-growth departure is equivalent to a greater climatic deviation. Although exact correspondences cannot be given, it is likely that departures exceeding ±2.0 standard deviation units represent climatic extremes beyond ±3.0 standard deviations (Charles W. Stockton, personal communication). Therefore, a lower level of potential significance is warranted, and a limit that specifies 25 per cent of tree-growth variation (the extreme 12.5 per cent of the variability above the mean and the 12.5 per cent below the mean) is used here. Thus, tree-growth departures that exceed 1.1 standard deviation units in either direction are considered potentially significant in the sense that, on a regional scale, such values indicate climatic conditions that were sufficiently rare and severe to have had processual consequences for physical, biotic, and human behavioral systems on the Colorado Plateaus.

A second type of HFP dendroclimatic variability is the temporal patterning revealed by the frequency structure of the regional decade departure sequence (Figure 5.7A; Plog et al., Chapter 8 below, Figure 8.1C). Rapid oscillations from high to low values characterize the 310–380, 750–1000, 1350–1560, and 1730–1825 intervals. The intervening periods exhibit greater persistence; that is, transitions from high to low extremes take place over longer intervals of time. The implications of the temporal structure of HFP paleoclimatic variability for physical, biotic, and human behavioral systems are developed elsewhere in this volume.

Mean index values for intervals of 10, 25, and 50 years (Figures 5.7C, D, E) differ from the departures in that they represent mean standardized tree growth for the periods in question rather than the average deviation from the mean of the entire series. As the interval increases, the mean index approaches that of the total chronology (~1.0); thus, progressively smaller vertical scales are used in plotting the 10-, 25-, and 50-year means. The three mean index series are included for comparison with reconstructions of low-frequency environmental variability provided by other paleoenvironmental analyses.

Another important property of Colorado Plateaus dendroclimate is the dispersion of individual values around the means of sub-intervals of the tree-ring chronology. A program developed by Donald A. Graybill was used to calculate decade-interval variances (Table 5.1, Figure 5.7F). High variance at the early end of the series may be a function of the low number of samples covering this period. Beyond 350, sample

Table 5.1. *Decade variance values, Colorado Plateaus regional tree-ring chronology*

Centuries A.D.	Decades									
	01–10	11–20	21–30	31–40	41–50	51–60	61–70	71–80	81–90	91–100
0000–0100	.28	.22	.30	.09	.06	.16	.23	.20	.11	.06
0100–0200	.08	.07	.06	.18	.13	.16	.21	.11	.05	.05
0200–0300	.09	.03	.04	.13	.05	.07	.21	.23	.10	.13
0300–0400	.19	.16	.11	.06	.06	.03	.04	.05	.06	.03
0400–0500	.04	.02	.08	.10	.08	.11	.04	.11	.04	.08
0500–0600	.05	.05	.12	.08	.17	.11	.07	.11	.09	.07
0600–0700	.02	.07	.14	.15	.14	.08	.12	.06	.09	.05
0700–0800	.07	.09	.15	.13	.09	.06	.09	.10	.09	.11
0800–0900	.19	.14	.23	.09	.07	.07	.08	.06	.07	.13
0900–1000	.09	.05	.11	.04	.03	.13	.05	.18	.33	.09
1000–1100	.10	.09	.03	.05	.07	.04	.19	.03	.10	.06
1100–1200	.05	.03	.11	.03	.10	.13	.14	.06	.09	.09
1200–1300	.05	.14	.10	.06	.07	.25	.07	.16	.09	.08
1300–1400	.08	.13	.08	.09	.06	.13	.08	.06	.07	.08
1400–1500	.06	.11	.13	.07	.07	.08	.10	.08	.07	.16
1500–1600	.04	.09	.05	.09	.07	.02	.04	.05	.09	.11
1600–1700	.06	.04	.12	.07	.04	.09	.07	.04	.14	.07
1700–1800	.06	.08	.18	.04	.21	.05	.06	.09	.08	.06
1800–1900	.04	.18	.10	.10	.15	.06	.21	.04	.06	.14
1900–1980	.24	.09	.04	.05	.10	.09	.06	.22		

depth is sufficient (>20 samples/year) to exert little or no control over the variance of different segments of the chronology.

Predictably, a moderate positive relationship exists between variance on the one hand and departures and mean decade indices on the other. During intervals characterized by low tree-growth, variance is suppressed; during intervals of high tree-growth, variance increases. Variance changes could reflect the behavior of the precipitation of the entire year or of the seasonal patterning of rainfall. Since the winter component accounts for much of the variability in modern Southwestern precipitation, low variance may coincide with winter-prominent conditions and high variances with summer-dominant conditions. Investigation of these possibilities must await quantitative dendroclimatic retrodictions of seasonal precipitation in various localities and throughout the region.

Spatial patterning is an important aspect of HFP dendroclimatic variability that heretofore has been neglected in paleoenvironmental

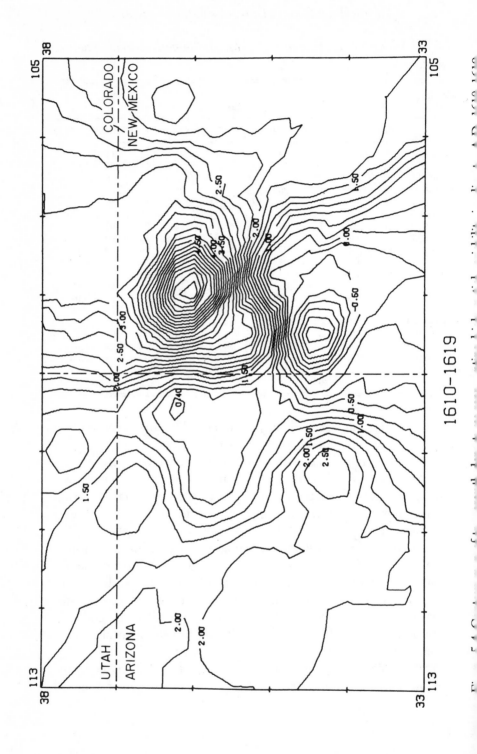

1610–1619

research. Contour maps of decadal dendroclimatic variability from A.D. 680 to 1970 (Dean and Robinson 1977) reveal that at certain times dendroclimatic conditions varied greatly from place to place on the Colorado Plateaus (Figure 5.4), while at other times conditions were relatively uniform from one locality to another within the region (Figure 5.5). Plog (1983) measured the degree of spatial variability represented in these maps by calculating the standard deviation of the station departure values for each decade. This measure varies through time to record periods characterized by high spatial variability in dendroclimatic conditions interspersed among intervals of greater uniformity across the region (Figure 5.7G; Plog *et al.*, Chapter 8 below, Figure 8.1D).

At the decadal level, spatial variability and tree growth tend to be positively related; that is, high spatial variability tends to be associated with high tree-growth departures, and spatial uniformity with low departures. This relationship reflects the fact that limiting climatic conditions allow less variability in tree growth than do favorable conditions (Dean and Robinson 1982:58). Apart from these high-frequency correspondences, spatial variability exhibits a high degree of persistence that is absent from the amplitude series. Fairly long periods are characterized by either high or low spatial variability, and the transitions between these states are relatively gradual. In addition, the spatial variability record is characterized by a slight but consistent trend from greater to less uniformity.

Tree-growth amplitude variation and the temporal and spatial patterning of Colorado Plateaus dendroclimatic variability (Figure 5.7; Plog *et al.*, Chapter 8 below, Figure 8.1C, D) provide an empirical foundation for examining the relationships between dendroclimatic reconstructions of past environmental variability and reconstructions based on other paleoenvironmental techniques. A comprehensive understanding of these relationships creates an integrated record of past LFP and HFP environmental variability that permits an investigation, in Chapter 8 below, of human behavioral adaptation to environmental stability and change on the Colorado Plateaus.

141

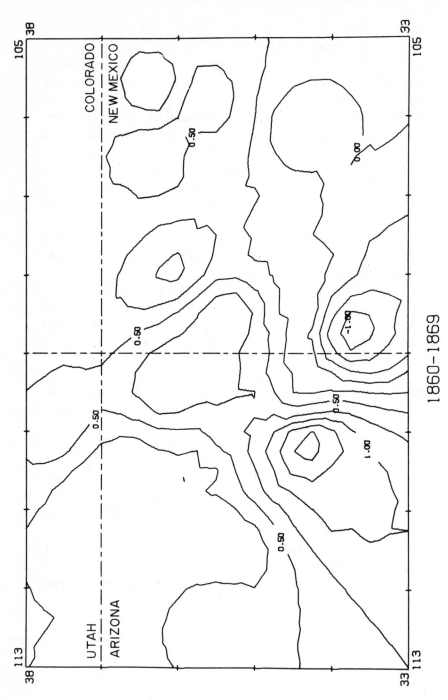

Figure 5.5. Contour map of tree-growth departures representing low spatial variability in climate, A.D. 1860–1869.

DENDROCHRONOLOGY AND PALYNOLOGY

Because a common set of environmental factors, mainly climatic, affects tree growth and the pollen rain, some sort of relationship between the paleoenvironmental evidence of palynology and dendroclimatology is to be expected. Depending on the conception of what pollen analysis reveals about past environmental conditions, two models of the relationship between palynology and dendroclimatology are possible. Temporal variability in local pollen sequences has been interpreted as reflecting either fluctuations in the areal and elevational distributions of various plants and plant communities (Peterson 1981; Schoenwetter 1966:20; 1970:41; Schoenwetter and Eddy 1964:98–102) or variation in pollen production by plants whose spatial distribution does not change appreciably (Hevly 1964a:184, Chapter 4 above). Both models relate pollen fluctuations to environmental conditions that stimulate or constrain the life processes of the plants involved. The first model generally specifies the fairly gradual expansion or contraction of the lower elevational ranges of various species in response to, respectively, favorable or unfavorable environmental (climatic) conditions. The second model views plant distributions as fairly stable over short periods of time and attributes pollen fluctuations to greater or less pollen production in response to favorable or unfavorable environmental conditions. Dendrochronology can be related to both these conceptual schemes, but, as is developed below, one of them is much more relevant than the other to the evaluation of dendroclimatic reconstructions.

The elevational change model of pollen variability is the more difficult to relate to the dendroclimatic record, primarily because the slow response time of forest border movement inhibits comparison with high-frequency tree-ring records. Because pinyon trees first produce pollen between 25 and 50 years of age (R. H. Hevly, personal communication), there is at best a 25-year lag between the onset of the conditions that allowed the expansion of the lower pinyon forest border and the deposition of pollen from the newly established trees. Similar lag effects probably accompany the retraction of the forest border. It is unlikely that the large-scale tree death that produces a retreat of the forest occurs immediately when adverse conditions set in. Mature trees growing on the extended lower forest border can survive adverse environmental conditions that would have prevented seedling establishment in the zone. Lag problems such as these place formidable barriers in the way of attempts to relate high-frequency dendroclimatic variability to palynological records of forest border displacements that may have begun decades before initiation or termination of pollen production. Shorter lags probably characterize elevational changes in the distribution of nonarboreal species that mature faster than trees. As a result, vegetation distribution changes comparable in frequency to tree-growth fluctuations may be revealed by arboreal/nonarboreal pollen ratios. Nevertheless, in the case of changes in the distributions of either arboreal or nonarboreal species, we are dealing with lags of unspecified magnitude that undoubtedly vary greatly from one situation to another. It is therefore difficult to develop models that relate radial tree growth to changes in the elevational distributions of various plant species. The lack of suitable models hinders comparison of tree-ring and pollen records because we have no certain indications of how the visible effects of these kinds of environmental change in the two records should relate to one another temporally.

A pollen production model of palynological processes is more amenable to dendrochronological testing because pollen production can respond much more rapidly to climatic fluctuations than can the position of the forest border. Immediate responses in pollen production would produce palynological records that are more nearly synchronous with dendroclimatic sequences than are records produced by slower changes in plant distributions. Furthermore, environmental conditions that promote pollen production also favor increased tree growth (Hevly 1964a:183–4). Therefore, there should be a positive relationship between tree-ring variability and fluctuations in the arboreal pollen record. Unfortunately, this relationship must remain somewhat conjectural because few relevant studies have been performed in environments similar to those of the Southwest or on Southwestern tree species. Until such studies are undertaken in this region, the idea of a positive relationship between arboreal pollen production and tree-ring width must remain probable but unverified. However, the assumption of synchrony in arboreal pollen production and tree-growth responses provides a basis for the evaluation of palynological and dendroclimatic records against one another.

Observed relationships between dendroclimatic and palynological environmental reconstructions can be used to evaluate both models of the genesis of palynological variability. If the vegetation zone distribution model is correct, there should be substantial and probably highly variable lags between dendroclimatic and palynological curves. In all probability, the variable nature of these lags would preclude any regular relationships, with the result that the two time series could be expected to exhibit little or no systematic covariation. Conversely, a pollen production origin of palynological variability should produce a positive, in-phase relationship between local pollen curves and nearby tree-ring chronologies. Given adequately dated quantitative data on pollen variability through time, satisfactory statistical tests of the above expectations could perhaps strengthen one model at the expense of the other. Lacking pollen data of this kind, I can only cite the evident similarity between the Black Mesa and Hay Hollow Valley pollen curves (Euler *et al.* 1979:Figure 4, Columns 3A and 4) and the regional tree-growth departures (Euler *et al.* 1979:Figure 4, Columns 1A and 1B) as moderately supportive of the second model. Additional evidence is provided by comparing Colorado Plateaus tree growth (Plog *et al.*, Chapter 8 below, Figure 8.1C) with generalized effective moisture reconstructions extrapolated from local pollen sequences by Hevly (Chapter 4 above; Plog *et al.*, Chapter 8 below, Figure 8.1B) and by Schoenwetter (1970, Figure 1). Most periods of deficient or excess effective moisture are fairly closely matched by intervals of negative or positive growth relationships that are especially evident in the 25-year mean-index series (Figure 5.7D). In contrast, not all positive or negative departures are matched by excess or deficient effective moisture. Given the fairly low level of temporal resolution and high-frequency insensitivity of the pollen record, this result is not too surprising. The very existence of correspondences between these two series contradicts the expectations of the plant distribution model of tree growth/pollen relationships and fulfills those of the pollen production model. Undoubtedly, however, rigid dichotomization of the two models simplifies a much more complex situation in which either model (or possibly both) may apply in different places at different times. Quantitative relationships between dendroclimatic and palynological records at various localities might permit the differentiation of forest border fluctuation effects from pollen production effects, thereby enhancing our understanding of the ways in which environmental variability is preserved in both pollen and tree-growth records.

DENDROCHRONOLOGY AND ALLUVIAL GEOLOGY

Dendrochronological and alluvial chronostratigraphic reconstructions of past environmental conditions should covary to the extent that both are controlled by a third variable, climate. In view of our extensive knowledge of the climatic contribution to the radial growth of Southwestern conifers, understanding the relationship between dendroclimatic and alluvial stratigraphic paleoenvironmental records depends to a great extent on the relationship between climate and fluvial processes. At present, the latter is a matter of some contention, with four disparate models of these relationships vying for acceptance. Until this situation is resolved, progress toward a synthesis of the paleoenvironment of the Colorado Plateaus will be slow.

One model of the climate–fluvial process relationship is based on the unassailable assumption that erosion is accomplished by moving water, usually immense quantities of moving water. Large-scale erosion is therefore considered to occur during intervals of greater-than-average precipitation, when plenty of water is available to transport heavy sediment loads out of the drainage systems (Hall 1977; Love 1980). This model derives in part from assumptions about stream competence and from relationships between certain pollen types and inferred alluvial conditions in the Southwest. Based on analogy with the modern situation in the Sonoran Desert, Martin (1963:60–1) reasoned that "high energy" convectional storms enhance runoff, which causes erosion, which promotes the growth of plants adapted to disturbed ground. The apparent dominance of disturbed-ground pollen types during periods characterized by breaks in local depositional sequences on the Colorado Plateaus was deemed to support Martin's inference (Schoenwetter 1962:197; 1967:102–3; Schoenwetter and Dittert 1968:44; Schoenwetter and Eddy 1964:98–102). These considerations led to the equation of erosion and the prevalence of disturbed-ground plant pollen with periods of increased "high energy" rainfall associated with "summer dominant" precipitation regimes. In periods dominated by winter precipitation, water from the "low energy" frontal storms does not run off rapidly and is retained by the soil, and aggradation occurs. The idea that arroyo cutting is associated with high precipitation, especially high summer rainfall, currently enjoys widespread acceptance among archaeologists.

146

The second model that relates fluvial processes to climate is diametrically opposed to the first in that erosion is attributed to aridity rather than to a surfeit of water. Generally, one of two causal mechanisms is invoked as the link between erosion and reduced precipitation. Decreased precipitation is seen to reduce plant cover, which increases runoff and exposes the ground to destructive erosion. Alternatively, decreased precipitation is seen to cause alluvial groundwater levels to drop, which renders the unconsolidated floodplain sediments susceptible to stripping and channelling. Depressed water tables and surficial erosion are seen as causes rather than results of reduced plant cover. The aridity model is favored by the geologists who have worked out the stratigraphy of the alluvial deposits on the Colorado Plateaus (Antevs 1952; Bryan 1940, 1954; Cooley 1962; Hack 1942, 1945). T. Karlstrom (Chapter 3 above) has formalized this model (see also E. Karlstrom 1983:329). Archaeologists have accorded the aridity model a less cordial reception than they have given to the excess precipitation model. Nevertheless, the aridity model has been successfully applied to the explanation of prehistoric settlement behavior and population movements in the Laguna Creek drainage of northeastern Arizona (Dean 1969:193–6, 1970; Dean, Lindsay, and Robinson 1978).

The third and fourth models minimize the role of climate as a principal causal factor in alluvial cut-and-fill processes. The third model, which is based primarily on laboratory simulations and on studies of modern streambed behavior, views channel cutting and filling as temporally random processes that are independent of climatic variability (Patton and Schumm 1981; Schumm and Hadley 1957; Thornthwaite *et al.* 1942). In general, sediment type, through its control of stream channel morphology and of sediment transport and deposition, assumes the role of primary causal variable in this model (Patton and Schumm 1981). The fourth model attributes channel cutting to destructive land-use practices by human beings. Generally, overgrazing is viewed as causing arroyo cutting through the reduction of plant cover, which increases runoff and exposes the ground surface to the erosive power of the running water (Cooke and Reeves 1976). Overgrazing emerges as the culprit because of the temporal coincidence between the onset of the current episode of arroyo cutting and the beginning of large-scale livestock operations in the Southwest (Swift 1926). Because they lack a climatic element, neither of these models is particularly susceptible to dendrochronological evaluation. However, a correlation between dendroclimatic variability and alternating episodes of alluviation and degradation would militate against both these models.

Only the first two fluvial-process models are sufficiently testable with dendrochronological data to warrant further consideration here. For three principal reasons, the second model, which specifies that erosion is associated with drier-than-average climate and that deposition is associated with increased supplies of water, is the focus of attention here. First, so many compelling arguments can be marshalled in support of the second model (Euler *et al.* 1979:205, Note 83; Karlstrom, Chapter 3 above) that it seems pointless to deal with the first model. Secondly, T. Karlstrom's (Chapter 3 above) and E. Karlstrom's (1983: 329) expositions of the second model provide a basis for generating test propositions that can be assessed with dendrochronological data. No such explicit formulation of the first model is available. Finally, the first model is such a perfect converse of the second that any positive test of the latter is a negative test of the former and vice versa. Therefore, in testing one model, we also test the other.

Given the above considerations, the relationships between dendroclimatic information and the second model of fluvial processes resolve themselves into two subsidiary conceptions that can be designated the continuous variability and the threshold models. Both are generated from inferred climatic implications of the dated stratigraphic sequence (Euler *et al.* 1979, Figure 4, Column 2A; T. Karlstrom 1983, Chapter 3 above) and the "hydrologic curve" (Euler *et al.* 1979, Figure 5, Column 1; Plog *et al.*, Chapter 8 below: Figure 8.1A) abstracted from the stratigraphic evidence. The hydrologic curve specifies the gradual rise and fall of alluvial groundwater levels through time, a process considered by Karlstrom to be periodic in nature with a fundamental cycle of approximately 550 years (Euler *et al.* 1979:1097; T. Karlstrom 1983, Chapter 3 above). Thus, the hydrologic curve depicts the rise and fall of alluvial water tables as a continuous, time transgressive, periodic process whose trace through time resembles a modified sine wave (Figure 5.6A, D). In effect, the curve is a model of possible relationships between hydrologic process and climate that can be at least partially evaluated with dendrochronological data.

The continuous variability model postulates an essentially one-to-one relationship between hydrologic variability and climate in which the hydrologic curve is taken to reflect similar, long-term trends in precipitation (Figure 5.6B). In other words, changes in climate, mainly

148

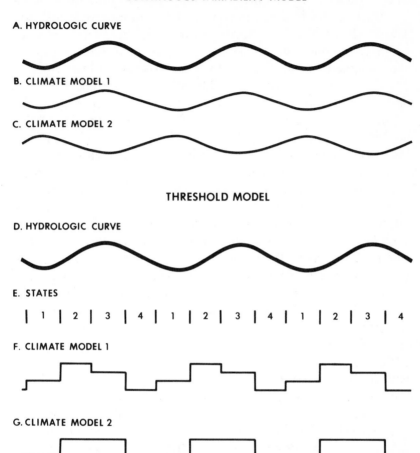

Figure 5.6 Models of possible relationships between climate and fluvial processes.

in precipitation, are expected to conform closely to the hydrologic curve. Rising water tables and aggradation are equated with, and caused by, gradually increasing precipitation. Falling water tables and erosion are associated with, and caused by, gradually decreasing precipitation. This relationship is qualitative in that the hydrologic curve provides no way of estimating the magnitude of change in available water (precipitation) associated with the hydrologic fluctuations, which themselves are not quantified. Tacit acceptance of the continuous variability model

149

led Euler *et al.* (1979, Figure 5, Column 1) to superimpose the high-frequency dendroclimatic curve on the hydrologic curve, which was considered to portray long-term climatic variability. The "negative" version of the continuous variability model, in which increased precipitation is associated with arroyo cutting, is indicated in Figure 5.6C.

Rather than continuous variability, the threshold model involves more or less abrupt transformations from one "state" to another. The continuous hydrologic curve can be divided into segments representing four "fluvial states" (Figure 5.6E): (1) stable low water tables; (2) rising water tables accompanied by aggradation; (3) stable high water tables; and (4) declining water tables accompanied by erosion. Each of these states could be regulated by climatic boundary conditions such that the transgression of a hydrologic threshold could provide the kick for a transformation from one state to another. Such boundary conditions could be established by various climatic variables acting singly or in combination. Among the possible controls are total precipitation and mean temperature of the whole year or parts of the year, annual or seasonal variability in precipitation and temperature, spatial variability in precipitation, and various combinations of these factors. Tree-ring data, as integrators of precipitation and temperature effects, should be suitable for testing this model.

While climatic change may provide the stimuli for some hydrologic state transformations, it need not account for all of them. Some fluvial processes may be self-regulating to the extent that some transitions are self-induced. This should be especially true for transitions from variable states to steady states. On the other hand, transformations from stable to variable states are more likely to be triggered by external factors, especially if the stable states represent equilibrium with prevailing environmental conditions. For example, the transition from a stable low water table state to one of aggradation and rising water tables is likely to be stimulated by environmental, probably climatic, changes that increase the amount of water entering the hydrologic system (E. Karlstrom 1983:329; T. Karlstrom 1983, Chapter 3 above). Unless the streambed is raised through deposition, however, over-bank accretion of sediments can proceed only as far as a limit established by the maximum flood under the prevailing climatic conditions (Hereford 1984). If streambed accretion accompanies overbank aggradation, sediments of great depth can accumulate. Nevertheless, there undoubtedly is a limit to this process, even under optimum Holocene climatic regimes.

150

Therefore, the transition from aggradation to high water table stability could be induced by the internal dynamics of the fluvial processes quite independently of climate. A transformation from a state of high groundwater stability to declining water tables and erosion could be triggered by climatic change, presumably one that reduces the amount of water entering the system (E. Karlstrom 1983:329; T. Karlstrom 1983, Chapter 3 above). The dropping water table/erosion state could be self-limiting in that a transition to the stable low water table state could occur when channel cutting reaches a structural base level, usually bedrock. Alternatively, all state transformations could be climate-induced, or, more probably, the transitions represent complex interactions of many factors. The alternative relationships of climate (precipitation) to the threshold model are illustrated in Figure 5.6F, G.

Based on the foregoing considerations, several dendrochronological tests of the two fluvial-process models are possible. These tests are not likely to be conclusive; however, they should provide some indications as to which of the alternative models is the more probable. Other types of paleoenvironmental evidence, such as palynology and pack rat midden analysis, may provide additional tests of the postulated relationships.

If the continuous variability model, which postulates a sinusoidal curve with a basic periodicity of approximately 550 years (Euler *et al.* 1979:1097; T. Karlstrom 1983, Chapter 3 above) is correct and if the hypothesis that there is a one-to-one relationship between hydrologic and climatic variability is true, we would expect Southwestern climatic variability to parallel that of the hydrologic curve. Thus, a hypothetical "climatic curve" should possess a 550-year periodicity that is in phase with the hydrologic curve. A climatic curve with an out-of-phase 550-year periodicity also would support the continuous variability model; however, the existence of such a relationship would deal a nearly fatal blow to the idea that erosion occurs during dry intervals and strengthen the alternative hypothesis that erosion occurs during wetter periods. Ideally, the dendroclimatic record should provide useful tests of these possible relationships. However, as pointed out earlier, because of the way tree-ring chronologies are constructed, they are relatively insensitive to low-frequency variability of the duration reflected by the primary hydrologic curve. It is possible, however, that cycles referable to higher-frequency hydrologic variations may be preserved in some tree-ring series. Identification of correspondences between low-frequency tree-growth variability and higher-frequency components of the hydrologic record would suggest a climatic cause for the latter. Such a result, however, would not support the inference that longer hydrologic periodicities up to and including the basic 550-year cycle denote similar variations in climate. In other words, dendrochronological confirmation of higher-frequency hydrologic periodicities would not constitute support for the 550-year cycle.

On the assumption that the hydrologic curve is a regional phenomenon related to broad-scale climatic processes, the Colorado Plateaus composite tree-ring chronology might be expected to contain variability similar to that of the hydrologic curve. The presence in the regional tree-ring sequence of low-frequency trends that either parallel or mirror oscillations of the hydrologic record would support respectively the parallel (Figure 5.6B) or offset (Figure 5.6C) versions of the continuous variability model. However, the absence from the tree-ring sequence of periodicities greater than approximately 150 years would not disprove the continuous variability model, given the procedural factors that reduce the low-frequency variability in tree-ring series.

In case the hydrologic curve is of local rather than regional relevance, the two tree-ring chronologies closest to the area where the hydrologic fluctuations were defined are examined for long-term trends. Both the Hopi Mesas and Tsegi Canyon chronologies (Figure 5.3) should be sensitive to the climatic conditions that produced the alluvial oscillations known to have occurred in the Black Mesa area. Should both the regional and local chronologies covary (either positively or negatively) with hydrologic fluctuations, we will have strong support for the continuous variability model and for the regional applicability of the hydrologic curve. If the local chronologies exhibit periodicities congruent with hydrologic variations while the regional tree-ring sequence does not, the case for a lack of synchrony in alluviation and erosion across the Colorado Plateaus will be strengthened. Finally, a lack of appropriate low-frequency trends in the regional *and* local chronologies would further weaken the status of the continuous variability model, although such an eventuality could be due to the method by which the tree-ring sequences were constructed.

Univariate spectral analyses at lags of 550, 275, 137, 68, 35, 17, 8, 4, and 2 years were performed to investigate the cyclic structure of the regional tree-ring chronology at the postulated basic hydrologic periodicity of 550 years and at higher frequency hydrologic cycles. These analyses detected strong periodicities only at the very high frequencies of one and two years, a result that reflects the minor, short-term persistence characteristic of most Southwestern tree-ring series. More importantly, none of the frequencies specified by the hydrologic reconstructions were represented by statistically significant autocorrelations or spectral densities. Spectral analysis also revealed the Hopi Mesas and Tsegi Canyon tree-ring chronologies to have marked persistence only at high frequencies and especially at the one- and two-year periodicities. Thus, spectral analysis of the Colorado Plateaus composite chronology and of Black Mesa area sequences provides no support for either version of the continuous variability model.

A more geographically restricted and perhaps more appropriate dendrochronological test of the continuous variability model is provided by tree-ring chronologies from the Dead Juniper Wash locality. One of these chronologies is composed of one living and five dead juniper trees rooted at various depths in the floodplain sediments. Because of their direct association with the alluvium, these trees should have been particularly responsive to fluctuating hydrologic conditions on the floodplain during the 613 years (1360–1972) encompassed by this chronology, and the effects of low-frequency hydrologic cycles should be especially evident in the growth of these trees. Both the average sample length (290 years) and the maximum representative lag (ca. 150 years) are suitable for the detection of the 137.5-year quarter-cycle and higher frequency harmonics of the basic 550-year cycle of hydrologic curve variability (Euler *et al.* 1979; T. Karlstrom 1983, Chapter 3 above). The second Dead Juniper Wash tree-ring chronology, which ranges from 1384 to 1972, comprises five living trees growing on the valleyside slopes above the floodplain. With an average sample length of 304 years, this sequence too is suitable for discriminating periodicities up to and including the 137.5-year subcycle. Since the slope trees are not rooted in the alluvium, they should be insensitive to hydrologic variation that is not related to climate. Thus, differences in the spectral composition of these two chronologies can be attributed to habitat differences and would indicate that hydrologic fluctuations do not necessarily coincide with climatic ones. On the other hand, a correlation between the periodic behavior of the alluvial and slope trees and that of hydrologic variability would support the idea of climatic control of fluvial processes, at least along Dead Juniper Wash.

Spectral analyses at a maximum lag of 137 years reveal the two Dead

Juniper Wash chronologies to possess virtually identical persistence structures. In both series, variance is concentrated at the higher-frequency end of the scale (one and two years), and no significant low-frequency components are evident. These results suggest that both the valley floor and slope trees along Dead Juniper Wash responded identically to similar short- and long-term environmental and physio-logical processes that are unrelated to hydrologic behavior. The absence of an identifiable hydrologic response in the floodplain trees could be due to three factors: (1) standardization of the ring series removed any hydrologic component from the floodplain chronology; (2) the alluvial water table remained below the root levels of the floodplain trees whose growth as a result responded primarily to local climatic variability; (3) the continuous variability model of tree-growth/hydrologic relation-ships is invalid. Further analysis will be required to discover which of the above inferences is correct; however, the Dead Juniper Wash tests provide no support for the continuous variability model.

Spectral analyses reveal that the Colorado Plateaus composite tree-ring chronology, two chronologies from the Black Mesa area, and two Dead Juniper Wash ring series have virtually identical persistence structures. In addition, these analyses fail to disclose any statistically significant low-frequency periodicities in any of the tree-ring chron-ologies. Thus, there is no dendrochronological support on the regional, areal, or local level for either version of the continuous variability model of climate/fluvial process relationships. Although these results do not permit the unequivocal rejection of the continuous variability model, they substantially reduce the probability that it accurately portrays the true situation.

Due to the nature of tree-ring chronologies and of dendroclimatic retrodictions, a dendrochronological evaluation of the threshold model is both more appropriate and more complicated than such an assess-ment of the continuous variability model. The first step is to select dendrochronological variables that might be expected to reflect the relationships specified in the model. If the relationships are due to the magnitudes of precipitation and temperature, ring-width indices, as integrators of both these climatic variables, are logical choices for analysis. Similarly, the variance of tree-ring chronologies might be appropriate for such an evaluation. Spatial variability in tree growth may provide useful tests of the model. Quantitative dendroclimatic retrodictions – such as those of precipitation in the Santa Fe area (Rose,

Dean, and Robinson 1981) and of streamflow in the Colorado River (Stockton 1975) and the Verde and Salt Rivers (Smith and Stockton 1981) – also should be relevant to this task.

Tree-growth index tests of the threshold model can be based on the Colorado Plateaus composite tree-ring chronology and on the Hopi Mesas and Tsegi Canyon chronologies. If *all* the fluvial state transformations postulated by this model are caused by changes in the *amount* of precipitation, each state would have a precipitation threshold unique to itself. These conditions produce the asymmetrically stepped Threshold Model 1 shown in Figure 5.6F. Any other possible form of Threshold Model 1 requires either a steady increase or steady decline in average annual precipitation (and tree-growth indices) over the years of record, a circumstance that is conclusively refuted by a preponderance of paleoenvironmental research. As it stands, Threshold Model 1 entails increases in mean tree-growth index values at the transitions from State 1 to State 2 and from State 4 to State 1 and decreases in mean index values at the transitions from States 2 to 3 and 3 to 4. In order to maintain a horizontal trend, the mean index changes at the States 1/2 and States 3/4 boundaries must be substantially larger than those at the States 2/3 and 4/1 boundaries. If the fluvial system is partially self-regulated, as shown by Threshold Model 2 (Figure 5.6G), we would expect the mean index values to increase at the States 1/2 transition and to decrease at the States 3/4 transition, the States 2/3 and 4/1 transformations being self-induced as described previously. The simplest dendrochronological test of these predictions would be to average the ring-width indices for the various steady-state intervals as inferred from the hydrologic curve (Plog *et al.*, Chapter 8 below:Figure 8.1A; Euler *et al.* 1979, Figure 5:Column 1). However, the boundaries of the fluvial states are not dated precisely enough to justify this procedure. Furthermore, lags between climatic changes and hydrologic responses may negate the one-to-one temporal equivalence assumed in the application of this procedure. Therefore, decade and 20-year departures and moving averages of 10, 25, and 50 years derived from the regional tree-ring chronology are used empirically to determine periods of high or low tree growth.

The higher-frequency (10–25 years) measures of regional dendroclimatic variability (Figure 5.7A–D) evince few systematic relationships ◆with either the aggradation (Figure 5.7H) or hydrologic curve (Figure 5.7I). In all probability, the high-frequency variability in these tree-ring

155

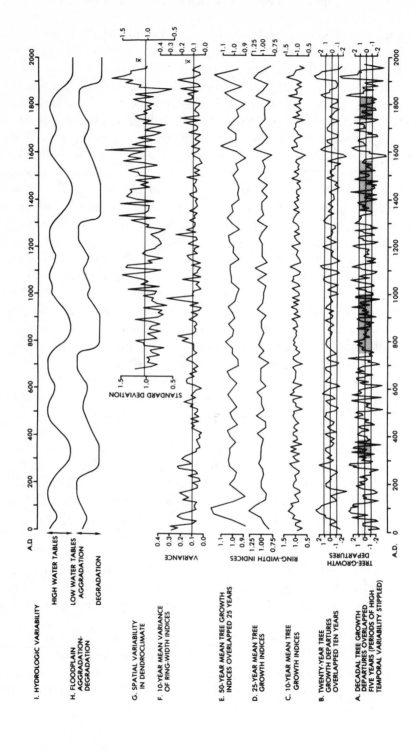

sequences masks any longer trends that may relate to hydrologic processes. More regular relationships emerge from a comparison of the 50-year mean index series (Figure 5.7E) with the two fluvial process curves. Each primary and secondary episode of falling/low water tables and erosion (States 4 and 1) is accompanied or immediately preceded by one or two consecutive 50-year intervals of low tree growth. The not uncommon occurrence of 50-year dendroclimatic minima during periods of rising groundwater levels, however, indicates that protracted intervals of below-average precipitation are not the sole cause of low water tables and erosion. Rising water tables and aggradation (State 2) are not systematically associated with increased tree growth at either the 50- or 25-year resolution levels. In fact, as just mentioned, groundwater accretion and sedimentation appear frequently to continue through periods of low annual precipitation. Thus, while long-term dendroclimatic minima may be related to the onset of alluvial groundwater depletion and floodplain erosion, dendroclimatic maxima do not appear to be associated with the transition from erosion to deposition. A fairly strong correspondence exists between stable high groundwater (State 3) and average or high 50-year tree-growth indices. Average-to-high tree growth, however, also occurs during periods of stable low groundwater and stream entrenchment (State 1). Thus, while average or above-average long-term precipitation probably helps maintain stable aggradational regimes (State 3), it does not appear by itself to be capable of terminating stable erosional conditions (State 1).

An interesting relationship prevails between the temporal variability in dendroclimate (Figure 5.7A) and the alluvial record. All four instances of high temporal variability occur during periods characterized by stable low water tables and erosion (State 1), rising ground-

---

← Figure 5.7 Dendroclimatic and hydrologic variability on the southern Colorado Plateaus, A.D. 1–1970: A, decadal tree-growth departures overlapped five years (stippling represents periods of high temporal variability); B, 20-year tree-growth departures overlapped ten years; C, decadal mean tree-growth indices; D, 25-year mean tree-growth indices; E, 50-year mean tree-growth indices; F, decadal mean variance of tree-growth indices; G, spatial variability in climate denoted by standard deviations of decadal tree-growth departures; H, floodplain aggradation–degradation curve; I, primary hydrologic variability.

water and deposition (State 2), or both. High temporal variability is never associated with stable high water tables (State 3) and only once with falling groundwater-erosion (State 4). Why these relationships should obtain is problematical. Perhaps greater climatic persistence helps maintain high water tables and hastens groundwater depletion and erosion once those processes begin. High temporal persistence would tend to prolong the periods of average or above average precipitation associated with State 3 and the intervals of below-average precipitation that seem to characterize the onset of State 4. The reduced persistence characteristic of intervals of high temporal variability could help maintain low water tables (State 1) by inhibiting the accumulation of groundwater in the sediments. This possibility, however, is weakened by the association of all four periods of high temporal variability with the early stages of State 2 groundwater accretion and alluvial deposition. Apparently, the transition from State 1 to State 2 is initiated by factors other than the temporal structure of climatic variability, although high temporal variability may establish conditions conducive to this transformation. Clearly, high temporal variability is not necessary to sustain State 2, for groundwater accretion and aggradation occur under both high and low temporal variability in dendroclimate.

Hydrologic fluctuations could be related to changes in the range of variability of precipitation as well as to changes in the amount of rainfall. For example, States 1 and 3 might be perpetuated in part by, respectively, high and low dendroclimatic variance. The limited dispersal of values that characterizes low-amplitude variability might help to stabilize the high water tables of State 3. Conversely, high variability, in which the dispersal of values is increased, may create in stable high-groundwater fluvial systems disequilibria that either establish conditions conducive to erosion or themselves trigger water table decretion and alluvial degradation. High variance could then help maintain low water tables (State 1) by perpetuating hydrologic disequilibria that preclude the accumulation of groundwater in alluvial sediments. If these relationships obtain, rising water tables and aggradation (States 2 and 3) should coincide with reduced dendroclimatic variance, and States 4 and 1 (falling water tables and stream entrenchment) should correspond with high variance. In addition, the transition from State 1 to State 2 should be accompanied by a decrease in dendroclimatic variance, while the States 3/4 transformation should coincide with an increase in variance.

Comparison of the regional tree-ring chronology variance plot (Figure 5.7F) and the two fluvial process curves (Figure 5.7H, I) reveals no systematic correspondences. States 1 and 3 are not associated with the predicted levels of amplitude variance, nor do the expected changes in variance occur at the States 3/4 and 1/2 transformations. Apparently, climatic changes of the type represented by dendroclimatic amplitude variance have little or no effect on the fluvial processes that control the rise and fall of alluvial water tables and the alternating episodes of floodplain aggradation and dissection.

Hydrologic fluctuations could be related to spatial variability in climate through the effects of the latter on the replenishment of alluvial groundwater. The unequal recharge of alluvial water tables resulting from the discontinuous distribution within and among watersheds of spatially varied precipitation could cause groundwater levels to fall as subsurface flow redistributes groundwater more evenly throughout fluvial systems. Falling water tables could then trigger erosion of the sediments. Conversely, when precipitation is uniformly distributed through space, groundwater differentials may not develop, a situation likely to lead to water-table accretion or stability and to aggradation. If these relationships prevail, we would expect increased spatial variability in dendroclimate during or just before State 4 and spatial uniformity near the onset of State 2. If spatial variability helps maintain hydrologic systems, high variability should be associated with States 1 and 4 and uniformity with States 2 and 3.

The most striking relationships between the fluvial process and spatial dendroclimatic variability curves (Figure 5.7) are the trend toward greater spatial uniformity during intervals of rising and stable high water tables and alluvial deposition (States 2 and 3). Decreased spatial variability is particularly characteristic of the State 3 segments of these intervals. Also impressive are (1) the tendency for primary downward fluctuations in alluvial groundwater levels (State 4) to coincide with sharply increased spatial variability and (2) the general association of stable low water tables and stream entrenchment (State 1) with high spatial variability. The failure of the A.D. 750–900 States 4 and 1 intervals to exhibit these relationships may be due to weaknesses in spatial variability measurement caused by decreased numbers or areal extent of dendroclimatic stations, to differences in the patterning of spatial variability, or to differences in the systemic relationships between spatial variability and fluvial processes. A longer record of spatial

159

variability in dendroclimate, when such becomes available, may help resolve these apparent inconsistencies.

Based on the fairly consistent relationships between past hydrologic and spatial dendroclimatic variability, it can be inferred that spatial variability in climate influences the rise and fall of alluvial water tables and alternating episodes of floodplain aggradation and degradation. Spatial uniformity appears to help maintain stable high water tables (State 3), while high spatial variability seems to help perpetuate low groundwater levels and erosion (State 1). Furthermore, an abrupt and substantial increase in spatial variability following a long period of spatial uniformity may be an important factor in triggering the transition from stable high water tables (State 3) to rapid groundwater depletion and erosion (State 4). The relationships between fluvial processes and trends in spatial variability in climate would seem to be a fruitful subject for further study in our efforts to understand long-term environmental variability on the Colorado Plateaus.

Further subjective evaluation of the hydrologic curve is possible through the use of dendrohydrologic retrodictions of annual Colorado River runoff at Lee's Ferry, Arizona, from 1564 to 1961 (Stockton 1975) and of annual Salt River streamflow near Roosevelt, Arizona, from 1580 to 1980 (Smith and Stockton 1981). Although the relationship between streamflow and fluvial processes should make retrodicted runoff a good independent test of the hydrologic curve, two problems arise in this regard. The first of these involves the nature of the dendrohydrologic retrodictions. Colorado River runoff at Lee's Ferry includes water from a region much larger than the Colorado Plateaus; therefore, the effects of precipitation in the Rocky Mountains might mask any relationships between Colorado River runoff and the Colorado Plateaus hydrologic curve. The Salt River has the virtue of lying entirely within the Southwest; however, only a fraction of the flow above Roosevelt originates on the Colorado Plateaus.

The second problem arises in developing expected relationships between the alluvial chronostratigraphic record and retrodicted runoff. At first glance, it seems logical to equate high and low runoff with, respectively, high and low water tables. Just the opposite might prevail, however, if the accumulation of subsurface water during periods of groundwater accretion and stable high water tables (States 2 and 3) reduces the amount of surface runoff. Gregory's (1916:129) observation that streamflow increased as arroyo cutting tapped and drained alluvial

160

water tables along Laguna and Moenkopi Creeks in northeastern Arizona is consistent with the latter possibility. Examination of the dendrohydrologic retrodictions may permit an empirical determination of which, if either, of these alternatives is the more probable.

None of the predicted correlations, positive or negative, between the Colorado Plateaus hydrologic curve and retrodicted annual runoff for the Colorado (Stockton 1975, Figure 6.3) and Salt (Smith and Stockton 1981, Figure 2) Rivers are apparent. Several explanations of this result can be advanced, including the possibility that neither model of the relationship between fluvial processes and surface runoff is correct. Alternatively, the dendrohydrologic retrodictions may represent frequencies too high to relate to the low-frequency hydrologic curve. Differences between the Colorado and Salt River reconstructions indicate that streamflow responds to local, high-frequency variables and, therefore, may not reflect the low-frequency trends evident in the hydrologic curve. The fact that much of the runoff involved in this test originated in areas outside the Colorado Plateaus could also contribute to the lack of convergence between the hydrologic and runoff curves. Conversely, the hydrologic curve may represent localized conditions in and around Black Mesa rather than regional phenomena. Whatever the reasons for the observed disparities, it is evident that the available dendrohydrologic runoff retrodictions provide inconclusive tests of postulated relationships between climate and fluvial processes on the Colorado Plateaus.

Qualitative comparisons of dendroclimatic variability with the hydrologic and aggradation curves provide several suggestive, though not always conclusive, tests of the various models of possible relationships between climate and fluvial processes on the Colorado Plateaus (Figure 5.6). Virtually no empirical support can be adduced for either version of the continuous variability model (Figure 5.6B, C), and it seems unlikely that there is either a positive or negative continuous relationship between climate on the one hand and the rise and fall of alluvial water tables on the other. This outcome strengthens the probability that some form of the threshold model (Figure 5.6F, G) best portrays the true situation. The meager evidence that bears directly on a choice between Threshold Model 1 (Figure 5.6F) and the more parsimonious Threshold Model 2 (Figure 5.6G) favors the latter, which seems to me the more likely of the two. Further comparisons of more detailed chronostratigraphic, palynological, and dendrochronological

161

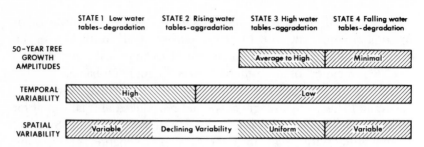

Figure 5.8 Correspondences between dendroclimatic variability and fluvial processes on the Colorado Plateaus.

data and reconstructions may allow an unequivocal choice between these two versions of the threshold model or may lead to the development and testing of additional models.

Within the context of a threshold model, some inferences can be drawn as to possible relationships between climate and fluvial processes on the Colorado Plateaus. Three aspects of dendroclimatic variability – long-term (50-year) amplitude values, temporal variation, and spatial variability – seem to exhibit regular relationships to hydrologic fluctuations and aggradation-degradation cycles. All four aggradation-hydrologic states and the transformations between them are associated with at least one of the foregoing climatic variables (Figure 5.8). A purely climatic stimulus for the transition from stable low water tables (State 1) to aggradation-rising groundwater (State 2) is not apparent. Once initiated, the general trend diagnostic of State 2 is not terminated by prolonged drought or by changes in the temporal structure of climatic variability. These facts may indicate that the fluvial system naturally tends toward groundwater accumulation and aggradation. That is, average (or above average) climatic conditions may maintain the fluvial system in States 2 or 3 until exceptional climatic circumstances breach systemic boundary conditions to initiate and perpetuate States 4 and 1. Given a systemic tendency toward aggradation and groundwater accretion, above-average precipitation apparently is not necessary either to trigger or to sustain State 2. Thus, State 2 may be initiated by fluvial system-specific factors and seems to be maintained by average precipitation amplitudes combined with low temporal variability and fluctuating but generally declining spatial variability in climate. Low temporal and declining spatial variability would favor groundwater accretion by reducing year-to-year and areal differentials in water input into the

162

hydrologic system. The transition to State 3 (stable high water tables) is probably caused primarily by the attainment of fluvial system boundary conditions established by maximum flood heights possible under the prevailing Holocene climatic regime. State 3 fairly clearly is sustained by average to above-average long-term precipitation coupled with low spatial and temporal variability in climate. The first condition would maintain sufficient water input into the alluvial groundwater system, while the second and third factors would inhibit the development of spatial and temporal input differentials.

The transition from the stable high water tables of State 3 to the falling groundwater levels and rapid erosion of State 4 is the most severe and abrupt change of the fluvial process cycle. Significantly, this is the only state transformation accompanied by major changes in two aspects of climate, in this case precipitation amplitude and spatial variability. It seems probable that this important change in the fluvial system is related to the combined effects of these two climatic factors. Droughts of 50 or more years, following long intervals of average to high precipitation, coupled with the termination of long periods of spatial uniformity by increased spatial variability would reduce input into the alluvial ground-water systems and create areal differentials in input that would have to be accommodated by the systems. The result of these developments would be falling water tables and rapid channel entrenchment. The transition from State 4 to the stable low water tables and lateral erosion characteristic of State 1 is probably induced by the attainment of systemic boundary conditions, in this case regional and local erosional base levels. State 4 is not necessarily terminated by above-average precipitation and seems to be maintained by high spatial and high temporal variability, both of which inhibit the accumulation of ground-water reserves under any precipitation regime.

The aforementioned correspondences between climate and fluvial states and transformations (Figure 5.8) specify an informal conceptual model of climate–fluvial relationships on the Colorado Plateaus. This is a tentative construct suitable for future operationalization and testing. Briefly, the model identifies a fluvial system with a natural tendency toward aggradation and groundwater accretion that is modified by various climatic factors, particularly precipitation and spatial climatic variability. Aspects of the fluvial system that are controlled primarily by intrinsic factors are the initiation and maintenance of State 2, the transition from State 2 to State 3, and the State 4/1 transformation. The

163

first aspect is attributed to the nature of the system, while the second and third are effects of the limiting conditions that bound the system. Aspects that are regulated principally by extrinsic climatic factors are the maintenance of State 3 by high precipitation, spatial uniformity, and low temporal variability; the transformation from State 3 to State 4, caused by long-term drought coupled with abrupt shifts from low to high spatial variability; and the maintenance of State 1 by high spatial and temporal variability.

Adequate evaluation of the provisional conceptual model of climate–fluvial relationships hinges on the realization of three conditions. First, the conceptual formulation must be converted into a quantitative construct that can be used to derive expectations of test data. Secondly, variables specified by the model must be operationalized so that satisfactory tests can be performed. Finally, additional, high-resolution chronostratigraphic data and alluvial–hydrologic reconstructions and quantitative dendroclimatic retrodictions of paleoenvironmental variability must be generated before such tests can be undertaken. Future evaluation of the model under these conditions undoubtedly will refine the current construct or perhaps even require its rejection. Whatever the outcome, reformulation of the model cannot fail to advance understanding of environmental stability and change on the Colorado Plateaus and of the processes responsible for the identified fluctuations.

CONCLUSIONS

Dendrochronology contributes to the study of past environmental variability on the Colorado Plateaus in several ways. Tree-ring dating, either directly or indirectly through its influence on archaeological chronometry, is a major component of the temporal control of the archaeological, palynological, chronostratigraphic, botanical, and faunal data that underlie the reconstruction of various aspects of paleoenvironmental variability during the last 2000 years. Qualitative dendroclimatic reconstruction for the Colorado Plateaus illuminates several aspects of paleoclimatic variability, of which three have proved useful here (Figure 5.7): tree-growth amplitudes that reflect relative annual precipitation at scales ranging from 10 to 50 years, temporal variability, and spatial variability. These parameters provide an empirical basis for evaluating relationships between climatic behavior and other kinds of environmental variability such as pollen production,

164

distributional changes in plant communities, alluvial water table fluctuations, and alternating episodes of floodplain aggradation and degradation. Comparison of dendroclimatic, palynological, and alluvial chronostratigraphic environmental reconstructions illuminates some of the problems inherent in correlating the output of techniques of differing environmental sensitivity and temporal resolution. General similarities are evident between tree-growth amplitudes and the higher-frequency pollen records from Hay Hollow Valley and Black Mesa. On the other hand, only considerable experimentation with averaging tree-growth measures over intervals of varying length finally produced a series (50-year mean index values) that appears comparable to the low-frquency pollen record from Hay Hollow Valley and the aggradation–hydrologic curves. Fewer problems arise in relating other aspects of paleoclimate, especially temporal and spatial variability, to the pollen and alluvial–hydrologic records, primarily because lower-frequency variation seems more prominent in these climatic series. Several possible relationships between dendroclimatic and palynological reconstructions are apparent, although consideration of the pivotal issue of changes in the seasonal distribution of precipitation must await more extensive quantitative dendroclimatic retrodictions. Comparison of various dendroclimatic measures with the aggradation–hydrologic curves allows the preliminary testing of alternative models of relationships between climatic variability and fluvial processes. These evaluations greatly reduce the probability of a continuous relationship between climate and fluvial processes and strengthen the likelihood that threshold phenomena regulate a series of cyclic transformations among fluvial states. Provisionally, three climatic variables – long-term precipitation amplitudes, spatial variability, and temporal variability – are identified, along with fluvial system specific boundary conditions, as being major determinants of these thresholds and of the transformations from one state to another. Future tests of these postulated relationships should help refine or reformulate the tentative model resulting from the rather crude comparisons undertaken here.

The problems involved in relating tree-growth amplitudes to the pollen and alluvial chronostratigraphic records result primarily from the different frequency ranges to which these paleoenvironmental techniques are sensitive. Comparisons are potentially meaningful only when the higher-frequency dendroclimatic reconstructions are con-

165

verted by the averaging of values over multiyear intervals into series that reflect lower-frequency variability similar to that contained in the LFP pollen and alluvial records. Averaging, however, reduces the amplitude values proportionately to the length of the averaged interval, and considerable information on climatic magnitudes is lost. Thus, a compromise between interval and amplitude information accounts for the use of 50 years as the maximum averaging period.

A second problem in this type of operation is the selection of the temporal intervals to be averaged. Spurious results commonly arise from the use of nonequivalent sampling intervals. The calculation of averages for overlapping periods only partially resolves the sampling interval problem. In the future, other smoothing techniques, such as moving averages or numerical filters, should be used to obviate the sampling interval problem in comparing high- and low-frequency paleoenvironmental reconstruction. A final weakness of the comparisons presented here is the failure to investigate temporal lags in the response of plant communities and alluvial hydrologic conditions to climatic variability. Such lags are to be expected as results of the response time of plant communities or of the water infiltration and translocation rates characteristic of hydrologic systems. Unfortunately, in the absence of independent estimates of these response times and rates, the search for appropriate lags would degenerate into a "curve matching" exercise of dubious value.

Considerable opportunity remains for further study of relationships among the environmental consequences of high- and low-frequency natural processes on the Colorado Plateaus. However, several conditions should be fulfilled before such studies can go much beyond the analyses contained in this volume. More detailed, more quantitative models of potential relationships among climate, plant community parameters, and fluvial processes are necessary to isolate the questions most relevant to the purpose and to identify data pertinent to answering those questions. Additional research is needed to establish the degree to which the Black Mesa area alluvial sequence is representative of the Colorado Plateaus as a whole. Comparable chronostratigraphic studies elsewhere on the Plateaus would satisfy this requirement and provide independent data bases for further investigation of climate–fluvial process relationships. Additional local pollen sequences could serve the same functions for further investigation of relationships between climate on the one hand and pollen production and vegetation distribu-

166

tions on the other. Both palynological and chronostratigraphic reconstructions of higher resolution than many of those now available would facilitate comparison with dendroclimatic series. By the same token, greater attention to lower-frequency components of dendroclimatic records would enhance comparability with LFP palynological and chronostratigraphic reconstructions. Comparison of local, high-frequency pollen sequences could contribute substantially to our comprehension of the spatial variability in climate revealed by the tree-ring record. Finally, geographically extensive, quantitative dendroclimatic retrodictions of variables such as annual and seasonal precipitation, temperatures, and Palmer Drought Severity Indices eventually will provide an even firmer foundation for directly evaluating the climatic components of the environmental variability specified by palynology and alluvial chronostratigraphy.

In addition to exemplifying paleoclimatic variability on the Colorado Plateaus and examining relationships among paleoenvironmental techniques and their reconstructions, my purpose in this chapter has been to lay a foundation for the use of various paleoenvironmental reconstructions in evaluating Anasazi behavioral responses to environmental stability and change. To this end, the reconstructed environmental variables have been characterized here in a way intended to maximize their utility in applying the model of Anasazi adaptive behavior (Dean, Chapter 2 above) to the prehistory of the Colorado Plateaus, a task undertaken by Dean *et al.* (1985) and by Plog *et al.* in Chapter 8 below.

6
Anasazi demographic patterns and organizational responses: assumptions and interpretive difficulties

SHIRLEY POWELL

Department of Anthropology
Northern Arizona University

INTRODUCTION

This chapter introduces the concept of paleodemography and its importance for reconstructing prehistoric adaptive and organizational systems. However, unlike the following chapter (Euler, Chapter 7 below), the empirical bases for reconstructing prehistoric Southwestern population dynamics are not discussed. Instead, this chapter addresses the theoretical and methodolical biases archaeologists bring to the study of Southwestern paleodemography and the effects these biases have on both population reconstructions and adaptive/organizational inferences based on those reconstructions. Chapter 8 integrates data on environmental variation and population dynamics and retrodicts cultural responses to these patterns.

Paleodemography or demographic archaeology investigates "the size, density, and growth rates of archaeological human populations," as well as "the role of human populations and their demographic dynamics in culture change" (Hassan 1978:49). People are seen as both dependent and independent variables in the study of cultural change – they form part of the environment to which they are adapting and they actively change that environment with their adaptations (Dean, Chapter 2 above). Thus, measures of population size are critical for assessing theories of why and how cultures change. However, reconstructing a prehistoric population's demographic patterns from archaeological evidence is a complex and difficult chore.

People create and leave the material residues that archaeologists reconstruct and interpret. The distribution of material remains – relative to other material items and to the natural landscape – is directly and indirectly caused by patterns of human behavior and by natural processes. Archaeologists have come to recognize the many variables that produce the archaeological record and the methodological difficulties in distinguishing among those variables. Yet, for all the effort directed at clarifying issues of archaeological/behavioral interrelationships, one of the most basic of the "people-related" questions remains difficult-to-impossible to answer. This question, "How many people produced the archaeological record?" is the focus of this paper.

In the pages that follow I review reconstructions of population dynamics in the American Southwest. My intent is not to generate "correct" methods for estimating prehistoric population size, but rather is (1) to identify some of the methodological problems that make regional demographic patterns so difficult to reconstruct, (2) to discuss interpretive difficulties arising from incorrect population estimates, and (3) to consider some of the theoretical implications of these problems.

METHODS

Many techniques have been used to measure population size, and all use the same basic procedures. First, a material culture item that has some arguable and constant relationship with population size is identified. Next, the material culture items are assigned dates or spans of dates. Finally, the material items are summed within selected time intervals (Powell 1983:8–9). Frequently used material indicators of population size include number of sites (Colton 1936), number of rooms on a site (Plog 1974), floor area (Layhe 1977, 1981), and artifactual debris (Cook 1972). Use of any of these material indicators coupled with the procedures for estimating population size is problematical.

    1. Variation in material indicator size is generally not considered. Small sites/rooms and large sites/rooms contribute equally to the population count regardless of the numbers of

individuals actually living there. Most measures (except site area, floor area, and artifactual density) are insensitive to size variation – variation which could be caused by the target variable, size of the population producing the rooms or artifacts.

2. Functional variation is not considered. For example, sites may have been used for purposes other than habitation, or groups of sites may have been used to house the same people at different times of the year. Thus, multiple sites used by the same group for different purposes (e.g., agricultural site, hunting and gathering station, and wintering site) are demographically redundant if all contribute to the population estimate. Similarly, multiple room types may be used by the same social group, or an expedient lithic technology may produce more archaeologically recoverable debris than a curated technology.

   If there is no variation over time in how the material indicator was used, summing demographically redundant items will lead to overinflated population counts; however, the population curve will accurately portray relative population levels since the inflation factor is constant. But if there is change over time in how the material indicator was used, both absolute and relative population estimates will be misleading because the inflation factor is not constant.

3. Site contemporaneity is often assumed, not demonstrated. Determining the correct span of usage of the material indicator is critical if contemporaneity is to be ascertained, as it must be when estimating population size from archaeological remains.

   Generally Southwestern sites are assigned to time periods ("phases") 100 to 300 years long; however, they may not have been occupied for the entire span of the phase (e.g., S. Plog 1986:229–31). A 30-room site occupied for 20 years at the beginning of a 100-year phase and a 50-room site occupied for 50 years at the end of a 100-year phase were not contemporaneous. In fact, the two sites were separated in time by 30 years, a substantial period in the life spans of neolithic humans. Yet if data from these two sites were combined in a phase-based population estimate, 80 rooms would be counted for a 100-year period instead of the correct count of 30 rooms, zero rooms, then 50 rooms. Thus, it should not be assumed that all sites were occupied for the entire phase, nor that they were contemporaneously occupied. This assumption also leads to overinflated population estimates, and if occupation spans vary over time, both absolute and relative population estimates will be incorrect. In addition to overinflating population counts, phase-based estimates are artificially smoothed (e.g., Plog 1975:99–100), masking considerable variation in the pattern of population change.

Also important in this regard is the rate at which the material items were produced. In the above example, we initially assumed that all rooms were built at the beginning of the phase and were occupied for the entire 100 years. But, it is far more likely that material items were produced at variable rates as the need for their production was identified – not all at the beginning of a phase. Further, demand and therefore production rates probably were variable, resulting in variable growth curves that might or might not approximate a normal distribution (e.g., Plog 1974:91).

4. Finally, population estimates based on material items are relative and have no readily demonstrable association with absolute population counts.

THEORY

Each technique for reconstructing prehistoric population size has attendant problems – problems that lead to questions about the relationship between the material indicator and actual population size and ultimately about the accuracy of the reconstruction. However, another entirely different class of problems leads to interpretive difficulties with paleodemographic studies. These problems spring from expectations and assumptions held by researchers.

These expectations or assumptions may be derived from theory, but once derived they are treated as real instead of being verified independently as a part of the research process. For example, ecological theory and evolutionary theory predict patterns of behavioral responses to certain classes of environmental conditions. Simply stated, a variable

171

behavioral repertoire is predicted if the physical and/or social environments are variable. Thus, environmental variability must be assessed
and, given the degree of variability observed, variability in behavioral or
cultural systems is predicted. (This, in fact, is the goal of this volume,
and the final chapter presents expected cultural responses to the physical
and social environmental conditions documented in the previous
chapters.)

Unfortunately, many archaeological studies do not measure
environmental variability, either over space or through time, they
simply assume that it exists. The subsequent analytical step verifies
"corresponding" cultural variation. Then, because cultural variation is
found, it is used as evidence for environmental variation. Such reasoning is tautological since the existence of behavioral variety is used as
"verification" of the conditional situation, environmental variety, e.g.,
because the cultural repertoire changes over time or varies spatially, the
physical environment must have been correspondingly variable to have
caused it. The theory predicts responses to a conditional situation, but
the conditional situation should be measured, not assumed.

Similarly, demographic variation, especially population growth, can
be used as the basis for predicting the existence of a variety of cultural
patterns. The search for labor-intensive subsistence systems, complex
organizational hierarchies, and cultural boundaries presumes the
existence of sufficient people to require and support such cultural
mechanisms. However, population growth sufficient to support or
cause these social institutions must be documented, not assumed. Use
of an archaeological measure of subsistence intensification to "verify"
population growth is tautological.

HOW POPULATION PARAMETERS ARE
INTERPRETED – ETHNOGRAPHIC
ANALOGS

Regardless of the methodological problems in selecting and measuring
variation in archaeological remains thought to be sensitive to population change, such remains are selected, measured, and the observed
variation is interpreted. The question then arises, "How are these
interpretations made, and on what are they based?"

Southwestern archaeologists are, at the same time, fortunate and
plagued by having rich ethnohistoric literature and ethnographic data

on which to base interpretations of archaeological remains. Use of historic and ethnographic sources has been so pervasive that historical reviews of archaeological research in the American Southwest reference the heavy reliance on analogical reasoning for interpreting prehistoric remains (Taylor 1954:561; Longacre 1970:2–4). Although Southwestern researchers have questioned the interpretive value of unverified analogs, some analyses that combine analogical models with rigorous independent testing have obtained highly productive results (Hill 1970). Nonetheless, noncritical acceptance of analogical interpretations has led to some potentially misleading – certainly unverified – "interpretations" of the archaeologial record. Population dynamics, subsistence, and settlement patterns all have been interpreted by Southwestern archaeologists with reference to ethnographic and ethnohistoric accounts.

The numerous ethnohistoric accounts and ethnographic studies of recent puebloan inhabitants of the Colorado Plateaus document large groups of people occupying large sites for long periods of time. Narratives of the initial Spanish contacts with puebloan populations suggest that tales of great mineral wealth, focused at the seven cities of Cibola, lured Spanish exploration northward. After contact had been made with Cibola (Zuni) in 1540, rumors continued to circulate of other "cities" located north and west of Zuni – the Hopi villages of the Tusayan province.

Descriptions of Hopi, based on actual contacts, suggested a population of between 10,000 and 50,000 individuals living in from five to twelve towns (Hammond and Rey 1940:226; Forrestal and Lynch 1954:x). Clearly the ethnohistoric literature records large numbers of individuals inhabiting relatively large villages or towns. There has been considerable debate concerning the accuracy of the Spanish accounts and the conquistadors' motives for inflating population estimates and descriptions of potential mineral wealth (Hodge 1912:324). However, researchers continue to base interpretations of archaeological remains, at least in part, on these accounts (e.g., Riley 1982; Upham 1982:35–51).

Ethnographic accounts also document reliance on cultivated corn, beans, and squash for subsistence; year-round occupation of the large pueblos (with possible seasonal movements to field houses to tend crops during the growing season); and long occupations of single sites. The pueblos of Acoma (Garcia-Mason 1979:452) and Old Oraibi (Titiev

173

1944) are touted as the oldest, continuously occupied settlements in North America, with initial occupations at about A.D. 1100. The large number of archaeological sites on the Colorado Plateaus attests to the frequency of site abandonments, however, for post-contact times there are comparatively few references to village abandonments. Inhabitants of several pueblos migrated during and after the Pueblo Revolt of 1680 (Schroeder 1979); Tiwa speakers moved from the central Rio Grande Valley to the El Paso area (Simmons 1979:186–7), and it was at this time that the Tewa village of Hano was founded at the Hopi Mesas (Dozier 1966). Ethnographic accounts of a more recent era (Titiev 1944) suggest that political schisms at Old Oraibi in the early 1900s resulted in the abandonment of part of Old Oraibi by the conservative faction and the subsequent founding of Bacobi and New Oraibi. Even these infrequent migration accounts suggest puebloan occupation spans of minimally 75 years for Bacobi and New Oraibi, and 275 years for Hano. Thus, migrations or village relocations are infrequently noted in the ethnohistoric and ethnographic literature (except during the Pueblo Revolt), and even when they do occur, they present little evidence against long puebloan occupation spans. The appearance of puebloan locational stability was further reinforced by European colonization on the Colorado Plateaus, of which one effect (among many) was to fix the pueblos in space.

INTERPRETATIONS OF ARCHAEOLOGICAL REMAINS

Given this series of descriptive generalizations derived from ethno-historic literature and ethnographic accounts, prehistoric archaeological sites on the Colorado Plateaus tend to be interpreted as the long-term abodes of sedentary agriculturalists. Because catastrophic social and political upheavals resulted in historically documented migrations, equally catastrophic events such as "great droughts" or invading hordes are similarly cited as causing prehistoric migrations. If small sites are recorded by archaeologists, they have most frequently been interpreted as (1) agricultural field houses used seasonally for tending crops by the inhabitants of large sites – like their historic puebloan counterparts; or (2) developmental precursors to large pueblos. This set of analogically based (but largely empirically unverified) "interpretations" in turn provides the basis for reconstructions of prehistoric cultural systems from archaeologial remains.

Recent research has suggested that cyclically deteriorating and ameliorating environmental conditions were answered by organizational systems that alternatively emphasized structural resiliency and growth (e.g., Plog 1983:295, 311). Although this scheme predicts varying responses to different environmental conditions, many of the subsistence/settlement assumptions discussed earlier are not addressed. This model suggests that, regardless of settlement size and organizational complexity, the occupants of the sites were relatively sedentary agriculturalists who relied on organizational solutions to their provisioning problems.

If, as the analogical interpretation leads us to believe, prehistoric puebloan sites were the abodes of sedentary people for long periods of time, large numbers of sites (with contemporaneous or overlapping occupation spans) must be interpreted as evidence for a large population. However, the if-clause of this statement combines at least two assumptions (although they are rarely stated as such) and will continue to do so until independent means are devised to evalute their empirical bases. (However, in most cases in which the long occupation span assumption has been tested, it has been shown to be false; sites occupied for more than 50 years are rare and reanalyses of prehistoric subsistence strategies are demonstrating great eclecticism [Ahlstrom 1985; Hantman 1983:101–63].) Further, the implications of this set of assumptions for interpreting archaeological remains and for reconstructing nonmaterial components of the cultural system are legion.

ASSUMPTION-BASED RECONSTRUCTIONS OF PREHISTORIC ADAPTIVE SYSTEMS

In the American Southwest, with its relatively low animal and plant biomass, a large human population would find it difficult to sustain itself using the available natural resources. Thus, it follows that adaptive cultural mechanisms would likely be labor-intensive (Boserup 1965). Strategies such as intensification of production (to increase productive output per unit of land) and commodities exchange (to equalize spatial inequalities in the distribution of resources) would be appropriate responses to physical and social environmental conditions that curtailed

175

spatially extensive responses such as direct mobility or diversification in the patterns of exploitation of the natural resource base.

In fact, the Southwestern archaeological record has been interpreted as evidence for the evolution of complex technology and social organization (e.g., Upham 1982). The large number of sites is interpreted as large population; plant food processing tools and preserved remains of cultigens serve as evidence for intensive agricultural production; site locations near permanent water sources indicate a hydraulic economy; and variation in settlement size and morphology is viewed as evidence for the social hierarchies necessary to organize and perpetuate these complex, labor-intensive subsistence strategies. However, as mentioned above, the interpretations of large populations and resultant population/resource imbalances are, for the most part, empirically unverified.

Figure 6.1 lists seven of the decisions that archaeologists must make when estimating population size from prehistoric remains; for simplicity's sake, each is plotted as having only two alternatives. Data exist to guide decision-making in each of the cases; however, generally they are qualitative, allowing for alternative, plausible interpretations. Archaeologists predisposed to the high population density assumption would tend to make reasonable decisions consistent with their original assumption: that the subsistence base was primarily agricultural, that the settlement pattern was logistic and that most sites were used for habitation, that sites were occupied for long periods of time and that birth-spacing was short, and that many persons lived in each structure. This set of decisions tracks down the left side of Figure 6.1. Archaeologists who lean to the low population density assumption would make equally (at least in their minds) reasonable decisions consistent with their assumption: that the subsistence base was eclectic, that the settlement pattern was residential, producing many different kinds of sites, that occupation spans were short and variable, that site dating for the purposes of demographic reconstructions must be site-based, and that birth-spacing was comparatively long, thus few people lived in each structure. This set of decisions leads down the right side of Figure 6.1.

Most archaeologists are familiar with the interpretive controversies surrounding each of the seven topics listed on Figure 6.1, and have come to some conclusions for dealing with this decision-making in their work. They also acknowledge that most of their interpretations are not unequivocal; there is great potential for ambiguity. This problem is bad

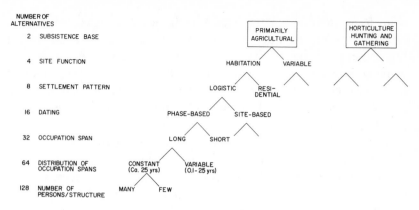

Figure 6.1 Decisions that archaeologists must make that affect population estimates.

enough at the level of a single decision. However, when multiple decisions enter into the equation, the number of possible "solutions" proliferates exponentially. In this case, the seven original decisions, each with two alternatives, results in 128 final alternatives. The set of decisions made consistent with a high population density model generates the upper estimation limit, while the set of decisions consistent with a low density model generates the lower estimation limit. What archaeologists have failed to acknowledge is that their individual decision-making leads to only one of many plausible alternatives.

ALTERNATIVE ASSUMPTIONS – ALTERNATIVE INTERPRETATIONS

Disregarding for the moment the question of appropriate methods for generating accurate and absolute population counts, let us reexamine behavioral strategies and the Southwestern archaeological record. However, because different assumptions lead to different interpretations of the same data, for the purposes of illustration, low prehistoric population levels will be assumed. In this example the decisions will follow the right side of Figure 6.1, the lowest possible population estimate.

The most far-reaching interpretive impact of low population is that coping strategies for spatial inequalities in the distribution of resources may be direct (people may move directly to resources when they are

177

ready to be procured). This contrasts with the relatively complex social mechanisms used to equalize resource distribution under conditions of high population density. Thus, with low population, subsistence may be based on widely distributed resources through direct exploitation of large catchment areas. Larger units of land are available to support each individual, therefore individuals or groups may procure resources directly.

Spatially extensive and direct procurement (through settlement relocation or logistical strategies) implies: heavy emphasis on wild plant and animal resources; mobility to procure these varied resources; and the existence of large, temporarily unexploited areas. With low population density and a corresponding high-mobility adaptation, the same archaeological remains that are cited as evidence for high population, intensive subsistence strategies, and complex social organization may be viewed much differently. First, the large number of sites would be the result of the shifting, short-term exploitation of the environment by relatively few individuals. As with the Navajo and other highly mobile groups, a single social unit would create or reoccupy two or more sites during their annual round, and thus would create many archaeological sites in a lifetime.

Secondly, spatially extensive population relocations, so-called migrations or abandonments, would have been feasible to avoid overexploitation of a region. With low population density, a mobile population might not use parts of its territory for many years running; this would be one possible and expectable response to an unpredictable, patchy environment and is different from a migration or an abandonment with its catastrophic implications. Such movements would be interpreted as areal abandonments because of the inappropriate spatial scale of analysis employed by archaeologists. This "migratory" pattern, too, would have contributed to the large number of observed archaeological sites. Further, the frequent shifting of site locations would suggest that prehistoric sites were actually occupied for much shorter spans than protohistoric or ethnographic puebloan villages.

With high population density, inter- and intrasite differentiation, especially if room or site size were an element of the differentiation, would be interpreted as evidence for complex vertical social hierarchies. Yet, such variation might as easily be due to seasonal variation in site structure or social group composition or to reoccupation of an especially advantageous locale.

EMPIRICAL EVIDENCE FOR LOW POPULATION

Several recent empirical analyses have shown that some of the above patterns occur in parts of the Southwest during some time periods. Because dense population and subsistence intensification are so closely interrelated, questions about the degree of reliance on agriculture also raise questions about population size and density. Descriptive generalizations about subsistence strategies have been revised greatly over the past several years (Ford 1984; Gasser 1982; Seme' 1984). Reanalysis of the archaeological contexts that produced early corn (ca. 3000 B.C.) has shown stratigraphic intermixing that casts doubt on the antiquity of cultigens in the northern Southwest, suggesting a much later date for the introduction of corn (ca. 1000–700 B.C.) on the Colorado Plateaus (Berry 1982; Ford 1984; Wills 1985). Since high population density presupposes reliance on cultigens, it may follow that absence of cultigens indicates low population.

Much of the archaeological evidence for reliance on cultigens for subsistence was indirect and inferential; however, the evidence for heavy reliance on wild foods is equally indirect and inferential. The presence of metates, manos, and food storage facilities was cited as indicative of subsistence based on cultigens. However, macrobotanical remains and pollen suggest a very eclectic vegetal resource base. In fact, some of the facilities thought to be incontrovertible evidence for corn agriculture are now known to have been used, at least in part, for processing wild plants (Gasser 1982; Murry 1983). Additionally, quantitative assessments of human osteological remains suggest variation in dietary composition ranging from few starchy cultigens (Berry 1983; Martin, Swedlund, and Armelagos 1982) to a diet based largely on starchy cultigens (El-Najjar *et al.* 1976). Thus corn is a later introduction and was used much more variably than previously thought.

Settlement pattern data and interpretations also have been subjected to recent queries and reinterpretations. Reconsiderations of settlement pattern data consistent with implicit low population assumptions have led to alternative interpretations emphasizing seasonal and regional mobility. Powell (1983) has analyzed changing site morphology over time on northern Black Mesa, Arizona, and argues that the archaeological record documents a change from seasonal mobility to a base-camp-and-special-activity-outlier pattern. On a pan-southwestern

179

scale, Berry (1982) has questioned the assumptions behind "phase-stacking" or inferring continuous occupational sequences from settlement data that are noncontinuously distributed over time. Berry reanalyzed chronological data from Anasazi sites and concluded that major occupational hiatuses were caused by periodic abandonments of the Colorado Plateaus (although his interpretations have been questioned and may be a result of his methods [Dean 1985]).

Reevaluations of site size and occupation span data have shown different patterns than previously presumed. Data collected by the Southwestern Anthropological Research Group (SARG) indicate that mean site size was 1.3 rooms prior to A.D. 800, 2.9 rooms between A.D. 800 to 1100, and 9.5 rooms after A.D. 1100 (Plog, Effland, and Green 1978:141). Reanalysis of building sequences and structural deterioration rates on tree-ring-dated sites shows that occupations ranged from eleven to 341 years, with a mean occupation span of 80 years (Hantman 1983:157–8; Neitzel and Hantman 1983). Further, sites with ten or fewer rooms have an average tree-ring-dated occupation span of 34 years (Hantman 1983:158). Comparisons of relatively and absolutely dated sites have been used to generate occupation span estimates for the former, suggesting that many sites may have been occupied for as little as one to 22 years (Hantman 1983:159; Synenki 1979). These patterns, in turn, suggest that many sites treated as contemporaneous in phase-based population estimates, in fact were not occupied at the same time.

Thus, reevaluation of archaeological data suggests that several commonly held assumptions – assumptions that mold subsequent reconstructions of prehistoric adaptive and organizational patterns – are not always correct: the subsistence base was far more diverse and variable than previously presumed; mobility, as well as exchange, may have been a viable spatial averaging mechanism; large sites were not the norm; and occupation spans were far more variable, and short occupations more common, than previously supposed.

SCALE OF ANALYSIS

Another major methodological and interpretive problem that has been recognized in sociological and socio-cultural anthropological research is the relationship between samples and populations (Babbie 1973; Arensberg 1961). Investigators of modern-day social phenomena are constantly faced with the discrepancy between the units they observe and the units they seek to generalize about, and they have devised methods for selecting samples and assessing their representativeness *vis-à-vis* the population they seek to study.

Archaeologists have faced these same problems, but have usually addressed them within a spatial framework (e.g., is my site or study area representative of the cultural area about which I wish to make generalizations?). As a result, there is a body of archaeological literature that considers spatial sampling techniques. However, as archaeologists tackle behavioral and social questions, they must identify relevant behavioral/social units and devise methods for sampling them. Obviously, regional population size and density are important considerations in sampling decisions.

The possibility of alternative interpretations of Southwestern demographic patterns raises questions about the appropriate size of study areas. Acceptance of the high population density assumption has led many archaeologists implicitly to treat the phenomena under observation as complete systems or subsystems. For example, settlement pattern analyses generally assume that the area investigated and the sample of recorded sites comprised an operative spatial and social unit. Investigations into social organization similarly assume that the target phenomenon is actually being observed (e.g., that a patri- or matrilocal residential unit actually inhabited a structure, or that a "community" actually lived at a site or in a study area). However, if population was distributed sparsely over the landscape, archaeologists may attempt to interpret inappropriately small areas and incomplete social/behavioral units.

Recent analyses have shown this pattern to be true (although not universal). The distribution of nonlocal lithic and ceramic materials within a 120 mi^2 area in northern Arizona showed that exchange networks extended beyond the bounds of the study area (Green 1982; Plog and Hantman 1982), and analysis of site configurations in the same area indicated that only part of the subsistence/settlement system was present (Powell 1983). Thus, it appears that spatial scale is an important variable that must be determined prior to interpreting archaeological remains.

MODELING ENVIRONMENTAL, POPULATION, AND BEHAVIORAL INTERRELATIONSHIPS

In the preceding pages, I have developed three points.

1. There are many methodological problems associated with estimating population size from archaeological data.
2. Interpretations of Southwestern cultural patterns are frequently based on the assumption of high population density, low plant and animal biomass, and resultant population/resource imbalances. Thus, mobility is assumed to occur only as rare, brief mass events on an otherwise sedentary social landscape.
3. An alternative assumption, low population density, results in far different interpretations of these same archaeological remains.

As yet, no prehistoric population estimates for the Southwest have been generated that eliminate the many methodological problems inherent in making demographic reconstructions from archaeological data. Despite that major empirical and methodological impediment, however, predictions of adaptive responses to patterns of environmental change under different population-density conditions can be made. Table 6.1 summarizes expected technological, subsistence, and organizational responses to changes in major environmental parameters and in the spatial distribution of natural resources. The table summarizes expected human responses to environmental changes caused by low-frequency (occurring every 250–300 years) and higher-frequency (25-year cycles) natural processes (LFP and HFP, respectively). Additionally, the distribution of resources over the landscape (either spatially homogeneous or heterogeneous) is considered. These two variables permit prediction of actual resource availability within a time–space framework; however, human perception of the environmental patterns, and therefore human responses to variation in the patterns, very likely was less than perfect. Finally, because of the interaction between demographic patterns and variation in resource availability, cultural responses are presented and discussed separately for low- and high-density conditions.

Table 6.1. *Proposed environmental and population interactions*

	Low population density	
	Low-frequency processes	High-frequency processes
Spatially heterogeneous	cyclic material culture change (same periodicity as LFP) spatial averaging mechanisms – high mobility coarse-grained ecological response	high intraassemblage variation spatial averaging mechanisms – high mobility coarse-grained ecological response
Spatially homogeneous	cyclic material culture change (same periodicity as LFP) large catchment areas – tethered wandering fine-grained ecological response	high intraassemblage variation large catchment areas – tethered wandering fine-grained ecological response
	High population density	
	Low-frequency processes	High-frequency processes
Spatially heterogeneous	cyclic material culture change (same periodicity as LFP) spatial averaging mechanisms – exchange subsistence intensification, Hopi-like strategy cultigens plus wild plants and animals	high intraassemblage variation spatial averaging mechanisms – exchange subsistence intensification, Hopi-like strategy cultigens plus wild plants and animals
Spatially homogeneous	cyclic material culture change (same periodicity as LFP) temporal averaging mechanisms – storage subsistence intensification – water control facilities	high intraassemblage variation temporal averaging mechanisms – storage subsistence intensification – water control facilities and Hopi-like strategy

183

LOW POPULATION DENSITY ADAPTIVE RESPONSES TO PATTERNS OF ENVIRONMENTAL VARIATION

The major adaptive responses to change in the periodicity of major environmental shifts are grounded in human perception or awareness of the environmental shift. High-frequency processes occur within a temporal scale perceivable by humans possessing no written records (Dean, Chapter 2 above). Further, because several such environmental shifts are occurring within the span of a human's lifetime, they would be perceived as part of the normal or expectable range of variation. Such variation can potentially be buffered by technological or social intervention. Thus, the cultural system would include a repertoire of responses appropriate to the highly variable conditions and would subsequently be perceived by archaeologists as variable (so long as the response repertoire left archaeologically observable remains).

Conversely, low-frequency environmental processes generally are not observable by humans responding to them. If gradual, environmental shifts would be accommodated culturally by equally gradual shifts in the adaptive system. Such cultural adjustments would be viewed by the archaeologist as cyclic cultural change paralleling or lagging slightly behind the environmental cycle. If abrupt, which LFP environmental changes probably were on the Colorado Plateaus, the shift might have been too great for accommodation within the existing cultural system. In this case, "catastrophic" change would be responded to with major technological or social innovations or by reduction or extinction of the population.

Human perceptions of environmental texture – either spatially heterogeneous or spatially homogeneous – would also structure the repertoire of cultural responses. A heterogeneous natural resource distribution might be responded to by attempts to equalize the distribution of those resources perceived to be essential for survival (spatial averaging). With low population density this would be accomplished with least organizational effort by moving individuals directly to resources – a high-mobility pattern (e.g., Powell 1983).

However, if resources were evenly distributed over the landscape, there would be no necessary advantage in moving to the resources since (with low biomass) no single resource patch would be sufficiently large to support the group for any length of time. Because of the sparse, but

184

even, resource distribution, a group would require access to a large area to ensure group survival, and transport efficiency would require a centrally located base camp associated with many special-activity outliers. Thus, a high-mobility settlement pattern might be composed either of seasonally occupied habitation camps or of base camps and special-activity outliers.

HIGH POPULATION DENSITY ADAPTIVE RESPONSES TO PATTERNS OF ENVIRONMENTAL VARIATION

Human perceptions (or lack of perceptions) of low- and high-frequency environmental processes are critical in structuring adaptive response irrespective of population density. With high population density, high-frequency processes would still be perceived as part of the expectable range of environmental variation and would be responded to with an equivalently variable repertoire of technological and organizational coping mechanisms.

Again, conversely, low-frequency processes probably would not be perceived. Instead, gradual cultural adjustments would be made to the gradually shifting physical environmental conditions. Abrupt shifts due to low-frequency natural processes would be outside the range of expectable environmental variation. This would produce an archaeological pattern of gradual cyclic material culture change with major technological and organizational innovations at the times of major environmental changes.

High population density would eliminate the option of a spatially extensive, high mobility/large catchment area response to the low biomass. However, perceptions of the distribution of resources over the landscape would still structure patterns of resource procurement. Spatially heterogeneous conditions would continue to select for spatial averaging mechanisms. However, because direct mobility is no longer an option, the mechanism for equalizing resource distributions would be commodities exchange (e.g., Braun and Plog 1982; Plog 1980b). Spatially homogeneous conditions would not provide the same strong impetus for resource exchange. However, temporal variation in resource distribution would select for food storage to equalize these inequalities, regardless of the grain of the spatial distribution (Binford 1980).

185

Under high-density conditions, subsistence strategies would incorporate the large labor pool; thus, increasingly labor-intensive exploitation of the landscape to increase productivity per land unit would be expected. Spatially heterogeneous conditions would select for variation in agricultural practices, and a system much like that employed by the present-day Hopis (Hack 1942) would be appropriate. Spatially homogeneous conditions, especially when occurring within an interval of low-frequency environmental change, would select for investment in permanent agricultural facilities such as water control devices. Water control facilities would also be expected under spatially homogeneous/ high-frequency conditions; however, these would be part of the variable repertoire predicted for that component of the cultural systems.

The preceding pages have documented the interplay between temporal and spatial conditions that affects the availability of resources over space and over time. The impact of the distribution of human populations over the landscape was also considered, and it is clear that population size and its distribution have a profound effect on the repertoire of response mechanisms available to those populations. It is also clear that, due to many methodological problems, absolute population counts do not exist for any area on the Colorado Plateaus. In the absence of absolute population measures and the methods for generating them, our only recourse is to use relative estimates with all their attendant problems and to try to accommodate the range of potential descriptive inaccuracies in our interpretations (Euler, Chapter 7 below; Plog *et al.*, Chapter 8 below).

IMPLICATIONS: THE CAUSES AND EFFECTS OF POPULATION GROWTH

The preceding pages have documented the interpretive implications of assuming either low or high population density in the absence of absolute population counts. However, assumptions about population size and distribution also affect theoretical studies. Because population growth may be viewed as a dependent or independent variable, considerable debate surrounds the assignment of causality in cultural change studies. Many archaeologists concern themselves with the relationship between population growth and the evolution of food-producing strategies and hierarchical social organization. One long-standing, and still unresolved, debate questions the role of population

186

growth in the origins of agriculture (Powell 1983:7–9). Borrowing concepts from Malthus, some archaeologists claim that population was limited by resource availability, until the invention of agriculture (Zubrow 1971). Food production increased carrying capacity and removed natural restrictions on population growth; as a result, population, responding as a dependent variable, increased.

The other side of the debate claims that population growth provided a major stimulus for the adoption of agriculture by creating imbalances in resource/population relationships (Boserup 1965). One cultural solution to these imbalances would be to increase the quantity of food produced per unit of land. However, because subsistence intensification, including agriculture, requires more labor input for each unit of food produced, there is little intrinsic incentive to intensify food production in the absence of population pressure. The major benefit of subsistence intensification is that more food is produced on a given unit of land; thus, a larger, more densely packed population may be supported.

Because food production concentrates resources in a limited area and might cause scheduling conflicts, mobility is restricted (Moore 1985). Further population growth then occurs as a result of the shorter birth spacing associated with sedentism. The increased value of children in an agricultural labor pool also provides an incentive for larger families. Following this reasoning, the very condition (population growth) that led to selection of an increasingly labor-intensive subsistence strategy (food production) also led to responses that selected for further population growth. In this example, population growth is initially an independent variable that sets into motion a systemic, positive-feedback situation.

Population growth has also been implicitly linked with the evolution of complex social organization. One theory links the development of social hierarchies to a human proclivity for subordinating other humans. Sociopolitical control is maintained by controlling the means of production – both labor and capital. Several studies have scrutinized population increase as a dependent variable in the evolution of hierarchical social organization and decision-making organizations in the American Southwest (Upham, Lightfoot, and Feinman 1981; Upham 1982; Lightfoot and Feinman 1982). In their view, short-term individual or family-based decisions to intensify food production "to finance social or religious activities" could have had several effects, including population growth and intensified land-use strategies (Upham, Lightfoot, and Feinman 1981:823). These, in turn, provided a potential for some individuals or families to produce food surpluses. These food surpluses would have provided the industrious intensifiers with opportunities "to participate in regional exchange networks, thereby consolidating their positions of influence in both local and regional settlement systems" (Upham, Lightfoot, and Feinman 1981:823). Participation in the regional settlement systems and the influence accrued from that participation would have provided social groups led by these entrepreneurial individuals a competitive edge over social groups lacking such individuals. "The long-term implications of such processes would have been that those groups which lacked some form of managerial organization would not have survived direct competition with larger better integrated, social systems" (Upham, Lightfoot, and Feinman 1981:823).

In this scenario, one overall, interactive effect of these processes is population growth. Production of food surpluses allows population growth, and intensification of land-use strategies both allows and encourages population growth. Finally, because individuals are viewed as a desirable resource in and of themselves, increases in group size would have provided a competitive edge to the larger group, encouraging the leader to recruit followers (Lightfoot and Feinman 1982:66). Thus, entrepreneurial behavior and the production of food surpluses provided the impetus for a series of events – events which also provided incentives for continuing population increase. Population increase is viewed as a dependent variable that responds positively (through immigration or intrinsic growth) to the organizational manipulation of a managerial elite.

Alternative approaches to the relationship between size and organizational complexity view population growth as an initial kick that sets off a systemic, positive-feedback situation between increasing population and organizational complexity. Recent analyses have shown that even simply organized social groups are not autonomous and do not live in isolation (e.g., Wobst 1974). Computer simulations suggest that mating networks must incorporate 175–475 individuals (Wobst 1974:168) if an individual is to have a reasonable chance to be matched with an appropriate mate at the appropriate time.

Population density estimates for the mobile Western Shoshoni (Bradfield 1973) have been used to reconstruct the spatial extents of a

188

hypothetical mating network. The two networks range in size from $19,700$ km^2, or a radius of 72.2 km, for the more mobile Shoshoni, to 2460 km^2, or a radius of 28 km, for the more sedentary Owens Valley Paiute (Plog and Powell 1984:212). Clearly, even for organizationally simple groups, large numbers of individuals are organized, however informally, into spatially extensive networks.

The fact that relatively large numbers of individuals (175–475 persons) must be integrated into a mating network to ensure any one individual an appropriate mate at the appropriate time says nothing about the organizational mechanisms that integrate such a network. Of importance here is the observation that a large number of individuals does not necessarily mean formal, hierarchical organizational strategies. There are numerous instances in the ethnographic literature of the use of kin ties (either fictive or real) or of the creation of artificial resource or commodity scarcities to ensure social interactions among large numbers of individuals spaced over large areas (Bradfield 1973; Chagnon 1968; Weissner 1977). The actual form of the organizational network appears related in part to demands on the speed and efficiency of information processing. Thus, size alone is not an accurate indicator of the formality or the complexity of organizational mechanisms necessary to integrate a social group.

Johnson (1983:175) has noted that "the ability of individuals and small groups to monitor and process information in decision-making contexts" limits group size and conditions group organization. He cites numerous studies that lead to a relatively unambiguous empirical generalization about consensual decision-making: "consensual decision-making groups of six and more individuals are under increasing scalar stress due to degrading decision performance" (Johnson 1983:177). For this reason, alternative organizational strategies must be sought for efficient information processing and decision-making as the number of interacting units exceeds six.

However, decision-making organizations may increase in complexity by two alternative, but not mutually exclusive, mechanisms.

Horizontal specialization increases the number of decision-making units at a given level of a decision hierarchy, whereas vertical specialization increases the number of hierarchic arranged levels of such an organization. (Johnson 1978:87–8)

Thus, numbers of individuals alone will not predict the hierarchical arrangements within the organization integrating those individuals.

Although those individuals may be organized within a multilevel vertical hierarchy, they may alternatively be integrated within a horizontal structure or a structure that combines elements of both.

CONCLUSIONS

I have tried to show the lack of consensus about the role of population growth in recent analyses of cultural change. Population growth is viewed as a dependent, independent, systemic, and/or contextual variable. The evaluation of many models of cultural change relies on the continuous and absolute measurement of temporal variation in population levels (e.g., Plog 1980, 1983:294). Among other things, meaningful temporal intervals for archaeological population reconstructions imply the contemporaneity of the units contributing to the population estimate.

Measurement of population density, growth rates, and the impact of population growth as a culture-changing variable, all must rely on accurate demographic reconstructions. Yet, even the most basic demographic variable, population size, is extremely difficult to measure. Archaeologists are cognizant of the complex and indirect relationships between archaeological remains and the size of the population that left the remains. The literature abounds with discussions of techniques for reconstructing population size as well as of the methodological problems that make archaeological census-taking so difficult. Such basic issues as site definition, survey intensity, regional sampling strategies, intrasite collection strategies, and individual measurement variation all affect the final characterization of archaeological survey data and regional population size (S. Plog, F. Plog, and Wait 1978). More complex demographic issues such as reconstructions of social organization from regional settlement patterns are even more problematical. Additionally, the investigator's theoretical orientation and descriptive preconceptions derived from that theory may color final interpretations.

Demographic patterns have a profound, but predictable, impact on the range of behavioral options available to the prehistoric inhabitants of the Colorado Plateaus, as can be seen in the last chapter of this volume. It is also clear that it is no simple matter to measure population from archaeological data. There has been great variation in the techniques employed and little consideration of how prehistoric behavioral variability – over time and over space – affects the reliability and compar-

ability of the estimates. Further, the theoretical and descriptive–
interpretive implications of assuming patterns of human distribution
over the landscape are far-reaching.

Much very worthwhile methodological effort is currently being
expended on refining population estimates and the chronological
frameworks within which these are placed. Several researchers are
attempting to factor out the effects of the two variables, occupation span
and number of individuals, that contribute to debris accumulation at
archaeological sites. If, in fact, people produce debris at a constant rate,
and if the total trash accumulation at a site is known, it will be a
relatively simple matter to calculate the number of individuals who
produced that trash – once we know how long they were producing it.
Preliminary research (Hantman 1983) has demonstrated the problems
and ambiguities in devising occupation span measures. However,
ideally, this will clarify the relationship between material culture and
the size of the population producing it – allowing generation of
absolute, regional population counts. But, until old analogically based
assumptions about prehistoric population distributions are verified, or
until new population figures are derived, we should exercise caution
using these assumptions when interpreting cultural patterns.

ACKNOWLEDGMENTS
Many thanks to David Braun, Jeff Dean, George Gumerman, Bob Leonard,
and Stead Upham, who read and commented on earlier drafts of this paper; to
R. Yvette Duncan for her editorial expertise; and to Kathy Morgan, who typed
the drafts of the manuscript.

7
Demography and cultural dynamics on the Colorado Plateaus

ROBERT C. EULER

Department of Anthropology
Arizona State University

INTRODUCTION

This chapter summarizes demographic and cultural dynamics across the Colorado Plateaus as these may ultimately interdigitate functionally with each other and with the natural environment. By examining the archaeological literature for this area, especially that occupied by the Anasazi, data were gathered to relate to the basic cultural and behavioral themes of this symposium as detailed in Chapter 8 below and to test the hypotheses presented there. Although this chapter was finalized before the themes as ultimately designed were formalized, correspondences are simple. I deal with initial *colonization and range expansion, abandonment, upland–lowland movement* as those terms are used in Chapter 8 below. *Interaction* relates to my paragraphs on exchange and alliances; *subsistence practices* are discussed in terms of storage and soil and water control features; *territoriality* by discussing defensive sites; and *social integration* in terms of dispersed or nucleated settlements and large and small sites.

I have attempted succinctly to show cultural relationships and change through time as they actually existed (Taylor 1948:143) and I have used my judgment in deciding what were the most fundamental and significant influences (Taylor 1948:149) resulting in demarcations of cultural change. In looking at these "boundary markers" of change as they have been put forth by various investigators, I shall be concerned with how they denote alterations in sociopolitical structure, economic orientation, demography, and, in terms of the concluding chapter of this volume, in adaptation to the natural environment.

Relating to culture change, I intend to discuss what for the purposes of this study are behaviorally significant, rather than merely stylistic alterations in these cultures; this is not to say that stylistic changes cannot be significant. I also want to see if there are "hinge points" of change across the Plateaus and, of course, the reasons for them.

The demographic data presented in the text and in the accompanying chart (Figure 7.1) are not intended to be absolute curves; numbers of people simply are not available or reliable nor are they necessary for the purposes of this study. Considerable controversy surrounds the role of demography in culture change. Since this has recently been reviewed at some length (Hassan 1981), it will not be belabored here.

Obviously, this literature does not provide information on all these topics for any particular region of the Plateaus. Often comparability is lacking, as is good chronological ordering. Many writers do not address all of these subjects or rely solely upon their own constructed "phase" systems or the Pecos Classification, as though the latter implies absolute temporal periods cast in 200-year concreteness. I have not relied upon either here.

There is, however, a need to generalize and to make some inferences even though there may be no consensus. I hope, however, that this synthesis of the demographic and cultural dynamics of the Colorado Plateaus will be sufficiently detailed to relate cogently to other chapters in this volume.

THE ANASAZI DOMAIN

Since the main thrust of this chapter relates to culture and demographic change on the Colorado Plateaus, it is concerned primarily with data from the several Anasazi traditions, those people who, at various times in the prehistoric past, occupied most of that vast geographic area. As the lifeways of other people, such as the Sinagua, Cohonina, or Mogollon, impinged upon or elucidate Anasazi patterns, they too will be brought to bear. These are listed in Figures 8.2 through 8.9.

Three major Anasazi traditions are recognized – Kayenta, Mesa

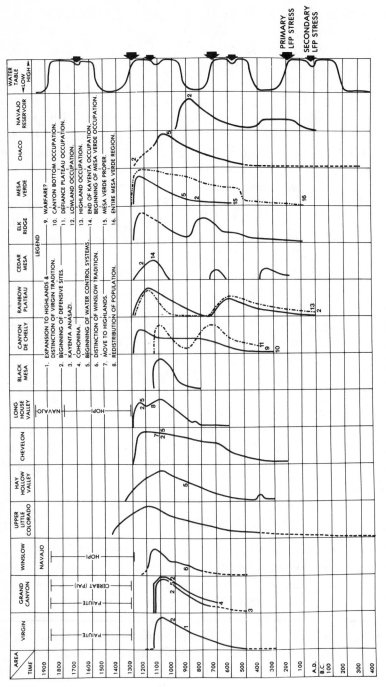

Figure 7.1 Relative population curves – Colorado Plateaus.

Verde, and Chaco – although it is becoming clear that distinctions between the latter two are often blurred. Two relatively minor Anasazi groups, the Virgin River or Western Anasazi (Thompson 1978) and the Winslow are also of concern. Parenthetically, the Western Anasazi terminology of Thompson refers specifically to people of the so-called Virgin tradition and not to the broader concept that includes Anasazi of the San Juan, Colorado, and Little Colorado drainages as proposed by Plog (1979:108–30).

Areas such as Cedar Mesa and the Red Rock Plateau in Utah, where both Kayenta and Mesa Verde peoples resided at different times, and the Hay Hollow Valley, Arizona, an area utilized by both Chaco Anasazi and Mogollon, will also be discussed. The Navajo Reservoir district of northwestern New Mexico and southwestern Colorado, with Chaco and Mesa Verde components, is also important to our presentation.

The Kayenta subtradition

The Kayenta Anasazi occupied much although not all of the Colorado Plateaus in northern Arizona and extended into southern Utah as well as into southeastern Nevada just off the Plateaus to the west. Within this broad area, some archaeologists would delineate smaller subdivisions. One is the "Virgin Branch" (Aikens 1966). These people lived in the westernmost area of Anasazi settlement, the Arizona Strip, that arid region north of Grand Canyon, extending north to the southern limits of the Great Basin and west to the drainage of the Virgin River. It is included in a discussion of the Kayenta because diagnostic differences between the two are indeed minor; prior to A.D. 900 they were non-existent (Aikens 1966:55) and after that date restricted to architectural patterns and small distinctions in ceramics.

While a number of surveys and excavations have been undertaken in Western Anasazi territory, we still know little about cultural dynamics there (Lipe and Thompson 1979:283). Aikens's (1966) summary, almost two decades old, is still the best available. He indicated that the Virgin area was first occupied by Anasazi ca. A.D. 200, a date that is perhaps too early, during a period marked by the introduction of horticulture (p. 21). Farther west, the lowland Virgin River drainage was inhabited by A.D. 500 (Lyneis 1981:3). From ca. A.D. 500 to 900, the time of first sustained population, the Anasazi of the Virgin region lived in small, dispersed pithouse settlements in well watered valley or canyon environments. Storage cists first appeared at Lost City, Nevada (Shutler 1961) and in western Grand Canyon (Thompson 1970) at this time. The society was probably organized in small lineages with no social stratification (Aikens 1966:35). Between A.D. 700 to 1150, Aikens (p. 36) postulated an increase in population and an expansion into highland areas such as the Shivwits Plateau. About A.D. 900, surface masonry pueblos in a circular or horseshoe patterned room block came into use, in addition to pithouses. Aikens (1966:55) did not infer any reasons for this architectural style differing from that of the Kayenta. One might suggest that degree of social cohesion, the function of religious versus secular rooms (kivas increased in numbers), or spatial requirements may have been factors to be considered. Aikens (1966:53) also suggested that the lineage-based social structure continued and that the production base remained in horticulture. Structures that may have been defensive were constructed in the ninth and twelfth centuries. It has been postulated that Cliff's Edge, a site dating ca. A.D. 830, situated on a high bluff overlooking the Virgin River, was located for defense (Jenkins 1981). Shutler (1961:68) noted that at Lost City, sites were located on ridges at the edge of the valley as though situated with "an eye to defense." Some sites of this period at Lost City had as many as 84 rooms.

Very few water control structures have been described from the Virgin area. Moffit and Chang (1978:197), in a rather superficial report of a survey near Mt Trumbull, mentioned a check dam but provided no dates for its construction.

By A.D. 1150, "the Virgin subculture ceased to exist" and the people probably joined the Kayenta proper farther east (Aikens 1966:56). Recently, Thompson (1983:20) has proposed a model which would reject "demographic cataclysm" for the abandonment of the Virgin area. While it would not be realistic to suggest that all Anasazi departed that area at once, Thompson's suggestion that a gradual re-emphasis on foraging rather than horticulture would have permitted a longer occupation and a more gradual withdrawal remains hypothetical.

Throughout the entire chronological life of the Virgin Anasazi, exchange with neighboring people seems to have been important. These people "served as a gateway community" and had strong trade linkages to the southern California coast (Lyneis 1981).

While Aikens's beginning and terminal dates (A.D. 200–1150) are generally accepted for the Virgin, excavations of a Virgin site in the

Tuweep district of Grand Canyon National Park have yielded six radiocarbon dates of between A.D. 100 and 320 for a pithouse structure and four radiocarbon dates of ca. "1250 A.D. to 1260 A.D." for other features of the site (Thompson and Thompson 1974:19–20, 34–5). All of the early dates except one were in clear association with ceramics. While no sherd identifications were given, the Thompsons (p. 32) indicated that "The painted designs are overwhelmingly in the stylistic traditions known as Lino B/G and Kana-a B/G." Although Berry (1982:55), in a recent effort to reassess prehistoric Anasazi chronologies, completely accepts these as firm dates, I prefer to remain skeptical and rely upon the tree-ring dated correlations of those two ceramic types of ca. A.D. 575–875 and ca. A.D. 725–950 respectively (Breternitz 1966:79, 82). In a later paper, Lipe and Thompson (1979:53) suggest that "The time of greatest Virgin Branch population was apparently between about A.D. 1000 and 1150" and that at the latter date the population "declined precipitously" and by "the middle 1200's, they had probably abandoned the Arizona Strip entirely."

That the dates of A.D. 200–1250 may be too early and too late, is indicated from a survey of 209 Virgin Anasazi sites in 32,640 acres (13,209 ha.) of the Tuweep District of Grand Canyon National Park. This study revealed no occupation "earlier than 600 A.D. or later than 1150 A.D." (Thompson 1979:251).

Lipe and Thompson (1979:54) also suggest that in southern Nevada, the Southern Paiute came into contact with the Virgin Anasazi "by A.D. 1100 and perhaps as early as 900." Thus, they postulate that the two groups were in contact for perhaps as much as 300 to 350 years (or as little as 50 years). As will be seen, such contact is not demonstrated by evidence from Grand Canyon immediately to the south and east.

At an Anasazi site at Kanab, Utah, Nickens and Kvamme (1981) noted an occupation radiocarbon-dated ca. A.D. 520 ± 120. After a hiatus, the site was reoccupied from ca. A.D. 980 ± 120 to A.D. 1150 ± 110 (pp. 67–9). They further suggest that occupation, abandonment, and reoccupation indicative of village instability was characteristic of Anasazi populations in the Kanab area and that abandonment may have been occasioned by climatic stress.

A recent volume describing excavations of Virgin tradition sites in the lowlands near St. George, Utah, provides our most up-to-date summary of the area as a whole (Dalley and McFadden 1985:42–4). The authors describe pithouses and many storage cists for what they term "Basketmaker III . . . more or less" from "A.D. 500–700" with sites in abundance in both lowlands and highlands. The same appears to be the case also in "the 700's and 800's," especially on Little Creek Mountain at a highland elevation of 5100 to 5900 feet (1554 to 1798 m) (Heid 1982:113, 115, 132). These gross patterns change very little, continuing perhaps to abandonment ca. A.D. 1150.

The Grand Canyon region

While the Grand Canyon was the scene of occupation by several cultural groups through time, the primary inhabitants in the prehistoric period were Kayenta Anasazi. There is evidence (Euler and Chandler 1978) that Kayenta peoples made initial exploration of the Canyon by ca. A.D. 600 or even earlier (Jones 1986). Occupation of the South Rim and Inner Canyon areas was sparse, however, until ca. A.D. 1000 when there was an influx of Kayenta in those two areas as well as on the North Rim. Based primarily upon ceramic dating, the majority of more than 1500 Anasazi sites so far recorded at Grand Canyon were occupied between A.D. 1050 and 1150.

Throughout most of Grand Canyon, the Kayenta utilized the varying ecological zones spanning more than 5000 vertical feet (1524 m) from rims to the Colorado River to hunt, gather edible wild foods as they became harvestable at different times and elevations, and to farm in favorable locations, both upland and lowland. Theirs was an excellent example of adaptation to an extreme physiographic variable. A social structure probably consisting of nuclear or extended families permitted a seasonal movement with geographic orientation being primarily to the Inner Canyon.

Of significance is the fact that of all Anasazi sites in Grand Canyon, fewer than ten kivas have been recorded; these are at sites occupied ca. A.D. 1050–1150. None is definitely known from the North Rim and only a few from the Inner Canyon and South Rim (Effland, Jones, and Euler 1981). This is probably also indicative of seasonal utilization with sites with kivas having been occupied in winter months.

Storage facilities, primarily masonry granaries tucked into overhangs in the cliff walls, are common for the same period. In some areas along the rims, storage capacities in these granaries appear to be greater than necessary for the few habitation structures located nearby; statistical data, however, have not yet been generated.

Another significant architectural feature of the A.D. 1050–1150 period at Grand Canyon is the presence of numerous defensible structures, primarily on the South Rim. These take the form of massive dry laid walls built on small buttes or "islands" isolated from the "mainland" of the rim itself. These walls are usually located on the side of the "island" facing the "mainland". These structures contain rooms or artifacts only infrequently. They seem for the most part to relate to both Kayenta and Cohonina occupation of the Canyon.

Larger settlements have been recorded. For example, at Unkar Delta, there is a village, including two kivas, undoubtedly occupied by several extended families or lineages.

A change from pithouse to surface masonry architecture apparently took place there about A.D. 1075, settlements on the delta were moved to non-arable areas ca. A.D. 1100, and the area was abandoned by A.D. 1150 (Schwartz, Chapman, and Kepp 1980).

On the North Rim, especially in the Walhalla Glades at an elevation of about 8000 feet (2438 m), there was a sizeable Kayenta occupation ca. A.D. 1050–1150. Hundreds of small, two to five room surface masonry structures were occupied (Schwartz, Kepp, and Chapman 1981; Effland, Jones, and Euler 1981). Associated with these small pueblos were many one-room field houses and extensive agricultural soil and water control devices such as linear borders, waffle gardens, and check dams (Jones 1983). Again, A.D. 1150 marked the abandonment of these high-elevation sites.

While the emphasis of this paper lies in Anasazi dynamics, it should be noted that the somewhat enigmatic and non-Anasazi Cohonina people also utilized Grand Canyon at about the same time as did the Kayenta. The earliest evidence for the Cohonina comes about A.D. 700, with an increase in population ca. A.D. 1050–1150.

Cartledge (1979:313), analyzing data from a survey on the slopes of Sitgreaves Mountain south of Grand Canyon, found, however, a greater Cohonina population between A.D. 750–950 than in the A.D. 950–1150 period. That area is several hundred meters higher than Grand Canyon. During their entire cultural history, the Cohonina occupied much of the South Rim west of the Kayenta and utilized portions of the Inner Canyon only seasonally. They were in friendly contact with both Virgin and Kayenta and, indeed, adopted a veneer of Anasazi culture. Cohonina sites, both earlier pithouse communities and later surface masonry structures were usually small, the largest

199

consisting of twelve to fifteen rooms (Cartledge 1979:305). While the Cohonina farmed the Coconino Plateau, water control devices were scarce; Effland and Green (1979) reported a few check dams which apparently date between A.D. 1000 and 1150. Aside from the defensible "island" sites noted above, the only other evidence for Cohonina "forts" is at Medicine Fort near Flagstaff, constructed ca. A.D. 1060 according to Colton (1946:81–4). By A.D. 1150 the Cohonina also disappear from the cultural record.

Recent evidence (Euler 1981) supports the hypothesis that all of Grand Canyon was essentially unoccupied by humans for approximately 150 years. By A.D. 1300, or perhaps somewhat later, the South Rim and Inner Canyon reaches were in the possession of peoples of the Cerbat tradition, ancestors of the Walapai and Havasupai. They remained in that geographic range, farming in well-watered localities and hunting and gathering elsewhere, until forcibly removed by U.S. Army troops in the late 1860s. During the same time span, the North Rim and its tributary canyons were taken over by ancestors of the Southern Paiute who followed an economic round quite similar to that of the Cerbat. Unfortunately, since ceramic cross dating post A.D. 1300 (Jeddito Yellow Ware) is not time-specific and since cultures of both Cerbat and Paiute changed very little through time, it is not possible to establish times of occupation for recorded sites in many instances. Therefore, data upon which to base population graphs are virtually nonexistent.

The Kayenta heartland

The region of northeastern Arizona including Tsegi Canyon, Marsh Pass, the Long House Valley, and Black Mesa can be considered the heartland of the Kayenta Anasazi. This is not to say that differences in cultural patterns, such as on Black Mesa or in Glen Canyon, did not exist. It is an indication that the Kayenta were most long-lived and culturally developed in these areas.

Although the Kayenta region has been a focus of archaeological studies for almost 80 years, and the general pattern of Kayenta cultural development is fairly well understood, there are a number of areas for which we lack information about cultural and demographic change. As Dean (1981:5) has remarked about the Kayenta, "we still have no good idea of *regional* population magnitudes and trends or of adjustments in population distributions."

Rather than attempt to summarize the culture history of the Kayenta Anasazi in their heartland, something that has been done many times elsewhere, I will examine specific areas for which there is relatively secure evidence of changing conditions.

Black Mesa

Of all Kayenta areas, the intensive sixteen-year record of the Black Mesa Archaeological Project, with data from thousands of surveyed and over 100 excavated sites, provides an excellent data base. At the same time, as in other areas that have been scrutinized by more than one investigator, multiple syntheses have been proffered.

Layhe (1981) provided a detailed projection of demographic and settlement change that indicated, with the exception of several Archaic sites (Smiley and Andrews 1983:50), that the earliest occupation of Black Mesa began ca. 700–600 B.C. The population was small but distributed in both upland and lowland environments. Farming was done along the flood plains and hunting and gathering in the uplands (Andrews 1982:41; Klesert and Layhe 1980).

By A.D. 200, however, Black Mesa, at least on its northeastern reaches, appears to have been abandoned; settlement did not again occur until ca. A.D. 800. There was then a gradual increase in the population until A.D. 1025 when a dramatic rise took place (Powell and Nichols 1983).

During the few centuries preceding A.D. 1025–1050, Powell's (1980:259) analysis showed only a summer seasonal use of the Mesa. More recent data (Powell 1983:127–8), indicate a mixed pattern of both winter and summer seasonal sites. S. Plog (1986:16), however, believes "there was not a major change between A.D. 800 and A.D. 1150 from seasonal . . . to year-round utilization of northern Black Mesa." Earlier analyses indicated an increasing occupation of upland areas beginning during the A.D. 850–970 period (Swedlund and Sessions 1976:146), although this may be subject to modification. Upland areas may have been utilized on a seasonal basis throughout the occupation, with an increasing number of permanent settlements in the upland areas after A.D. 900–950. S. Plog (1986:33–5) believes that in the period from A.D. 850–950 there was occupation in the lowlands near major drainages with limited activity sites higher. From A.D. 950–1000, sites were located in less favorable agricultural zones at higher elevations and more distant from drainages. However, between A.D. 1000 and 1050, both patterns were present although there appears to have been more settlement of the upper reaches of the major drainages. In the ensuing century the trend was reversed to levels comparable to that of the A.D. 850–950 period with habitation sites at lower elevations. In contrast, Powell's (1980:265) analysis indicated that there was "no apparent settlement location shift from lowland to upland locales." This discrepancy may simply be due to impreciseness in definitions of those two physiographic terms.

In any event, there appears to have been a dramatic increase in population ca. A.D. 1025, followed by a decline ca. A.D. 1075, and abandonment ca. A.D. 1150. Mobility was important prior to A.D. 1000 or 1050, but restricted after that (Powell and Nichols 1983).

Earlier investigations on Black Mesa postulated a society living in virtual isolation. More recent studies, however, suggest a considerable volume of exchange, especially from A.D. 800 to 900. From A.D. 1050 to 1150 this exchange network was reduced (Fernstrom 1980). Studies of lithic raw material procurement (Green 1982:213–6) have indicated that until A.D. 200 local lithics were used. From A.D. 800 to 1000 there was infrequent importation but from A.D. 1000 to 1100 there was an intensification of exchange ties with exotic lithics being brought in to the Mesa. After A.D. 1100 local materials were again used.

After A.D. 1150, some of the Black Mesa population may have moved to the better watered Tsegi Canyon drainage to the north. It is also becoming increasingly clear that about A.D. 1150, there was a movement toward the southern reaches of the Mesa. Several sites of this time span have been recorded in areas where there are good springs today. Little is known for these later periods on Black Mesa since no representative sites have been excavated. Indeed, Dean (1981:4) recently has remarked, "the most intriguing temporal gap . . . is the interval between A.D. 1150 and 1250, which encompassed major population movements within the Kayenta region."

Long House Valley

Immediately north of Black Mesa, intensive surveys have been carried out in Long House Valley (Dean, Lindsay, and Robinson 1978). These indicate a Kayenta occupation from perhaps as early as 2500 B.C. (p. 28) to A.D. 1300, sporadic Hopi utilization from ca. A.D. 1300 to 1800, with Navajo occupation following that. While the authors say little about population dynamics prior to A.D. 1000, they do note that the period between then and 1150 is "characterized by a major population increase as indicated by a monumental increase in the number of sites" (p. 33).

Subsistence was based upon intensive agriculture supplemented, obviously, by hunting and gathering. Some fields were watered by an irrigation ditch constructed about A.D. 1150 (Dean, personal communication).

There was also a redistribution of the population after A.D. 1150 from the alluvial flats of the valley floor to the Navajo sandstone benches and scarps on the north edge of the valley. Other water control devices, in the form of masonry walled reservoirs, were built at this time. Several large sites, such as Long House, were built on defensible promontories. Abandonment of Long House Valley by the Kayenta took place by A.D. 1300.

Rainbow Plateau and Navajo Mountain

Farther north, on the Rainbow Plateau at an elevation of ca. 6000 feet (1829 m) and around Navajo Mountain, Kayenta occupation has been noted from pre-A.D. 1 until some time in the 1270s (Lindsay *et al.* 1968:364–5) although there was a temporary abandonment from about A.D. 700 to 800. Even in the succeeding two centuries (A.D. 800–1000), population was sparse in the uplands; the Shonto Plateau, Laguna Creek, and Navajo Canyon at lower elevations were occupied. Higher-elevation settlement resumed and there was an increase in population from ca. A.D. 1000–1225. Abandonment began about A.D. 1250 although Rainbow Plateau continued to be used by the Kayenta until the 1270s.

Water and soil control structures in the form of irrigation ditches and linear borders were constructed between A.D. 1150 and 1250 (Lindsay *et al.* 1968:364).

Between A.D. 1200 and 1250, large villages of upwards of 100 rooms were occupied. These settlements were located "on eminences including buttes, ridges, and small mesas" (Lindsay *et al.* 1968:365) and may have been defensible.

Glen Canyon

For Glen Canyon and its environs near the upper Colorado River, Jennings (1966) has summarized the culture history. He remarked (p. 34):

If one considers the full area [lowlands and uplands] one does find the entire chronological sweep of Anasazi occupancy represented, but the distribution is spotty and discontinuous until Pueblo II and III times.

Jennings further noted, without giving specific times, that his "Basket-maker III and Pueblo I stages" (p. 35) were represented only in the lowlands of Navajo Canyon, that throughout the Glen Canyon region there was a heavy lowland settlement below 5000 feet (1525 m) from "Pueblo II to late Pueblo III," that the same pattern prevailed in the upland areas up to 7500 feet (2270 m).

According to Lipe and Lindsay (1983), there was an extensive Anasazi settlement in the Glen Canyon basin during the early centuries A.D. ("Basketmaker II") but then little or no occupation until the middle to late 1000s (p. 4). The Kaiparowits Plateau also had a high site density from that time or the early 1100s but little settlement after about A.D. 1150. The Kayenta-affiliated Coombs site was in use from the late A.D. 1000s until at least the A.D. 1160s when the last tree-ring dates are recorded. Cummings Mesa, the Rainbow Plateau, and the northern portions of Paiute Mesa were occupied from the late A.D. 1000s or early 1100s through the middle 1200s with some sites still inhabited in the 1270s. These dates also apply to Anasazi utilization of the lowland canyons, the lower San Juan, and the lower Glen Canyon proper (Lipe and Lindsay 1983:5). The neighboring Red Rock Plateau was occupied from about A.D. 1100 to 1150 and again from about A.D. 1210 to 1260 (p. 6). With the exception of the Coombs site and perhaps a few other locales that continued a few years longer, the western Glen Canyon basin was abandoned about A.D. 1150 although areas east of the Colorado River were still in use after that date and habitation in lowland areas increased (Lipe 1970). Most of the Anasazi occupation of Glen Canyon, then, took place between A.D. 1050 and 1270 (Lipe and Lindsay 1983).

After A.D. 1150, the Glen Canyon people constructed several water control structures: a masonry dam at the Creeping Dune site, stone-lined ditches at Beaver Creek, and numerous terraces (Jennings

1966:44–5; Lindsay 1961), all indicating forms of agricultural intensification. These were concentrated in the southern highlands and nearby canyons (Lipe and Lindsay 1983:35).

Storage technology became elaborated during the late 1100s and 1200s and defensive structures were associated with complexes of granaries (Lipe and Lindsay 1983:35), especially in the 1200s.

The Sinagua

The Sinagua, who were centered in the Flagstaff–Sunset Crater area of the Colorado Plateaus, are not considered Anasazi. Because of their geographic position and their exchange relationships with the Kayenta Anasazi and people to the south of them, however, they will be mentioned briefly here.

Pilles (1979:475) considered the Sinagua to be a "part of the Mogollon tradition"; I would prefer not to "pigeon-hole" them, but to simply consider them as a separate and distinct group for the present.

The early work of Colton (1936) indicated a small population of Sinagua beginning about A.D. 500 in the Flagstaff area. This population remained relatively stable until the eruption of Sunset Crater ca. A.D. 1064. Shortly after this volcanic episode, new farm lands brought about by moisture-retaining ash fall created a prehistoric land rush that caused a tremendous population increase over the following century. In the thirteenth century, according to Colton's reconstruction, because of localized drought and prevailing high winds, the moisture-retaining ash was dispersed and the number of inhabitants declined. By A.D. 1300, the Flagstaff area was abandoned; only a few sites south of there, such as Chavez Pass, continued to be occupied.

Recently, Pilles (1979) proposed an alternative interpretation based upon additional survey coupled with new physiographic data. These indicate that the Sinagua pattern was first recognizable between A.D. 500 and 700 east of Flagstaff near an ecotone between ponderosa pine and pinyon–juniper woodlands. About A.D. 900, Sinagua farmers moved to higher elevations along the flanks of the San Francisco Peaks. Here, according to Pilles, the Sinagua lived in pithouses and surface masonry field houses. Some villages contained 15 to 25 structures.

Pilles believed that the ash fall from eruptions of Sunset Crater did not necessarily act as a mulch to provide moisture for farming but that between A.D. 1050 and 1150 the Sinagua were able to move back to lower elevations in the pinyon–juniper forests for other reasons. New data indicate that the Sunset Crater eruptions began in A.D. 1064 and continued intermittently until A.D. 1250 (Shoemaker 1977). The post-eruptive Sinagua population was not the result of a land rush according to Pilles (1979:479), but rather "a shift of the indigenous population to a different resource zone."

While there may have been an increase in the Sinagua population after the eruptions, Pilles (1979:480) believed that earlier estimates were exaggerated and that these changes were "probably more influenced by new environmental, sociological, and climatic conditions."

Nevertheless, defensible sites did appear in the Sinagua area in the twelfth century. These were often built with defensive walls on the rugged crests of cinder cones (Colton 1946:66–7; DeBoer 1980:119) or on the necks of buttes formed by stream meanders such as in Walnut Canyon (Euler 1964:1).

Water control devices, primarily check dams, were constructed by Sinagua farmers from ca. A.D. 950 to 1200, but apparently were only minor adjuncts to the agricultural economy (DeBoer 1980:120).

It has also been suggested that, about A.D. 1130, there is evidence at Sinagua sites for a "significant increase of variability in mortuary ritual" and that this date marked the beginning of "new trade networks, population aggregation, and the intensification of agricultural pursuits" (Hohmann 1983:74).

The Winslow and Hopi Buttes area

Portions of the Little Colorado high desert south of Black Mesa and north of the Little Colorado River were occupied by those Anasazi often referred to as of the Winslow tradition. This was a minor and little-known culture that seems to have had its genesis in a Kayenta base and became distinctive like the Virgin tradition, about A.D. 900. Before that time, the area was very sparsely occupied by Kayenta peoples. By A.D. 900, however, the population expanded and developed a distinctive architectural and ceramic style (Gumerman and Skinner 1968). The Little Colorado desert has no major streams except for the Little Colorado River itself. Consequently, the settlement pattern was one of many small, dispersed communities situated to take advantage of the localized water sources and arable land of the region. Unlike most other Kayenta traditions, the Winslow people constructed a few specialized sites as ceremonial centers, with great kivas, which apparently served as integrators for this dispersed group (Gumerman 1968, 1983). Population increased dramatically after A.D. 1050 (Gumerman 1975) and continued to expand until approximately A.D. 1250, when it was no longer possible to sustain inhabitants in this largely arid desert area away from the river proper, and the region was abandoned (Gumerman 1983:10). The Winslow people moved to areas adjacent to the Little Colorado River, such as the Homolovi ruins, or to the Hopi Mesas where there were more dependable water supplies.

The Upper Little Colorado River area

In this region of eastern Arizona, there was a mixed Chaco Anasazi and Mogollon occupation. Longacre (1964:203–11) provided a brief synopsis of the culture history of this region in which, following a long occupation by people of the 1500 B.C. to A.D. 300 Concho Complex, he saw the period from A.D. 300 to 500 as one in which the indigenous population was low. The inhabitants farmed and lived in small villages of shallow pithouses, each with an associated storage pit. During the next 200 years, farming became a dominant pursuit and sites were located in or near valleys by fertile flood plains. Population remained stable, but began to increase between A.D. 700 and 900 when villages of twelve to fifteen pithouses were common. From A.D. 900 to 1100, the first above-ground architecture and great kivas came into vogue. Following that, from A.D. 1100 to 1300, sites were located primarily along major streams. These villages were mostly large masonry pueblos. By A.D. 1450, most of the area had been abandoned except for two major stream valleys, the Little Colorado and Silver Creek. There the population clustered in large villages of 50 to 100 rooms each.

At least one defensive site, Casa Malpais (Danson and Malde 1950), may have been constructed during this period although more recent dendrochronological data would suggest a building date in the late 1200s (Dean, personal communication); another, in a similar high position, near St. Johns, may also have been defensive (Beeson 1966:199).

Longacre's (1964:206) postulated population curve, based upon the number of sites multiplied by the mean number of rooms per phase, illustrates this development quite clearly, with the greatest number of inhabitants ca. A.D. 1150 followed by a rather rapid decline.

Hay Hollow Valley

One area of the upper Little Colorado River Valley that has been intensively studied is the Hay Hollow Valley. While Plog (1974:36) believed that its chronology was different from that of the Upper Little Colorado (Longacre 1964), his "phases" appear to be quite similar and his Hay Hollow population curve generally typifies "the population changes for the Upper Little Colorado Region" (Plog 1974:93). Plog (1974:37–40) suggested that between 1500 B.C. and A.D. 300, there was a low population concerned more with hunting and gathering than with horticulture. Sites were located on the valley floor with nuclear families occupying each pit house. About A.D. 1, settlements were few and small (Plog, Hill, and Read 1976:149). From A.D. 300 to 500, pithouse villages were constructed on mesa tops. While Plog (1974:37–40) postulated a low population for this period, elsewhere (Plog, Hill and Read 1976:149) he noted that sites consisted of large 50- to 75-room pithouse villages. In any event, the "peak of the population for the Basketmaker culture was reached at about A.D. 400" (Plog 1974:94).

The time between A.D. 500 and 750 (Plog 1974:37–40) or 800 (p. 97), was marked by pithouse settlements again located on the valley floor. Perhaps, however, there were seasonal shifts in these patterns. The population apparently decreased and then stabilized.

Pithouse villages and surface masonry pueblos, an architectural innovation, marked the period of A.D. 750 to 900. While 40 settlements have been recorded in Hay Hollow Valley at this time, there appear to have been no central sites; each was the residence of more than one nuclear family, perhaps small matrilocal units.

Population began to rise and between A.D. 900 and 1100 there were more sites and more habitation rooms. Large sites with a mean number of seventeen rooms each, perhaps occupied by multiple lineages, were surrounded by smaller sites and field houses. Irrigation ditches were dug and agriculture loomed large in the economy.

From A.D. 1100 to 1400 there were fewer but larger sites in Hay Hollow. Pueblos of 100 to 300 rooms (Plog, Hill, and Read 1976:149), such as Broken K, were scattered over the region. The population was beginning to decline, however, and by A.D. 1350, the valley was abandoned even though the Upper Little Colorado region was occupied for another century and a half (Plog 1974:37–40).

Plog (1975:101) has postulated that this abandonment was brought about by a growing population expanding into marginal areas. The society, he believed, was still experimenting with its subsistence strategies to the extent that slight environmental shifts may have caused the population to leave.

Chevelon

Some 50 miles west of the Hay Hollow Valley, along the Chevelon Creek drainage, the "evolutionary trajectory of the populations" (Plog, Hill, and Read 1976:149) was different from that in the Upper Little Colorado River region. Here, at elevations varying from 5495 feet (1675 m) to 8989 feet (2740 m), the population remained low and scattered until ca. A.D. 700 to 800 (Plog, Hill, and Read 1976:150). The few pithouses and small villages occupied about A.D. 200 to 300 grew in size, however, between A.D. 500 and 700 (Plog 1978:55). After A.D. 800, the dominant settlement appears to have been limited to one or two U-shaped structures (Plog, Hill, and Read 1976:150), although by A.D. 1050, small sites, pithouses or slab-based structures, were built "in every conceivable location" (Plog 1978:55). During this same time, site densities shifted south to higher elevations. About A.D. 1150 to 1250 "defensive" masonry sites were built on rincons in Chevelon Canyon (F. Plog, personal communication).

The period from A.D. 1050 to 1250 saw the greatest numbers of sites in the Chevelon drainage. Pueblos of five to ten rooms, and then of ten to 40 rooms were constructed.

Abandonment of the area came ca. A.D. 1300. The inhabitants moved either south of the Mogollon rim or to large sites such as Chevelon Ruin along the Little Colorado River.

Canyon de Chelly

According to a recent synthesis, sites in Canyon de Chelly and the adjacent uplands of the Defiance Plateau often reveal "components of Chaco, Kayenta, and Mesa Verde Anasazi" (McDonald 1976:58). A few structures in the lower sections of the canyon were occupied from about 200 B.C. to A.D. 400. At some of these sites, burials indicated a violent death for the inhabitants, perhaps indicative of hostilities (p. 37). Shortly after A.D. 500, there was a movement up Canyon de Chelly as well as to the uplands of the Defiance Plateau. From ca. A.D. 700 to

900, there was an increase in population in the canyon proper (p. 49). On the plateau, while there was a heavy early use, almost no sites have been recorded from A.D. 700 to shortly after 900. Plateau population increased markedly, however, between A.D. 1000 and 1100 (McDonald 1976:54) or A.D. 1050 and 1150 (Morris 1983). The Defiance Plateau was abandoned some time about A.D. 1140 and the people returned to the canyon bottoms. The largest population in the canyon appears to have been between A.D. 1140 and 1300 according to McDonald (1976:59), followed by general Anasazi abandonment ca. A.D. 1300. At Antelope House, construction increased markedly about A.D. 1140 and the site was abandoned by A.D. 1270 (Morris 1979:865–6). Morris (1983) has noted that the century preceding A.D. 1150 in de Chelly was marked by rapid population growth followed by an extended decline that culminated in the A.D. 1300 abandonment. Exchange and perhaps other contacts with Mesa Verde and Chaco took place from about A.D. 1200 to 1270.

Cedar Mesa

Cedar Mesa is an area of some 500 square miles (1295 km^2) north of the San Juan River. At its north end, the elevation of the mesa is about 7000 feet (2134 m), sloping west and east to about 5320 feet (1622 m) (Lipe and Matson 1971:126).

Anasazi occupation there began ca. A.D. 200 and sites of that period until ca. A.D. 400 were numerous near the mesa rims (Matson and Lipe 1978:3). Then the mesa was abandoned until the late 600s when Anasazi returned in small numbers. There is, however, an increase in sites of this period as one goes north and east on the mesa "where there is more effective moisture" (Matson and Lipe 1978:6–7). About A.D. 750 there was total abandonment again until about A.D. 1080 to 1100.

From then until A.D. 1150, there was an intensive occupation of Cedar Mesa by both Mesa Verde and Kayenta peoples. Shortly after that date, and certainly by A.D. 1200, however, the Kayenta had left. Only sites of the Mesa Verde tradition were inhabited from then until final Anasazi abandonment ca. A.D. 1270. Some of these were relatively large structures containing 20 to 30 units, some of which were situated in defensible locations (Matson and Lipe 1978:9–10).

Elk Ridge

Immediately north of Cedar Mesa is Elk Ridge, with an elevational range from 6500 feet (1981 m) to 8000 feet (2438 m). Here, some 2000 sites have been recorded. Ceramic data indicate close ties to the Mesa Verde although the occupation "appears to be some blend or mix of Kayenta and Mesa Verde" (DeBloois and Green 1978:13).

While there are no firm dates for an early occupation, pre-A.D. 700 "remains occur in low frequencies" (p. 13). From ca. A.D. 700 to 900 "there was a dramatic increase in the number of sites in the Elk Ridge area" (p. 14) but in the ensuing period from A.D. 900 to 1100 "there is a marked decrease in site densities" (p. 13). From A.D. 1100 to 1260 "the number of sites again decreases but there is also an increase in site size" (p. 13). The Anasazi apparently abandoned Elk Ridge about A.D. 1260.

The Red Rock Plateau

West of Cedar Mesa and Elk Ridge, in the triangle formed by the San Juan and Colorado rivers, lies the Red Rock Plateau. This is an environmentally marginal area, generally less than 5500 feet (1676 m) elevation, consisting of exposed bedrock and sand but dissected by many canyons containing arable soils and ample water. Within this region, Anasazi occupation was sparse during three periods which were interrupted by periods of total abandonment (Lipe 1970).

From ca. A.D. 200 to 300 there was a small occupation, perhaps no more than a single small band in the canyons. Farming was carried on at this time, but hunting and gathering were also important, more so than in later periods. Following that brief utilization, the area was abandoned until ca. A.D. 1100, when Kayenta peoples occupied the broad canyon bottoms. Sites consisted of small residences of two to three nuclear families each.

About A.D. 1150, the area was again abandoned for 50 to 60 years (Lipe 1970:113). Then, ca. A.D. 1210 to 1260, both Kayenta and Mesa Verde peoples moved to the broad canyon bottoms as well as to the deeper narrower and more inaccessible canyons. At least four defensive sites have been recorded in the Lake Canyon area for this period (Lipe 1970:111). After abandonment by the Anasazi, Red Rock Plateau was visited sporadically by the Hopi from ca. A.D. 1300 to 1600 (p. 137).

211

The Mesa Verde region

While distinctions between the Mesa Verde and Chaco Anasazi traditions are no longer defined as sharply as they were a few years ago, archaeologists attempting syntheses of the Mesa Verde usually mean the Mesa Verde proper, and when they do similar summaries for Chaco, they usually refer to Chaco Canyon itself. When Chaco "traits" such as great kivas are found in the Mesa Verde area, it is usually suggested that Chaco people moved there. When Mesa Verde "traits" such as distinctive masonry or ceramics have been found in Chaco, it is thought that Mesa Verde people migrated there. This might have been the case, but in recent years such movement has been questioned. In the past it was also assumed that boundaries between the two, generally along the San Juan River, were sharp. Current thinking (Judge, personal communication; Rohn, personal communication) suggests that the geographical and cultural boundaries may not have been so precise, that movements of people may not have been so clear-cut, and that traits such as great kivas or distinctive masonry styles may not have been restricted to one or the other tradition.

Therefore, I shall refer primarily to the Mesa Verde and the Chaco as two broad regions. Perhaps they could more properly be termed the Northern and Southern San Juan. Indeed, Nickens and Hull (1980:148) and Rohn (1983) have suggested that Mesa Verde is but a portion of the Northern San Juan.

The Mesa Verde region has received considerable attention in recent years. Studies by the University of Colorado (Breternitz 1973; Lister 1966), the Wetherill Mesa Project (Hayes 1964), those on Chapin Mesa (Rohn 1977), and in the Montezuma Valley north of the Mesa Verde itself (Rohn 1975) have added to our knowledge of the culture history of those Anasazi living north of the San Juan. More data in the near future will come from the work of the Dolores Archaeological Project (Kane 1979).

From the first to the early fourth century A.D. Anasazi were established in the Animas River Valley north of Durango (Morris and Burgh 1954:85). These Indians lived in structures with a cribbed wall and roof construction, but otherwise were similar to other Anasazi of this period.

In the sixth century A.D. there was a geographical spread of Mesa Verde people, and Mesa Verde itself was occupied in the last quarter of that century (Breternitz 1973:9). In the middle 600s, there appears to have been an influx of people to the Mesa. Pithouse sites consisting of seven to eight structures per village were situated on low ridges of the Mesa. From A.D. 700 to 900, these sites were near areas of abundant arable soils (Cordell 1981:123). In the Montezuma Valley north of Mesa Verde, a number of sites of the seventh century A.D. period have been recorded. Some were encircled by stockades (Rohn 1975) which may indicate defense.

Recent surveys between the Animas and La Plata rivers south of the La Plata Mountains have demonstrated a fairly dense occupation of that highland area between ca. A.D. 750 and 880, and very little utilization after that date (Ware 1981:25).

Most archaeologists who have worked in the Mesa Verde area agree that there was a transition ca. A.D. 750. In the succeeding period more sites, including surface jacal structures, were occupied on the Mesa. Structures were built on low ridges in a loose L-shaped plan similar to that of Site 13 on Alkalai Ridge (Brew 1946; Hayes 1964:89; Rohn 1977:235). Between about A.D. 900 and 975, sites on Wetherill Mesa were smaller and more widely dispersed among various landforms. From A.D. 970 to 1050, sites were fewer in number and more widely scattered (Cordell 1981:124).

North of the Mesa Verde, in the area from Hovenweep east across the Montezuma Valley to the rim of Dolores Canyon, we see a clearer pattern of settlement dynamics. In the Hovenweep area at about 5500 feet (1676 m) there appears to have been virtually no occupation ca. A.D. 750 to 900. East of there, in the Montezuma Valley at about 6800 feet (2073 m) this period saw a moderate utilization. Still farther east and at the higher elevation of 7800 feet (2377 m), there was a much greater settlement at this time (Rohn, personal communication).

In the Dolores River Valley, Anasazi occupation appears to have been limited to the A.D. 650 to 1150 period. Population estimates have been derived by two methods: household clusters and rubble/pithouse areas (Kane, Orcutt, and Kohler 1982). The first of these indicates a low population until ca. A.D. 775, then a rapid climb to A.D. 850 to 900, and an equally rapid decline by A.D. 950. The second approach projects a relatively smooth and steep increase from A.D. 600 to ca. A.D. 875, a sharp decline to A.D. 1000, and a very minor increase to ca. A.D. 1150, with abandonment at ca. A.D. 1200. Obviously, one of these reconstructions must be in error. Earlier, Orcutt (1981) had indicated a Dolores area population of about 1500 people between A.D. 650 and 850, increasing to 2300 between A.D. 850 and 975, and dropping precipitously to about 250 between A.D. 1050 and 1150. She also graphed population against elevation. For the same three time periods, in the earliest, the greatest number of people lived at between 6850 (2088 m) and 6950 feet (2118 m); for the middle period, the most people lived at a slightly lower elevation, between 6750 (2057 m) and 6850 feet (2088 m); for the last period, when the Dolores area population had declined dramatically, the maximum population, numbering not more than 250 individuals, stayed at the same elevation. It should be noted that I have only had access to Orcutt's (1981) graphs, not the rationale behind them.

More recently, Kane (1983:31) has suggested that ca. A.D. 975 "there was a rapid population exodus" from along the Dolores River in what he termed the Escalante Sector in the Yellowjacket District of the Mesa Verde Region. Subsequently, ca. A.D. 1050–1200, there were "low population levels" presumably culminating in abandonment about A.D. 1200.

From A.D. 900 to 1100, much of the Mesa Verde region was occupied. Surface jacal structures continued to be used as well as some masonry. Kivas were built. The Ewing site in the Montezuma Valley, the only completely excavated settlement of this period in the Mesa Verde area, revealed a group of two unit pueblos and three kivas surrounded by a "post stockade" and was built on the crest of a low ridge (Rohn 1983:13). Water and soil control devices such as reservoirs, terraces, and check dams were constructed on the Mesa Verde and elsewhere in the northern San Juan and continued to be used until abandonment (Hayes 1964:76–81; Herold 1961:102ff). The Mummy Lake reservoir and related ditch system may have been built in the tenth and used through the twelfth century (Rohn 1963, 1972). Irrigation appears to be directly correlated with population increase (Herold 1961:121).

According to Hayes (1964:109), data from Wetherill Mesa indicate that the maximum Mesa Verde population was reached at this time. Rohn (1977), viewing demographic trends from Chapin Mesa, however, is of the opinion that the A.D. 750 to 900 period saw a continuing increase in population, with a maximum not being reached until ca. A.D. 1250.

Hayes and Rohn are not in agreement regarding certain aspects of

214

succeeding periods either. Hayes (1964:94, 109) postulated a period from ca. A.D. 950 to 1075 with a continuing decrease in population. Rohn (1977:238–40) suggested a time from ca. A.D. 1000 to 1100, when much of the Montezuma Valley was inhabited, as was the Mesa Verde proper. Reservoirs, stone check dams, terraces, and small field houses were "definitely in use" (Rohn 1977:239) and, for the first time, "actual occupation of the northern [higher] portions of Chapin Mesa" (Rohn 1977:240) took place both on the mesa top and on benches in the canyon bottoms. Rohn also postulated that, since these are some of the least desirable agricultural lands, "their use may indicate population pressure on the better lands or their partial destruction through erosion" (p. 240). Soon after A.D. 1100, people were moving into cliff dwellings in Johnson Canyon, a southern section of the Mesa Verde. There, a suite of 299 dated tree-ring samples indicates two distinct periods of construction, from the 1130s to about 1160 and from about 1195 to 1215 with construction ending and abandonment of Johnson Canyon occurring about A.D. 1240 (Nickens 1981:17).

From A.D. 1100 to 1200 (Rohn 1977:241), on the Mesa and in the Montezuma Valley there was a greater population than in the Dolores area (Rohn, personal communication). On the Mesa, sites were located toward the ends of low ridges closer to the rim. Some cave or rockshelter sites were occupied as, indeed, they had been earlier. Architecturally there was a more formalized site pattern with each community often housed within a single multiroom and multikiva structure. Ceremonial buildings, such as towers, began to be constructed.

Hayes (1964:94), again basing his reconstruction on the Wetherill Mesa survey, has postulated that the time from A.D. 1050 to 1150 saw the construction of unit pueblos, fewer but larger sites, and a continuing decrease in population.

A potentially significant development took place in the Hovenweep area ca. A.D. 1150. There, sites were built at the heads of box canyons near springs. The inhabitants constructed rock and earthen dams in the drainages above these springs, presumably to catch runoff that would then percolate through the sandstone to recharge the springs below (Rohn 1972). Similar construction was also carried out on Chapin Mesa at the same time (Rohn, personal communication).

In the survey reports of Hayes (1964) and Rohn (1977), there is again a minor disagreement as to the commencement of the latest occupation of the region. Hayes suggested (p. 100) that this took place from A.D. 1150

215

to 1300, while Rohn (p. 243) placed it totally within the thirteenth century.

Obviously, on the Mesa, this was a period of movement into the cliffs on its south end; on Wetherill Mesa, only 33 per cent of the latest sites were on the mesa top (Hayes 1964:100) and most of these were ceremonial structures (Rohn 1977:243).

There is little direct evidence for defensive sites during this period; Cattanach (1980:415) considered "a low wall or defensive 'breastwork', with 21 loopholes" at Long House to have been such.

What many students of the Mesa Verde Anasazi overlook is that, during the thirteenth century, dozens of very large open sites were inhabited in the Montezuma Valley. These include Goodman Point, Mud Springs, Toltec Ruin, Yucca House, Lowry Ruin, Wilson Ruin, Cannonball Ruin, Easter Ruin, and Yellow Jacket Ruin to name several. Yellow Jacket, to give an example of size of sites in this area, is at least one-half mile long by one-quarter mile wide (0.8 × 0.4 km) and contains one great kiva and at least 103 smaller kiva depressions. The largest of these sites may have begun to function as ceremonial centers possibly in conjunction with great kivas and/or tri-walled structures (Rohn 1981). Clearly, this must have been the time of greatest population in the Mesa Verde area as a whole (Rohn 1983:25).

By A.D. 1300, as in so many Anasazi areas, the Mesa Verde region was abandoned.

The Chaco region

In spite of the tremendous archaeological effort expended in the Chaco Canyon area and its environs, the cultural and demographic dynamics of its Anasazi inhabitants remain, if not obscure, at least confusing.

Most of the research has been done in Chaco Canyon proper, with the exception of a project along the lower Chaco River (Reher 1977) and a recent study of a larger area of the San Juan Basin (Gillespie and Powers 1983).

The latter is based upon a computerized data bank of 28,000 sites recorded from 8 to 10 per cent of the area of the Basin. Elevational correlations indicate that from A.D. 500 to 750, 54 per cent of the sites were located between 6000 and 6600 feet (1829 and 2012 m) and 36 per cent between 5400 and 6000 feet (1646 and 1829 m). From A.D. 750 to 900, 14 per cent of the sites were at an altitude of 6600 to 7200 feet (2012

216

to 2195 m), 59 per cent from 6000 to 6600 feet (1829 to 2012 m), and 22 per cent from 5400 to 6000 feet (1646 to 1829 m). During the period from A.D. 900 to 1100, 6 per cent of the habitation structures were at an elevation of more than 7200 feet (2195 m), 20 per cent from 6600 to 7200 feet (2012 to 2195 m), 34 per cent from 6000 to 6600 feet (1829 to 2012 m), and 3 per cent from 5400 to 6000 feet (1646 to 1829 m). Later, between A.D. 1100 and 1300, 5 per cent of the sites were above 7200 feet (2195 m), 23 per cent were at 6600 to 7200 feet (2012 to 2195 m), 40 per cent were from 6000 to 6600 feet (1829 to 2012 m), and 25 per cent from 5400 to 6000 feet (1646 to 1829 m).

Four areas of the San Juan Basin (Chuska Valley, Chaco, Rio Puerco East, and Rio San Jose) had large Anasazi populations from A.D. 900 to 1100, followed by a decrease in the ensuing two centuries. These preliminary data (Gillespie and Powers 1983) may, however, be skewed by variations in survey intensity throughout the Basin. The authors noted that the land between 5400 and 6600 feet (1646 and 2012 m) contains 90 per cent of the sites occupied from A.D. 500 to 750 and 65 per cent of structures in use from A.D. 1100 to 1300. When two intensively surveyed regions (Chuska Valley and Chaco) are removed from this tabulation, the other two areas contain but 68 per cent of the A.D. 500 to 750 sites, 56 per cent of those built between A.D. 750 and 900, 38 per cent between A.D. 900 and 1100, and 44 per cent A.D. 1100 and 1300.

The Chaco proper and its outliers yield more A.D. 750 to 900 sites in lower elevations near to floodwater farming locations and here actual movement of people may have been no more than 1 km, and 100 to several hundred feet (30 to ca. 200 m) in elevation.

On the Rio Puerco, according to Gillespie and Powers (1983), settlement from A.D. 500 to 900 was along the drainage, although Irwin-Williams (1983) indicates that it was in the uplands.

Sites occupied from A.D. 750 to 900 were often at higher elevations, such as on Barker Dome in the San Juan–Animas area, presumably where dry farming was carried on.

Site frequency throughout the San Juan Basin doubled from the A.D. 500–750 period to the subsequent A.D. 750–900 time span. It then tripled in the A.D. 900 to 1100 period and then dropped by 32 per cent between 1100 and 1300 although site construction continued to increase at least until A.D. 1130. "By as early as A.D. 1150, and certainly by 1175, numerous sites and even entire communities were

217

abandoned" (Gillespie and Powers 1983). After that time, the better watered San Juan–Animas area loomed more significant than did the Chaco Canyon. There was a resurgence in site construction in the middle 1200s, especially in areas where floodwater farming could be successful as well as in scattered highlands at 7000 feet (2134 m) or higher.

Chaco Canyon itself is incised some 400 to 500 feet (121 to 152 m) in the Chaco Plateau for a distance of about 20 miles (32 km) at an elevation of about 6000 feet (1829 m) (Hayes 1981:2). In this area, the earliest evidence of Anasazi culture, "characteristic Basketmaker II remains," may have occurred as early as 950 B.C. (Mathews and Neller 1979:873).

The results of an intensive survey of Chaco Canyon (Hayes 1981) indicate that pithouse villages were in use ca. A.D. 450 to 500 and continued to be so until A.D. 700 or 750 (p. 23). Some 135 such sites have been recorded.

During the succeeding period, from ca. A.D. 750 to 900, there appear to have been "gradual but significant changes in housing arrangements" (pp. 24–5) which set a pattern of stability for the next 600 years. 373 sites of this time range have been recorded. At the same time, there was a decreased use of the mesas surrounding Chaco Canyon and by ca. A.D. 1100 most sites were located in the bottomlands (Judge et al. 1981:70). Apparently, the early components of Chaco culture developed in essentially the same way as did the manifestations of those time periods elsewhere on the Colorado Plateaus.

From ca. A.D. 900 to 975, 353 sites are known, and these were distributed much as structures were in the preceding period. There were, in general, fewer but larger communities. Indications are that the site frequency stabilized but the population continued to increase (p. 70).

About A.D. 925 to 1050, construction began on the large towns and there was an "emergence of what apparently was a new and adaptive system in Chaco in the early 900s" (p. 76). According to Judge and his colleagues, moisture conditions "may have been improving during the tenth century" (p. 77) and the Chacoans may have increased the amount of acreage under cultivation by expanding into marginal areas (pp. 77–8).

Hayes (1981:29) has reported that this development ("some new stimulus") did not take place until ca. A.D. 1050. He believed that this was the time of beginning of construction of multi-storied pueblos contemporaneous with the habitation of smaller sites across the canyon, (p. 30), in spite of tree-ring evidence that early building of Pueblo Bonito began in A.D. 919 (Robinson, Harrill, and Warren 1974).

Elsewhere, Hayes (1981:55) reported that between A.D. 1030 and 1100, a large assemblage of new traits was introduced to Chaco. Certainly, this period saw the greatest development of multi-storied towns, roads, water control devices, and separate ceremonial centers in Chaco. Some 50 or more Chacoan "outliers" were probably built during this period also (Judge *et al.* 1981:88).

The water control devices were particularly elaborate and consisted of canals, reservoirs, dams, grid borders, and farming terraces (Vivian 1970:69–73). These were individual community enterprises that began "sometime after A.D. 1000" (p. 75) or slightly earlier in the early tenth century (Vivian 1983).

Judge and his associates (1981:81) have suggested that the large towns of Una Vida, Pueblo Bonito, and Penasco Blanco were built to serve as redistributive centers in the early part of the tenth century. An alternative model has been proposed by Vivian (1983). He suggests that these so-called "central places" were constructed to control agricultural land and water resources and that these and Chacoan outliers were built to redistribute population rather than food.

Windes (1981) "suggests a relatively low population [perhaps 2000 or less] existed in towns, perhaps at times intermittently or seasonally" and that the period from A.D. 900 to 1050 was the most populous period for the Chaco (Windes 1982).

Hayes (1981:32–4) reported a decreasing population in Chaco Canyon in the late 1100s, Mesa Verde people coming to the Canyon (p. 68), and abandonment in the 1300s. The most recent work in Chaco has generated a model of a late Chacoan occupation from A.D. 1125 to 1225 and a Mesa Verde incursion from A.D. 1225 to 1300. One of the late sites has a date (presumably archaeomagnetic) for occupation at that unit of A.D. 1250 ± 28 (Judge *et al.* 1981:71; Toll, Windes, and McKenna 1980:95). Similar sites have heretofore been assigned to a later Mesa Verde occupation. This has been rejected, however, with the suggestion that the ceramics, showing affinities to the Chuska Valley and Mesa Verde, indicate merely a change in extant ceramic patterns and an economic shift to the San Juan Basin (Toll, Windes, and McKenna 1980:114).

Much of the dating of these supposed post-A.D. 1125 occupations, whether Chacoan or Mesa Verdean, is based on archaeomagnetic determinations. These fly in the face of careful tree-ring dating which indicates that the building boom in Chaco of the last half of the eleventh century had essentially ended by ca. A.D. 1140 (Robinson, Harrill, and Warren 1974).

To add to the confusion generated by archaeologists involved in the most recent and intensive work in Chaco, there is a suggestion that the Mesa Verde reoccupants by A.D. 1300 had moved to "fortified sites" on Chacra Mesa to the east, where they resided until not later than A.D. 1400 (Vivian, written communication 1970). In any event, the Chaco was abandoned by the Anasazi and not again occupied until Navajos entered the area ca. A.D. 1700 (Hayes 1981:34).

The Zuni area

This region was one of the few reaches of the Colorado Plateaus that was not abandoned in prehistoric times. While the early occupation prior to A.D. 1000 is not well known, pithouse villages occur in the lower, western portions of the area. About A.D. 1000 a major change in settlements took place with surface pueblos tending to replace subsurface dwellings. Some of the larger sites exhibit architectural characteristics of Chacoan Outliers (Anyon and Ferguson 1983:4). There appears to have been a move to higher valleys and uplands about 6000 feet (1829 m). The period from A.D. 1000 to 1175 is characterized by the occupation of a great number of small sites in an extensive range of topographical and geographical locations, many on alluvial terraces and stabilized sand dunes. It is suggested that this was a gradually expanding population with a mobile agricultural strategy (Anyon and Ferguson 1983:12).

About A.D. 1200, there was a movement to areas above 7000 feet (2134 m) and hundreds of structures averaging ten to twenty rooms were built in the high valleys (p. 4).

By A.D. 1275, there was a "nucleation of settlements into larger, multi-storied, plaza-oriented pueblos" of 200 to 785 rooms; most other sites were abandoned. Between A.D. 1275 and 1540, over 36 nucleated pueblos were constructed in the Zuni area (p. 5) although there are indications that no more than eight to ten were occupied at any one time; only six were inhabited at the time of Spanish contact in 1540 (p. 6).

Demography and cultural dynamics

After A.D. 1400, "sites in the Zuni area are all located near permanent water sources along drainages with large watersheds" and good irrigable soils (Anyon and Ferguson 1983:10).

The Navajo Reservoir district

Along the San Juan River north of the center of Chaco development and east of the Mesa Verde heartland, intensive survey and excavation were carried out prior to construction of the Navajo Reservoir (Dittert, Hester, and Eddy 1961). Analysis of materials recovered during these and following studies (Eddy 1966) indicated five periods of cultural development from ca. A.D. 1 to A.D. 1000 when the area was abandoned by Anasazi people.

According to Eddy (1974:75–84), from the first through the eighth centuries A.D., settlements were lower down on the river. Eddy's suggested demographic curve indicated a small population present prior to A.D. 750 followed "by a marked explosive increase in number and size of settlements from A.D. 800 to 900" (p. 79). This was also a time when stockades were present at some sites and "large intercommunity kivas" were in use (Eddy 1966:492). Internecine warfare may have existed at this time (Eddy 1983:32). Trade also was extensive (p. 498). Following that, there was "a decided decline in numbers of people and settlements to abandonment of the district after A.D. 1000" (p. 498). Eddy (1974:80–1) has also suggested that about A.D. 800 the bulk of the Anasazi population was located along the San Juan near the mouth of the Pine River. About A.D. 800 to 900 there was a move upriver and by A.D. 900 to 1000 a still higher movement to the Piedra River area. After abandonment of the "reservoir district," there were still further relocations up the Piedra. Chimney Rock Pueblo, a Chacoan outlier, was occupied from A.D. 1076 to 1125 (Eddy 1983:13).

The Middle Puerco

Turning finally to the extreme southeastern section of the Colorado Plateaus, there was a low and relatively stable population in the uplands of tributary drainages between A.D. 795 and 875. In the succeeding 75 years (A.D. 875–950) there was a slight increase in numbers of people but, more importantly, a shift in settlement patterns to locations on colluvial slopes at their junctures with principal valley floors. Agri-

221

cultural check dams aided simple runoff of water to fields (Irwin-Williams 1983).

The construction along the Middle Puerco of a Chacoan outlier in the early tenth century was also marked by the first of "an extensive series of complex water control devices" (Irwin-Williams 1983). These included check dams, contoured terraces, and ditches. Population again increased to the point that by A.D. 1080 to 1100 it was about three times greater than in the early ninth century. After that, from ca. A.D. 1130 to 1180 according to Irwin-Williams (1983), there was a sharp decline and dispersal of the inhabitants, followed late in the twelfth century by some recovery. Between 1180 and 1235 there was again a dramatic increase in numbers of people. After A.D. 1240, however, there was another major decline although labor-intensive irrigation systems were again in use. Some sites reached a size of ca. 90 rooms. By A.D. 1300, the Anasazi abandoned the Rio Puerco Valley (Irwin-Williams 1983). Thus, two population peaks, based upon room counts, are seen: one about A.D. 1100, followed by decline, and a second about A.D. 1225, followed by abandonment.

SUMMARY

Demography

As has been noted earlier, the population estimates presented here are not reflective of absolute figures, but are designed to indicate relative population fluctuations and trends of movements of people, keeping in mind the problems expressed by Powell (Chapter 6 above). I am also aware that populations did not fluctuate in smooth-line curves throughout the region; there were a number of minor fluctuations in each area. It should also be pointed out that there is a close correlation between these curves (Fig. 7.1) and a SARG-generated graph showing number of rooms occupied per 25-year period (Fig. 7.2).

In general, across the Colorado Plateaus, if estimates are correct, population was low from prior to A.D. 1 until A.D. 875 or 900. There are, however, a few exceptions. For example, in Hay Hollow Valley, there was a slight increase ca. A.D. 400, followed by a decrease. On the Rainbow Plateau, an increase in population in both lower and higher elevations took place about A.D. 675, followed by a decrease at A.D. 750. Cedar Mesa apparently had a small population from about A.D.

222

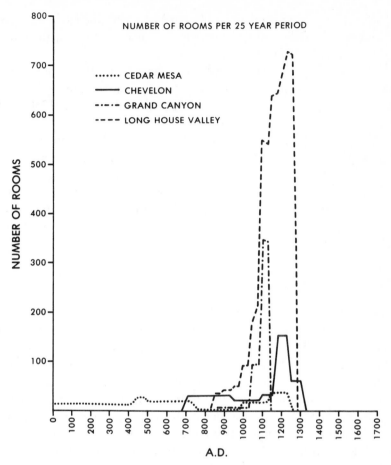

Figure 7.2 Number of rooms per 25-year period.

200 to 400, followed by complete abandonment until ca. A.D. 1050. Again, in general terms, there appears to have been a rather large increase across the Plateaus, especially in the west, about A.D. 1000. Farther east, the population did not peak until ca. A.D. 1200 or 1250. Again, there are some exceptions to this trend. The Rainbow Plateau continued to show anomalies with a low population from A.D. 750 until about A.D. 1100. In Canyon de Chelly, settlement increased in the canyon bottom from ca. A.D. 700 until a peak was reached about 1250, while there was a corresponding decrease in the highlands of the flanking Defiance Plateau from ca. A.D. 750 until 1050. The demo-

graphic picture on the uplands of Cedar Mesa continued to be aberrant. From A.D. 1050 to 1300 there was a reoccupation, with a peak occurring at A.D. 1150.

To the east, in the Mesa Verde and Chaco areas, there continues to be no good agreement regarding population fluctuations. Probably, numbers of people in the Mesa Verde peaked about A.D. 1250 while the high point in the Chaco occurred ca. A.D. 1100.

In northwestern Arizona, including the Grand Canyon, on Black Mesa, the uplands of the Defiance Plateau, the Dolores area, and probably Chaco, the Anasazi had abandoned their territories by A.D. 1150. The Navajo Reservoir area had been vacated by A.D. 1000 or shortly thereafter. Elsewhere, virtually complete depopulation came about by A.D. 1300 except for some sections of the Upper Little Colorado region and Zuni.

Exchange

While trade among the prehistoric Anasazi appears to have been extensive (F. Plog 1983), much discussion in the contemporary literature revolves about "models" (Fry 1980), without presenting empirical data as to what goods were exchanged for what others in return. F. Plog (1983:303), while discussing extensive trade in non-perishable items, also noted that there is a lack of data on subsistence trade and that there are insufficient dates "to determine precisely how episodic extensive trading may have been." It would seem, however, that there was substantial exchange activity in the ninth, eleventh, and fourteenth centuries. Upham (1982) and F. Plog (1984) based their concept of prehistoric alliances in part on exchange, especially during periods of high spatial environmental variability. Upham and his colleagues (Upham, Lightfoot, and Feinman 1981) have noted, in addition, regional exchange in the Little Colorado and Navajo Reservoir area as early as ca. A.D. 400 and increasing through time. Upham (1983:230) has also suggested that "agricultural intensification and expanding regional exchange were processes that occurred concurrently" in the Chavez Pass region between A.D. 1110 and 1300. Lightfoot (1979:322–3) suggested that economic sharing, based upon ceramic design and petrographic analyses, took place between the Winslow and Chevelon areas between about A.D. 1050 and 1250. On Black Mesa, there was a broad and apparently voluminous exchange

224

network between A.D. 800 and 900 (Fernstrom 1980) and again between A.D. 1000 to 1100 (Green 1982, 1985; Deutchman 1980). This appears to have been considerably reduced from then until abandonment about A.D. 1150. This would seem to indicate that there may have been some "local productive uncertainty" followed by the development of "more intensive regional social networks" (Braun and Plog 1982:515).

Storage

The archaeological literature, with few exceptions, does not discuss variability in amounts of functional storage space through time; quantification is very difficult. Obviously, most Anasazi developed some type of storage facilities, such as pits or cists, early in their history. On Black Mesa, to continue using that area as an example, such features were constructed prior to A.D. 1. These, with modifications after the advent of coursed masonry, continued throughout Anasazi occupation of the Plateaus. Undoubtedly, storage capacities varied with different types of stress. Therefore, it is unfortunate that we do not have adequate data from the several geographic and cultural areas discussed earlier in this chapter. We can, however, discuss this phenomenon through time for at least two regions, Black Mesa (Powell 1982) and the Upper Little Colorado (F. Plog, personal communication).

On Black Mesa there are indications of a marked increase in storage facilities about A.D. 875. After that time there was a decline in the number and/or capacities of these until another, even greater expansion was reached about 1050.

In the Upper Little Colorado region, much the same pattern can be seen although slightly later in time. There, storage reached a peak at A.D. 1000, then declined sharply until ca. A.D. 1125, and peaked again at A.D. 1200. As has been noted, storage associated with defensive structures increased in the Glen Canyon area in the late 1100s.

Water control

In many areas of the Anasazi domain one sees evidences of water and soil control devices such as check dams, irrigation ditches, reservoirs, and terraces (Plog and Garrett 1972; Vivian 1974).

They seem to have appeared earliest in the Hay Hollow Valley, ca. A.D. 900. In the Mesa Verde area (Mummy Lake) and along the

225

Middle Puerco, water control systems also may have been constructed in the early 900s (Rohn 1977; Irwin-Williams 1983).

In the west, in Grand Canyon, they are known to date from ca. A.D. 1075. The same is true of Chaco, but in Chaco the water control systems are large-scale rather than small check dams or linear borders (Vivian 1970:75).

In the Kayenta region, ditches are known to have been constructed by A.D. 1150 or 1175, although the reservoirs in Long House Valley date from the early thirteenth century.

While water control mechanisms appeared ca. A.D. 900, they became predominant about A.D. 1150.

Defense

Of all the factors considered here, perhaps the incidence of potentially defensive or defensible sites across the Anasazi territory is most apparent. These, however, do not necessarily indicate the presence of overt hostilities; they may simply be a sign of territorial imperative.

With one or two exceptions, such features are relatively late on the Plateaus. As has been noted, there is some evidence of violent death in Canyon de Chelly as early as ca. A.D. 375. Secondly, if the early stockaded pithouse villages in the Navajo Reservoir District and the Montezuma Valley of the Mesa Verde region reported by Eddy (1966, 1983) and Rohn (1975) were indeed defensible, some hostilities may have been operational there ca. A.D. 850. Defense also seems to have been a factor in the Virgin area at the same time.

Beyond that, the evidence for defense among the Anasazi falls into two later time periods. In the west (Grand Canyon, Cohonina, Sinagua, Chevelon), sites of this nature are seen ca. A.D. 1100. In Glen Canyon they appear during the late 1100s. Farther east (Upper Little Colorado, Long House Valley, Rainbow Plateau, Cedar Mesa, and Mesa Verde), the phenomenon begins about A.D. 1250. At Chaco, defensive sites seem to have been present only on Chacra Mesa post-A.D. 1300.

Thus, it can be seen that defensive structures were common at two distinct periods, A.D. 850 and A.D. 1175.

Large sites and kivas

Much the same can be said for the establishment of large villages, often with many kivas. In the west (Virgin, Upper Little Colorado, Hay

Hollow, Chevelon), these appeared ca. A.D. 1050 to 1100 or slightly earlier. There are some indications that sites of up to 100 houses or more were occupied in the Little Colorado region by A.D. 900 (Upham, Lightfoot, and Feinman 1981:824).

In the east (Long House Valley, Rainbow Plateau, Cedar Mesa, Canyon de Chelly), they are not generally seen until ca. A.D. 1250, although Sambrito Village in the Navajo Reservoir area is an early large site (Eddy 1966).

Chaco is also an exception, where large villages and many kivas, including great kivas, were built ca. A.D. 1050–1100 or slightly earlier. The Mesa Verde area saw the development of large communities such as Far View or those in the Montezuma Valley by A.D. 1050 or 1100 (Rohn, personal communication).

Across the Colorado Plateaus, kivas appear to have been predominant about A.D. 1150.

BROAD PATTERNS

Fred Plog (1983), in a paper that formulated political and economic alliances on the Colorado Plateaus, has suggested that in the period from A.D. 600 to 1450, at least ten broad or strong cultural patterns appeared. It is worthwhile to conclude this chapter with a brief summary of these.

In chronological order, these are as follows:

Adamana

Between ca. A.D. 400 and 700 in the Upper Little Colorado River area there emerged a pattern characterized by shallow pithouses on the tops of mesas. Some of the sites included what have been described as "great houses" (Plog 1983). Ceramics were predominately the paddle-and-anvil Adamana Brown.

White Mound

This broad pattern, which existed from roughly A.D. 775 to 870, is characterized by arc-shaped rows of surface jacal storage rooms, pit-house residences, and a kiva or proto-kiva in front of the arc. Ceramics were of the Kana-a style. This pattern was found in many areas of the

227

Colorado Plateaus and Plog (1983:313) has suggested that it is an indication "of some large organizational entity that tied together the more diverse local populations."

Chaco

This is one of the most obvious of all the broad patterns in the Anasazi area. The large towns in Chaco Canyon and the numerous outliers form a distinct architectural style. These are often connected by an extensive road network. Extensive trade in turquoise, shell, and obsidian was featured. Marked water control systems, essentially in the form of irrigation canals, were also a part of this pattern which existed from about A.D. 950 to 1100.

Little Colorado

As the name implies, this pattern is marked by a distinct group of ceramic types made along the Little Colorado River from about A.D. 1050 to 1150. Other features are less well defined.

Mesa Verde

This broad pattern centering in the northern San Juan area existed from roughly A.D. 1050 to 1300. Architecturally, it is marked by surface masonry pueblos and towers constructed of shaped rectangular sandstone blocks. Ceramics were in a Mesa Verde White Ware tradition. Water and soil control features were very extensive.

Kayenta

Throughout much of northern Arizona and southern Utah from ca. A.D. 1050 to 1150, another distinct pattern is recognizable. Aboveground pueblos, jacal wing units attached to a small group of masonry storage rooms characterize the architecture. Ceramics are marked by both gray/white and red/orange wares. There is no great evidence for extensive trade, and soil/water control features are limited.

Tsegi

The Tsegi alliance occurred in extreme northern Arizona and southern Utah between A.D. 1250 and 1300. It is defined by utilization of cliff dwellings as habitation loci and probably by relatively homogeneous residential units as discussed by Dean (1969). Ceramics were predominantly negative paint black-on-white styles and the "northern polychromes" (Plog, personal communication).

Jeddito

This pattern, between A.D. 1300 and 1450, centers on a series of very large (up to 1000 rooms) pueblos along and near the Little Colorado River in the vicinity of present-day Winslow. Yellow and orange wares characterize the pattern, or alliance, as Upham (1982) has termed it. In aspects of trade and water control systems, the Jeddito area is second in importance only to Chaco.

White Mountain

White Mountain Red Ware is the principal component of this pattern found along the Mogollon Rim and Upper Little Colorado River Valley between A.D. 1250 and 1350. Sites are often large with one or more great kivas. Water control features are found in the lower but not in the higher elevations and Plog (1983:316) suggests that "upland–lowland exchange may have been crucial for these people." Trade in obsidian and shell was common.

Zuni

From ca. A.D. 1350 to the time of Spanish contact, the Zuni area was the center of an alliance marked by glaze-ware ceramics and architecture similar to that of the Little Colorado River Valley (Plog 1983).

The above patterns by Plog may or may not correlate well with the environmental emphasis of other aspects of this volume; that will be discussed in the concluding chapter.

8
Anasazi adaptive strategies: the model, predictions, and results

FRED PLOG, GEORGE J. GUMERMAN,
ROBERT C. EULER, JEFFREY S. DEAN,
RICHARD H. HEVLY, and
THOR N. V. KARLSTROM

INTRODUCTION

This chapter summarizes the various environmental and cultural themes developed in the preceding chapters. The behavioral and environmental models are reviewed, and various behaviors are predicted for broad classes of environmental and demographic conditions. These predictions are then tested against the data.

Our intention is to provide clear and succinct statements of the main issues. For brevity and clarity, we summarize the information in the form of graphs and tables. Many of the issues are comprehensively addressed in the preceding chapters. Statements of the supporting data and arguments appear in Dean *et al.* (1985), a work that contains additional examples of environmental–behavioral correlations of the types developed here.

A GENERAL BEHAVIORAL MODEL

Interaction among three major variable categories – environmental, demographic, and behavioral – is viewed as a means of understanding aspects of systemic cultural change among the Anasazi of the southern Colorado Plateaus (Dean, Chapter 2 above). While recognizing that these variables can be dependent or independent, for our purposes we emphasize the independent qualities of environment and population and the dependent qualities of human behavior. That is, we focus on behavior as a mechanism of adaptation to environmental and population variability.

Boundary conditions that define and regulate a behavioral adaptive system are expressed in terms of a limited definition of carrying capacity that is determined by the interrelationships among the variables of the three categories. Carrying capacity is functionally defined as the number of individuals that can be supported by particular environmental conditions and by a given subsistence technology. Thus, systemic behavioral change is stimulated when the boundary conditions that regulate an adaptive system are transcended by variables from one or more of the three categories. Environmental changes that reduce the carrying capacities of particular habitats or population growth that exceeds carrying-capacity levels are the most common violations of systemic limits.

Crossing carrying-capacity thresholds requires behavioral adaptive responses that either reduce populations to supportable levels or raise carrying-capacity thresholds. Adjustments of the latter sort constitute the kind of systemic sociocultural change of particular interest here. Behavioral variability that occurs within the threshold boundaries of an adaptive system is mainly "stylistic" in nature and constitutes a reservoir of possible different responses to situations in which systemic thresholds are crossed.

Two kinds of limiting variability characterize the environment of the Colorado Plateaus: first, that due to low-frequency natural processes (LFP), which are defined as those having periodicities of greater than 25 years, and secondly, that due to fluctuations caused by high-frequency processes (HFP), which have periods of less than 25 years. Environmental transformations brought about by each have important consequences for the survival of human populations and should stimulate adaptive behavioral responses from those affected. The magnitudes of behavioral responses to LFP and HFP environmental transformations are directly related to the severity and the rates of the changes and to the sizes and densities of the human populations. As populations approach local carrying-capacity thresholds, they become more susceptible to environmental change because relatively minor fluctuations can exceed systemic limits. Thus, primary and secondary LFP or HFP

231

environmental degradational transformations that coincide with high population have greater potential effect on adaptive behavior than do similar changes associated with low population (Powell, Chapter 6 above).

Based on the foregoing considerations, known relationships between LFP and HFP paleoenvironmental variability and prehistoric human population on the southern Colorado Plateaus can be employed to isolate periods of high and low systemic stress. Archaeological data representing these intervals can then be used to evaluate the model.

ENVIRONMENTAL RECONSTRUCTIONS: THE ALLUVIAL HYDROLOGIC RECORD

The chronostratigraphic record of alluvial deposits, terraces, and soils is the major source of information on LFP environmental variability on the Colorado Plateaus for the last two millennia. Basic chronostratigraphic data are translated into reconstructions of past variability in aggradational, erosional, and associated hydrologic conditions by means of theoretical models of process change. This geologic model specifies interactions among the environmental variables of alluviation, erosion, soil formation, and terrace and arroyo or channel morphology. Such models tend to be diachronic or synchronic; the diachronic models are derived from stratigraphic studies of long-range variability in alluvial conditions (Antevs 1952; Bryan 1954; Hack 1942; Haynes 1968; Karlstrom, Chapter 3 above), and the synchronic models are based on short-range studies of contemporary stream behavior and floodplain processes (Cooke and Reeves 1976; Graf 1983; Schumm and Hadley 1957). Explanations based on these models often seem so contradictory that if one model is correct the other must be false (Schumm and Hadley 1957). In reality, however, these models apply to different frequency aspects of the alluvial–hydrologic system. Diachronic models of current stream and floodplain processes describe only the higher-frequency components of the latest of a series of sequent states encompassed by the integrative, lower-frequency synchronic models. Doubtless, other models will be found to apply to other states of the alluvial–hydrologic system when such states are analyzed in greater detail. Lacking critical empirical evidence for all frequency levels of alluvial–hydrologic variability, it seems counterproductive to assert that apparent contradictions between the synchronic and diachronic behavior of alluvial systems invalidate the former, especially in the face of considerable evidence that short-term alluvial behavior is not necessarily representative of the long-term behavior in such systems.

The aggradational and hydrologic reconstructions presented here are based on an explicit model of climatologic–hydrologic–alluvial relationships (Euler *et al.* 1979:1097; E. Karlstrom 1983:329; Karlstrom, Chapter 3 above). Water infiltration into near-surface alluvial groundwater reservoirs is viewed as a critical factor in the operation of the surface hydrologic system. Increased input and retention of water in alluvial groundwater raise water-table levels and, by inhibiting infiltration rates and augmenting surface water supplies by increased spring and seep activity, create conditions favorable for deposition, especially in undissected headwater locales in wider, low-gradient valley segments and at drainage confluences. Under conditions of continuing high groundwater levels and increased sediment yields, the accumulation of sediments is propagated from these nodes throughout the drainage system. General floodplain accretion results when the confines of the drainage channels are repeatedly exceeded by flood levels, and overbank deposition occurs. Decreased groundwater input or retention lowers water tables and increases the susceptibility of floodplain sediments to erosion. Arroyo cutting begins at loci where groundwater depletion is most rapid and where valley floors are constricted and gradients are highest. Usually, floodplain dissection proceeds by the headward cutting of arroyos, although local incision commonly expands from mid-drainage nodes.

Based on Karlstrom's model (Chapter 3 above), chronostratigraphic evidence for channel incision, surface stability, and soil formation is equated with depressed alluvial water tables. Evidence for channel filling, floodplain accretion, and lack of soil development is equated with high groundwater levels. In this way, a stratigraphic record of alternating deposition and erosion of alluvium is translated into a hydroclimatic reconstruction of rising and falling alluvial groundwater levels, which in turn generally reflect rising and falling precipitation ratios.

While other models of aggradation/erosion relationships have been applied in the Southwest (Hall 1977; Love 1980; Graf 1983), the formulation adopted here enjoys substantial empirical support (Euler *et al.* 1979:1100; Karlstrom 1976; Chapter 3 above). Palynological (Hevly, Chapter 4 above) and dendrochronological (Dean, Chapter 5 above) reconstructions favor the causal processes specified by this model. It is also buttressed by the association of soil development with terrace surface stability and arroyo cutting and by sediment trends in alluvial deposits (Karlstrom, Chapter 3 above). Hereford's (1983, 1984) study of recent floodplain accretion and degradation along the Little Colorado River and Paria River provides additional support.

The data used to reconstruct past alluvial variability result from detailed analyses of more than 40 stratigraphic sections in the Black Mesa area. Although channel and terrace morphology, sediment composition, unconformities, and soil horizons specify the structure of the alluvial formations, the temporal placement of depositional units and hiatuses and the correlation of different sections is based on point boundary dates associated with the stratigraphic units (Euler *et al.* 1979:1096–7; T. Karlstrom 1983; Chapter 3 above). Traditional methods of equating stratigraphic units from different localities on the basis of similarities in terrace morphology and sediment composition have not been employed here; cross-correlation is accomplished on the basis of independent temporal placement of sequentially corresponding horizons, indicated by radiocarbon, ceramic, and tree-ring dates. This approach has disclosed temporal correspondences between alluvial units of widely differing thickness and terrace association and has provided a clearer and more consistent picture of alluvial–hydrologic relationships in the study area than is available anywhere else in the Southwest.

The stratigraphic and chronological data are transformed by the hydroclimatic model into reconstructions of hydrologic and aggradation–degradation variability in the Black Mesa area for the last 2000 years (Euler *et al.* 1979, Figures 4 and 5; Hevly and Karlstrom 1974; Karlstrom, Gumerman, and Euler 1974, 1976; T. Karlstrom 1983; Chapter 3 above). These reconstructions are summarized in Figure 8.1A. The aggradation–degradation curve (solid line) represents the

Figure 8.1 Environmental and demographic variability on →
the southern Colorado Plateaus. A indicates hydrologic
fluctuations and changes in flood plain; B primary (solid) and
secondary (dashed) fluctuations in effective moisture reflected
in the pollen data; C decadal tree-growth departures in standard
deviation units; D spatial variability indicated by dendroclimate;
E postulated relative population trends from A.D. 1–1450.

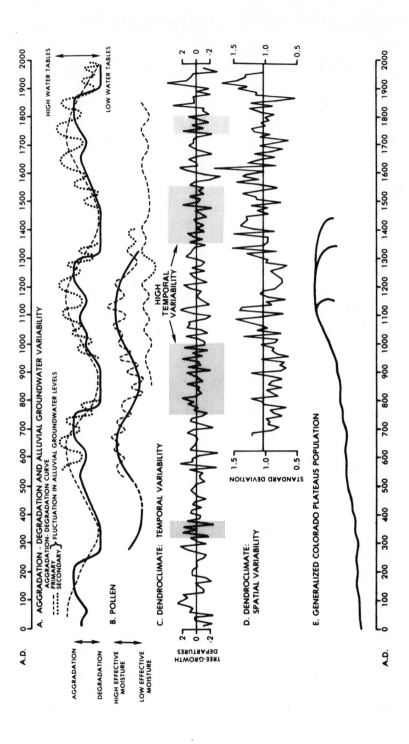

accumulation and erosion of floodplain sediments. Positive slopes denote intervals characterized predominantly by aggradation, while negative slopes indicate periods when degradation was the norm. High and low segments of the curve represent, respectively, high water tables coupled with higher sediment yield and aggradation and low water tables combined with lower sediment yield and degradation. Primary troughs in the curve designate first-order depositional hiatuses when arroyo cutting, terrace surface stability, and weak to moderate soil-formation typified the system. Secondary troughs in the positive segments of the curve indicate second-order depositional interruptions characterized by limited erosion, temporary surface stability, and incipient to weak soil development. Primary (Figure 8.1A, dashed line) and secondary (dotted line) fluctuations in alluvial water tables are also shown. In accordance with the model, the rise and fall of alluvial water tables is depicted as an integrative, smooth, time-transitional process. The differences between the hydrologic and aggradation curves reflect the fact that a temporally continuous process, groundwater fluctuation, can produce a discontinuous series of events, aggradation and degradation, when hydrogeologic threshold conditions are exceeded.

The geographical range encompassed by the Black Mesa area reconstructions (Figure 8.1A) is difficult to assess because of the lack of comparable chronostratigraphic research in other areas. Differences in research orientation, analytical procedures, the number of point boundary dates, and temporal resolution diminish the degree of comparability between the Black Mesa reconstructions and the results of studies in other areas. Parallelisms with other paleoclimatic records of comparable resolution and statistical analysis of regional point boundary dates, however, indicate the general applicability of the Black Mesa sequence throughout the northern Colorado Plateaus and surrounding regions (Karlstrom, Chapter 3 above).

THE POLLEN RECORD

Environmental trends of varied nature, magnitude, and duration may be recognized in the pollen records from alluvial and archaeological sediments from the Colorado Plateaus; however, not all localities yield equally sensitive records, and the records vary as to the relative effects of anthropogenic and climatic factors. Each locality differs in terms of the vegetation surrounding the site of pollen deposition and in other, more remote source areas from which pollen may be derived. Therefore, it is not surprising that different environments yield pollen data of variable utility for reconstructing past conditions and that different pollen statistics must sometimes be developed to suit the particular environmental situation or query. The alluvial and archaeological sediments employed in this study are fragmentary; therefore, temporal continuity of more than a few centuries and temporal overlap from one locality to another are rarely achieved. However, the precision of dating obtainable with tree rings, archaeology, and C-14 makes it possible to compare environmental trends detectable in proxy data like pollen with evidence of environmental change provided by dendroclimatology and geology.

Obvious changes in the proportions of arboreal pollen (AP) relative to nonarboreal pollen (NAP) in alluvial sediments potentially reflect responses of the local plant community to environmental changes (Fall 1981; Hevly, Chapter 4 above; Schoenwetter and Eddy 1964). However, at several localities on and near the southern Colorado Plateaus, these changes can be shown to parallel changes of sediment size and hence potentially reflect relative transport of pollen by water (Hall 1977; Hevly, Chapter 4 above). Examination of nearby archaeological pollen records permits an assessment of these two not necessarily exclusive alternatives.

Archaeological records parallel the alluvial pollen records in most instances, although the proportions of arboreal pollen may differ in archaeological and alluvial contexts (Hevly, Chapter 4 above; Schoenwetter and Eddy 1964). In many instances the archaeological pollen records are dominated by NAP, reflecting in all probability the local plant community, which was certainly disturbed by human activity and is characterized by an enrichment of such pioneer taxa as Cheno–Ams and low spine Compositae. Alluvial pollen records, which are usually characterized by a higher relative abundance of AP, manifest increased relative abundance of NAP during episodes of floodplain stability and/or dissection (Fall 1981; Hall 1977; Hevly, Chapter 4 above). On the other hand, episodes of alluviation contain pollen records exhibiting increased relative abundance of AP and, at least on Black Mesa, also of increased pine in a sum of pine and juniper and of large pine in a sum of all intact pine pollen. While this probably reflects water transport of pollen from upstream sources, the occurrence of contemporaneous increases of pine in sums of pine and juniper in nearby archaeological sites suggests that the production of pine pollen may have been increased as well.

The changes of proportions in various sums of arboreal pollen are not restricted to Black Mesa but occur at other localities as well, e.g., Flagstaff (Elden Pueblo), Canyon de Chelly (Antelope House), Chimney Rock Mesa, Hay Hollow Valley, and the Navajo Reservoir. At some localities, such as Hay Hollow Valley, it is possible to detect arboreal pollen sums in which the component taxa fluctuate through time at different wave lengths (Hevly, Chapter 4 above). One of these, the proportion of small pine in a sum of all pine, parallels the alluvial record of Black Mesa and its associated pollen record (Figure 8.1B, solid line), which is not unlike the temporal variability in dendroclimate, whose wave length spans several centuries (Figure 8.1C). On the other hand, the proportion of all pine in a sum of pine and juniper (Figure 8.1B, dashed line) appears to parallel dendroclimatic amplitude variability, whose trends span at most only a few decades. Similar trends of selected AP indicators may be observed in the pollen records of other sites. The failure of all sites to exhibit identical trends for the same pollen statistics at all periods of time may be related not only to habitat variations but also to spatial variability in climate, as indicated by the dendroclimatic data (Figure 8.1D).

Some pollen statistics cannot be related readily to the dendroclimatic data. On Black Mesa the archaeological AP proportions parallel only generally those of the alluvial record; and during the Lomoki–Toreva phases, which were characterized by increased building activity and presumably increased population as well, they are inverse to alluvial AP proportions and not parallel to the dendroclimatic record. In Hay Hollow Valley a different pollen statistic, the proportion of juniper in a sum of juniper and large pine pollen, also manifests an inverse relationship with archaeological indications of increased population, and is contrary to trends exhibited by other proxy climatic data. Thus the pollen record of these two localities appears to reflect the impact of burgeoning human population, whose effect seems to have been primarily local, since all other data, particularly that from alluvial proveniences, seem to indicate the persistence of vegetation similar to that observed today. Nevertheless, changes did occur in biotic productivity (at least in pollen production and tree growth), alluvial history, and sometimes human settlement pattern and demography. In part these changes resulted from human exploitation of biotic resources as well as disturbance and mineral depletion of soils; but some variation also arose from minor climatic perturbations involving relative effective moisture.

THE TREE-RING RECORD

HFP paleoenvironmental variability on the Colorado Plateaus is monitored by the radial growth of climate-sensitive trees. The annual nature of the rings in Southwestern conifers coupled with synchronous ring-width variation in trees that lived during the same time interval allows the construction of millennia-long composite chronologies with a temporal resolution of one year. Empirically derived and tested models of the relationships between environmental variables and the physiological processes of tree growth (Fritts 1976:231–8) specify the environmental information contained in tree-ring series. Basically, these models indicate a direct relationship with the precipitation and an indirect relationship with the temperature of a fourteen-month "tree year." The tree year, which comprises the twelve months prior to the beginning of growth plus the current growing season, lasts from June 1 of the previous year through July of the current year. Although both relative and quantitative dendroclimatic reconstructions are possible, only the former are available for the prehistoric period throughout the southern Colorado Plateaus.

The dendroclimatic reconstructions used here are based on a specially constructed regional climatic tree-ring chronology that spans the period A.D. 1 to 1970 and encompasses the southern Colorado Plateaus. This chronology combines 23 of the 26 local ring sequences included in the geographical network of stations used by Dean and Robinson (1977) to reconstruct relative spatial and temporal variability in the dendroclimate of the northern Southwest. The regional climatic chronology suppresses local variability in order to exemplify patterns common to the study area as a whole. Although the composite chronology itself is composed of annual increments, the reconstructions used here are expressed in decade units to enhance comparability with other, lower-resolution paleoenvironmental reconstructions.

Three kinds of dendroclimatic variability are illustrated in Figure 8.1. Figure 8.1C depicts the amplitudes of relative dendroclimatic variability as tree-growth departures, which are expressed in standard deviation units. This curve represents the average departure of tree growth

239

from the long-term mean for each decade of the study period. Positive departures represent above-average precipitation; negative values specify below-average precipitation. Departures that fall outside the range of ±1.1 standard deviation units probably represent climatic variations large enough and rare enough to have affected human behavior. The stippling in Figure 8.1C indicates intervals of high temporal variability in dendroclimate, characterized by rapid fluctuations from high to low values. Intervening periods are characterized by greater temporal persistence; that is, change from high to low values is more gradual. Intervals of high and low temporal variability are delineated on the basis of attributes of the composite chronology and of the individual locality sequences of which it is composed. Figure 8.1D illustrates spatial variability in dendroclimate in which intervals of uniform climatic conditions across the region alternate with periods of greater spatial heterogeneity. Spatial variability is measured by calculating the standard deviation of individual station departures on the decade dendroclimatic maps in Dean and Robinson (1977).

ENVIRONMENT, SUBSISTENCE, AND SETTLEMENT ON THE COLORADO PLATEAUS

In Table 8.1, the relationships developed in the preceding chapters between various environmental patterns and selected cultural variables are summarized. Because the hydrologic curve (Figure 8.1A) is a primary index of LFP variability, parts A and B of the table are organized around the four states of that curve: rising groundwater levels, high groundwater levels, falling groundwater levels, and low groundwater levels. Since the same hydrologic state has different implications for valley floors than for upland areas, the conditions in these two zones are considered separately. Each state is characterized in terms of flood heights, channel configuration, the development of alluvial fans and overbank deposits, gradient changes, changes in sediment grain size, and the relation of alluvial to eolian deposition.

Table 8.1B indicates the effects of the hydrological states on perennial and annual plants, trees, animals, agricultural practices, hunting–gathering, the potential of hunting–gathering relative to agriculture, and settlement. Table 8.1C presents probable hydrologic, depositional–erosional, vegetational, faunal, and human subsistence consequences

240

of HFP dendroclimatic amplitude and temporal and spatial variability.

The projected adaptive conditions and consequences outlined in Table 8.1 are offered as hypotheses, the testing of which requires detailed analyses of specific sites and local sequences not feasible at the regional level. For example, a landform that defines uplands in one area may be a lowland form in another area. Similarly, reliance on agricultural resources may be early in one area and late in another. Elsewhere (Dean *et al.* 1985), we suggest some specific tests of this type.

Adaptive mechanisms

Humans employ a large number of behavioral responses to meet environmental contingencies. Many responses, such as weekly or monthly shifts in the subsistence round, leave no easily discernible traces in the archaeological record. Our concern perforce is with strategies likely to leave interpretable evidence in the archaeological record. Even so, Anasazi use of some potentially decisional strategies cannot be pursued for lack of sufficient evidence. Six major categories of strategy (settlement behavior, subsistence mix, interaction, subsistence practices, territoriality, and social integration) are related to each of the following variables: hydrology and effective moisture, relative amplitude of precipitation (wetness/dryness), temporal variability (high/low) of climate, spatial variability of climate, and regional population levels.

Potential effects of the independent environmental and population variables on Anasazi adaptive behavior can be estimated from the relationships delineated in Table 8.1. In Figures 8.2 through 8.9, the predicted effects are expressed in terms of the relative probability – high, moderate, or low – of particular aspects of environmental and population variability stimulating a specific behavioral response. Probability "bands" are superposed on the traces of four environmental variables (aggradation/effective moisture, dendroclimatic amplitude, and temporal and spatial variability in climate) and regional population trends. Dendroclimate amplitude and spatial variability curves are smoothed with running means to emphasize trends that probably have greater regional impact than do the more rapid oscillations shown in Figure 8.1. Determination that a particular independent variable has no effect on a specific behavior – for example, temporal climatic variability in reference to colonization/range expansion (Figure 8.2) – is not arbitrary.

241

Table 8.1. *Summary of environmental conditions and behavioral responses*

A. Groundwater and aggradational relationships

Hydrologic trends	Valley Floors	Upland slopes and surfaces
Rising water tables (Fluvial State 2)	Increasing mean flood heights and lengthening sustained flood regimes; augmented and reactivated springs; straighter, wider, and shallower channels with channel filling and progressively higher episodic overbank deposition on bordering valley bottom surfaces concurrently throughout the drainage net. Alluvial fan development at mouths of tributaries completely or partly dam main stem segments, creating local pond and lake environments or valley floor segments of lower gradients, facilitating aggradation of finer-grained sediments and/or cienega deposits. Actively aggrading valley floors provide important unvegetated source areas for windblown silt and sand deposited downwind on lee slopes and adjacent upland surfaces (cliff-head dunes and loess deposits).	Increasing slope-wash activity; augmented and reactivated springs; increasing saturation of surface sediments approaching or exceeding field capacity – increasing landsliding and gullying of water-saturated, fine-grained sediments. Increasing landslide, slope wash and gullying activity in turn increases sediment yield (Qs) from slopes into valley bottoms, resulting in stream overloading and aggradation. Moderate to steep slopes = Zone I; gentler basal slopes and valley bottoms = Zone II.
High water tables (Fluvial State 3)	Floodplains tend to stabilize in equilibrium with high water-table levels and sustained flood regimes. If effective moisture rates are greater than local transmission and evaporation rates, water tables will continue to rise with accompanying overbank deposition; if less, water tables and surface supplies start falling, accompanied by local dissection and gullying concentrated particularly in areas at steeper valley floor gradients.	Slope processes in equilibrium with water-saturated sediments and higher water-table levels (see above). There may be a tendency toward reduced landsliding and slope wash except during periods of exceptionally prolonged precipitation.

Falling water tables (Fluvial State 4)	Decreasing mean flood heights; lessened sustained flow; initiation and development of arroyos along axial channel segments. More flash floods, increasingly confined to lengthening and widening, progressively more sinuous arroyos, with a corresponding decrease in overbank deposition on bordering valley-floor surfaces. Valley-floor surfaces increasingly subject to revegetation, surface stability, and soil-forming processes. With time, arroyo segments integrate progressively into a continuous arroyo network from lower reaches into tributary heads. Active arroyo-cutting provides a significant part of sediment supply to system with the finest transported downstream and out of the system and with deposition of the coarser bed load fractions on arroyo floors (a-type deposits). Thus valley bottoms located in Zone I and downstream localities with lower gradients and widening channel cross-sections become temporary Zone II's. Stabilized and revegetated valley bottoms deter deflation and removal of sediments by wind action.	Decreasing slope-wash activity, ground saturation, spring flow, landsliding and lowering water-table levels – increasing slope stability and lessening sediment yield (Q_s) to valley bottoms.
Low water tables (Fluvial State 1)	Floodplains and arroyo floors tend to stabilize in equilibrium with lower water-table levels and flash-flood regimes. If effective moisture rates are more than local transmission and evaporation rates, arroyo floors will tend to aggrade; if less, local downcutting and widening will continue. Sediment yield (Q_s) is increasingly derived from arroyo walls and headcuts (Zone I).	Slope processes are in general equilibrium with undersaturated surface sediments and lower water-table levels (see above), minimum slope-wash and landslide activity, and maximum slope stability. Arroyos in valley bottoms extend headward into marginal slope areas.

Table 8.1. *Continued*

B. Vegetational relationships and subsistence potential

Hydrologic trends	Valley Floors	Upland slopes and surfaces
	Away from arroyos, stabilized terraces would support nearly continuous cover by pioneer and early serial vegetation. Reduced growth and pollen production in hygric and riparian components. *Animals*. Browsers displaced; grazers probably persist. *Agricultural potential*. Equal at first to preceding stage. After erosion threshold exceeded, declines rapidly to a level equal to or worse than following stage. *Agricultural practices*. Rainfall and floodwater farming with planting in more limited and less diverse loci. Least likelihood of irrigation. *Settlement patterns*. Rapid and great restriction of location; larger settlements. *Gathering*. Diminishing resources; potential for specialization reduced. *Hunting*. Diminishing resources; potential for specialization reduced. *Hunting–gathering/agriculture*. Decreasing agriculture productivity. Increasing reliance on hunting–gathering.	*Animals*. Browsers probably displaced; changed composition and reduced numbers of grazers. *Agricultural potential*. Diminishing due to lowered water tables and decreased effective moisture. *Agricultural practices*. Rainfall and floodwater farming along stream courses. Progressive abandonment of fields on interdivide alluvial and eolian sediment. *Settlement patterns*. Rapid restriction of location; not necessarily larger settlements. *Gathering*. Diminishing resources. Potential for specialization reduced. *Hunting*. Diminishing resources. Potential for specialization reduced. *Hunting–gathering/agriculture*. Decreasing agricultural productivity. Hunting–gathering more important than agriculture.
Low water tables (Fluvial State 1)	*Nonaggradation*. Stable, continuing on marginal stabilized terrace surfaces. *Trees*. Some junipers established on newly stabilized surfaces in arroyo channels and on stabilized faces of arroyo banks and bordering terrace surfaces. *Perennials and annuals*. Stability, with higher density, cover, and productivity than during previous periods of initial cutting or	*Nondeposition–nonaggradation*. All biota basically similar to above, with continued upslope movement of mesic components and replacement by xeric components.

aggradation. Less density, cover, and productivity than during other "stable" periods. Serial or climax species predominate over pioneer taxa. Xeric taxa favored.
Agricultural potential. Poor, but probably better than under previous regime. Enhanced use of nonagricultural resources.
Agriculture practices. Rainfall farming in pockets of good agricultural land. Greatest likelihood of irrigation.
Settlement patterns. Stability of restricted pattern.
Gathering. Resources limited, reduced specialization.
Hunting. Resources limited, reduced specialization.
Hunting–gathering/agriculture. Hunting–gathering more important than agriculture. Agriculture can be important with irrigation.

Agricultural potential. Poor, due to lack of available or accessible groundwater and low effective moisture.
Agriculture practices. Rainfall and floodwater farming along restricted favorable sites in stream channels. Few fields on interdrainage divides.
Settlement patterns. Stability of restricted pattern.
Gathering. Resources limited, reduced specialization.
Hunting. Resources limited, reduced specialization.
Hunting–gathering/agriculture. Hunting–gathering more important than agriculture.

C. Dendroclimatic conditions and relationships

Amplitudes	Valley Floors	Upland slopes and surfaces
High precipitation, low temperatures	Increased soil moisture; minor increase in sediment saturation; local and minor augmentation of groundwater. Increased deposition or erosion under, respectively, aggradational or degradational regimes. Increased productivity and density of natural plant populations not heavily impacted by agricultural activity. Growth of small-animal populations. Increased productivity of crops and commensal plants. Increased potential for hunting–gathering or farming, but not both.	Increased soil moisture. Increased erosion or deposition under, respectively, aggradational or degradational regimes. Increased productivity of natural plant communities and animal populations. Increased crop and commensal productivity in habitats suitable for farming but not susceptible to lower temperatures. Increased potential for hunting and gathering and for farming in suitable locales.
Low precipitation, high temperatures	Decreased soil moisture, sediment saturation, and local groundwater levels. Decreased deposition or erosion under aggradational or degradational regimes. Decreased productivity of natural plant communities, animal populations, and crops. Decreased potential for hunting–gathering and agriculture.	Decreased soil moisture. Decreased erosion or deposition under aggradational or degradational regimes. Decreased productivity of natural plant communities, animal populations, and decreased potential for hunting–gathering. Agricultural potential increased relative to valley floors, due to higher upland precipitation and higher temperatures associated with aridity.

Table 8.1. Continued

B. Vegetational relationships and subsistence potential

Hydrologic trends	Valley Floors	Upland slopes and surfaces
Rising water tables (Fluvial State 2)	*General aggradation*. As long as episodic aggradation continues, the following vegetative trends are most probable. *Trees*. Conifers already growing on floodplain eventually killed by saturation of roots or by burial. Some water-tolerant species, such as cottonwood, ash, willow, and walnut, could germinate and survive in favorable local microhabitats. Basically few to no woody species on the aggrading floodplain. *Perennials*. Decreased density, cover, and productivity due to burial (excluding species tolerant of incremental burial). *Annuals*. Enhanced abundance of pioneer taxa favored by surface disturbance (e.g., Chenopodiaceae, Amaranthaceae and Compositae such as cocklebur and small ragweed). *Animals*. Tendency for browsers to be displaced to more favorable habitats, with possible reduction in numbers due to increased competition for limited resources. Tendency for grazers utilizing pioneer species to increase in number. *Agricultural potential*. Highly favorable between floods, including *akchin* farming on subdued fans formed at mouths of tributaries; diminished reliance on nonagricultural food sources by humans. *Agricultural practices*. Rainfall and floodwater farming with planting in increasingly diverse loci (e.g. along valley bottoms and on interdivide areas underlain by deeper alluvium and eolian deposits). *Settlement patterns*. Growth nodes near springs, more permanent streams; gradual extensions as water table rises.	*General erosion*. Persistence except where removed by erosion (landsliding and slope wash). *Perennials and trees*. Same as perennials. Established trees tend to stabilize clumps of soil. Seed germination and seedling establishment inhibited by surface instability. Decreased variance in radial growth due to increased ground-water supply. *Annuals*. Density, cover, and productivity reduced due to soil disturbance, excluding pioneer species favored by disturbance of soil. *Animals*. Tendency for browsers to be displaced to more favorable habitats, with possible reduction in numbers due to increased competition for limited resources. Tendency for grazers utilizing pioneer species to increase in number. *Agricultural potential*. Moderate on flat uplands, less on steep slopes. *Agricultural practices*. Construction of soil control devices to offset slope wash. Rainfall and floodwater farming with increasing utility of sites along drainages and flat interdivide areas underlain by deeper alluvium and eolian sediments. *Settlement patterns*. Growth nodes near springs, more permanent streams; gradual extensions but slower than in lowlands.

High water tables (Fluvial State 3)	*Gathering.* Reliance on perennials diminishes; reliance on annuals increases; selection for few preferred taxa. *Hunting.* Browsers reduced; grazers increasing; selection for few preferred taxa. *Hunting–gathering/agriculture.* Agriculture more important than hunting–gathering. *Nonaggradation.* Stable, persistence of ponds, lakes, and cienegas. *Trees.* Same as for perennial and annual species. Establishment and expansion of riparian species on stable floodplains (e.g., including such recently introduced taxa as salt cedar and Russian olive). *Perennials and annuals.* Increased density, cover, and productivity, with a tendency for succession from annual pioneer to serial and climax species. *Agricultural potential.* Excellent; diminished reliance on nonagricultural resources. *Agricultural practices.* Rainfall and floodwater farming, with fields located in diverse circumstances. *Settlement patterns.* High diversity of locations. *Gathering.* High diversity and abundance; specialization probable. *Hunting.* High diversity and abundance; specialization probable. *Hunting–gathering/agriculture.* Both agriculture and hunting–gathering favorable.	*Gathering.* Reliance on perennials persists; reliance on annuals decreases; selection for few preferred taxa. *Hunting.* Increasing diversity and abundance, selection for few preferred taxa. *Hunting–gathering/agriculture.* Agriculture more important than hunting–gathering. *General nonaggradation or nondeposition.* *All vegetation.* Increased density cover, and productivity. Seedling establishment. Diminished variance in tree growth; enhanced pollen production. Torrential streams could initiate landsliding and local destruction of dense vegetation. *Animals.* Increased number and diversity. *Agricultural potential.* Moderate, slightly better than during preceding regime. *Agricultural practices.* Rainfall and floodwater farming along stream channels and in deeper alluvium. *Settlement patterns.* High diversity of locations. *Gathering.* High diversity and abundance; specialization probable. *Hunting.* High diversity and abundance; specialization probable. *Hunting–gathering/agriculture.* Both agriculture and hunting–gathering favorable.
Falling water tables (Fluvial State 4)	*Erosion.* Soil formation on stabilized surfaces. *Trees.* Riparian species die out as water table drops below root zone. Dissection would impede establishment of conifer woodlands on arroyo floors. *Perennials.* Decreased density, cover, and productivity. Pioneer taxa favored locally. *Annuals.* Decreased density, cover, and productivity except for pioneer species adapted to surface disturbance. Increased dominance of xeric elements in both perennial and annual components.	*Erosion.* If present, confined to gullies. Decreased slope wash on intergully areas. Decreased land sliding. *Trees.* Maturation of pinyon–juniper seedlings established in preceding period. Increased variance in tree growth as precipitation assumes greater role in water supply. *Mesic perennials and annuals.* Reduced diversity cover and productivity due to lower effective moisture. Increase in xeric components. Upslope movement of mesic elements.

Table 8.1. Continued

C. Dendroclimatic conditions and relationships

Temporal variability	Valley Floors	Upland slopes and surfaces
High	Decreased or stabilized soil moisture due to high frequency of change in precipitation. Inhibited accumulation of groundwater. Reduced rate of aggradation, increased rate of erosion. Decreased productivity and density of natural plant communities, animal populations, and crops. Decreased potential for hunting–gathering and farming. Agricultural potential greater relative to uplands as a result of cumulative effects of alluvial groundwater. Increased efficacy of intensified production systems.	Decreased or stabilized soil moisture. Increased erosion rate due to stabilization of groundwater and reduction of vegetation density. Decreased productivity and density of natural plant and animal communities and of crops. Decreased potential for hunting–gathering and farming.
Low	Effects depend on whether persistent trend is toward more or less precipitation.	
Increasing	Reinforces accumulation of groundwater and deposition under aggradational regimes, inhibits erosion under degradational regimes. Increases productivity of plant and animal populations and of crops. Increasing potential for hunting–gathering or agriculture.	Same as for valley floors except trend toward decreasing temperatures reduces farming potential of uplands relative to valley floors.
Decreasing	Inhibits accumulation of groundwater and deposition under aggradational regimes; enhances erosion under degradational regimes. Decreasing productivity of natural plant and animal communities and of crops. Decreasing potential for hunting–gathering and farming.	Same as for valley bottoms except trend toward increasing temperatures may enhance farming potential.

The increased ability to predict future conditions on the basis of present conditions, as a result of temporal persistence, has adaptive advantages, whether good or bad conditions expected. For example, expectation of worsening conditions may justify and repay investments in costly intensification behavior or facilities.

Spatial variability	Valley Floors	Upland slopes and surfaces
High	Decreased accumulation of groundwater due to spatial differentials in infiltration. Promotes degradation due to effect on water tables. Creates spatial differentials in natural plant and animal communities and in crop production. Enhances adaptive significance of interareal exchange and interaction, especially during periods of hydrological stress, low precipitation, amplitudes, and low temporal variability in precipitation. No direct effect on subsistence potential of local valley floor habitats.	Similar to effects in lowlands adjusted for elevational differences in temperature, precipitation, and natural resources.
Low	Increased accumulation of groundwater due to spatial uniformity in infiltration; this tendency especially strong during periods of high precipitation and low temporal variability. Enhances spatial uniformity in productivity of natural plant and animal communities and of crops. Reduces adaptive efficacy of exchange and interaction. No direct effect on local subsistence potentials.	As above.

In some instances, it is impossible to develop a logical relationship between an environmental or population condition and a behavioral response. In other cases, the relationship between an independent variable and a behavior is ambiguous in that the independent variable could entail either a high or low probability of the response. Certain environmental and population conditions are depicted as facilitating rather than causing specific behavioral adaptations. Although the condition itself is not likely to trigger a particular response, it enhances the probability that the behavior will succeed once it is activated in response to some other stimulus.

For each behavioral strategy, we attempted to define an "interactive model," one that treated the possible effects of combinations of individual environmental and population variables. Interactive models proved to be of limited utility, and, except for one example (Figure 8.2), they are omitted from the analyses. However, we emphasize that this possibility was explored and that individual environmental or population variables, or small sets thereof, exhibited greater explanatory power than did the entire set.

For the sake of simplicity, we have treated individual behavioral responses as if they occurred independently of one another, when in reality they could have occurred as combinations of behavioral strategies. Furthermore, the choice of one strategy, such as intensification of agriculture, may have eliminated other behavioral possibilities, such as mobility. A discussion of the effects of the various behavioral strategies on one another and also on their environment requires additional study.

The predicted probability relationships between environment, population, and behavior are tested against pertinent archaeological data (Euler, Chapter 7 above) for the A.D. 600–1300 interval. The analyses are limited to this period for two reasons. First, archaeological data for earlier and later periods are inadequate for the evaluation of environment–population–behavior relationships. Secondly, low population levels and discontinuous population distributions prior to 600 probably reduced the impact of environmental variability on Anasazi behavior.

Even within the A.D. 600–1300 time period, problems exist with data comparability. It has been necessary to use published data concerning Anasazi behavioral responses that were collected and interpreted by different investigators at different times using many different methods. We have necessarily assumed that a sufficient degree of comparability exists for our purposes. Our "tests" are not formal statistical procedures. Given incomplete understanding of the archaeological record and the imprecise dating, formal statistical testing seems inappropriate. At the same time, we follow the general method of such tests. The percentage of the total time period during which environmental or population conditions favoring a particular behavioral adaptation prevailed is used to compute the number or duration of occurrences of the behavior that would be expected if the relationship between the variable and the behavior were random. Thus, if environmental circumstances favorable to a particular behavior prevailed during half the period of record, we would expect 50 per cent of the instances or the duration of that behavior to fall within the favorable period on the basis of a random relationship. In this way it is possible to identify cases in which the association between environmental and behavioral variables exceeds, equals, or falls short of a random relationship.

Although we do not perform statistical tests, we provide information to permit such an approach, should anyone desire to evaluate our results. Similarly, our conclusions regarding variables that we considered to have no predictable effect on the behavioral responses can be assessed. A number of cases in which inspection of the data suggested that our theoretical expectations were incorrect were checked and were found to conform to our expectations. A summary of the results of the tests is found in Table 8.2.

In testing the postulated relationships between the environment and prehistoric behavioral responses, the responses are characterized in two different ways – as events and as processes. Some of the responses that we consider occurred at specific points in time: the construction of a water control system or a defensive site, for example. These are treated as events. Other responses, such as alliances, endured for substantial periods and are treated as processes by aggregating the behavior in question. For example, if three different alliances existed during a particular 100-year period, this occurrence is treated as 300 years of "aggregated alliance behavior."

In the case of events, we ask whether the events occurred during the periods when we predict they should have occurred, given the causal environmental variable(s). For processes, we ask whether the aggregated behavior occurred during the predicted periods that are based on the causal environmental variable(s). This task is accomplished by comparing expectations with observations in the following manner:

251

1. Identifying the number of pertinent events for which we have documentation
2. For each postulated environmental cause, determining the percentage of the 700-year sequence during which those events should have occurred, given the arguments formulated for each pertinent variable
3. Determining how many such events would fall into these periods, given random conditions alone
4. Counting the events falling into and outside these periods
5. Checking to see whether the number of such events (4) is greater than the expectation (3).

Thus, if an event occurred sixteen times during the 700-year period and the postulated conditions favoring that event were present during 30

Table 8.2. *Results of tests of hypotheses*

I. Settlement behavior	
A. Colonization/range expansion	
1. Directly correlated with aggradation, high effective moisture	REJECT
2. Directly correlated with spatial variation in precipitation	CONFIRM
3. Directly correlated with population growth	CONFIRM
4. Inversely correlated with population size/density	REJECT
B. Mobility	
1. Directly correlated with aggradation, high effective moisture	REJECT
2. Directly correlated with high-frequency temporal variability in precipitation	REJECT
3. Directly correlated with high spatial variability in precipitation	REJECT
4. Directly correlated with low to moderate population levels	REJECT
C. Abandonment	
1. Inversely correlated with aggradation, high effective moisture	CONFIRM
2. Facilitated by high population levels	CONFIRM
E. Upland–lowland movement	
1. Populations move upland during periods of aggradation, high effective moisture	CONFIRM
2. Populations move down during periods of degradation, low effective moisture	CONFIRM
III. Interaction	
1. Inversely correlated with aggradation, high effective moisture	WEAK
2. Directly correlated with high spatial variability in precipitation	CONFIRM
3. Directly correlated with high temporal variability in precipitation	CONFIRM
4. Directly correlated with high population	CONFIRM

per cent of the sequence, one would expect five $(0.30 \times 16 = 4.8)$ occurrences to fall into the favored time periods even if the event was randomly distributed in relation to the environmental variable. If far more than five cases fall into the time periods, then the postulated relationship between the event and the environmental variable is indicated.

The procedure in regard to aggregated behavior is the same. If 1200 years of aggregated behavior indicating the use of a particular strategy was noted and that strategy, on the basis of a particular variable, is most likely to have occurred during 30 per cent of the 700-year period under study, then one would predict that 360 years would fall into the favored time period under random conditions. To the extent that far more than 360 years do fall into the favored time periods, the postulated relationship between the environmental variable and the strategy is supported.

Table 8.2. *continued*

IV. Subsistence practices	
A.1 Initiation of intensification	
1. Inversely correlated with aggradation, high effective moisture	MODERATE
2. Directly correlated with high temporal variability in precipitation	REJECT
3. Directly correlated with high spatial variability in precipitation	REJECT
4. Directly correlated with high population levels	CONFIRM
A.2 Persistence of intensification	
1. Directly correlated with aggradation, high effective moisture	REJECT
2. Inversely correlated with high temporal variability in precipitation	REJECT
3. Inversely correlated with high spatial variability in precipitation	REJECT
4. Directly correlated with high population levels	REJECT
V. Territoriality	
1. Directly correlated with aggradation, high effective moisture	REJECT
2. Inversely correlated with aggradation, high effective moisture	REJECT
3. Directly correlated with amplitude of precipitation	REJECT
4. Inversely correlated with amplitude of precipitation	REJECT
5. Inversely correlated with high spatial variability in precipitation	REJECT
6. Inversely correlated with high temporal variability in precipitation	MODERATELY CONFIRM
7. Directly correlated with high population levels	CONFIRM

TESTS OF PREDICTED RELATIONSHIPS

I. Settlement behavior

A. *Colonization/range expansion (Figure 8.2)*. Colonization and range expansion are opposite sides of the same coin. From the perspective of an inhabited area, the outward movement of peoples into previously unoccupied areas is range expansion. From the perspective of the unoccupied area, that same process is colonization.

The principal environmental circumstance under which such behavior occurs is high spatial variability in precipitation. Given increasing or high spatial variability it should prove advantageous for a group of people to occupy surrounding areas in order to homogenize the effects of high variability. As long as space is available, population growth also should stimulate this behavior, even under conditions of spatial uniformity. Colonization/range expansion is limited by the availability of open space and is less likely under conditions of high population or high population density. Fluvial States 2 and 3 (Table 8.1) facilitate range expansion in that they increase the availability and extent of valley floor farmland; however, mere availability is unlikely to cause expansion in the absence of other stimuli. On the other hand, the spatial concentration of resources, particularly arable bottomland, during Fluvial States 1 and 4 is likely to inhibit colonization/range expansion. There are no necessary causal links with the amplitude or temporal variability of precipitation, as range expansion does not necessarily alleviate the negative effects of these variables.

High spatial variability in precipitation prevailed during about 41 per cent of the study period. If a random relationship existed between high spatial variability and range expansion/colonization, one would expect about 41 per cent, or seven, of the seventeen occurrences of this behavior to fall into high spatial variability periods. At least ten and, given the inadequacies of dating, as many as twelve do so. Thus, the postulated relationship is supported.

Under random conditions, 36 per cent, or about six, of the seventeen cases of colonization/range expansion should occur during Fluvial States 1 and 4. The actual association of four such cases with these conditions provides only weak support for our prediction that this behavior is inhibited by depressed alluvial water tables, floodplain erosion, and low effective moisture. It is probably significant, however,

254

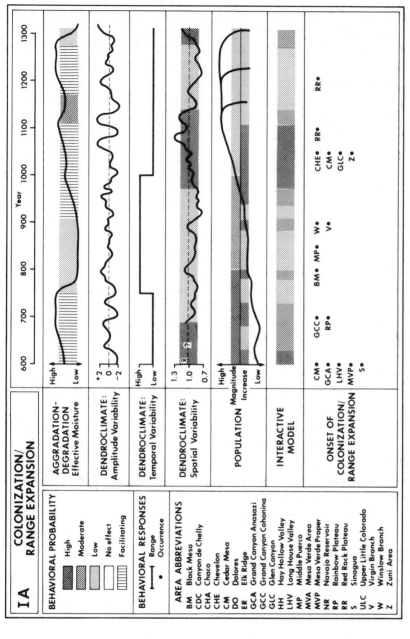

Figure 8.2 Test of postulated relationship between environment, population, and behavior (colonization/range expansion).

that all four cases fall during the A.D. 750–910 erosion interval, when some favorable locales might have been unoccupied because of the relatively small and discontinuous populations of the period. The facilitative rather than causal role of rising water tables, aggradation, and high effective moisture relative to colonization/range expansion is supported by the association of thirteen instances of this behavior with Fluvial States 2 and 3 in comparison to the eleven such cases expected under random conditions.

Given the random model, one would expect seven or eight of the cases of colonization/range expansion to occur during the 44 per cent of the sequence characterized by increasing population. The actual association of fifteen instances of this behavior with population growth empirically confirms this intuitively obvious expectation. The predicted inverse relationship between population size and colonization/range expansion is refuted by the association of six instances of this behavior with high population as compared with the seven cases that under random conditions should occur during the 43 per cent of the sequence characterized by high population. This result suggests that population in the region as a whole was never so high as to preclude range expansion.

An interactive model was developed for range expansion/colonization (Figure 8.2, IA). Since we subsequently excluded such models because they hindered rather than enhanced explanation, the treatment of interactive models is illustrated only in this case. Given the interactive model, the period during which there is a high probability of range expansion covers about 22 per cent of the sequence. Thus, one would expect four cases to fall into such intervals. The actual occurrence of ten such cases indicates a strong relationship, which is due to the combined causal effects of spatial variability and population growth and the facilitative effect of hydrology–aggradation. Thus, the interactive model adds little to the explanatory power of the independent variables considered separately.

B. *Mobility (Figure 8.3).* Mobility refers to whether people reside principally in one place or in multiple loci during a year. Sedentary peoples reside all or most of a year in a single location, while mobile peoples spend more of the year moving between two or more less permanent residential loci. Our measure of mobility is based primarily on the dendrochronologial record of site construction in the region. The

256

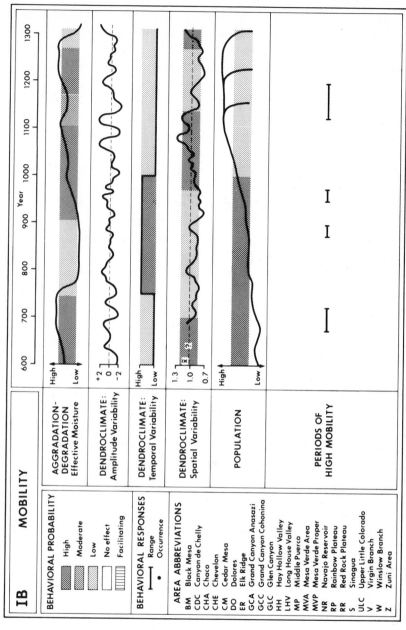

Figure 8.3 Test of postulated relationship between environment, population, and settlement behavior (mobility).

675–725, 875–900, 950–975, and 1125–1200 periods exhibit substantial reductions in the number of dated sites, which partly reflects the ephemeral sites produced by more mobile settlement behavior. Although other archaeological indicators of mobility may exist, they are poorly understood.

The primary environmental factors affecting the degree of mobility/sedentism are hydrology/effective moisture and temporal and spatial variability in precipitation. Prior to A.D. 600, mobility was probably the predominant pattern in the Southwest (Powell, Chapter 6 above). Since mobility had been the life-style for thousands of years, it is unlikely that a sedentary pattern would have been adopted without specific motivation. Floodplain erosion and low effective moisture would have reduced habitats available for exploitation and stimulated sedentism in the vicinity of those habitats. For the same reasons, rising water tables and aggradation could have increased mobility.

High temporal variability in precipitation would have reduced the overall abundance of plant and animal resources. Enhanced mobility in order to acquire resources that had not been utilized previously or to increase the utilization of particular resources is a possible response. In periods of increasing and high spatial variability, greater mobility could have offset interlocality variations in resource availability. The use of mobility under any of these conditions would have depended on population densities low enough to permit increased movement. No observable relationship between mobility and the amplitude of rainfall is postulated.

Given that fluvial conditions diagnostic of a high probability for mobility prevailed during 64 per cent of the total sequence, 112 of the 175 years of high mobility should be associated with such conditions. In fact, 100 years are associated, suggesting a slightly negative relationship between aggradation/high effective moisture and mobility.

High temporal variability in precipitation occurred during roughly 38 per cent of the sequence. Thus, 68 of the 175 years of high mobility should coincide with high temporal variability. The occurrence of only 50 of these years during the predicted periods suggests that mobility was a response to relative temporal stability of resources.

Assuming that mobility is more likely during periods of increasing and high spatial variability, which cover about 41 per cent of the sequence, one would predict that 72 of the 175 years of high mobility would be associated with such epochs. The occurrence of only 50 years of mobility with high spatial variability indicates that this behavior was actually associated with low spatial variability.

Low and moderate populations characterize about 57 per cent of the sequence, leading to the prediction that 100 years of high mobility should occur when population is low or moderate. In fact, 100 of the 175 years occur in association with such conditions, which suggests that no relationship exists between mobility and population size. This outcome indicates that population was never high enough to preclude mobility. These analyses suggest that temporal and spatial resource stability are the major stimuli of mobility.

C. Abandonment (Figure 8.4). Abandonment involves the temporary or permanent withdrawal of a resident population from an area. Undoubtedly, many "abandoned" areas continued to be utilized for purposes other than settlement. The operative consideration, however, is that the area was not a locus of permanent habitation. In our view, abandonment is primarily a response to LFP environmental degradation and high population levels and densities. Falling alluvial water tables, widespread floodplain erosion, and low effective moisture are the only environmental factors general enough and severe enough to cause habitat deterioration on a scale sufficient to precipitate abandonment. High population levels by themselves are more likely to facilitate rather than cause abandonments; however, social factors attendant on high population densities could cause aggregated settlement patterns that result in the abandonment of hinterland areas. Therefore, high population is considered to increase the probability of abandonment either as an indirect cause or as a facilitator of this behavior. In general, HFP environmental variability is likely to be too episodic to stimulate any but the most localized of abandonments. In accordance with the behavioral model, amplitude, temporal, and spatial variability in climate are likely only to reinforce or mitigate the primary effects of LFP environmental variability and population.

Under random conditions, we would expect eight of the 22 cases of abandonment to fall during the 37 per cent of the sequence characterized by fluvial conditions that specify moderate to high probability of this response. The actual association of fifteen (and perhaps seventeen, given the uncertainties of dating) such cases with moderate or high probability intervals provides strong support for the predicted relationship between abandonment and LFP environmental variability. Given

259

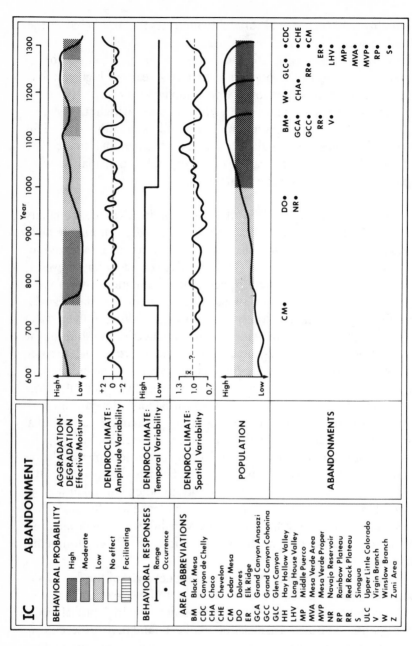

Figure 8.4 Test of postulated relationship between environment, population, and behavior (abandonment).

a random model, ten of the 22 instances should be associated with the 43 per cent of the period characterized by high regional population levels. The observed occurrence of nineteen episodes of abandonment during the interval of high population strongly supports the postulated causal or facilitative relationship between population and this behavior.

D. *Migration.* Migration refers to long-distance movement of relatively large numbers of people. Although migration commonly is involved in the abandonment of areas, it need not be. Because migration can occur in the absence of complete withdrawal from an area, it is considered separately from abandonment. Migration is probably triggered by the same LFP environmental factors that cause abandonment; that is, falling water tables, floodplain degradation, and low effective moisture. Population is both a potential cause and facilitator of migration. It is difficult to imagine environmental deterioration of sufficient severity to stimulate a long-distance move in the absence of high populations. If surrounding areas were not heavily populated, it is likely that the less disruptive responses of range expansion or increased mobility were employed. Finally, if migration occurred, there must have been empty areas or areas with populations sufficiently below carrying capacities to absorb the immigrants. We do not see migration as a likely response to changes in the amplitude, frequency, or spatial variability of precipitation.

At present, the only well-documented prehistoric migration is that of Kayenta or Tusayan peoples into Point of Pines (Haury 1958) and the San Pedro Valley (DiPeso 1958). The occurrence of this migration around A.D. 1280, immediately after the initiation of arroyo cutting on the southern Colorado Plateaus, supports the predicted relationship between migration and hydrology.

E. *Upland–lowland movement (Figure 8.5).* On the southern Colorado Plateaus, higher areas tend to be cooler and wetter than lower localities. Furthermore, a reciprocal relationship exists in the stability of valley floor and upland surfaces under different hydrologic regimes (Table 8.1A). Therefore, under certain circumstances local or regional shifts of habitation elevation are advantageous. We believe elevational shifts to be related primarily to hydrology–aggradation and effective moisture. During depositional intervals people would probably have moved to the uplands because the aggrading, semisaturated valley floor

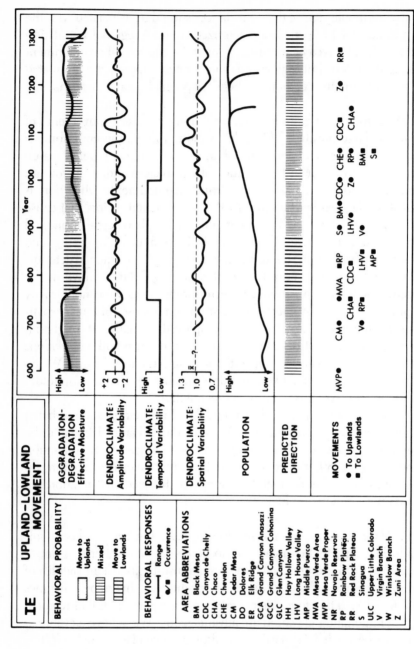

Figure 8.5 Test of postulated relationship between environment, population, and settlement behavior (upland–lowland movement).

sediments would have been poor construction surfaces. The increased stability of alluvial surfaces during periods of degradation would have concentrated high-quality agricultural land in the valley bottoms. Populations low enough to have left some empty space would have facilitated elevational shifts. Most elevational shifts due to precipitation variables, primarily amplitude, would have been too episodic and localized to be detectable in the regional archaeological data.

The sequences can be divided into three parts: those during which movement into the uplands is predicted (because of rising water tables), those during which movement into the lowlands is predicted (because of falling water tables), and those during which movement could conceivably be in either direction (because the long-term curve is rising, but the short-term curve is falling). We discovered 24 cases of movement in the literature. Of the twelve instances of movement during periods when movement to the uplands is predicted, ten are in the predicted direction. Of the five instances of movement during periods when movement to the lowlands is predicted, all are in the predicted direction. Three cases fall in the period when either response might be appropriate; one to the lowlands, two to the uplands. Of those cases that fail to follow the predicted pattern, two are close enough to boundaries that a slight error in dating the site or in placing the boundary would result in all cases being in accord with expectation. In any case, the overwhelming majority of cases follow the predicted pattern.

It is evident that upland–lowland movement fits the postulated relationship with hydrology and effective moisture very closely.

II. Subsistence mix

Subsistence mix is the relative importance of hunted, gathered, and agricultural resources in the diet. Because of a lack of data, we do not deal with this issue beyond noting its potential importance. With the exception of spatial variability in precipitation, all the environmental variables could affect subsistence mix. Furthermore, because the mix of resources was likely to vary in response to local, high-frequency environmental variability, tightly controlled local diet data are required to investigate this strategy.

III. Interaction (Figure 8.6)

Interaction is expressed as the intensity of social interchange between different groups. Interaction may be measured archaeologically by the

263

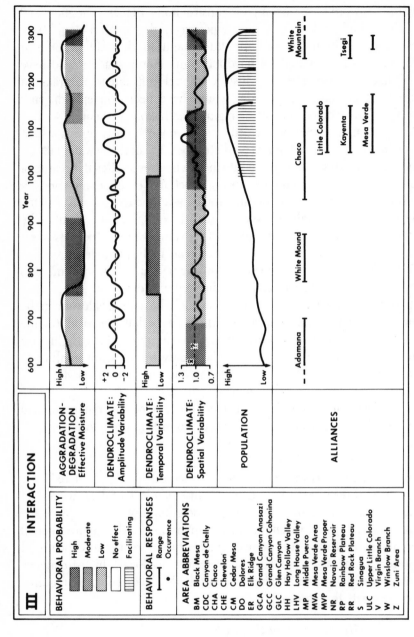

Figure 8.6 Test of postulated relationship between environment, population, and social interaction.

occurrence of "alliances" as defined by F. Plog (1983); i.e., organizational entities characterized by social ties powerful enough to produce strong normative patterns in material culture and by the social mechanisms typically associated with such ties including central places, social stratification, and economic intensification.

Hydrology–aggradation, effective moisture, and temporal and spatial variability in precipitation are the most likely triggers of this behavior. Hydrology and effective moisture are potential causes because the greater abundance and wider distribution of resources caused by aggradation and increased effective moisture reduce the stimulus to interaction. On the other hand, the increased chronological and areal variability in population distributions that may arise under conditions of degradation and low effective moisture creates differentials among nearby groups, which in turn tend to stimulate interaction. This response could be stimulated by the diminished productivity associated with high temporal variability in climate. Rising and high spatial variability in climate is perhaps the major determinant of interaction through the development of local differentials in resource availability and productivity. The tendency toward increased interaction should be especially strong when high spatial variability in precipitation coincides with LFP environmental and demographic conditions that favor interaction, and should be weaker when LFP and demographic conditions reduce the need for exchange. No relationship between interaction and precipitation amplitude is postulated. Demographic conditions facilitate interaction in that this behavior is more likely when population is high and continuously distributed over the landscape.

Summing the time spans of the nine alliances that fall within the study period yields a total of 850 years of interactive behavior. Fluvial conditions predicted to favor interactive behavior occurred during 36 per cent of the sequence. Under random conditions, one could expect about 306 years of this behavior to occur under these circumstances. The association of 315 years of interaction with these conditions suggests a weak positive relationship.

Given that high temporal variability in precipitation occurs during 36 per cent of the sequence, one would expect that 288 years of interactive behavior would be associated with such epochs. The observed figure of 150 years suggests that low rather than high temporal variability in precipitation favors interaction.

Rising and high spatial variability in precipitation covers about 41 per

265

cent of the sequence. Thus, one would expect 328 years of associated interactive behavior compared with the 565 observed. A strong association between high spatial variability and interaction is indicated.

Enhanced interaction was postulated for the 43 per cent of the sequence during which population was high. Random association requires that 344 years of interactive behavior be associated with high population, which contrasts with the 550 years actually observed. Interaction and alliance behavior are most likely to occur when population and spatial variability in climate are both high and temporal climatic variability is low.

IV. Subsistence practices

This term refers to the manner in which the Anasazi manipulated the subsistence resources available to them. Two such practices are of primary concern, intensification and storage.

A. *Intensification (Figures 8.7 and 8.8).* Intensification refers to increased labor investment per unit of land in the production of resources. While it is logically possible that hunting and gathering as well as agriculture can be intensified, our primary concern is the agricultural intensification manifested by soil and water control devices. All the environmental factors except precipitation amplitude, which fluctuates too rapidly to reward investment in costly facilities, could have affected intensification. However, the relationships of environmental variability to intensification are complex.

Floodplain erosion and decreased effective moisture would stimulate the construction of soil and water control facilities but would diminish the likelihood that such efforts would succeed. Aggradation and increased effective moisture would reduce the stimulus for such facilities but would enhance the likelihood of their success. High temporal variability in precipitation would stimulate intensification in order to increase food production during wet years to offset the reduced production of dry years; however, high temporal persistence would enhance the predictability of yields from intensified agricultural systems. The expectable effects of increasing spatial climatic variability on intensification are also ambiguous. Spatial variability in precipitation may stimulate intensification; however, spatial variability itself diminishes the likelihood of success. Terracing and ditching are of little avail if the rain falls elsewhere. High population should stimulate the initiation and maintenance of intensified agricultural systems (Boserup 1965).

266

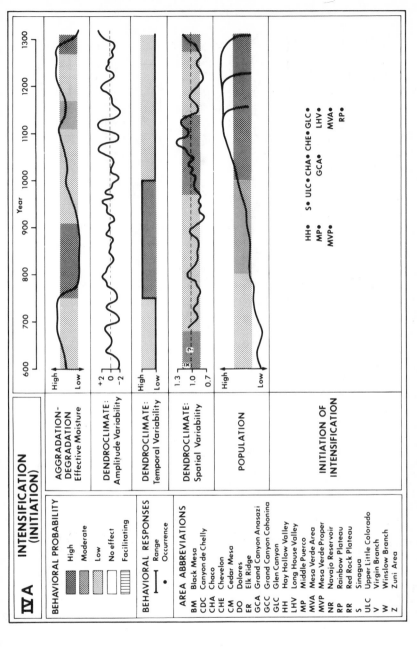

Figure 8.7 Test of postulated relationship between environment, population, and agricultural behavior (intensification).

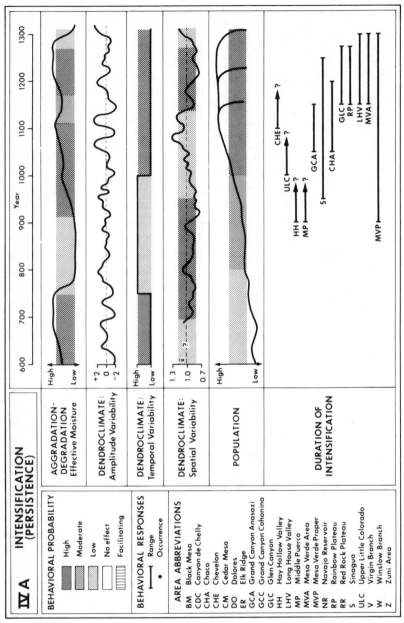

Figure 8.8 Test of postulated relationship between environment, population, and agricultural behavior (persistence).

It is apparent from the preceding discussion that the effects of LFP and HFP environmental variability on intensification differ with respect to the initiation and continuation of intensification. Figures 8.7 and 8.8 illustrate these two aspects of the situation. In Figure 8.7 the relationships between the environmental variables and the initiation of intensification in different areas are examined. In Figure 8.8 the environmental conditions associated with the persistence of intensification are considered.

Fluvial and effective moisture conditions favoring the beginning of intensification occur during approximately 36 per cent of the sequence (Figure 8.7). Thus, one would expect four of the twelve recorded instances of the initiation of intensification to occur during these periods. Seven occur, suggesting a moderate relationship between degradation/low effective moisture and the initiation of intensification. Given that high temporal climatic variability occurs during about 36 per cent of the sequence, the four associated occurrences of intensification do not depart from the expectations of the random model. The initiation of four instances of intensification during conditions of rising and high spatial variability does not depart substantially from the five occurrences specified by the random model.

The situation in regard to demography is quite different. The moderate to high populations that should cause the adoption of intensification characterize 71 per cent of the sequence; therefore nine instances of this response should be associated with these conditions. The initiation of all twelve cases of intensified agriculture indicates that population increase, along with depressed water tables and degradation, is a primary cause of the adoption of this behavior.

None of the environmental variables explains the persistence of intensification. Aggregating the data shown in Figure 8.8, there were 1700 years during which intensified strategies were practiced somewhere in the area. Using aggradation–high effective moisture as a predictor, 1275 of these years should fall during the high probability periods. The actual figure is 1100. If high temporal variability in precipitation is related to the practice of intensified strategies in the manner postulated, 1275 of these years should fall during high-probability periods. The actual figure is 1400. For spatial variability in precipitation, the predicted figure is 850 years and the observed is 1000. On the basis of population, one would expect 1275 years to fall during the high probability periods. The actual figure is 1275 years. Thus, in no case do the observations depart significantly from those expected under random conditions. Only in the cases of the two precipitation variables is there the possibility of even a weak association. These results suggest that, once initiated, intensification continued to be used as a strategy regardless of environmental conditions. Historical and social factors may, of course, complicate our understanding of this situation.

B. *Storage*. Storage involves setting aside the products of one growing season for use in subsequent seasons. This strategy could be related to each of the environmental variables. The relatively high availability of resources under conditions of aggradation and high effective moisture reduces the likelihood of this strategy. Conversely, degradation and decreased effective moisture should stimulate storage. HFP amplitude of variation in precipitation would have parallel effects. Deleterious effects of high temporal or spatial variability in precipitation could be offset by increasing the amount of stored resources. Interactive responses to increasing spatial variability in precipitation might entail storing the surplus resources to be exchanged. While the level of population might affect the form of storage, we see no reason why population levels as such would alter per capita amounts stored.

We offer no tests of the storage expectations. There are several studies of storage behavior in particular areas (Plog 1974; Powell 1983), and other investigators have noted changes in the quantity and/or form of storage. However, having pursued this line of investigation, we concluded that descriptions of storage variability are too diffuse for useful tests of the predictions. Nonetheless, we are convinced of the ultimate worth of further investigations of the proposed storage relationships.

V. Territoriality (Figure 8.9)

Territoriality refers to the degree to which human groups explicitly identify with and defend territories. This adaptive strategy is difficult to deal with archaeologically; however, defensive sites provide some pertinent evidence. Our reasoning in regard to the use of this evidence derives from Dyson-Hudson and Smith's conclusion that human groups invest the energy to defend territories only when the resources available within the territories are sufficiently secure to justify the cost (1978).

All the environmental variables have potential effects on territoriality. The greater abundance of resources under conditions of

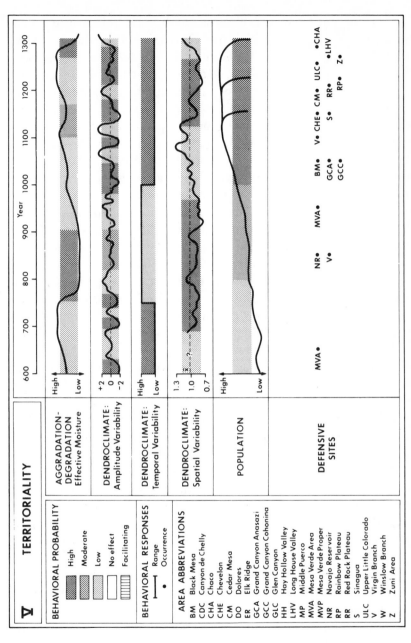

Figure 8.9 Test of postulated relationship between environment, population, and territoriality.

aggradation and increased effective moisture should favor territorial behavior. However, the spatial restriction of resources during periods of degradation or low effective moisture are likely to stimulate territorial behavior around those small areas still possessing high resource potential. Changes in the amplitude of precipitation would cause short-term changes parallel to those just discussed. Increased territorial behavior during periods of reduced spatial and temporal variability in precipitation would be expected. With increased temporal and spatial variability, resource stability would probably be insufficient to warrant territorial behavior. Finally, territorial behavior is more likely when population levels are high than when they are low.

Seventeen instances of defensive behavior are specified in the literature. Under random conditions, six of these should occur during the 36 per cent of the sequence characterized by fluvial conditions of moderate to high probability for this behavior. The actual occurrence of seven indicates that no relationship exists between LFP variability and territoriality. If the correlation were inverse one would expect eleven cases to be associated with periods of low effective moisture and degradation compared to the twelve observed. No such relationship is indicated.

Low precipitation amplitude conditions that might result in territorial behavior occur during about 44 per cent of the sequence, leading to the prediction that under random conditions seven or eight instances of territorial behavior should associate with below-average departures. The observed occurrence is eight cases, indicating no relationship. The same conclusion is reached in regard to the postulated inverse relationship.

Low temporal variability in precipitation occurs during about 64 per cent of the sequence. Given a random model, one would expect eleven of the seventeen cases of territorial behavior to associate with low temporal variability. The observed fourteen instances suggest a moderate correspondence between territoriality and temporal persistence in climate.

During the roughly 59 per cent of the sequence characterized by declining and low spatial variability, ten cases of territorial behavior, given a random model, would be expected. The actual occurrence of nine such cases indicates no relationship between territoriality and spatial variability in climate.

Conditions of moderate or high population favoring territorial behavior occur during about 71 per cent of the sequence. The twelve instances expected, given a random model, compare with an observed total of sixteen, which indicates a fairly strong relationship between territorial behavior and high population.

In general, these results support Dyson-Hudson and Smith's conclusions. It is, however, important to realize that Dyson-Hudson and Smith operated primarily with a spatial notion of causality. This analysis suggests that temporal persistence coupled with high population can increase the likelihood of territorial behavior.

VI. Social integration

In general, this term refers to the strength of the ties that link members of different family or kin groups. Clearly, this variable is difficult to measure archaeologically. However, the extent to which people lived in aggregated settlements as opposed to being dispersed over the landscape is an appropriate measure. With the exception of precipitation amplitude, all the environmental variables might be related to aggregation and dispersion. Falling alluvial groundwater, floodplain degradation, and low effective moisture would create restricted patches of high-quality agricultural land. Populations may aggregate around such pockets of productive land.

Aggregation is likely to be associated with low temporal and spatial variability. During periods of high variability the concentration of population in a limited area would be difficult.

High population by itself does not necessarily cause aggregation. However, high population facilitates this behavior because aggregation is more likely with large numbers of people than with small.

At least since Julian Steward's (1937) calculation of variation in room:kiva ratios and continuing into recent applications of rank:size rules, the extent of social integration has concerned Southwestern prehistorians. Given the diversity of current approaches to this topic, including disagreements over the definition of aggregation, we do not examine this response further. As more precise concepts and measures of aggregation are developed, testing of relationships between environmental variables and social integration will become possible.

CONCLUSIONS

The following paragraphs conclude both the volume and this chapter. We attempt to make clear what has and has not been done in this volume and what can and cannot be done to understand more accurately the relationships between prehistoric peoples and their environments.

We do not believe, of course, that the behavioral responses we examine are the only ones used by the Anasazi to monitor and respond to environmental variability. They are, however, detectable in the archaeological record, even though in many cases we lack sufficient information of the kind necessary to test our expectations adequately. Furthermore, some of these predictions cannot be properly evaluated on a regional scale and require testing at local levels. We therefore encourage researchers to test our models against locally pertinent data. In this way archaeologists can more clearly understand the strength and weakness of the model and isolate those aspects of the model that need refinement.

Further testing and refinement of our models will require better understanding of certain demographic and behavioral factors. Perhaps most critically lacking are accurate estimates of regional demographic trends on the southern Colorado Plateaus. A few local population curves are well documented; however, demography requires a regional perspective because humans can and often do move. The role of population in Anasazi culture-history probably will be found to have been more significant than heretofore imagined (Powell, Chapter 6 above).

Another topic for further investigation is the role of human modification of the natural environment. While Anasazi behavior must have triggered varying degrees of edaphic change in different areas, at present we have only a vague notion of the magnitude and direction of those changes.

More attention should also be focused on quantifying changes in subsistence mix, storage behavior, direction and intensity of interactive behavior, and degree of aggregation. Clearly, it is now necessary to develop archaeological data of the quality and quantity of some of the environmental data.

This volume should not be perceived as an effort to argue that prehistoric cultural patterns in the Southwest can be understood exclusively through the analysis of relationships between people and their natural environments. Throughout this volume we have stressed our intention to treat environmental variables as independent and behavioral variables as dependent. None of us believe that the totality of human adaptation to the area can be understood without adequate attention to the effect of humans on their natural environment and of humans and human groups upon one another. If our efforts appear to create the basis for a "new environmental determinism," we deny this intent. The thrust of our efforts has been to define precisely and evaluate carefully the nature of environmental variation in the prehistoric past and the effects of this variation on human behavior. Other archaeologists are invited to be as explicit as possible in characterizing the effects of humans on the environment and on one another. Only through such efforts will we achieve the balanced understanding of causality in the prehistoric past that all of us wish to see.

Our characterization of the environment attempts to balance the effects of particular events with those of processes. Both events and processes are crucial to understanding human and environmental interaction. In essence, this effort is an attempt to utilize the best of "catastrophism" and "gradualism" in the study of evolution. While changes in environmental patterns are not characteristically catastrophic, sudden events – the eruption of a volcano or rapid erosion – can and did have important behavioral consequences. At the same time, less sudden shifts – in the temporal and spatial variability of climate, in the quantity of precipitation, or in human population levels – also had enormous consequences. We have tried to be equally sensitive to both high- and low-frequency environmental processes (the latter appearing as discrete events to the peoples experiencing them). Analyses that fail to attend to both types of environmental processes, as most traditional, cultural ecological studies do, are unlikely to offer great insight into the interaction between humans and their environments.

We have also argued that greater attention must be given to what might be called variability within variability. Precipitation, for example, ranged from high to low values. There were, however, periods during which this variation was characterized by quite short cycles and others during which the cycles were longer. From the perspective of individuals attempting to adjust their subsistence strategies to meet environmental contingencies, these were quite different patterns. Even if limited in degree (amplitude), the former were not predictable and the latter, if extreme in degree, were more predictable year to year. Increased attention to this issue is essential if prehistoric adaptive patterns are to be better understood.

We have attempted a similar effort in regard to behavioral responses to environmental change. Archaeologists have devoted too much effort to explaining specific behavioral events – a migration, an abandonment, increased or decreased interaction. In the approach advocated here, these and other cultural and behavioral phenomena are treated as recurrent strategies used by different peoples in different times and places to adapt to changing environmental conditions. At issue is whether there are commonalities in the circumstances under which these strategies were selected. Only in this fashion can a truly processual understanding of the prehistoric past be achieved. While our efforts have focused largely on the natural environment, we challenge archaeologists to use a similar treatment with cultural phenomena.

Finally, we have proposed a different approach to evaluating the relationships between behavioral and environmental phenomena. Building on the above and recognizing that both events and processes have duration and frequency, we have used a procedure that identifies those portions of the prehistoric record during which particular responses are expected to occur and compares these predictions with the best available data. In the traditional approach an event is identified, and environmental correlates are sought. There are two problems with such an approach. First, all events have correlates, usually many. Identifying the specific correlate that caused the event becomes quite difficult. Secondly, the correlates of a specific event at a specific time and place may be different from the correlates of similar events at other times and places. Only by building independent overall records of environmental and behavioral patterns can one overcome this difficulty.

This is not to claim that our efforts have been entirely successful. Had this situation arisen, we would have worried over the potential triviality of the predictions. Table 8.2 summarizes the results of the analyses, showing which predictions succeeded and which failed. Some of the apparent successes may reflect the manner in which the data were interpreted, and these predictions may ultimately prove less successful than appears to be the case at present. Nevertheless, these initial tests provide a useful structure for future work. We hope that the manner in which we have undertaken these analyses and the tentative conclusions we have reached will stimulate archaeologists to refine data, interpretations of data, and analytical procedures. If such refinements evolve from this volume, we will feel that our effort has been well spent even if many of our conclusions prove incorrect.

Afterword

GEORGE J. GUMERMAN

Concluding thoughts about this volume are difficult because of its extremely broad scope. The authors have ranged throughout the Christian era and across the southern Colorado Plateaus. The theory and method from alluvial hydrology, dendrochronology, palynology, and archaeology have been discussed. Data from these diverse disciplines have been gathered, interpreted, and compared to construct a natural and cultural model of the last two millennia on the southern Colorado Plateaus. Expected Anasazi reactions to specific environmental and demographic conditions were generated, and the expectations were tested against the actual situation as best as we could reconstruct it.

In summation, it is worthwhile to discuss briefly the contributions, the strengths, and the weaknesses of each discipline represented in this volume. All the disciplines have clearly advanced beyond the hoary excuse of needing more data to evaluate their models and interpretations. In fact, in occasional cases the amount of data is overwhelming and tends to obscure trends. For example, the annual level of resolution of tree-ring data hinders comparison with the lower-frequency reconstruction of other paleoenvironmental techniques. Certainly there are areas where more data would be helpful, such as more accurate demographic figures or additional pollen profiles. Of special concern is

277

the reliance on locales which by fortuitous circumstance have been the scenes of most recent archaeological efforts. For this reason there is a heavy dependence on data from Black Mesa. Nevertheless, major questions to be addressed simply do not need more data thrown at them. Instead, a refinement of method and theory to evaluate the data better is required.

The following critique of the various chapters in this volume is a very abbreviated summary of the discussants' comments which space does not permit to be published verbatim. James Schoenwetter critiqued the floral section of the volume, Larry Agenbroad the hydrostratigraphic section, Charles Stockton the dendrochronology, and Patrick Kirch and James Judge the archaeology.

The greatest need for a reevaluation of method, theory, and data is in palynology, in spite of the fact that Hevly's vegetative retrodiction for this volume supports, in general, both the alluvial–hydrologic and the dendroclimatic record. Schoenwetter, however, has criticized Hevly's efforts on several grounds. Schoenwetter feels that Hevly has not adequately demonstrated that pollen frequency fluctuations are time dependent rather than the result of past human behavior or of the palynological model used for interpreting the data. Furthermore, he suggests that the dating of the pollen samples is too imprecise to permit an understanding of the relationship of the pollen data to the other lines of evidence. In short, Schoenwetter believes that Hevly has not adequately proved his case, not necessarily that he is wrong.

It appears timely for the palynologists to come together in a series of frank discussions to attempt to resolve some of their differences and devise methods to test their basic assumptions. Until that is done, it would appear that other scientists must treat environmental interpretations derived from pollen data as suspect, at least for the Southwest.

Interpretation of the alluvial–hydrologic record has been almost as controversial as that of the pollen data. As the authors of the last chapter point out, however, the interpretations based on the two models of fluvial processes may not be so conflicting as generally supposed. Rather, one model, based on contemporary observation of fluvial processes, produces a record of short-term alluvial action. The other model, derived from the chronostratigraphic record, produces a long-term, low-frequency profile of these processes. Since the short- and long-term alluvial processes may be quite different, the two models can be compatible.

The hydrostratigraphic record is the most important source of low-frequency environmental process information and permits the reconstruction of depositional, erosional, and water-table conditions affecting human populations. The importance of the hydrostratigraphic record for the purposes of this volume cannot be overstated. While not all surficial geologists may agree with the entirety of the hydrostratigraphic model, the data are now presented so that other scholars may test the model for themselves. Karlstrom's study of the alluvial units on the Colorado Plateaus is the most detailed since Hack's classic work of 45 years ago. His study essentially confirms Hack's three-fold alluvial subdivision. In addition, Karlstrom defined an additional series of depositional subunits within each major alluvial section.

Central to Karlstrom's interpretation of hydrological cycles from alluvial deposits is the assumption that change in stream flow is a response to the wide precipitation variability on the Colorado Plateaus, and that the alluvial chronology is generally synchronous in different drainages throughout the region.

The hydrologic cycle is vital for understanding not only the low-frequency environmental processes as reflected in the hydrostratigraphic record but also the high-frequency environmental processes derived from tree-ring data. However, as Charles Stockton has noted in discussing the interpretation of tree-ring data, the effect of climatic variation on the processes of the hydrologic cycle is very complex and poorly understood.

The method, theory, and data of dendrochronology hardly need discussion here, although there are a number of questions regarding interpretations. In spite of what most southwestern archaeologists believe, tree-ring growth, while far superior to any other method now available to us, is an imperfect indicator of climate variability. Consequently the inference of climatic variability and its relationship to hydrologic states from the proxy data of tree-rings is tenuous. Nevertheless, dendrochronology provides the highest resolution and best-dated temporal and spatial high-frequency environmental record.

Southwestern archaeology seems to have entered a period of some pessimism in the last few years regarding our ability to obtain our goals. There is, however, little disagreement regarding archaeological method and theory, although there are differences in emphases. There are also few acrimonious debates regarding interpretation in the Southwest. More often there are interpretive disagreements, but even in these cases the difficulty of replication in archaeology and the relative independence of each archaeological project diffuses much disagreement.

Of greater and more basic concern is archaeology's ability to reconstruct systems of past human behavior, i.e., the very task we say is our *raison d'être*. We find it necessary to make too many assumptions, to hold too many factors constant, and too often to reduce variables to a manageable few, excluding perhaps critical ones. In short, our model and data set may be constructs which distort in major ways our interpretation of past behaviors. Because of this situation and the complexity of the interrelationship of the data, the model, and the variables the author tests, certain changes in any aspect of this study could substantially change the conclusions. For these reasons, it is necessary that we straightforwardly evaluate not only our strengths but also our weaknesses. Patrick Kirch and James Judge, in reviewing our efforts, have concentrated their efforts on problems involving the model, data measurement, and interpretation.

The model is criticized by Kirch for assuming the independence of environmental and behavioral variables. He makes the cogent point that, as has been demonstrated recently, peoples with the simplest level of technology have profoundly affected their natural environment; the human role in environmental change is not a passive one. Kirch argues that there is some evidence for human-induced environmental change in the Southwest and that we should attempt to determine the combined role of human and climate-induced environmental change.

Judge expresses concern that archaeologists do not control the needed demographic and behavioral data that are necessary to test our hypotheses adequately. There is no question that the quality and quantity of data could be improved. Furthermore, we were hampered by the necessity to use published data of variable quality and degrees of comparability. Our interpretation of published data may also be open to question. Even the areas we chose to use were predetermined by the historical vagaries of where archaeologists had previously worked and published the results of their investigations. Given the opportunity, we would have liked to utilize data from other localities on the Colorado Plateaus. Studies of this nature, however, must rely on the natural and cultural data that are available. It was simply impossible to delay our study until the quality and quantity of Colorado Plateaus data were of a much higher order.

The question of the overall interpretation of the data, addressed by us largely in the last chapter, is a critical one. Judge criticizes us for not taking the complexity of the situation into account and for ignoring the complexity of human behavior. As noted, however, in Chapter 8 above, we did attempt to construct an "interactive model," one in which combinations of environmental and population variables interact with one another and with behavioral variables. The results of that attempt obscured rather than clarified the situation, which underscores the basic question. In dealing with such voluminous and varied data, to what degree is simplification possible without invalidating interpretations? We feel that to introduce much greater complexity into the tests of the model would obscure the major trends. Obviously, it is possible to elaborate on the model, the data, tests, and interpretations. We invite interested scholars to do so.

The complexity of human–environment interaction is perhaps why Judge believes we should have tested our model on a local, rather than a regional, level. We reject that notion. This is a task for the future. Since the early, classic formulations of Anasazi prehistory, exemplified by the all encompassing frameworks of Kidder's work and the Pecos Classification, attempts at explanation dealing with large volumes of data have almost always been at a local level. While these locality-based studies have contributed greatly to our understanding of the incredible range of nuances in Anasazi behavior, they are, by necessity, unable to deal with those behaviors that are regulated by the system-wide nature of the Anasazi world.

The relationship between local and regional studies is one of interplay. The studies of geographically constricted areas are vitally important, for they have provided much of the data we used in our study. Now the results of this study can be used to help interpret behavior in specific localities, and the data from these localities can be used to refine our model.

This volume is the result of hundreds of people's efforts in many disciplines. It has evolved over the years and has been enhanced by the accumulation of knowledge, reflecting the growth of our disciplines and ourselves. In a number of ways, its form was dictated by decisions we made many years ago. This volume documents a stage in the study of human–environment relationships in southwestern archaeology, a stage that is not yet complete. As with our earlier statements, this effort is unfinished.

References

Adam, David P., C. W. Ferguson, and V. C. Lamarche, Jr 1967. Enclosed bark as a pollen trap. *Science* 157:1067–8.

Adam, David P., and Peter J. Mehringer, Jr 1975. Modern pollen surface – an analysis of subsamples. *Journal of Research* 3(6):733–6. Washington, D.C.: United States Geological Survey.

Adams, Richard N. 1981. Natural selection, energetics, and 'cultural materialism'. *Current Anthropology* 22(6):603–8.

Ahlstrom, Richard V. N. 1980. Measuring time in archaeology. Unpublished manuscript on file, Department of Anthropology, University of Arizona, Tucson.

1985. The interpretation of archaeological tree-ring dates. Unpublished Ph.D. diss., University of Arizona. Ann Arbor: University Microfilms International.

Aikens, C. Melvin 1966. *Virgin–Kayenta cultural relationships*. University of Utah Anthropological Papers no. 79. Salt Lake City: University of Utah Press.

Anderson, James N. 1973. Ecological anthropology and anthropological ecology. In *Handbook of Social and Cultural Anthropology*. Ed. J. Honigmann, pp. 179–240. Chicago: Rand McNally.

Andrews, Peter P. 1982. Research and culture history. In *Excavations on Black Mesa, 1980: a descriptive report*. Eds. Peter P. Andrews, Robert Layhe, Deborah Nichols, and Shirley Powell. Research paper no. 24. Carbondale: Center for Archaeological Investigations, Southern Illinois University.

282

References

Antevs, Ernst 1948. Climatic changes and pre-white man. In *The Great Basin, with emphasis on glacial and post-glacial times*. Ed. N. Adams. University of Utah Bulletin, vol. 58, no. 20. Salt Lake City: University of Utah.

— 1952. Arroyo-cutting and filling. *Journal of Geology* 60:375–85.

— 1955. Geologic-climatic method of dating. *Arizona Physical Science Bulletin* 2:151–69.

Anyon, Roger, and T. J. Ferguson 1983. Settlement patterns and changing adaptations in the Zuni area after A.D. 1000. Paper presented at the 2nd Anasazi Symposium, Farmington, New Mexico.

Arensberg, Conrad M. 1961. The community as object and as sample. *American Anthropologist* 63:241–64.

Babbie, Earl L. 1973. *Survey research methods*. Belmont, CA: Wadsworth Publishing Company.

Bannister, Bryant 1962. The interpretation of tree-ring dates. *American Antiquity* 27:508–14.

— 1969. Dendrochronology. In *Science in archaeology: a survey of progress and research*. Revised edition. Eds. Don Brothwell and Eric Higgs. London: Thames and Hudson.

Bannister, Bryant, Jeffry W. Dean, and William J. Robinson 1968. *Tree-ring dates from Arizona C-D*. Tucson: Laboratory of Tree-Ring Research, University of Arizona.

Baumhoff, M. D., and R. F. Heizer 1965. Postglacial climate and archaeology in the desert west. In *The Quaternary of the United States*. Eds. H. E. Wright and D. G. Frey. Princeton: Princeton University Press.

Beals, Ralph L., George W. Brainerd, and Watson Smith 1945. *Archaeological studies in northeast Arizona*. University of California Publications in American Archaeology and Ethnology 44(1):1–171.

Beeson, William J. 1966, Archaeological survey near St. Johns, Arizona: a methodological study. Unpublished Ph.D. diss., University of Arizona.

Berlin, G. L., J. R. Ambler, R. H. Hevly, and G. G. Shaber 1977. Identification of a Sinagua agricultural field by areal thermography, soil chemistry, pollen-plant analysis, and archaeology. *American Antiquity* 42:588–600.

Berry, David R. 1983. Skeletal remains from RB 568. In *Honoring the dead, Anasazi ceramics from the Rainbow Bridge–Monument Valley expedition*, by Helen K. Crotty. Monograph Series no. 22. University of California, Los Angeles, Museum of Cultural History.

Berry, Michael S. 1982, *Time, space, and transition in Anasazi prehistory*. Salt Lake City: University of Utah Press.

Binford, Lewis R. 1965. Archaeological systematics and the study of culture process. *American Antiquity* 31:203–10.

— 1980. Willow smoke and dogs' tails: hunter–gatherer settlement systems and archaeological site formation. *American Antiquity* 45:4–20.

Blasing, Terence Jack 1975. Methods for analyzing climatic variations in the north Pacific sector and western North America for the last few centuries. Unpublished Ph.D. diss., University of Wisconsin, Ann Arbor.

Blasing, T. J., and Harold C. Fritts 1976. Reconstructing past climatic anomalies in the northern Pacific and western North America from tree-ring data. *Quaternary Research* 6:563–79.

Bohrer, V. L. 1972. Paleoecology of the Hay Hollow Site, Arizona. *Fieldiana: Anthropology* 63(1):1–30.

1975. The prehistoric and historic role of cool season grasses in the Southwest. *Economic Botany* 29:199–207.

1981. Methods of recognizing cultural activity from pollen in archaeological sites. *The Kiva* 46(3):135–42.

1982. Plant remains from rooms at Grasshopper Pueblo. In *Multidisciplinary research at Grasshopper Pueblo, Arizona*. Eds. William Longacre *et al.* Anthropological Papers of the University of Arizona no. 40. Tucson: University of Arizona Press.

Boison, Paul J., and P. C. Patton 1983. Late Pleistocene and Holocene alluvial stratigraphy of three tributaries of the Escalante River, southcentral Utah. In *Chaco Canyon country*. Eds. S. G. Wells *et al.* Albuquerque: Adobe Press.

Boserup, Esther 1965. *The conditions of agricultural growth: the economics of agrarian change under population pressure.* Chicago: Aldine Atherton.

Bradfield, Maitland M. 1963. *A natural history of associations*, vol. II. London: Duckworth.

1971. Changing patterns of Hopi agriculture. *Journal of the Royal Anthropological Institute* 30.

1973. Rock cut cisterns and pollen 'rain' in the vicinity of Old Oraibi, Arizona. *Plateau* 46:68–71.

Brady, L. F. 1936. The arroyo of the Rio de Flag: a study of an erosion cycle. *Museum Notes* 9(6):33–7.

Braun, David P., and Stephen Plog 1982. Evolution of 'tribal' social networks: theory and prehistoric North American evidence. *American Antiquity* 47:504–25.

Breternitz, David A. 1966. *An appraisal of tree-ring dated pottery in the Southwest*. Anthropological Papers of the University of Arizona, no. 10. Tucson: University of Arizona Press.

1973. Tree-ring dated Basketmaker III and Pueblo I sites in Mesa Verde National Park. Unpublished manuscript, Mesa Verde Research Center, University of Colorado, Boulder.

Brew, John Otis 1946. *Archaeology of Alkali Ridge, southeastern Utah*. Papers of the Peabody Museum of American Archaeology and Ethnology, Harvard University, vol. 21. Cambridge, Mass.: Harvard University Press.

Bronitsky, Gordon J. 1977. An ecological model of trade: prehistoric

284

economic change in the northern Rio Grande region of New Mexico. Unpublished Ph.D. diss., University of Arizona.

Bryan, Kirk 1925. Dates of channel trenching (arroyo-cutting) in the arid Southwest. *Science* 62:338–44.

1928. Change in plant associations by changes in ground water level. *Ecology* 9:474–8.

1940. Erosion in the valleys of the Southwest. *New Mexico Quarterly Review* 10:227–32.

1954. *The geology of Chaco Canyon, New Mexico, in relation to the life and remains of the prehistoric peoples of Pueblo Bonito.* Smithsonian Miscellaneous Collections, vol. 122, no. 7. Washington, D.C.: Smithsonian Institution.

Buge, D. E., and J. Schoenwetter 1977. Pollen studies at Chimney Rock Mesa. Appendix B in *Archaeologic investigations at Chimney Rock Mesa, 1970–71*, pp. 77–80. Memoirs of the Colorado Archaeological Society no. 1, by Frank Eddy.

Burns, Barney Tillman 1983. Simulated Anasazi storage behavior using crop yields reconstructed from tree rings: A.D. 652–1968. Unpublished Ph.D. diss., University of Arizona.

Cartledge, Thomas R. 1979. Cohonina adaptation to the Coconino Plateau: a re-evaluation. *The Kiva* 44(4):297–317.

Cattanach, George S., Jr 1980. *Long House: Mesa Verde National Park, Colorado.* Publications in Archaeology 7H. Wetherill Mesa studies, National Park Service. Washington, D.C.: Government Printing Office.

Chagnon, Napoleon A. 1968. *Yanomamo, the fierce people.* New York: Holt, Rinehart, and Winston.

Cohen, Mark Nathan 1977. *The food crisis in prehistory: overpopulation and the origins of agriculture.* New Haven: Yale University Press.

Colton, Harold S. 1932. *A survey of prehistoric sites in the region of Flagstaff, Arizona.* Bureau of American Ethnology, Bulletin 104. Washington, D.C.: Smithsonian Institution.

1936. The rise and fall of the prehistoric populations of northern Arizona. *Science* 84(2181):337–43.

1946. *The Sinagua.* Museum of Northern Arizona, Bulletin 22. Flagstaff: Museum of Northern Arizona Press.

Cook, Sherburne F. 1972. *Prehistoric demography.* Reading, Mass.: Addison-Wesley Module in Anthropology 16.

Cooke, R. U., and R. W. Reeves 1976. *Arroyos and environmental change in the American South-West.* Oxford: Oxford University Press.

Cooley, Maurice E. 1962. Late Pleistocene and recent erosion and alluviation in parts of the Colorado River system, Arizona and Utah. In *Geological Survey research 1962: short papers in geology, hydrology, and topography, articles 1–59.* Washington, D.C.: United States Geological Survey, Professional Paper 450–B.

Cooley, Maurice E., J. W. Harshbarger, J. P. Akers, and W. F. Hardt

285

1969. *Regional hydrogeology of the Navajo and Hopi Indian reservations, Arizona, New Mexico, and Utah.* Washington, D.C.: United States Geological Survey, Professional Paper 521–A.

Cordell, Linda S. 1981. The Wetherill Mesa simulation: a retrospective. In *Simulation in archaeology.* Ed. Jeremy Sabloff. Albuquerque: University of New Mexico Press.

Cordell, Linda S., and Fred Plog 1979. Escaping the confines of normative thought: a reevaluation of Puebloan prehistory. *American Antiquity* 44:405–29.

Dalley, Gardiner F., and Douglas A. McFadden 1985. *The archaeology of the Red Cliffs site.* Bureau of Land Management, Utah, Cultural Resource Series no. 17. Salt Lake City: Bureau of Land Management, Utah State Office.

Dansereau, P. 1957. *Biogeography – an ecological perspective.* New York: Ronald Press Co.

Danson, Edward B., and H. E. Malde 1950. Casa Malpais, a fortified pueblo site at Springerville, Arizona. *Plateau* 22(4):61–7.

Daubenmire, Rexford F. 1954. Alpine timberlines in the Americas and their interpretation. *Butler University Botanical Studies* 11:119–36.

1960. A seven-year study of cone production as related to xylem layers and temperature in *Pinus ponderosa. American Midland Naturalist* 64:187–93.

Davis, Emma Lou 1965. Small pressures and cultural drift as explanations for abandonment of the San Juan area, New Mexico and Arizona. *American Antiquity* 30:353–5.

Davis, Owen K., R. H. Hevly, and R. D. Foust 1985. A comparison of historic and prehistoric vegetation change caused by man in central Arizona. *American Association of Stratigraphic Palynologists Contribution Series* 16:63–76.

Dean, Jeffrey S. 1969. *Chronological analysis of Tsegi Phase sites in northeastern Arizona.* Papers of the Laboratory of Tree-Ring Research no. 3. Tucson: University of Arizona Press.

1970. Aspects of Tsegi Phase social organization: a trial reconstruction. In *Reconstructing prehistoric Pueblo societies.* Ed. William A. Longacre. Albuquerque: University of New Mexico Press.

1978a. Tree-ring dating in archaeology. In *Miscellaneous collected papers 19–24.* Ed. Jesse D. Jennings. University of Utah Anthropological Papers, no. 99. Salt Lake City: University of Utah Press.

1978b. Independent dating in archaeological analysis. In *Advances in archaeological method and theory,* vol. 1. Ed. Michael B. Schiffer. New York: Academic Press.

1981. Research problems in Kayenta Anasazi archaeology. Paper presented at the 45th annual meeting of the Society for American Archaeology, San Diego, California.

References

1985. Review of *Time, space, and transition in Anasazi prehistory*, by Michael S. Berry. *American Antiquity* 50:704–5.

Dean, Jeffrey S., and William J. Robinson 1977. *Dendroclimatic variability in the American Southwest, A.D. 680 to 1970*. Tucson: Laboratory of Tree-Ring Research, University of Arizona.

1978. *Expanding tree-ring chronologies of the southwestern United States*. Tucson: Laboratory of Tree-Ring Research, University of Arizona, Chronology Series III.

1979. Computer cartography and the reconstruction of dendroclimatic variability in the American Southwest, A.D. 680 to 1970. In *Statistical cartographic applications to spatial analysis in archaeological contexts*. Ed. Steadman Upham. Anthropological Research Papers no. 15. Tempe: Arizona State University.

1982. Dendrochronology of Grasshopper Pueblo. In *Multidisciplinary research at Grasshopper Pueblo, Arizona*. Eds. William A. Longacre, Sally J. Holbrook, and Michael W. Graves. Anthropological Papers of the University of Arizona no. 40. Tucson: University of Arizona Press.

Dean, Jeffrey S., Alexander J. Lindsay, Jr, and William J. Robinson 1978. Prehistoric settlement in Long House Valley, northeastern Arizona. In *Investigations of the Southwestern Anthropological Research Group: an experiment in archaeological cooperation*. Eds. Robert C. Euler and George J. Gumerman. Flagstaff: Museum of Northern Arizona.

Dean, Jeffrey S., Robert C. Euler, George J. Gumerman, Fred Plog, Richard H. Hevly, and Thor N. V. Karlstrom 1985. Human behavior, demography, and paleoenvironment on the Colorado Plateaus. *American Antiquity*, 50(3):537–54.

DeBloois, Evan I., and Dee F. Green 1978. SARG research on the Elk Ridge Project Manti-Lasal National Forest, Utah. In *Investigations of the Southwestern Anthropological Research Group: an experiment in archaeological cooperation*. Eds. Robert C. Euler and George J. Gumerman. Flagstaff: Museum of Northern Arizona.

DeBoer, Warren R. 1980. *The prehistoric Sinagua: the view from Elden Mountain*. Cultural Resources Report no. 34. Albuquerque: USDA Forest Service, Southwestern Regional Office.

Denton, George H., and Wibjorn Karlen 1973. Holocene climatic variations – their pattern and possible cause. *Quaternary Research* 3:155–205.

1977. Holocene glacial and tree-line variations in the White River Valley and Skolai Pass, Alaska and Yukon territory. *Quaternary Research* 7:63–111.

Deutchman, Haree L. 1980. Chemical evidence of ceramic exchange on Black Mesa. In *Models and methods in regional exchange*. Ed. Robert E. Fray. Washington, D.C.: Papers of the Society for American Archaeology no. 1, pp. 119–34.

Dickey, Archie Murl 1971. Palynology of Hay Hollow Valley. Unpublished M.S. thesis, University of Northern Arizona.

REFERENCES

Diggs, Robert E. 1982. Ten thousand years of land use at the Hall Ranch locality near Springerville, Arizona. Unpublished M.A. thesis, University of Northern Arizona.

DiPeso, Charles C. 1958. *The Reeve Ruin of southeastern Arizona: a study of a prehistoric western Pueblo migration into the middle San Pedro Valley.* Dragoon: The Amerind Foundation Inc. no. 8.

Dittert, Alfred E., Jr, Jim J. Hester, and Frank W. Eddy 1961. *An archaeological survey of the Navajo Reservoir district, Northwestern New Mexico.* Monographs of the School of American Research and the Museum of New Mexico no. 23. Santa Fe: Museum of New Mexico.

Dixon, Hobart 1962, Vegetation, pollen rain, and pollen preservation, Sangre de Cristo Mountains, New Mexico. Unpublished M.S. thesis, University of New Mexico.

Dobyns, F. 1979. Altitude sorting of ethnic groups in the Southwest. *Plateau* 47:42–8.

Douglass, Andrew Ellicott 1914. A method of estimating rainfall by the growth of trees. In *The climatic factor as illustrated in arid America* by Ellsworth Huntington. Washington, D.C.: Carnegie Institution, Publication no. 192.

Dozier, Edward P. 1966. *Hano: a Tewa Indian community in Arizona.* New York: Holt, Rinehart, and Winston.

    1970. *The Pueblo Indians of North America.* New York: Holt, Rinehart, and Winston.

Dyson-Hudson, Rada, and Eric A. Smith 1978. Human territoriality: an ecological reassessment. *American Anthropologist* 80:21–42.

Earle, Timothy K., and Andrew L. Christenson, Eds. 1980. *Modeling change in prehistoric subsistence economics.* New York: Academic Press.

Eddy, Frank W. 1966. *Prehistory of the Navajo Reservoir district, northwestern New Mexico.* Museum of New Mexico Papers in Anthropology no. 15. Santa Fe: Museum of New Mexico.

    1974. Population dislocation in the Navajo Reservoir district, New Mexico and Colorado. *American Antiquity* 39:75–84.

    1983. Anasazi cultural responses to a marginal environment in the upper San Juan Basin, New Mexico and Colorado. Paper presented at the 2nd Anasazi Symposium, Farmington, New Mexico.

Effland, Richard W., and Margerie Green 1979. *A cultural resource sensitivity study of the Tusayan Ranger district, Kaibab National Forest.* Tempe, Arizona: Archaeological Consulting Services, Ltd.

Effland, Richard W., Jr, A. Trinkle Jones, and Robert C. Euler 1981. *The archaeology of Powell Plateau, Grand Canyon, Arizona.* Monograph no. 3. Grand Canyon, Arizona: Grand Canyon Natural History Association.

Eggan, Fred 1950. *Social organization of the western Pueblos.* Chicago: University of Chicago Press.

References

1966. *The American Indian perspectives for the study of social change.* Chicago: Aldine.

El-Najjar, Mahmoud Y., Dennis J. Ryan, Christy G. Turner II, and Betsy Lozoff 1976. The etiology of porotic hyperostosis among the prehistoric and historic Anasazi Indians of southwestern United States. *American Journal of Physical Anthropology* 44:477–88.

Euler, Robert C. 1964. *An archaeological survey of the south rim of Walnut Canyon National Monument, Arizona.* Arizona State College Anthropological Papers, no. 1. Flagstaff: Northland Press.

1981. Cohonina–Havasupai relationships in Grand Canyon. In *Collected papers in honor of Erik Kellerman Reed.* Ed. Albert H. Schroeder. Papers of the Archaeological Society of New Mexico no. 6. Albuquerque: Albuquerque Archaeological Society Press.

Euler, Robert C., and Susan M. Chandler 1978. Aspects of prehistoric settlement pattern in Grand Canyon. In *Investigations of the Southwestern Anthropological Research Group: an experiment in archaeological cooperation.* Eds. Robert C. Euler and George J. Gumerman. Flagstaff: Museum of Northern Arizona.

Euler, Robert C., and George J. Gumerman, Eds. 1978. *Investigations of the Southwestern Anthropological Research Group: an experiment in archaeological cooperation.* Flagstaff: Museum of Northern Arizona.

Euler, Robert C., George J. Gumerman, Thor N. V. Karlstrom, Jeffrey S. Dean, and Richard H. Hevly 1979. The Colorado Plateaus: cultural dynamics and paleoenvironment. *Science* 205:1089–101.

Fall, Patricia 1981. Modern pollen spectra and their application to alluvial pollen sedimentation. Unpublished M.S. thesis, University of Arizona.

Fall, Patricia L., Gerald Kelso, and Vera Markgraf 1981. Paleoenvironmental reconstruction at Canyon del Muerto, Arizona, based on principal-component analysis. *Journal of Archaeological Science* 8:297–307.

Fernstrom, Katharine 1980. The effect of ecological fluctuations on exchange networks. Unpublished M.A. thesis, Southern Illinois University at Carbondale.

Flannery, Kent V. 1968. Archaeological systems theory and early Mesoamerica. In *Anthropological archaeology in the Americas.* Ed. Betty J. Meggars. Washington, D.C.: Anthropological Society of Washington.

1972. The cultural evolution of civilizations. *Annual Review of Ecology and Systematics* 3:399–426.

Ford, Richard I. 1972. An ecological perspective on the eastern Pueblos. In *New perspective on the Pueblos.* Ed. Alfonso Ortiz. Albuquerque: University of New Mexico Press.

1981. Gardening and farming before A.D. 1000: patterns of prehistoric cultivation north of Mexico. *Journal of Ethnobiology* 1:5–27.

1984. Ecological consequences of early agriculture in the Southwest. In

Papers on the archaeology of Black Mesa, Arizona, vol. 2. Eds. Stephen Plog and Shirley Powell. Carbondale: Southern Illinois University Press.

Forrestal, Peter P., and Cyprian J. Lynch 1954. *Benavides' memorial of 1630*. Washington, D.C.: Academy of American Franciscan History.

Frisbie, C. 1980. *Southwestern Indian ritual drama*. Albuquerque: University of New Mexico Press.

Fritts, Harold C. 1965. Tree-ring evidence for climatic changes in western North America. *Monthly Weather Review* 93:421–43.

——— 1971. Dendroclimatology and dendroecology. *Quaternary Research* 1:419–49.

——— 1976. *Tree rings and climate*. New York: Academic Press.

——— 1981. Statistical climatic reconstructions from tree-ring widths. In *Climatic variations and variability: facts and theories*. Ed. A. Berger. Dordrecht, Netherlands: D. Reidel Publishing Company.

Fritts, Harold C., Terence J. Blasing, Bruce P. Hayden, and John E. Kutzbach 1971. Multivariate techniques for specifying tree-growth and climatic relations and for reconstructing anomalies in paleoclimate. *Journal of Applied Meteorology* 10:845–64.

Fritts, Harold C., D. G. Smith, and M. A. Stokes 1965. Tree-ring characteristics along a vegetation gradient in northern Arizona, San Francisco Peaks area. *Ecology* 46:393–400.

Fritz, John M. 1972. Archaeological systems for indirect observation of the past. In *Contemporary archaeology, a guide to theory and contributions*. Ed. Mark P. Leone. Carbondale: Southern Illinois University Press.

Fry, Robert E. Ed., 1980. *Models and methods in regional exchange*. Washington, D.C.: Papers of the Society for American Archaeology no. 1.

Garcia-Mason, Velma 1979. Acoma Pueblo. In *Handbook of North American Indians, Vol. 9, the Southwest*. Ed. Alfonso Ortiz. Washington, D.C.: Smithsonian Institution.

Garza, Patricia L. 1978. Retrodiction of subsistence stress on the Pajarito Plateau: a computer-based model. Unpublished Master's thesis, University of California, Los Angeles.

Gasser, Robert E. 1982. Anasazi diet. In *The Coronado project archaeological investigations: the specialists' volume: biocultural analyses*. Compiler R. E. Gasser. Research Paper no. 23. Flagstaff: Museum of Northern Arizona.

Gasser, Robert E., and E. Charles Adams 1981. Aspects of deterioration of plant remains in archaeological sites: the Walpi archaeological project. *Journal of Ethnobiology* 1(1):182–92.

Gatewood, J. S., Alfonso Wilson, H. E. Thomas, and L. R. Kisler 1963. *General effects of droughts on water resources of the Southwest, 1942–56*. Washington, D.C.: U.S. Geological Survey, Professional Paper 372–B.

References

Gillespie, William B., and Robert P. Powers 1983. Regional settlement changes and past environment in the San Juan Basin, northwestern New Mexico. Paper presented at the 2nd Anasazi Symposium, Farmington, New Mexico.

Graf, W. L. 1983. The arroyo problem – palaeohydrology and palaeohydraulics in the short term. In *Background to palaeohydrology: a perspective*. Ed. K. J. Gregory. London: John Wiley & Sons.

Green, Margerie 1982. Chipped stone raw materials and the study of interaction. Unpublished Ph.D. diss., Arizona State University.

— 1985. *Chipped stone raw materials and the study of interaction on Black Mesa, Arizona*. Occasional Paper no. 11. Carbondale: Center for Archaeological Investigations, Southern Illinois University.

Gregory, Herbert E. 1916. *The Navajo country: a geographic and hydrographic reconnaissance of parts of Arizona, New Mexico, and Utah*. Water Supply Paper 380. Washington, D.C.: United States Geological Survey.

— 1917. *Geology of the Navajo country: a reconnaissance of parts of Arizona, New Mexico, and Utah*. Professional Paper 93. Washington, D.C.: U.S. Geological Survey.

Griffin, William B. 1969. *Culture change and shifting populations in central northern Mexico*. Anthropological Papers of the University of Arizona no. 13. Tucson: University of Arizona Press.

Gumerman, George J. 1968. The archaeology of the Hopi Buttes district, Arizona. Unpublished Ph.D. diss., University of Arizona, Tucson.

— 1975. Alternative cultural models for demographic change: southwestern examples. In *Population studies in archaeology and biological anthropology: a symposium*. Ed. Alan C. Swedlund. American Antiquity Memoir 30, vol. 40, no. 2, pt. 2.

— 1983. Prehistoric social and economic survival on the Little Colorado Desert. Paper presented at the 2nd Anasazi Symposium, Farmington, New Mexico.

Gumerman, George J., Ed. 1971. *The distribution of prehistoric population aggregates*. Prescott College Anthropological Reports No. 1. Prescott, Arizona: Prescott College Press.

Gumerman, George J., and Robert C. Euler 1976. Black Mesa: retrospect and prospect. In *Papers on the archaeology of Black Mesa, Arizona*. Eds. George J. Gumerman and Robert C. Euler, pp. 162–70. Carbondale: Southern Illinois University Press.

Gumerman, George J., and S. Alan Skinner 1968. A synthesis of the central Little Colorado Valley, Arizona. *American Antiquity* 33:185–99.

Hack, John T. 1941. Dunes of the Western Navajo country. *Geographical Review* 31:240–63.

— 1942. *The changing physical environment of the Hopi Indians of Arizona*. Papers of the Peabody Museum of American Archaeology and Ethnology, Harvard University, vol. 35, no. 1. Cambridge, Mass.: Harvard University Press.

1945. Recent geology of the Tsegi Canyon. Appendix I of *Archaeological studies in northeast Arizona*. Eds. Ralph L. Beals, George W. Brainerd, and Watson Smith. Publications in American Archaeology and Ethnology, vol. 44, no. 1. Berkeley and Los Angeles: University of California Press.

Halbirt, Carl Dale 1985. Pollen analysis of metate wash samples: evaluating techniques for determining metate function. Unpublished M.A. thesis, Northern Arizona University.

Hall, Stephen A. 1977. Late Quaternary sedimentation and paleoecologic history of Chaco Canyon, New Mexico. *Geological Society of America Bulletin* 88:1593–618.

1981. Deteriorated pollen grains and the interpretation of Quaternary pollen diagrams. *Review of Paleobotany and Palynology* 32:193–206.

1985. Quaternary pollen analysis and vegetation history of the Southwest. In *Pollen records of late-Quaternary North American sediments*. Eds. V. M. Bryant, Jr, and R. G. Holloway. Dallas: American Association of Stratigraphic Palynologists Foundation.

Hammond, George P., and Agapito Rey 1940. *Narrative of the Coronado Expedition, 1540–1542*. Coronado Cuarto Centennial Publications, 1540–1940, vol. 5. Albuquerque: University of New Mexico Press.

Hantman, Jeffrey L. 1983. Social networks and stylistic distributions in the prehistoric plateau southwest. Unpublished Ph.D. diss., Arizona State University.

Hargrave, Lyndon Lane 1935. *Report on archaeological reconnaissance in the Rainbow Plateau area of northern Arizona and southern Utah*. Berkeley: University of California Press.

Harris, Marvin 1968. *The rise of anthropological theory*. New York: Thomas Y. Crowell.

Hassan, Fekri A. 1978. Demographic archaeology. In *Advances in archaeological method and theory*, vol. 1. Ed. Michael B. Schiffer. New York: Academic Press.

1981. *Demographic archaeology*. New York: Academic Press.

Haury, Emil W. 1945. *The excavations of Los Muertos and neighboring ruins of the Salt River Valley, southern Arizona*. Papers of the Peabody Museum of Archaeology and Ethnology, vol. 24, no. 1. Cambridge, Mass.: Harvard University Press.

1958. Evidence at Point of Pines for a prehistoric migration from northern Arizona. In *Migrations in New World culture history*. Ed. Raymond H. Thompson. Social Science Bulletin no. 27. Tucson: University of Arizona Press.

Havinga, H. 1971. An experimental investigation into the decay of pollen and spores in various soil types. In *Sporopollenin*. Eds. Brooks *et al.* New York: Academic Press.

Hayes, Alden C. 1964. *The archaeological survey of Wetherill Mesa, Mesa Verde National Park, Colorado*. Archaeological Research Series no.

References

7–A. Washington, D.C.: National Park Service, Government Printing Office.

1981. A survey of Chaco Canyon archaeology. In *Archaeological surveys of Chaco Canyon, New Mexico*. Eds. Alden C. Hayes, David M. Brugge, and W. James Judge. Publications in Archaeology, 18A, Chaco Canyon Studies. Washington, D.C.: National Park Service, Government Printing Office.

Haynes, C. Vance, Jr 1968. Geochronology in late Quaternary alluvium. In *Means of correlation of Quaternary successions*. Eds. R. B. Morrison, and H. E. Wright, Jr. Salt Lake City: University of Utah Press.

Heid, James 1982. Settlement patterns on Little Creek Mountain, Utah. *Western Anasazi Reports* 3(2):87–179.

Hereford, Richard 1983. Effect of climate and geomorphic threshold on the historic, geomorphic, and alluvial stratigraphy of the Paria and Little Colorado Rivers, southwest Colorado Plateaus. In *Chaco Canyon Country*. Eds. S. A. Wells, *et al*. Albuquerque: Adobe Press.

1984. Climate and ephemeral-stream processes: twentieth century geomorphology and alluvial stratigraphy of the Little Colorado River, Arizona. *Geological Society of America Bulletin* 95:654–68.

Herold, Joyce 1961. *Prehistoric settlement and physical environment in the Mesa Verde area*. University of Utah Anthropological Papers no. 53. Salt Lake City: University of Utah Press.

Hevly, Richard H. 1964a. Pollen analysis of Quaternary archaeology and lacustrine sediments from the Colorado Plateau. Unpublished Ph.D. diss., University of Arizona, Tucson.

1964b. Paleoecology of Laguna Salada. *Fieldiana: Anthropology 53. Chapters in the prehistory of eastern Arizona, II* by Paul S. Martin, *et al*. Chicago: Natural History Museum.

1968. Studies of the modern pollen rain in northern Arizona. *Journal of the Arizona Academy of Science* 5(2):116–27.

1981. Pollen production, transport, and preservation: potentials and limitations in archaeological palynology. *Journal of Ethnobiology* 1(1):39–54.

1983. Pollen studies of Holocene sediments of Black Mesa, Arizona. Unpublished manuscript. in possession of author.

1985. A 50,000 year record of Quaternary environments, Walker Lake, Coconino County, Arizona. *American Association of Stratigraphic Palynologist Contribution Series* 16:141–54.

Hevly, Richard H., and Thor N. V. Karlstrom 1974. Southwest Paleoclimate and continental correlations. In *Geology of northern Arizona with notes on archaeology and paleoclimate, part II – area studies and field guides*. Eds. Thor N. V. Karlstrom, Gordon A. Swann, and Raymond L. Eastwood. Flagstaff: Geological Society of America.

Hevly, Richard H., R. E. Kelly, G. Anderson, and S. J. Olsen 1979.

Comparative effects of climatic change, cultural impact and volcanism in the paleoecology of Flagstaff, Arizona, A.D. 900–1300. In *Volcanism and human ecology.* Eds. P. D. Sheets and D. C. Grayson. New York: Academic Press.

Hevly, Richard H., and Lawrence Renner 1984. *Atmospheric pollen and spores in Flagstaff, Arizona.* Journal of the Arizona Nevada Academy of Science.

Hill, James N. 1970. *Broken K Pueblo: prehistoric social organization in the American Southwest.* Anthropological Papers of the University of Arizona no. 18. Tucson: University of Arizona Press.

Hill, James, and Richard H. Hevly 1968. Pollen at Broken K Pueblo: some new interpretations. *American Antiquity* 33(2):200–10.

Hodge, F. W. 1912. *Handbook of American Indians north of Mexico,* parts 1 and 2. Bulletin no. 30. Washington, D.C.: Bureau of American Ethnology.

Hohmann, John W. 1983. *Sinagua social differentiation: inferences based on prehistoric mortuary practices.* Arizona Archaeologist no. 17. Phoenix: Arizona Archaeological Society.

Holling, C. S. 1973. Resilience and stability of ecological systems. *Annual Review of Ecology and Systematics* 4:1–23.

Horn, Lyle H., Reid A. Bryson, and William P. Lowry 1957. *An objective precipitation climatology of the United States.* Scientific Report no. 6. Madison: Department of Meteorology, University of Wisconsin.

Irwin-Williams, Cynthia 1983. Puebloan demographic adaptation in response to climatic stress on the middle Rio Puerco: 700 A.D.–1300 A.D. Paper presented at the 2nd Anasazi Symposium, Farmington, New Mexico.

Jacobs, B. F. 1985. A middle Wisconsin pollen record from Hay Lake, Arizona. *Quaternary Research* 24:121–30.

Jelenik, Arthur J. 1966. Correlation of archaeological and palynological data in the middle Pecos River Valley of central eastern New Mexico. *Science* 152:1507–9.

Jenkins, Dennis L. 1981. Cliff's Edge: a Pueblo I site on the Lower Virgin River. Unpublished M.A. thesis, University of Nevada at Las Vegas.

Jennings, Jesse D. 1966. *Glen Canyon: a summary.* University of Utah Anthropological Papers no. 81. Salt Lake City: University of Utah Press.

Jett, Stephen C. 1964. Pueblo Indian migrations: an evaluation of the possible physical and cultural determinants. *American Antiquity* 29:281–300.

1965 Comment on Davis' hypothesis of Pueblo Indian migrations. *American Antiquity* 31:276–7.

Jochim, Michael L. 1976. *Hunter-gatherer subsistence and settlements: a predictive model.* New York: Academic Press.

1979. Breaking down the system: recent ecological approaches in archaeology. In *Advances in archaeological method and theory*, vol. 2. Ed. Michael B. Schiffer. New York: Academic Press.

1981. *Strategies for survival: cultural behavior in an ecological context.* New York: Academic Press.

Johnsen, Thomas N., Jr 1962. One-seed juniper invasion of northern Arizona grassland. *Ecological Monograph* 32:187–207.

Johnson, Gregory A. 1978. Information sources and the development of decision-making organizations. In *Social archaeology: beyond subsistence and dating.* Eds. C. Redman, M. J. Berman, E. Curtin, W. Langehorne, Jr, N. Versaggi, and J. Wanser. New York: Academic Press.

1983. Decision-making organization and pastoral nomad camp size. *Human Ecology* 11(2):175–99.

Jones, Anne Trinkle 1983. Agricultural systems at Grand Canyon: Walhalla Glades. Unpublished manuscript on file, Department of Anthropology, Arizona State University, Tempe.

1986. *A cross section of Grand Canyon archaeology: excavations at five sites along the Colorado River.* Western Archaeological and Conservation Center Publications in Archaeology no. 28. Tucson.

Jorde, L. B. 1977. Precipitation cycles and cultural buffering in the prehistoric Southwest. In *For theory building in archaeology.* Ed. Lewis R. Binford. New York: Academic Press.

Judge, W. J., W. B. Gillespie, S. H. Lekson, and H. W. Toll 1981. Tenth century developments in Chaco Canyon. In *Collected papers in honor of Erik Kellerman Reed.* Ed. Albert H. Schroeder. Papers of the Archaeological Society of New Mexico no. 6. Albuquerque: Albuquerque Archaeological Society Press.

Kane, Allen E. 1979. *The Dolores Archaeological Program in 1978: introduction and implementation of the research design.* Salt Lake City: Bureau of Reclamation.

1983. Introduction to field investigations and analysis. In *Dolores Archaeological Program: field investigations and analysis – 1978.* Denver: United States Department of the Interior, Bureau of Reclamation Engineering and Research Center.

Kane, Allen E., Janet D. Orcutt, and Timothy A. Kohler 1982. Dolores Archaeological Program: approaches to paleodemographic reconstructions. Paper presented at the Society for American Archaeology Annual Meeting, Minneapolis, Minnesota.

Karlstrom, Erik T. 1983. Soils and geomorphology of northern Black Mesa. In *Excavations on Black Mesa, 1981: a descriptive report.* Eds. F. E. Smiley, Deborah L. Nichols, and Peter P. Andrews. Research Paper no. 36. Carbondale: Center for Archaeological Investigations, Southern Illinois University.

Karlstrom, Thor N. V. 1961. The glacial history of Alaska: its bearing on paleoclimatic theory. *Annals New York Academy of Science* 1:290–340.

1976. Quaternary and upper tertiary time-stratigraphy of the Colorado Plateaus, continental correlations and some paleoclimatic implications. In *Quaternary stratigraphy of North America*. Ed. W. C. Mahaney. Stroudberg, Philadelphia: Dowden, Hutchinson and Ross, Inc.

1978. Stratigraphy and paleoclimate of the Black Mesa Basin. In *The Energy Lands Program of the U.S. Geological Survey, fiscal year 1976*. Compiler John O. Maberry. Washington, D.C.: U.S. Geological Survey, Circular 778.

1980. Detailed Holocene record of paleoclimate from western North America, marine–terrestrial correlations and glaceostatic implications. In *Quaternary Paleoclimate*. Ed. W. C. Mahaney. Norwich, England: Geo. Abstracts.

1982. Dating of the type Tsegi and Naha deposits of Holocene age in the American Southwest. Abstracts with programs, Geological Society of America annual meeting.

1983. Holocene chronostratigraphy and the alluvial chronology of the Black Mesa region, and Holocene hydroclimate history. Unpublished manuscript on file, U.S. Geological Survey, Flagstaff.

in press. Alluvial chronology of Black Mesa, northeast Arizona, and description of chronometric samples. In Black Mesa book to be published. Carbondale: Center for Archaeological Investigations, Southern Illinois University.

Karlstrom, Thor N. V., George J. Gumerman, and Robert C. Euler 1974. Paleoenvironmental and cultural changes in the Black Mesa region, northeastern Arizona. In *Geology of northern Arizona with notes on archaeology and paleoclimate*. Eds. Thor N. V. Karlstrom, G. A. Swan, and R. L. Eastwood. Flagstaff: Northern Arizona University.

1976. Paleoenvironment and cultural correlates in the Black Mesa region. In *Papers on the archaeology of Black Mesa, Arizona*. Eds. George J. Gumerman and Robert C. Euler. Carbondale: Southern Illinois University Press.

Kelso, Gerald K. 1976. Absolute pollen frequencies applied to the interpretation of human activities in northern Arizona. Unpublished Ph.D. diss., University of Arizona, Tucson.

Kirch, Patrick V. 1980. The archaeological study of adaptation: theoretical and methodological issues. In *Advances in archaeological method and theory*, vol. 3. Ed. Michael B. Schiffer. New York: Academic Press.

Klesert, Anthony L., and Robert Layhe 1980. Black Mesa culture history and research design. In *Excavation on Black Mesa, 1979: a descriptive report*. Eds. Shirley Powell, Robert Layhe, and Anthony L. Klesert. Research paper no. 18. Carbondale: Center for Archaeological Investigations, Southern Illinois University.

Kochel, R. C., and V. R. Baker 1982. Paleoflood hydrology. *Science* 215:353–61.

Kottlowski, F. E., M. E. Cooley, and R. V. Ruhe 1965. Quaternary

References

geology of the Southwest. In *The Quaternary of the United States.*
Eds. H. E. Wright and D. G. Frey. Princeton: Princeton University
Press.
Kunitz, Stephen J., and Robert C. Euler 1972. *Aspects of Southwestern
paleoepidemiology.* Prescott College, Anthropological Reports no. 2.
Prescott, Arizona: Prescott College Press.
Kurtz, E. B., Jr, J. L. Liverman, and H. Tucker 1960. Some problems
concerning fossil and modern corn. *Bulletin of the Torrey Botanical
Club* 87:85–94.
Kushner, Gilbert 1970. A consideration of some processual designs for
archaeology as anthropology. *American Antiquity* 35:125–32.
LaMarche, Valmore C., Jr 1973. Holocene climatic variation from timber
line fluctuations in the White Mountain, California. *Quaternary
Research* 3:632–8.
Lambrechtse, E. 1982. Vegetation and rodent changes during secondary
succession in the pinyon–juniper woodland. Unpublished M.S.
thesis, University of Northern Arizona.
Layhe, Robert W. 1977. A multivariate approach for estimating prehistoric
population change, Black Mesa, northeastern Arizona. Unpublished
M.A. thesis, Southern Illinois University at Carbondale.
1981. A locational model for demographic and settlement system
change: an example from the American Southwest. Unpublished
Ph.D. diss., Southern Illinois University at Carbondale.
Leiberg, J. B., T. F. Rixon, and A. Dodwell 1904. *Forest conditions of the
San Francisco Mountain Reserve, Arizona,* no. 22. Washington,
D.C.: United States Geological Society.
Leopold, Luna B., E. B. Leopold, and Fred Wendorf 1963. Some
climatic indicators in the period A.D. 1200–1400, New Mexico. In
Changes of climate. Arid Zone Research Series 20. Paris: UNESCO
and World Meteorological Organization Symposium.
Leopold, Luna B., M. G. Wolman, and J. P. Miller 1964. *Fluvial
processes in geomorphology.* San Francisco: W. H. Freeman.
Lightfoot, Kent G. 1979. Food redistribution among prehistoric Pueblo
groups. *The Kiva* 44(4):319–39.
Lightfoot, Kent G., and Gary M. Feinman 1982. Social differentiation
and leadership development in early pithouse villages in the Mogollon
region of the American Southwest. *American Antiquity* 47:64–86.
Lindsay, Alexander J., Jr 1961. The Beaver Creek agricultural community
on the San Juan River, Utah. *American Antiquity* 27(2):174–87.
Lindsay, Alexander J., Jr, J. Richard Ambler, Mary Anne Stein, and
Philip M. Hobler 1968. *Survey and excavations north and east of
Navajo Mountain, Utah, 1959–1962.* Bulletin no. 45. Flagstaff:
Museum of Northern Arizona.
Lindsay, Lamar W. 1980a. *Pollen analysis of Cowboy Cave cultural
deposits.* University of Utah Anthropological Papers no. 104. Salt
Lake City: University of Utah Press.

1980b. *Pollen analysis of sudden shelter site deposits.* University of Utah Anthropological Papers no. 103. Salt Lake City: University of Utah Press.

Lipe, William D. 1970. Anasazi communities in the Red Rock Plateau, southeastern Utah. In *Reconstructing prehistoric pueblo societies.* Ed. William A. Longacre. Albuquerque: University of New Mexico Press.

Lipe, William D., and Alexander J. Lindsay, Jr 1983. Pueblo adaptations in the Glen Canyon area. Paper presented at the 2nd Anasazi Symposium, Farmington, New Mexico.

Lipe, William D., and R. G. Matson 1971. Human settlement and resources in the Cedar Mesa area, S.E. Utah. In *The distribution of prehistoric population aggregates.* Ed. George J. Gumerman. Prescott College Anthropological Reports no. 1. Prescott, Arizona: Prescott College Press.

Lipe, William D., and Richard A. Thompson 1979. A cultural resource assessment of the Grand Wash Planning Unit of the Arizona Strip District of the Bureau of Land Management. *Western Anasazi Reports* 2(1).

Lister, Robert H. 1966. *Contributions to Mesa Verde archaeology: III, site 866, and the cultural sequence at four villages in the Far View group, Mesa Verde National Park, Colorado.* University of Colorado Studies, Series in Anthropology no. 12. Boulder: University of Colorado.

Longacre, William A. 1964. A synthesis of upper Little Colorado prehistory, eastern Arizona. *Fieldiana: Anthropology 55. Chapters in the prehistory of eastern Arizona, II.* Chicago: Natural History Museum.

1970. A historical review. In *Reconstructing prehistoric pueblo societies.* Ed. W. A. Longacre. Albuquerque: University of New Mexico Press.

Love, David Waxham 1980. Quaternary geology of Chaco Canyon, northwestern New Mexico. Unpublished Ph.D. diss., University of New Mexico.

Low, Gilbert W. 1981. Using system dynamics to simulate the past. In *Simulations in archaeology.* Ed. Jeremy A. Sabloff. Albuquerque: University of New Mexico Press.

Lowe, Charles H., and David Brown 1977. *Biotic communities of the Southwest.* Washington, D.C.: USDA Forest Service.

Lyneis, Margaret M. 1981. The western Anasazi frontier: cultural processes along a prehistoric boundary. Paper presented at the 46th annual meeting of the Society for American Archaeology, San Diego.

Lytle-Webb, J. 1978. The environment of Miami Wash, Gila county, Arizona A.D. 1100 to 1400. Unpublished Ph.D. diss., University of Arizona.

MacDougal, William B. 1967. Botany of the museum and Colton ranch area. *Plateau* 39:134–42.

MacKey, James C., and Sally J. Holbrook 1978. Environmental

298

References

reconstruction and abandonment of the Largo–Gallina area, New Mexico. *Journal of Field Archaeology* 5:29–50.

Maher, Louis J., Jr 1963. Pollen analysis of surface materials from the southern San Juan Mountains, Colorado. *Geological Society of America Bulletin* 74:1485–503.

Malde, H. E. 1964. Environment and man in arid America. *Science* 145–123:9.

Martin, Debra L., Alan C. Swedlund, and George J. Armelagos 1982. Population dynamics, resources, and skeletal biology on Black Mesa. Paper presented at the 47th annual meeting of the Society for American Archaeology, Minneapolis.

Martin, P. S. 1963. *The last 10,000 years: a fossil pollen record of the American Southwest*. Tucson: University of Arizona Press.

Martin, P. S., and William Byers 1965. Pollen and archaeology at Wetherill Mesa. *Memoirs of the Society for American Archaeology* 19:122–35.

Mathews, T. W., and E. H. Neller 1979. Atlatl Cave: Archaic-Basketmaker II investigations in Chaco Canyon National Monument. In *Proceedings of the first conference on scientific research in the National Parks*. Ed. Robert M. Linn. NPS Transactions and Proceedings Series no. 5. Washington, D.C.: Government Printing Office.

Matson, R. G., and W. D. Lipe 1978. Settlement patterns on Cedar Mesa: boom and bust on the northern periphery. In *Investigations of the Southwestern Anthropological Research Group: an experiment in archaeological cooperation*. Eds. Robert C. Euler and George J. Gumerman. Flagstaff: Museum of Northern Arizona.

McDonald, James E. 1956. *Variability of precipitation in an arid region: a survey of characteristics for Arizona*. Technical Report no. 1. Tucson: Arizona Institute of Atmospheric Physics.

McDonald, James A. 1976. *An archaeological assessment of Canyon de Chelly National Monument*. Publications in Anthropology no. 5. Tucson: National Park Service, Western Archaeological Center.

McGavok, E. H., and Gary W. Levings 1974. Groundwater in the Navajo sandstone in the Black Mesa area, Arizona. In *Geology of northern Arizona with notes on archaeology and paleoclimate*. Eds. T. N. V. Karlstrom, G. A. Swan, and R. L. Eastwood. Flagstaff: Northern Arizona University.

Meko, David M., Charles W. Stockton, and William R. Boggess 1980. A tree-ring reconstruction of drought in southern California. *Water Resources Bulletin* 16:594–600.

Minnis, Paul E. 1978. Paleoethnobotanical indicators of prehistoric disturbance: a case study. In *The nature and status of ethnobotany*. Ed. R. Ford. Anthropological Papers no. 67:347–66. Ann Arbor: University of Michigan, Museum of Anthropology.

1985. *Social Adaptation to Food Stress*. Chicago: University of Chicago Press.

Nickens, Paul R., and Kenneth L. Kvamme 1981. *Archaeological investigations at the Kanab site, Kane County, Utah*. Montrose, Colorado: Nickens and Associates.

Orcutt, Janet D. 1981. Paleodemography and settlement patterns. Appendix A in Dolores Archaeological Program synthetic report, and T. A. Seliga. Dordrecht, Netherlands: D. Reidel Publishing Company.

Mitchell, V. L. 1976. The regionalization of climate in the western United States. *Journal of Applied Meteorology* 15(9):290–7.

Moffitt, Kathleen, and Claudia Chang 1978. The Mount Trumbull archaeological survey. *Western Anasazi Reports* 1(3):185–250.

Moore, James A. 1985. Forager/farmer interactions: information, social organization, and the frontier. In *The archaeology of frontiers and boundaries*. Eds. S. Green and S. Perlman. New York: Academic Press.

Morris, Don P. 1983. Settlement pattern adjustments and node relationships, Canyon de Chelly, Arizona. Paper presented at the 2nd Anasazi Symposium, Farmington, New Mexico.

Morris, Earl H., and Robert F. Burgh 1954. *Basketmaker II sites near Durango, Colorado*. Carnegie Institution of Washington, publication 604. Washington, D.C.: Carnegie Institution.

Murry, Robert Early, Jr 1983. Pollen analysis of Anasazi sites at Black Mesa, Arizona. Unpublished M.A. thesis, Texas A & M University.

Neitzel, Jill, and Jeffrey L. Hantman 1983. An evaluation of demographic reconstructions on the Colorado Plateau. Paper presented at the 48th annual meeting of the Society for American Archaeology, Pittsburg, Pennsylvania.

Nelson, Ben A. 1980. Cultural responses to population change: a comparison of two prehistoric occupations of the Mimbres Valley, New Mexico. Unpublished Ph.D. diss., Southern Illinois University at Carbondale.

Netting, Robert N. 1965. Household organization and intensive agriculture: the Kofyar case. *Africa* 35:422–8.

1974. Agrarian ecology. *Annual Review of Anthropology* 3:21–56.

1977. *Cultural ecology*. Menlo Park: Cummings.

Nichol, A. A. 1952. The natural vegetation of Arizona. *University of Arizona, College of Agriculture Technical Bulletin* 127:189–230.

Nickens, Paul R. 1981. *Pueblo III communities in transition: environment and adaptation in Johnson Canyon*. Memoirs of the Colorado Archaeological Society no. 2. Boulder: Colorado Archaeological Society.

Nickens, Paul R., and Deborah A. Hull 1980. *Archaeological resources of southwestern Colorado: an overview of the Bureau of Land*

300

References

Management's San Juan resource area. Montrose, Colorado: Nickens and Associates.

Mitchell, J. Murray, Jr, Charles W. Stockton, and David M. Meko 1979. Evidence of a 22-year rhythm of drought in the western United States related to the Hale solar cycles since the 17th century. In *Solar-terrestrial influences on weather and climate*. Eds. B. M. McCormac 1978–1981. Unpublished manuscript on file, Dolores Archaeological Project, Dove Creek, Colorado.

Patton, Peter C., and Stanley A. Schumm 1981. Ephemeral-stream processes: implications for studies of Quaternary valley fills. *Quaternary Research* 15:24–43.

Pearson, G. A. 1931. *Forest types in the Southwest as determined by climate and soil*. Technical Bulletin 247. Washington, D.C.: United States Department of Agriculture.

1950. *Management of ponderosa pine in the Southwest*. Monograph 6. Washington, D.C.: United States Department of Agriculture.

Peterson, Kenneth Lee 1981. 10,000 years of climatic change reconstructed from fossil pollen, La Plata Mountains, southwestern Colorado. Unpublished Ph.D. diss., Washington State University.

1985. Climatic reconstruction for the Dolores Project area. In *Dolores Archaeological Program: studies in environmental archaeology*, Chapter 20, pp. 207–16. Compiled by K. L. Peterson and Vickie L. Clay. Denver: United States Department of the Interior, Bureau of Reclamation.

Pilles, Pete J., Jr 1979. Sunset Crater and the Sinagua: a new interpretation. In *Volcanic activity and human ecology*. Eds. Payson D. Sheets and Donald K. Grayson. New York: Academic Press.

Pirazzoli, P. A. 1982. High stands of Holocene sea levels in the Northwest Pacific. *Quaternary Research* 10(1):1–29.

Plog, Fred T. 1974. *The study of prehistoric change*. New York: Academic Press.

1975. Demographic studies in Southwestern prehistory. In *Population studies in archaeology and biological anthropology: a symposium*. Ed. Alan C. Swedlund. American Antiquity Memoir 30, vol. 40, no. 2, pt. 2.

1978. The Keresan Bridge: an ecological and archaeological account. In *Social archaeology: beyond subsistence and dating*. Eds. Charles L. Redman, Mary Jane Berman, Edward V. Curtin, William T. Langhorne, Jr, Nina M. Versaggi, and Jeffery C. Wanser. New York: Academic Press.

1978. An analysis of variability in site locations in the Chevelon drainage, Arizona. In *Investigations of the Southwestern Anthropological Research Group: an experiment in archaeological cooperation*. Eds. Robert C. Euler and George J. Gumerman. Flagstaff: Museum of Northern Arizona.

REFERENCES

1979. Prehistory: western Anasazi. In *Handbook of North American Indians, vol. 9, the Southwest.* Ed. Alfonso Ortiz. Washington, D.C.: U.S. Government Printing Office.

1980. Alternative models of prehistoric change. In *Transformations: mathematical approaches to culture change.* Ed. C. Renfrew. New York: Academic Press.

1983. Political and economic alliance on the Colorado Plateaus, A.D. 400–1450. In *Advances in world archaeology,* vol. 2. Eds. Fred Wendorf and A. E. Close. New York: Academic Press.

1986. Exchange, tribes, and alliances: the northern Southwest. *American Archaeology* 4(3):217–23.

Plog, Fred T., and Cheryl K. Garrett 1972. Explaining variability in prehistoric Southwestern water control systems. In *Contemporary archaeology.* Ed. Mark P. Leone. Carbondale: Southern Illinois University Press.

Plog, Fred T., James N. Hill, and Dwight W. Read 1976. Future research plans. In *Chevelon Archaeological Research Project: 1971–1972.* Eds. Fred T. Plog, James N. Hill, and Dwight W. Read. Monograph II. Los Angeles: University of California, Department of Anthropology, Archaeological Survey.

Plog, Fred, Richard Effland, and Dee F. Green 1978. Inferences using the SARG data bank. In *Investigations of the Southwestern Anthropological Research Group: the proceedings of the 1976 conference.* Eds. R. C. Euler and G. J. Gumerman. Flagstaff: Museum of Northern Arizona.

Plog, Stephen 1980a. *Stylistic variation in prehistoric ceramics: design analysis in the American Southwest.* Cambridge: Cambridge University Press.

1980b. Village autonomy in the American Southwest. *Society for American Archaeology Papers* 1:135–46.

1986. Patterns of demographic growth and decline. In *Spatial organization and exchange: archaeological survey on northern Black Mesa.* Ed. S. Plog. Carbondale: Southern Illinois University Press.

Plog, Stephen, Ed. 1986. *Spatial organization and exchange: archaeological survey on northern Black Mesa.* Carbondale: Southern Illinois University Press.

Plog, Stephen, and Jeffrey L. Hantman 1982. The relationship of stylistic similarity to patterns of material exchange. In *Contexts for prehistoric exchange.* Eds. J. E. Ericson, and T. K. Earle. New York: Academic Press.

Plog, Stephen, Fred Plog, and Walter Wait 1978. Decision making in modern surveys. In *Advances in archaeological method and theory,* vol. 1. Ed. Michael B. Schiffer. New York: Academic Press.

Plog, Stephen, and Shirley Powell 1981. The scale and complexity of prehistoric exchange networks on the Colorado Plateau. Paper

References

presented at the 46th annual meeting of the Society for American Archaeology, San Diego.

1984. Patterns of cultural change: alternative interpretations. In *Papers on the archaeology of Black Mesa, Arizona*, vol. 2. Eds. S. Plog and S. Powell. Carbondale: Southern Illinois University Press.

Pomeroy, Lawrence R. 1981. Review of analysis of marine ecosystems. *Science* 213:1368–9.

Porter, S. C., and G. H. Denton 1967. Chronology of neoglaciation in the North American Cordillera. *American Journal of Science* 265:177–210.

Potter, Loren D. 1967. Differential pollen accumulation in water tank sediments and adjacent soils. *Ecology* 48:1041–3.

Potter, Loren D., and Joanne Rowley 1960. Pollen rain and vegetation, San Augustine Plains, New Mexico. *Botanical Gazette* 122:1–25.

Powell, Shirley 1980. Material culture and behavior: a prehistoric example for the American Southwest. Unpublished Ph.D. diss., Arizona State University. University Microfilms, Ann Arbor.

1982. Food storage and environmental uncertainty. Paper prepared for a School of American Research Advanced Seminar, "The Biography of Black Mesa."

1983. *Mobility and adaptation: the Anasazi of Black Mesa, Arizona.* Carbondale: Center for Archaeological Investigations, Southern Illinois University Press.

Powell, Shirley, and Deborah L. Nichols 1983. Physical environment technology, and cultural change: the Black Mesa Anasazi. Paper presented at the 2nd Anasazi Symposium, Farmington, New Mexico.

Pulliman, R. H. 1981. On predicting human diets. *Journal of Ethnobiology* 1:61–8.

Rappaport, Roy A. 1979. *Ecology, meaning, and religion.* Richmond, California: North Atlantic Books.

Ray, L. L., and T. N. V. Karlstrom 1968. Theoretical concepts in time-stratigraphic subdivision of glacial deposits. In *Means of correlation of Quaternary successions.* Eds. R. B. Morrison and H. E. Wright, Jr. Salt Lake City: University of Utah Press.

Reher, Charles A., Ed. 1977. *Settlement and subsistence along the lower Chaco River: the CGP survey.* Albuquerque: University of New Mexico Press.

Richmond, Gerald M., Ronald Fryxell, G. E. Neff, and P. L. Weis 1965. The Cordilleran ice sheet of the northern Rocky Mountains, and related Quaternary history of the Columbia Plateau. In *The Quaternary of the United States.* Eds. H. E. Wright and D. G. Frey. Princeton: Princeton University Press.

Riley, Carroll L. 1982. *The frontier people.* Occasional paper no. 1. Carbondale: Center for Archaeological Investigations, Southern Illinois University.

Robinson, W. J., B. G. Harrill, and R. L. Warren 1974. *Tree-ring dates from New Mexico B: Chaco-Gobernador area*. Tucson: Laboratory of Tree-Ring Research, University of Arizona.

Rohn, Arthur H. 1963. Prehistoric soil and water conservation in Chapin Mesa. *American Antiquity* 28:441–55.

——— 1972. Social implications of pueblo water management in the northern San Juan. *Sonderdruck: Zeitschrift fur Ethnologie* 97(2):212–19.

——— 1975. A stockaded Basketmaker III village at Yellow Jacket, Colorado. *The Kiva* 40(3):113–19.

——— 1977. *Cultural change and continuity on Chapin Mesa*. Lawrence: The Regents Press of Kansas.

——— 1981. Budding urban settlements in the northern San Juan. Paper presented at the 1st Anasazi Symposium, Mesa Verde National Park, Colorado.

——— 1983. Pueblo Indian social history seen from the northern San Juan. Paper presented at the 2nd Anasazi Symposium, Farmington, New Mexico.

Rose, Martin R. in prep. Dendroclimatic reconstruction for the southeastern Colorado Plateaus. Ph.D. diss. in preparation, University of Arizona, Tucson.

Rose, Martin R., Jeffrey S. Dean, and William J. Robinson 1981. *The past climate of Arroyo Hondo, New Mexico, reconstructed from tree rings*. Arroyo Hondo Archaeological Series, vol. 4. Santa Fe: School of American Research Press.

Rose, Martin R., William J. Robinson, and Jeffrey S. Dean 1982. Dendroclimatic reconstruction for the southeastern Colorado Plateau. Unpublished manuscript on file, Laboratory of Tree-Ring Research, University of Arizona, Tucson.

Rosenberg, B., and J. W. Gish 1975. Preliminary pollen analysis of sediments from Gallinas Springs, Cibola National Forest, New Mexico. Report to Palynology Laboratory, Department of Anthropology, Arizona State University.

Sabloff, J., and Lamberg-Karlovsky, C. C. 1975. *Ancient civilization and trade*. Albuquerque: University of New Mexico Press.

Samuels, Michael L., and Julio Betancourt 1982. Modeling the long-term effects of fuelwood harvest on pinyon–juniper woodlands. *Environmental Management* 6:505–15.

Sanders, William T., and David Webster 1978. Unilinealism, multilinealism, and the evolution of complex societies. In *Social archaeology: beyond subsistence and dating*. Eds. Charles L. Redman, Mary Jane Berman, Edward V. Curtin, William T. Langhorne, Jr, Nina M. Versaggi, and Jeffery C. Wanser. New York: Academic Press.

Schafer, John P., Thor N. V. Karlstrom, Maurice E. Cooley, and Gary W. Levings 1974. Field guide for the Black Mesa Little Colorado River area, northeastern Arizona. In *Geology of northern Arizona and*

References

notes on archaeology and paleoclimate. Eds. T. N. V. Karlstrom, G. A. Swan, and R. L. Eastwood. Flagstaff: Northern Arizona University.

Schoenwetter, James 1962. The pollen analysis of eighteen archaeological sites in Arizona and New Mexico. *Fieldiana: Anthropology 53. Chapters in the prehistory of eastern Arizona, I*, by Paul S. Martin, John B. Rinaldo, William A. Longacre, Constance Cronin, Leslie G. Freeman, Jr, and James Schoenwetter. Chicago: Natural History Museum.

1966. A re-evaluation of the Navajo Reservoir pollen chronology. *El Palacio* 73:19–26.

1967. Pollen survey of the Chuska Valley. In *An archaeological survey of the Chuska Valley and the Chaco Plateau, New Mexico. Part I, Natural science studies*, by Arthur H. Harris, James Schoenwetter, and A. H. Warren. New Mexico Research Records no. 4. Santa Fe: Museum of New Mexico Press.

1970. Archaeological pollen studies of the Colorado Plateau. *American Antiquity* 35:35–48.

1980. Contributions of pollen analysis to investigations of New World agriculture. *IV International Palynology Conference Proceedings*: 269–78.

Schoenwetter, James, and Frank W. Eddy 1964. *Alluvial and palynological reconstruction of environments, Navajo Reservoir district*. Papers in Anthropology no. 13. Santa Fe: Museum of New Mexico Press.

Schoenwetter, James, and Alfred E. Dittert, Jr 1968. An ecological interpretation of Anasazi settlement patterns. In *Anthropological archaeology in the Americas*. Ed. Betty J. Meggers. Washington, D.C.: The Anthropological Society of Washington.

Schroeder, Albert H. 1956. *Dendroclimatic changes in semiarid America*. Tucson: University of Arizona Press.

1979. Pueblos abandoned in historic times. In *Handbook of Northern American Indians, Vol. 9, the Southwest*. Ed. Alfonso Ortiz. Washington, D.C.: U.S. Government Printing Office.

Schulman, Edmund 1956. *Dendroclimatic changes in semiarid America*. Tucson: University of Arizona Press.

Schultz, J. D. 1983. Geomorphic and Quaternary history of the southeastern Chaco dune field, northwestern New Mexico. In *Chaco Canyon country*. Albuquerque: Adobe Press.

Schumm, S. A. 1977. *The fluvial system*. New York: Wiley and Sons.

Schumm, S. A., and R. F. Hadley 1957. Arroyos and the semiarid cycle of erosion. *American Journal of Science* 255:161–74.

Schwartz, Douglas W., Richard C. Chapman, and Jane Kepp 1980. *Archaeology of the Grand Canyon: Unkar Delta*. Grand Canyon Archaeological Series, vol. 2. Santa Fe: School of American Research Press.

Schwartz, Douglas W., Jane Kepp, and Richard C. Chapman 1981. *Archaeology of the Grand Canyon: the Walhalla Plateau.* Grand Canyon Archaeological Series, vol. 3. Santa Fe: School of American Research Press.

Scott, Linda J. 1979. Pollen analysis in selected rooms at Walpi and along modern transects near First Mesa. Second annual conference of ethnobiology. Flagstaff, Arizona, April 6–7, 1979.

Sears, Paul B. 1937. Pollen analysis as an aid in dating cultural deposits in the United States. In *Early man as depicted by leading authorities at the international symposium, the Academy of Natural Sciences, Philadelphia, March 1937.* Ed. George Grant MacCurdy. London: J. B. Lippincott Company.

——— 1961. Palynology and the climatic record of the Southwest. *Annals of the New York Academy of Sciences* 95:632–41.

Sellers, William D., and Richard H. Hill 1974. *Arizona climate: 1931–1972.* Tucson: University of Arizona Press.

Seme', Michele 1984. The effects of agricultural fields on faunal assemblage variation. In *Papers on the archaeology of Black Mesa, Arizona,* vol. II. Eds. S. Plog and S. Powell. Carbondale: Southern Illinois University Press.

Sessions, Steven 1978. Prehistoric population growth on Black Mesa. Unpublished manuscript on file. Center for Archaeological Investigations, Southern Illinois University at Carbondale.

Shoemaker, E. M. 1977. Eruption history of Sunset Crater, Arizona. Unpublished manuscript on file. Wupatki Sunset Crater National Monument.

Shutler, Richard, Jr 1961. *Lost city, Pueblo Grande de Nevada.* Anthropological Papers no. 5. Carson City, Nevada: Nevada State Museum.

Simmons, Marc 1979. History of the pueblos since 1821. In *Handbook of North American Indians, vol. 9, the Southwest.* Ed. Alfonso Ortiz. Washington, D.C.: Smithsonian Institution.

Slobodkin, Lawrence B., and Anatol Rappaport 1974. An optimal strategy of evolution. *Quarterly Review of Biology* 49:181–200. *Academy of Arts and Sciences* 44:291–305.

Slobodkin, Lawrence B., and Anatol Rapaport 1974. An optimal strategy of evolution. *Quarterly Review of Biology* 41:181–200.

Smiley, Terah L. 1955. The geochronological approach. In *Geochronology: with special reference to southwestern United States.* Ed. Terah L. Smiley. *Physical Science Bulletin* 26(2). Tucson: University of Arizona Bulletin Series.

Smiley, F. E., and Peter P. Andrews 1983. An overview of Black Mesa archaeological research. In *Excavations on Black Mesa, 1981: a descriptive report.* Eds. F. E. Smiley, Deborah L. Nichols, and Peter P. Andrews. Research paper no. 36. Carbondale: Center for Archaeological Investigations, Southern Illinois University.

References

Smith, H. V. 1956. The climate of Arizona. *Arizona Agricultural Experiment Station Bulletin* 279:1–99.

Smith, Lawrence P., and Charles W. Stockton 1981. Reconstructed stream flow for the Salt and Verde Rivers from tree-ring data. *Water Resources Bulletin* 17(6):939–47.

Solomon, A. M., T. J. Blasing, and J. A. Solomon 1982. Interpretation of floodplain pollen in alluvial sediments from an arid region. *Quaternary Research* 18:52–71.

Spooner, Brian, Ed. 1972. *Population growth: anthropological implications.* Cambridge, Mass.: MIT Press.

Steward, Julian H. 1936. The economic and social basis of primitive bands. In *Essays in anthropology presented to A. L. Kroeber.* Ed. R. Lowie. Berkeley: University of California Press.

1937. Ecological aspects of southwestern society. *Anthropos* 32:87–104.

1955. *Theory of culture change: the methodology of multilinear evolution.* Urbana: University of Illinois Press.

Stiger, Mark A. 1977. Anasazi diet: the coprolite evidence. Unpublished M.A. thesis, University of Colorado.

Stockton, C. W. 1975. *Long-term streamflow records reconstructed from tree rings.* Papers of the Laboratory of Tree-Ring Research no. 5. Tucson: University of Arizona Press.

Struvier, Mary B. 1977. Relation of pollen and flotation analysis to archaeological excavations, Chaco Canyon. Unpublished M.A. thesis, University of New Mexico, Albuquerque.

Swedlund, Alan C., and Steven E. Sessions 1976. A developmental model of prehistoric population growth on Black Mesa, Northeastern Arizona. In *Papers on the Archaeology of Black Mesa, Arizona.* Eds. G. J. Gumerman and R. C. Euler. Carbondale: Southern Illinois University Press.

Swift, T. T. 1926. Rate of channel trenching in the Southwest. *Science* 63:70–1.

Synenki, Alan T. 1979. Ritual, organization, and production: monitoring variability in aspects of societal complexity. Unpublished manuscript on file, Department of Anthropology, Southern Illinois University at Carbondale.

Tauber, Henrik 1967. Differential pollen dispersal and filtration. In *Quaternary Paleoecology.* Eds. J. Cushing and Herbert E. Wright, Jr. New Haven: Yale University Press.

Taylor, Walter W. 1948. *A study of archeology.* Menasha, Wisconsin: American Anthropological Association Memoir no. 69.

1954. Southwestern archaeology, its history and theory. *American Anthropologist* 54(4):561–75.

1958. *Two archaeological studies in northern Arizona: the pueblo ecology study: hail and farewell and a brief survey through the Grand Canyon of the Colorado River.* Museum of Northern Arizona Bulletin 30. Flagstaff: Northern Arizona Society of Science and Art, Inc.

307

Thompson, Richard A. 1970. *Prehistoric settlement in the Grand Canyon National Monument.* Faculty Research Series no. 1. Cedar City, Utah: Museum of Southern Utah.

1978. The western Anasazi workshop, September 10, 1977. *Western Anasazi Reports* 1(1):3–12.

1979. A projection of archaeological site densities in the slide mountain, Tuckup Point, and Jensen Tank areas of the Grand Canyon National Park. *Western Anasazi Reports* 2(3):234–55.

1983. Consideration of virgin Anasazi subsistence and settlement. Paper presented at the 2nd Anasazi Symposium, Farmington, New Mexico.

Thompson, Richard A., and Georgia Beth Thompson 1974. A preliminary report of excavations in the Grand Canyon National Monument. Report submitted to the National Park Service. Cedar City, Utah: Museum of Southern Utah.

Thornthwaite, C. Warren, C. F. Stewart Sharpe, and Earl F. Dosch 1942. *Climate and accelerated erosion in the arid and semi-arid Southwest, with special reference to the Polacca Wash drainage basin, Arizona.* Technical Bulletin no. 808. Washington, D.C.: U.S. Department of Agriculture.

Titiev, Mischa 1944. *Old Oraibi: study of the Hopi Indians of Third Mesa.* Papers of the Peabody Museum of American Archaeology and Ethnology, vol. 22, no. 1. Cambridge, Mass.: Harvard University Press.

Toll, H. Wolcott, III 1981. Ceramic comparisons concerning redistribution in Chaco Canyon, New Mexico. In *Production and distribution: a ceramic viewpoint.* Eds. H. Howard and E. L. Morris, pp. 83–121. Oxford: British Archaeological Reports 120.

Toll, H. W., T. C. Windes, and P. J. McKenna 1980. Late ceramic patterns in Chaco Canyon: the pragmatics of modeling ceramic exchange. In *Models and methods in regional exchange.* Ed. Robert E. Fry. Washington, D.C.: Papers of the Society for American Archaeology no. 1.

Trewartha, G. T. 1954. *An introduction to climate.* New York: McGraw–Hill.

Upham, Steadman 1982. *Politics and power: an economic and political history of the western pueblo.* New York: Academic Press.

1983. Intensification and exchange: an evolutionary model of non-egalitarian socio-political organization for the prehistoric Plateau Southwest. In *Ecological models in economic prehistory.* Ed. Gordon Bronitsky. Anthropological Research Papers no. 29, pp. 219–45. Tempe: Arizona State University.

Upham, Steadman, Kent G. Lightfoot, and Gary M. Feinman 1981. Explaining socially determined ceramic distributions in the prehistoric plateau southwest. *American Antiquity* 46:822–33.

Vayda, Andrew, and Bonnie J. McCay 1975. New directions in ecology

308

and ecological anthropology. *Annual Review of Anthropology* 4:293–306.

Vayda, Andrew P., and Roy A. Rappaport 1968. Ecology: cultural and non-cultural. In *Introduction to cultural anthropology*. Ed. J. A. Clifton. Boston: Houghton Mifflin.

Vivian, R. Gwinn 1970. An inquiry into prehistoric social organization in Chaco Canyon, New Mexico. In *Reconstructing prehistoric pueblo societies*. Ed. William A. Longacre. Albuquerque: University of New Mexico Press.

1974. Conservation and diversion: water control systems in the Anasazi southwest. In *Irrigation's impact on society*. Eds. Theodore E. Downing and McGuire Gibson. Anthropological Papers of the University of Arizona no. 25. Tucson: University of Arizona Press.

1983. The Chacoan phenomenon: culture growth in the San Juan Basin. Paper presented at the 2nd Anasazi Symposium, Farmington, New Mexico.

Ward, Jerome 1975. Intrasite subsistence patterns at the joint site as a function of paleoclimate. Unpublished M.S. thesis, Northern Arizona University.

Ware, John A. 1981. Archaeological investigations in the Durango district, southwestern Colorado. *Contract Abstracts and CRM Archaeology* 2(2).

Weissner, Pauline W. 1977. Hxaro: a regional system of reciprocity for reducing risk among the Kung San. Unpublished Ph.D. diss., University of Michigan.

Wells, S. G., T. F. Bullard, and L. N. Smith 1983. Chronology, rates, and magnitudes of late Quaternary landscape changes in southeastern Colorado Plateau. In *Chaco Canyon country*. Albuquerque: Adobe Press.

West, Gerald James 1978. Recent palynology of the Cedar Mesa area, Utah. Unpublished Ph.D. diss., University of Utah.

Wetterstrom, Wilma 1978. *Food, Diet and Population at Arroyo Hondo Pueblo, New Mexico*. Santa Fe: School of American Research.

Wilcox, David R. 1976. How the pueblos came to be as they are: the problem today. Unpublished manuscript on file, Department of Anthropology, University of Arizona, Tucson.

1981. The entry of Athapaskans into the American Southwest: the problem today. In *The protohistoric period in the North American southwest, A.D. 1450–1700*. Eds. David R. Wilcox and W. Bruce Masse. Anthropological Research Papers no. 24. Tempe: Arizona State University.

Windes, Thomas C. 1982. A second look at population in Chaco Canyon. Paper presented at the 47th annual meeting of the Society for American Archaeology, Minneapolis.

Winterhalder, Bruce 1980. Environmental analysis in human evolution and adaptation research. *Human Ecology* 8(2):135–70.

REFERENCES

Wobst, H. Martin 1974. Boundary conditions for paleolithic social systems: a simulation approach. *American Antiquity* **39**:147–78.

Womack, W. R., and S. A. Schumm 1977. An example of episodic erosion. *Geology* **5**:72–6.

Young, C. E. 1980. Tree-rings and north Kaibab deer hunting. *Journal of the Arizona–Nevada Academy of Science* **14**:61–5.

Zubrow, Ezra B. W. 1971. Carrying capacity and dynamic equilibrium in the prehistoric Southwest. *American Antiquity* **36**:127–38.

1975. *Prehistoric carrying capacity: a model.* Menlo Park, California: Cummings.

Index

311

Index

Index

Index